THE
COMPLETE BOOK OF
SUCCESSFUL GARDENING

David Carr
H. G. Witham Fogg

OCTOPUS

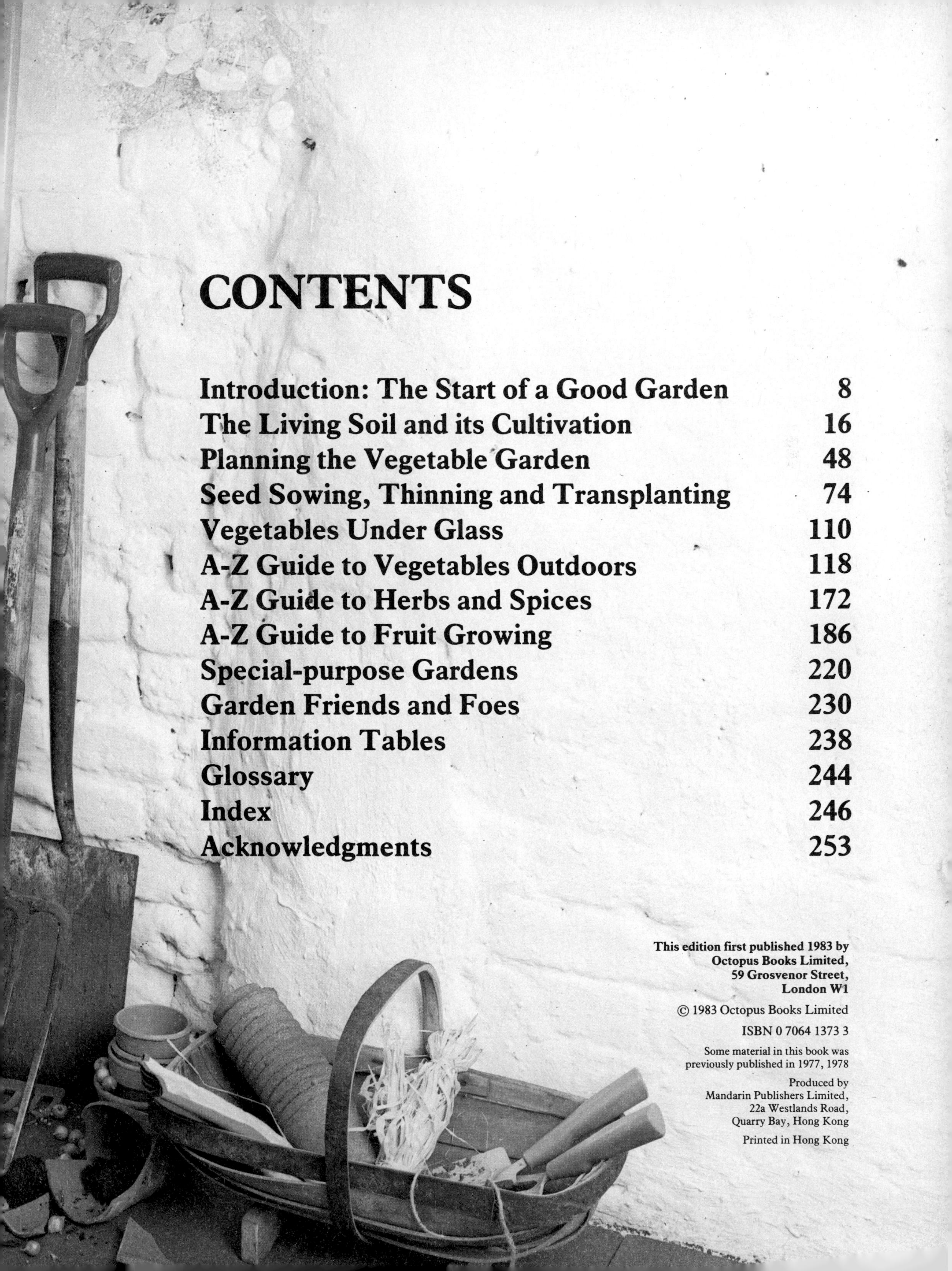

CONTENTS

This edition first published 1983 by
Octopus Books Limited,
59 Grosvenor Street,
London W1

© 1983 Octopus Books Limited

ISBN 0 7064 1373 3

Some material in this book was
previously published in 1977, 1978

Produced by
Mandarin Publishers Limited,
22a Westlands Road,
Quarry Bay, Hong Kong

Printed in Hong Kong

INTRODUCTION: THE START OF A GOOD GARDEN

Good gardens do not just happen – they are made. The best are constructed to a carefully thought-out plan, but there can be no blue-print for a perfect garden. Not only will site, soil, and size vary, so will personal preferences. This is what makes individual gardens so interesting. There are, however, broad principles of design and good garden management; how you apply these depends on how your imagination is fired by the ideas you read about and see. This book aims to give you practical advice and stimulating ideas – if you merge the two successfully there is no reason why you should not have your ideal garden – whatever the size.

On pages 56 to 67 we tell you in more detail how to plan

Decorative food plants like runner beans look perfectly at home in the flower garden

and plant your garden, but before you embark on any major reconstruction – and spend the often considerable amount of money necessary to carry it out – it makes sense to consider carefully your aims and priorities. If you are clear about what you want, there is every chance that you will be successful, but problems arise when you simply buy on impulse and site the plants and garden features wherever there seems to be a suitable space.

Planning today, planting for tomorrow
In a well-balanced garden there will be room for both permanent and temporary plants, but the balance will depend on your expectations of the garden, the time you can spare for regular maintenance and the length of time you expect to stay in your present home.

In the days of the 'family home', when several successive generations might take over the running of the garden, there was every incentive to plan and plant for long-term results. With the greater mobility of modern life however, many people move house after just a few years and it therefore pays to consider first whether you are planning and planting to see results this year, next year or in the more distant future. This is not to say that if you are likely to move house after such a short time you should not plant trees – but it could well affect your choice. A laburnum, many of the thorns (crataegus) and *Prunus* 'Amanogawa' are examples of trees that are relatively small anyway and will also almost certainly flower within a couple of years of planting, probably in their first season. They will not make imposing specimens of course, but at least you will be able to derive some pleasure and satisfaction from them in the short term, while later owners will have the long-term benefit of your planting. A sense of maturity is something you can not easily buy. Large trees *can* be bought – local authorities use them because they are more vandal-proof than saplings – but they are expensive and seldom do as well as much smaller specimens planted young and allowed to develop a good root system on site ... even within a few years the much smaller tree may overtake the larger one. But knowing that is little consolation if you have to face a bleak garden outlook in the meantime. You can, of course, fill your garden with hardy annuals and have a very colourful display, but you will then be on the treadmill of constant replenishment, and the garden will lack the 'backbone' that only well chosen trees and shrubs can provide.

If you do expect to move within a few years, one answer is to create the framework of your garden using quick-growing shrubs and large herbaceous plants, with a few suitable trees such as those already mentioned and *Betula pendula* 'Youngii' a quick-growing tree that has an interesting weeping habit, as well as height, with the bonus of quite attractive bark.

If however, you plan to stay in your present home for a long time you can elect to include a few of the more slow-growing plants and trees in your garden plans, avoiding an initial sparse look by using 'filler' plants such as quick-growing herbaceous perennials or even tall, bushy annuals such as mallows and lavateras.

Where money is not an inhibiting factor and you have the self-discipline to be able to remove some of the trees and shrubs later when they become too large, there is also the possibility of planting close initially and then removing the more expendable ones before they compete for light and space with the more prized specimens.

Expressing your individuality

The personal preferences to be taken into account when assessing the site are discussed on page 10, but even before you begin to assess a particular site, it is worth looking critically at how other people approach their gardening.

Gardens are traditionally divided into 'ornamental' and 'utility' or 'kitchen' sections – and gardeners tend to be either 'fruit and veg' or 'flower' people. Yet there is no reason why the two have to be segregated; they *can* be combined harmoniously if you cease to think in rigid terms.

A well-kept vegetable plot can be an attractive sight, and it certainly need not be hidden from view behind a hedge or at the very end of the garden; in rural areas one sometimes sees front gardens entirely devoted to vegetables. And, if your garden is small and space therefore at a premium, there is no reason why vegetables cannot be grown *among* the flowers. The illustration on pages 168 and 169 shows how success-fully the two can be merged. If this example still looks too regimented for your tastes, you could consider the possibili-ties of using some of the vegetables as ornamental plants. For example, the runner bean is still used primarily as a decorative climber in some parts of the world, and it is perfectly acceptable to combine its decorative features with a useful crop, as the illustration opposite demonstrates.

Carrots and beetroots make excellent foliage plants among flowers, and carrots in particular have the advantage of not having to be picked early as they mature, leaving premature gaps in the flower beds in the middle of summer.

All these examples demonstrate the value of 'thinking flexibly' and show how you can design the garden to suit your needs and express your personality.

Getting advice

Nobody has a monopoly on good ideas, and even a seasoned gardener – faced with a new plot – can still learn a thing or two. Fortunately plenty of help is available. Whether you want advice about design or about which plants to grow in

Even a small garden can produce a variety of vegetables

the local soil, it is worth seeking help *before* you spend money on materials and plants.

Books are an excellent source of general advice and will provide lots of ideas; particularly helpful are those which give practical advice coupled with lavish use of illustrations to guide you in your choice of plants in terms of heights, shapes and colours. And you can go back to the book again and again to check things out. What no book can do adequately, however, is deal with your specific problems. Your garden is unique, and your tastes personal. The soil, site and climate may be very different to those found even a short distance away. Books and magazines cannot 'fine tune' to that extent, and that is where local knowledge can be invaluable.

If you have just moved into a district, and your neighbours are obviously gardening enthusiasts, they can be a very helpful source of advice and information on what will and will not grow in your particular plot. If they are not, consider joining the local horticultural society (which is a good idea anyway). Fellow members will probably be delighted to talk to you about your gardening problems.

Another possible source of helpful advice is your local parks department – where you will be getting your help from professionals with a local knowledge. Some local authorities are more helpful than others.

National societies are also a mine of information. Most of them are for enthusiasts of particular groups of plants, however, and it may be more general advice that you need. By joining either the Royal Horticultural Society (Vincent Square, London SW1P 2PE) or the Northern Horticultural Society (Harlow Car Gardens, Harrogate, Yorkshire) you will have access to some of the country's top experts.

Both the first-time gardener and the experienced gardener confronted with a new garden are full of bright hopes and grand ideas. Realizing them is another matter, but great expectations certainly form the base of many fine creations.

Be prepared to modify your aspirations to what is practical, but do not be afraid to have ambition. Start by listing your ideas, eliminating what is clearly not feasible, then try to work the rest into your scheme – bearing in mind the principles of good design.

You may have to pay a fee for soil analysis or for detailed garden plans, but the major societies will help with all kinds of queries, from pest and disease problems, to where to buy plants or equipment.

Making a start on design

A garden is shaped by practical limitations and personal taste, but most garden designers are agreed on three requirements: function, appearance, and harmony.

A functional garden should serve its purpose and meet the needs of its owner.

Appearance depends on neatness, effective use of colour, and a design which provides points of interest in keeping with their surroundings.

Harmony is achieved when the garden is planned in relation to the house and its surroundings. Although an attractive setting makes designing easier, gardens of great merit are found in differing environments, both in the city and in the countryside. Charm and excellence do not depend only on size or situation.

Do not be tempted to flatten everything in sight in your new garden and start from scratch. Apart from making a lot of unnecessary work for yourself, it is almost certain that the existing garden will have at least one good feature worth preserving; perhaps a fine old tree or an unusual rose bush. Problem features can be minimized by drawing attention away from them or by disguising them altogether.

The selection and care of appropriate plants can be undertaken confidently once the principles of plant requirements are grasped.

Assessing the site

You will need a considerable amount of information about the site and its surroundings before assessing ideas for the design and development of your gar-

den. All gardens are limited to some extent by four considerations: personal preference, natural features of the site, climatic influence and drainage.

Personal preference

There are as many roles for a garden as there are gardeners, and only you know what you want from your piece of land. Most people aim for a garden that beautifies the space around or behind the house. This cosmetic role may be specific in certain instances, such as the disguise of blank walls, manhole covers or ugly buildings. Sometimes areas are set aside for growing food and these need particular care. When, for example, you are choosing a spot with sufficient light for Brussels sprouts, bear in mind that you are unlikely to want serried ranks of them in full view of the house. Similarly, flowers grown for cutting (or, in more ambitious years, for exhibition) will not best serve the overall design of the garden if they are too conspicuous.

For many people the best reward for an hour's gardening is another hour spent idling: a garden is its owner's play space, and the most important features of the leisure area are privacy and comfort. Young children will need a safe corner in sight of the house, perhaps with a little flower-bed of their own. The main problem with modern gardens is a lack of size which makes it difficult to set aside areas for special use, but fortunately there are such space-saving devices as trough gardens, movable tubs, and climbing plants, which will clothe generous expanses of wall or fence in return for their modest ground space.

The first-time gardener may not know enough about plants to know what he likes! In this case, colour is as good a starting point as any, until experience of differences in foliage and form leads to a more sophisticated choice. The table on page 82 offers basic information for choosing subjects for your flower garden.

'Instant' gardens need immediate and sometimes heavy expenditure and many people prefer to develop a garden gradually, thus lowering initial costs and spreading expenditure over a longer period. Any unfinished area can be put down to grass until it is developed.

RIGHT A small garden provides an attractive and practical outdoor room. The hard path is functional, and the planting provides a variety of colour and form.

Features of the site

Your garden will have an area, shape and natural qualities of its own such as the rise and fall of the land, any rocks or water, and the vegetation. Size is crucial as it affects the choice of what can be fitted in, since all plants need room to breathe. As small areas are used intensively, hard-wearing walking surfaces, although more expensive to lay than grass, should be used in confined spaces, especially for year-round purposes. On plots of regular shape, such as squares or rectangles, and particularly on small sites, designs tend to be more formal or regimented than on plots of irregular outline or large area, but with care and judgement in the beginning, the small garden need not lack character.

Changes in ground level can add interest; gentle slopes can be mown or planted, or, if funds permit, they can be stepped or terraced to make an attractive feature. Large differences in level can be treated with retaining walls, or formed into banks covered with colourful or interesting plants, which is an economical solution. Slopes steeper than one in three are best left as they are and not cultivated as heavy rain is likely to cause soil erosion.

The kind of soil in your garden can restrict the choice of plants; it would not be wise, for example, to plant rhododendrons on shallow chalk soils (see page 34, plants for particular soil types). Clay soils can cause flooding in wet weather because the rainwater is unable to drain away quickly.

If you have an intriguing view or such features as rocks and water or fine trees, highlight them in your design. Shelter, screening and divisions are important elements in any garden, to create privacy, protection from strong winds or sun, to hide eyesores or to protect children and pets from danger. Look around your garden and see where divisions are needed before choosing new materials and plants, remembering the significance of texture, colour and outline in plants, buildings and fencing structures.

Climate

The climate of the region in which you live will influence the successful growing of plants in your garden. For gardening purposes there are three broad categories of climate in Britain: arctic-alpine, oceanic, and continental.

Scotland and northern England, with harder winters and shorter growing seasons, have the *arctic-alpine* type of climate, except some of the Western

ABOVE A rock garden on a gentle slope. RIGHT A retaining wall planted with *Alyssum saxatile* and *Phlox subulata*. BELOW Ways of dealing with changes in level.

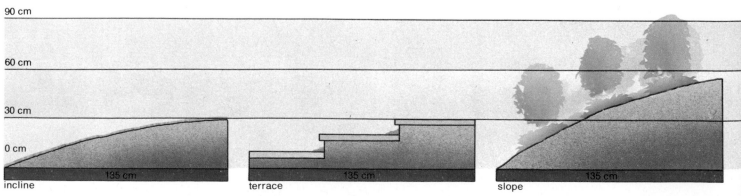

incline   terrace   slope

Isles, parts of Dumfriesshire, and coastal areas of Cumbria. The upland areas of central England and northern Wales also fall into this category.

The south-west and lowland coastal areas of western England and Wales have milder winters, more humid weather and higher rainfall than south and eastern England. The former are in the *oceanic* region and the latter falls within the *continental* category, having hotter, drier summers than the rest of Britain.

The map reveals a pattern of decreasing average temperatures from south-west England to north-east Scotland. This is due to the warm Gulf Stream air being progressively cooled as it moves in a north-easterly direction. High ground in Wales, northern

latitude

average winter-summer temperature

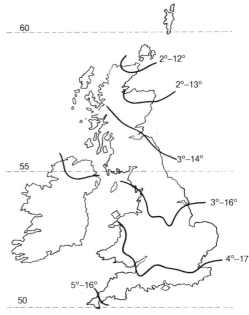

England and Scotland distorts, but does not alter, the general trend.

The influence of land and water, particularly on temperature, is very marked. The west coast is comparatively warm and moist, due to the influence of the Atlantic, and has fewer days of frost. The east coast, influenced by the continent, is generally drier and cooler. Inland areas of south-eastern and central England are hotter in summer and cooler in winter. Sites on high ground are not only cooler and wetter, but experience fogs and mists more frequently.

Towns and cities, with their roads,

paving, roofing and rapid surface drainage, are drier and warmer than the surrounding area by a few degrees; they encourage earlier flowering, but also tend to be draughtier. Gardens sheltered from north and east winds and south-facing can be an average of several degrees warmer than other less favoured sites, and their plants can crop weeks earlier even in the same street.

Coastal districts are usually noted for breezes; wind coming in off the sea meets no physical obstruction to reduce the air flow, and seashore buildings and vegetation take the full force. There is also the constant air flow between sea and land caused by their different temperatures. In summer, for example, on sunny days, the land is hotter; warm air rises, drawing in cooler air off the sea. At night this process is reversed, unless stronger regional air currents are at work.

Different kinds of plants, through selection and adaptation, have their own requirements for warmth, light and shade, water and humidity and this accounts for the variation in vegetation not only between regions and districts, but also within the same garden.

retaining wall

135 cm

Temperature Small variations of warmth have a big effect on growth: the difference between the north of Scotland and southern England is an annual average temperature of about 5.5°C (10°F) at sea level. The effect of altitude is a drop of about 0.5°C (1°F) for each 90m (300ft) rise. For hardy plants, growth virtually ceases below 5°C (41°F) and their growing season is restricted to the period when the temperature is above that point. Plants shaded by buildings or trees can be 5.5°C (10°F) or more cooler than those in sunny situations even within the same garden.

Light and shade Sunlight affects plants in many ways. During the winter months the rays of the sun are weaker because they strike the ground at a lower angle. South-facing slopes are warmer than north-facing ground because the rays hit the slopes more directly. Some crops flower in the spring or autumn, others flower during the summer, triggered off by the mechanism within plants which responds to the number of hours of daylight or darkness to which they are subjected. This is one of the reasons why some varieties of vegetables, such as soya beans, Australian varieties of cauliflowers, and some lettuces, cannot be grown satisfactorily out of their natural season. The same is true of some flowers, so it is necessary to choose varieties with care. The number of daylight hours in Scotland is up to two hours less in mid-winter and two hours more in mid-summer than in southern England. The big difference between plants growing on east or west

ABOVE A sunny day in winter. Shadows are longer and weaker than in summer.
BELOW Seasonal intensity of shade from the midday sun. The difference is caused by the height of the sun and the angle of its rays.

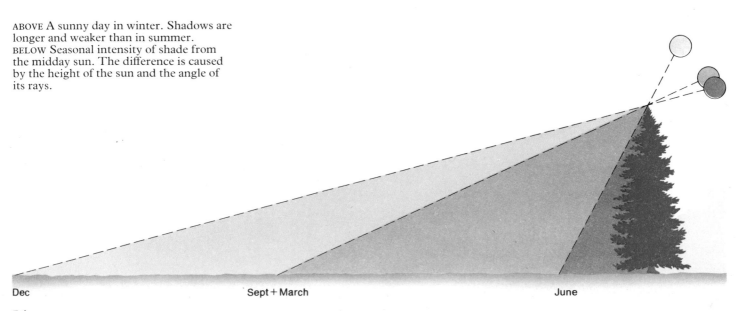

Dec   Sept + March   June

walls compared to a south aspect can be attributed to fewer hours of direct sunlight – they get about half the number. In 1977, a clematis plant growing on south and east-facing walls flowered 17 days earlier on the south-facing wall than on the one facing east.

Plants grown in full sunlight are stocky and sturdy, unlike their spindly counterparts on shaded sites.

Wind and shelter Plants protected by windbreaks can be several degrees warmer than others which are less sheltered. The lopsided windswept specimens seen in most coastal districts are examples of retarded growth on the windward side. More normal development occurs on the leeward side.

Rainfall and humidity Clouds, humid conditions, rain, and expanses of water such as the sea, exert a moderating influence, causing the weather to be less hot in summer and less cold in winter. The higher rainfall and humid conditions in western districts favour the growth of ferns, plums and black-currants, and the drier south-east is better for dessert apples. Damp humid conditions tend to encourage certain diseases; potato blight is an example.

ABOVE A garden in August with strong shadows. Plants should be positioned according to their preferences for light and shade.
RIGHT The effect of exposure and prevailing winds on a tamarisk in a seaside garden.

THE LIVING SOIL AND ITS CULTIVATION

The majority of garden owners have to continue coping with the particular soil they inherit. In the case of a newly built house there may be special problems caused by the relics of building works that have churned up the site and left immovable rocks behind. Thorough cleaning of the site is essential; if really serious damage has been done it may be necessary to pave over the area. Nevertheless, there are many ways in which a poor patch of ground can be improved and made more healthy to give heavier crops. First we should realize that the soil does not consist of inert dead matter but myriads of living organisms, which must be present if crops are to flourish.

The various types of soil are usually based on clay, sand, loam, chalk or peat, as explained in detail later in this chapter.

Clay soils become sticky and glue-like when wet. On drying, they harden into lumps, making it difficult for roots to penetrate.

Sandy soils are porous and easy to work but they drain rapidly and are liable to dry out badly in summer. Chalky or limy soils are usually shallow, lacking in humus and need feeding heavily. In dry seasons, particularly, the leaves of crops turn yellow, growth is stunted and yields are poor. Such soils can be made productive by adding plentiful supplies of organic matter each year.

Peaty soils are usually very sour. They contain plenty of organic matter, and because they often remain wet, they need to be drained. This is especially so in the case of the black heavy boggy peats.

The air spaces in the soil are also most important; air is essential for plants' roots have to breathe to live and grow. If the soil becomes too wet air is driven out and roots stop growing.

The so-called loamy soils are the best for they contain an ideal blend of clay and sand. The sand keeps the soil warm allowing moisture to seep through, while the clay prevents quick drying out as well as helping to retain plant food. Whatever the type of soil being cultivated, get to know its organic content so that the right feeding programme to sustain plant life can be worked out. Loams differ in

their composition, and regular applications of humus in the form of old manure or garden compost as well as an occasional liming, will normally ensure that good crops are produced.

It is not easy to state exactly what humus really is, but it has been described as a complex residue of partly oxidized animal and vegetable matter, together with substances synthesized by fungi and bacteria used to break down these wastes. It is hardly surprising that it is of complex character, since it is formed by the work of worms, animals, insects and many kinds of bacteria with numerous live and dead organisms combined with the residues of plants and animals. These produce the marvel we know as humus and upon which the organic gardener relies. It is not dead, in the way we usually understand that word but is part of an organic cycle in which constant changes and processes are going on.

The scarcity of farmyard manure should not cause us to give up our quest for bulk manures for there are substitutes which make it possible to build up good, fertile, 'easy-to-work' soil. These include composted vegetable refuse – including kitchen waste and leaves, which should not be burned – seaweed, sewage sludge, shoddy, spent hops and poultry manure. To these may be added organic fertilizers such as bone meal, hoof and horn and soot.

Very often manure is dug in too deeply, for many of our most useful plants and trees have a rooting system fairly near the surface. This is why mulching is so valuable and why it is so needful for the top 45 cm (18 ins) of soil to contain a high percentage of the organic materials that provide the humus material essential for proper development.

The beneficial soil organisms are the vital link in the chain of fertility, for it is through their functions in the decomposition of organic matter in the soil that a circulation of the necessary elements for plant life is possible. Most of the many soil organisms are to be found near the surface and in the area close to plant roots. Their

To manufacture the carbohydrates necessary for healthy growth by the process known as photosynthesis plants must have fresh air, adequate light from the sun, and water. Fine root hairs (shown many times magnified) absorb mineral salts in solution from the earth.

number falls off rapidly in soil deficient in organic matter. We can only refer to a few of the living agents in the soil, not only for space reasons, but because little is known of some of the others.

There are the mycorrhiza, a name covering various fungi which among other activities excrete substances which appear to stimulate growth. Quite a number of plants grow much better when these fungi are present. There is reason to believe that they thrive on decaying vegetable matter and do not live on the actual soil.

The soil bacteria vary considerably in size and function, while algae are soil plants without roots or distinctive form. They are in various ways connected with the protozoa some of which are not at all helpful to plant life. Another group of soil inhabitants is known as the actinomyces which appear to be related to both bacteria and fungi. Other lesser known organisms act in a different way in that instead of breaking down material, they build it up making it useful to plant life. Since we do have so many microbes working for us in the soil it is to our advantage to see that we provide the organic matter essential for this work to be carried on.

If there are multitudes of soil inhabitants we cannot see with the naked eye, there are other beneficial living agents working for us and whose appearance we know well. The most important of these are the earthworms. While they may not be wanted in the lawn because of the casts they throw up, elsewhere they should be made welcome and encouraged. The tunnels that they make as they burrow through the soil increase aeration and assist drainage, creating an environment in which beneficial bacteria can thrive, and worm-casts have a useful manurial effect.

The earthworm greatly helps to renew and maintain the film of top soil. While it is difficult to fully understand how the earthworm can make the soil more fertile, as a result of experiments in the USA and in Britain, worm casts have been found to contain more nitrogen, phosphates and potash than is present in the top 12–15 cm (5–6 ins) of normal garden soil.

Worm burrows may penetrate up to 1.20–1.50 m (4–5 ft) into the ground. The size and appearance of worms seen when moving the ground will give a good guide as to the fertility of the soil. Fat, red rather tacky glistening worms indicate a good soil, where these creatures can work and breed freely. Greyish-red slow moving perhaps curling specimens suggest that the ground is in great need of humus matter.

A useful function of their work which can often be seen happening is the pulling down of decaying leaves and other organic matter into the soil. Old pieces of grass or weeds as well as other pieces of vegetable matter such as loose skins off shallots or onion sets are also pulled into the ground where they are broken down and dampened by the excretions of worms and become useful to the plant as well as improving the physical condition of the soil.

Various chemical fertilizers may retard the increase of the worm population which is why they need using with care and should never be applied heavily.

It is possible to have soils analysed to obtain an accurate idea of their constituents. The horticultural departments of most county colleges will perform this service for a small fee. Alternatively small soil testing outfits are readily available and for a small plot these are usually quite satisfactory (see page 25). Weeds can also be a useful guide to the state of the soil.

The very common chickweed which can be seen thriving in fertile soil indicates that there is plenty of nitrogen available. Nettles flourish in ground containing plenty of humus and do not grow nearly so well where the soil is sandy, stony or very chalky. There is

Fat hen, or white goosefoot, was once eaten as a spinach substitute

Sheep's sorrel will not grow on chalky soils

therefore much truth in the saying that where nettles thrive the ground is good and crops are likely to flourish – after the nettles have been removed!

Fat hen is another extremely common annual weed which can be found growing freely in light loamy soil and indicates the ground contains plenty of plant foods. The presence of horsetail on the other hand, tells us that the soil is wet and badly drained. Sorrel and dock plants have deep roots which like dampness at the roots and grow strongly in deep clay.

The presence of self-sown clover in a lawn shows that the soil is alkaline. In this case apply a dressing of sulphate of ammonia which will destroy the large leaves of clover, make the soil more acid and strengthen the grass. Care is needed not to apply too much of this fertilizer since only a little (25 g (1 oz) per sq yd is usually adequate) may be needed to correct the imbalance between acidity and alkalinity.

Not all soil organisms are beneficial to plant growth: some compete for soil, space and nutrients in the battle for existence. Certain soil fungi are responsible for diseases such as damping off, mildews, root and stem rots. Nematodes or eelworms will attack roots and the upper parts of plants, while certain bacteria may cause galls and leaf spot diseases.

Everything that is done to keep the soil in good condition by feeding and by the improvement of the chemical and physical properties favours the well-being of beneficial soil organisms, so helping to maintain their dominance in the soil population.

Experience shows that the presence of organic matter leads to an increase in desirable soil fungi which play their part in pest control and in increasing soil fertility for the higher plants.

A now well-recognized method of helping to keep the soil in good condition, preventing the surface from drying out and encouraging the increase of the beneficial living soil inhabitants, is the practice of mulching.

The word 'mulch' simply means a layer of material placed over the soil, usually to cover the root area of the plants. Mulching serves several purposes including the conservation of moisture and preventing the drying out of the surface soil especially where there may be only a few young fibrous roots, while some mulches are applied as a means of feeding plants. Moisture from rain or watering

cans infiltrates more readily through mulches without the repeated stirring necessary to keep the surface soil broken and receptive to water.

Mulches have other functions in that they help to keep down weeds and according to what is used, feeding matter is eventually washed down to a good depth. Earthworms flourish in the humus formed by organic mulching materials, further improving the soil.

Crops which are gross feeders will derive most benefit from a surface covering of material which supplies plant food as well as preventing loss of moisture from the surface. Well-grown runner beans, late peas, cauliflowers, marrows and cucumbers and tomatoes under glass are specially responsive to mulching.

Do not apply mulches too early but wait until the soil begins to

Horsetail will take over damp areas if not checked by hoeing

Applying a springtime mulch to a plum tree

Heavy harvests will be the reward from well-nourished soils

warm. The middle of May is usually early enough for cauliflowers, mid-July for runner beans and for peas from June until late July, according to variety. Outdoors, tomatoes on light soil should be mulched by late June. Cucumbers under glass will benefit from several applications since this will prevent the roots from surfacing.

Make sure the soil is moist before applying any surface covering. Apart from materials which provide feeding matter and soil improvers, such as compost, leaf mould, peat moss and hop manure, there are many others which can be used. These include black plastic sheeting, which hinders weed growth, and sawdust which, when fresh, leaches nitrogen from the soil which needs to be replaced. It may also attract woodlice and ants. Grass clippings are also useful but they sometimes become messy and harbour flies. Small stones too, can be used. Anyone who has moved stones, in the driest of weather will have been surprised at the amount of moisture in the soil beneath them.

Frequent hoeing often produces a dust which acts as a mulch to the soil beneath, a practice once greatly relied upon. While material with feeding value is much more beneficial, we should not too lightly disregard successful methods relied on for many years.

For some years experiments have been made in growing vegetables and other crops by the no-digging method. This is not because certain gardeners are lazy and do not like the idea of the work involved in turning over the soil, but because they are keen to get the best results. Gardeners who have seriously tried 'no digging', are unlikely to go back to moving the soil.

Instead of using a spade, fork or hoe in the autumn, the non-

digger places a layer of compost all over the vacant ground in his garden. Advocates of this system, which in certain cases has much good to be said for it, argue that in nature, plant wastes are not buried but become incorporated with the soil by the effects of the weather and the functions of worms and other soil inhabitants. Bulky material is reduced by natural decomposition without the help of man. In addition, surface applications of compost provide the right conditions for the fungi which are present in fertile soil. Many weed seeds brought to the surface by ordinary digging could lie buried in unturned soil for many years.

There is reason to believe that surface mulching gives greater freedom from pests and diseases, while regular dressings of composted material placed on the surface result in better flavoured vegetables even though the size of the crop may sometimes be smaller. It is worthwhile trying a no-digging experiment on a small plot to compare results with conventional methods of cultivating the soil.

The success of the organic surface cultivation really depends on the amount of compost available. Mulching places the raw materials where nature allows the natural workers to process it. If it is buried very deeply organic material cannot be properly processed: it must be near the surface. Among other advantages of organic surface cultivation are that weeds are gradually eliminated and are not dug up again as they would be if the soil were turned over. Worms are not disturbed and therefore go on with their valuable work of aerating the soil, while soil bacteria are kept sufficiently near to the surface to function properly.

Plants grown by this method of cultivation show a vigour that is never seen where the gardener depends on continued supplies of artificial fertilizers, which not only cause the soil to become thin and lifeless but never encourage the production of a bunch of fibrous roots which plants need if they are to produce good crops.

How to Build a Compost Heap

One of the best substitutes for organic manures may be the plant food organic waste provided by a compost heap. This is made by composting all garden and kitchen waste so that it is acted upon by soil bacteria and fungi and so converted into humus.

The basic technique of compost making is described on this page, but you will find a step-by-step visual guide using alternative containers on pages 26 and 27.

The heap should not be fully exposed to the sun, wind or rain, and a low lying position, or one where there are drips from over-hanging trees, should be avoided. Where low ground is the only position available, it is not necessary or even wise to dig a hole; in fact, if this is done, water will collect and hinder the process of decomposition.

On level ground, a shallow excavation may be made for the base of the heap and in very dry areas where rainfall is always low, pits of 45–75 cm (18–30 ins) may be taken out. Fork over the foundation of the heap and if brushwood, cabbage stalks, coarse hedge trimmings or bricks are first laid in position, they will provide valuable aeration and drainage. Over this base, place a layer of peat and well-rotted manure or even ripe compost from the previous rotting down. Once this has been done, the various materials are placed upon the base and mixed so that decay is quick and even. Therefore coarse and fine, wet and dry, fresh and old material should be used together, and will lead to proper breaking down.

The shape and size of the heap affects the rate of decomposition and the ultimate quality of the compost. For preference make the heap in the shape of a pyramid or a rectangle avoiding a flat shape-less mass, as is so often seen. For the average garden a heap 1 m (3 ft) long, 45 cm (1½ ft) wide and 1 m (3 ft) high is the easiest size to manage. Wooden compost boxes may be employed to keep the material in place. Alternatively, use proprietory compost bins which retain heat, yet ensure adequate aeration of the decomposing waste.

To build up the heap spread a layer of manure, or sprinkle soil and dried blood or some other organic manure, on each layer of waste matter. After the next layer, use more soil and a sprinkling of ground chalk. Sandwich the layers until the heap is complete. Then leave it for three weeks before turning it, placing the outside to the middle. Then cover the heap entirely with a layer of soil, which will increase fermentation, or in the case of bins, plastic or even wood may be placed on the top to keep the heat in.

Depending on the materials used, a compost heap takes anything from three to 12 months to become ready for use. It is therefore a good plan to make a new heap every autumn, so the material is ripe for use by adding to the soil when winter digging. Two heaps are needed, one being built up as the other becomes ready to use.

Anything organic that rots down easily can be put on the heap, including plant remains, leaves, grass mowings, kitchen peelings, and tea leaves. Woody, bulky material such as cabbage plants can also be added to the heap but before doing so, it is wise to crush these with a hammer so that they rot down more easily. Although the heat from a well-made compost heap is sufficient to destroy many weed seeds, generally speaking perennial weeds such as couch grass, docks and bindweed are best burned.

Twigs laid beneath the first layer of compost ensure aeration. A sturdy framework keeps the heap neat and maintains its temperature

Build up alternate layers of soft material and soil, using fertilizers or ground chalk as described. Water each layer when it is completed.

After three weeks turn the heap over, outside to centre, before covering with soil and leaving it to rot down completely.

Understanding the soil

Sound soil management is essential to the success of any gardening venture, but first the nature of the soil has to be understood.

Soil has to be improved, modified or manipulated so that the best conditions for plant life can be created. Good conditions offer anchorage and support, sufficient food and warmth, adequate moisture and oxygen, and room for plants to develop.

The critical soil factors for effective gardening are: land drainage and porosity (the rate at which water drains through soil), and moisture retention, available plant foods, acidity and chalk content and warmth. Each type of soil has its own characteristics and is more suited to some kinds of plants than others, and garden soil can be measured sufficiently accurately with inexpensive do-it-yourself kits.

The composition of fertile soil

Fertile soil is easily worked, friable, and crumbly in texture. The fine crumbly surface layer of such soil is known as a good tilth. It is dark in colour, well-drained and yet retains moisture for growth. It contains reserves of plant food, and is warm enough to support sturdy balanced plant growth. Close examination of a handful of good soil will show that it is composed of moist crumbs or particles of solid matter, pieces of old root fibre, possibly a few small pebbles, a worm or two, and perhaps a quick-moving shiny-brown centipede. Fertile soil, far from being an inert lump of dirt, is literally teeming with life. In addition to the plants that can be seen growing on the land, and the worms and centipedes inhabiting it, there are more lowly forms of plant and animal life invisible to the naked eye. Bacteria form the largest part of the soil population, amounting to many millions in a mere handful of healthy soil.

ABOVE RIGHT The composition of good garden soil showing relative amounts of solids, air and water.
RIGHT Healthy garden soil viewed through a magnifying glass might look like this.

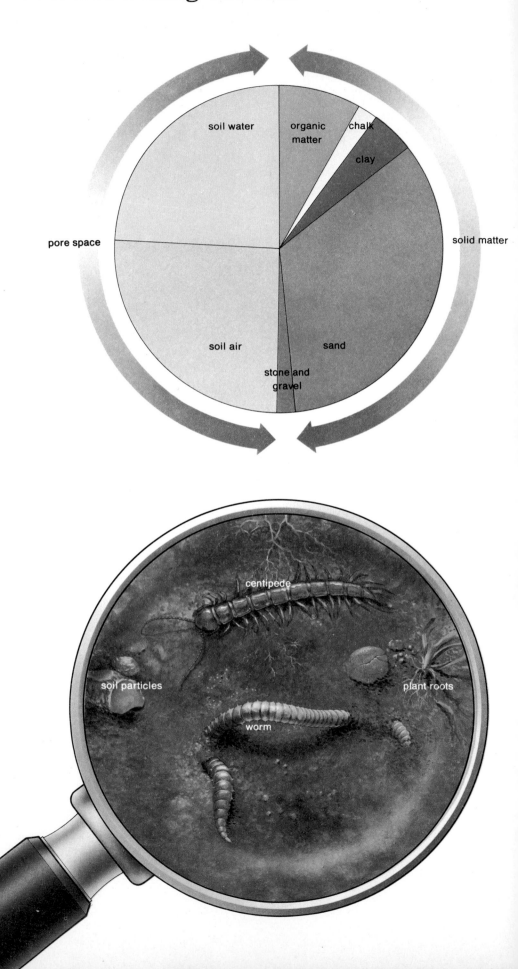

22

Clay soil from the Weald of Kent shows the general greyish colour and rusty mottled characteristic of waterlogged subsoils.

Deep, loamy soil, retentive of moisture and nutrients, on fertile 'brick earth'. The even brown colour indicates good subsoil drainage.

Sandy soil over Bagshot sands is loose and dry. In its natural state it lacks lime and plant nutrients.

There is a narrow margin between fertile and poor soils. By upsetting one factor – by overliming, or working a waterlogged soil, for example – yields can be considerably reduced for a year or more. Given care and attention, however, the land can be kept in good condition and improved upon without difficulty.

Pore Space

The spaces between the crumbs of soil are collectively called pore space. In a fertile soil about half the total volume consists of pore space, which is occupied in turn by water vapour, air, and water. The balance between water and air is crucial to plants. If the pore space is filled with water, roots will suffocate, while if it is full of air, plants die for lack of water. In a fertile soil, water is present around each particle as a thin film of moisture containing dissolved fertilizer and mineral salts. Air spaces separate each particle except during and immediately after rain or irrigation. When surplus rain or other water is drained away, fresh air and oxygen is sucked into the pore space. Clay soils have too much soil water, and sands and gravels have too little, for gardening purposes.

This shallow dry soil on the chalk of the Berkshire Downs still has a dark colour from the humus content built up under old grassland.

This heavy, fertile loam has little depth over the hard but brittle Cotswold limestone.

Soil solids

These can conveniently be considered under two headings: mineral, and organic matter.

Mineral matter For practical purposes, the mineral part of soil consists of: clay, sand, chalk, and plant nutrients. Fertile land contains all these materials in varying amounts, but within fairly narrow limits.

Clay is composed of very fine particles of matter which, even in small quantities can affect the soil properties. Clay soils can hold far more water and dissolved plant foods than sand, and are slow to drain. They are sticky when wet, and set rock hard when dry. Their management requires cultivation to be carried out only when the moisture content falls between these two extremes. Liming greatly improves its texture and clay also benefits from the addition of sand and manure.

Sand consists of comparatively coarse grains, and is free-draining, but low in plant nutrients. Sand helps to balance some of the undesirable effects of clay. Both *chalk and limestone* are neutral or alkaline and form a major constituent of soils in chalk and limestone districts. These materials can occur in soil as fine grains or coarse lumps.

Plant nutrients are chemicals in relatively small quantities in soil, either as solids or dissolved in water. The main elements needed for plant nutrition and which are supplied by fertilizer applications, are nitrogen, phosphorus and potassium, together with iron, magnesium and manganese. Substances such as sulphur, zinc and copper fall into the group known as trace elements, so-called because they are only required in minute amounts.

Organic matter Living and dead organisms and animal and plant remains come under this general heading.

The living material consists primarily of plants and roots, bacteria, and lower forms of life. The dead and decomposing remains are mainly manure and plant residues which perform the vital role of maintaining soils in good physical condition, assisting natural drainage, and releasing bacteria which break down harmful compounds in the soil. In certain parts of the country, such as the moss lands of Lancashire and the peat fens of Norfolk and Lincolnshire, land consisting predominantly of peat and other vegetable matter has been made highly fertile through the use of adequate liming, drainage and fertilizers.

Well-decayed organic matter is a rich dark brown colour and is called *humus*. It is a sweet-smelling and most valuable constituent of healthy soils.

Flora and fauna

No healthy, productive soil would be complete without beneficial bacteria and simple forms of animals and insect life. Bacteria break down organic matter, and assist in the weathering of soil particles which releases necessary nutrients, and they purify the soil and soil air by breaking down complex compounds and rendering them harmless. They also fix nitrogen from the atmosphere for the benefit of plants.

Although they can be a nuisance on lawns, earthworms perform a useful service in aerating the soil and assisting drainage. They aid the formation of humus by drawing fallen leaves underground into their burrows, and enrich the soil with their 'casts' or excreta.

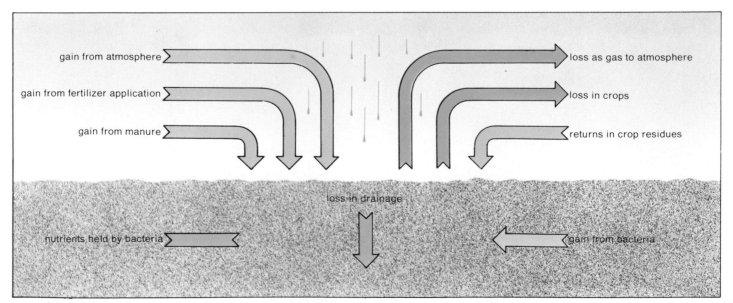

gain from atmosphere → loss as gas to atmosphere
gain from fertilizer application → loss in crops
gain from manure → returns in crop residues
loss in drainage
nutrients held by bacteria → gain from bacteria

Recognizing soil types

Soils vary greatly, even within a field or garden. Successful cultivation and treatment depends on recognition of types of soil. There are many ways of classifying land, such as being heavy or light to work, and early or late depending on when it produces crops, but for practical purposes a system based on texture and composition is quite adequate.

Texture system

There are seven main types of soil: clay soils, heavy loams, medium loams, sandy loams, sandy soils, chalk and limestone soils, and peat soils. Any of these may be acid, neutral or alkaline in reaction, except chalk and limestone soils, which are usually alkaline. Each soil type behaves differently, and plants respond by showing preferences for one soil or another.

Soil type can be identified simply and with some certainty by safe chemical and physical tests, and by observation.

Chemical tests These are used to determine two sets of soil factors rather than identify soil type. Firstly they show the soil reaction or the pH value – how acid or alkaline the land is; and secondly the plant food levels (nitrogen, phosphate and potash) in a soil.

These tests can either be carried out professionally or at home. Most modern do-it-yourself kits (available from garden centres and hardware stores) are well tried and sufficiently accurate for the amateur gardener. To carry out your own tests, dig up one or more small soil samples from your garden and remove any stones or large lumps. Put some of the soil sample in a glass test tube and pour in the chemical reagent supplied in the kit. After corking the tube, shake up the soil and chemical together and allow the mixture to settle. Compare the colour of the solution against the supplier's colour chart to discover the pH, or acidity of your soil. Some charts also indicate

how much lime is needed to correct any imbalance.

The degree of acidity or alkalinity which plants can tolerate comfortably is quite narrow. The degree of acidity or alkalinity is measured on a scale in which pH 7 is neutral; numbers below 7 indicate acidity and those above 7,

alkalinity. For many subjects a pH level of 6 to 7 is about the limit.

Plant nutrient levels can be discovered by using other do-it-yourself kits, or by using specially treated tapers which, when dipped in a solution of soil and chemical, change colour and are read off a chart in a similar manner.

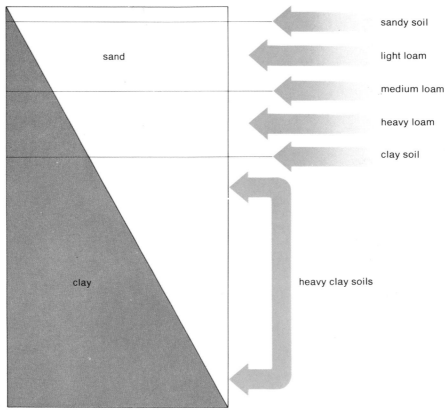

soil composition: sand and clay balance

ABOVE LEFT Humus in soil.
LEFT Ways in which soil gains and loses nutrients.
ABOVE RIGHT Soil composition: the effect of varying the proportions of sand and clay on the physical properties of soil.
RIGHT Soil testing with a simple kit.

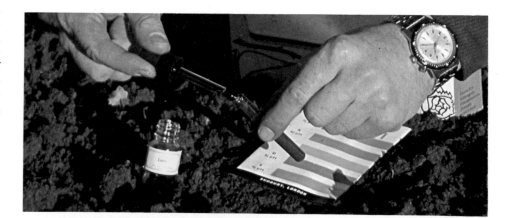

Step-by-step making compost

Burn twigs, tree prunings and wood which would take a very long time to rot down. Scatter the ash over the ground afterwards.

For a large quantity of compost, cover the pile with a plastic sheet and weight it down at the corners.

Three suitable compost makers are the box bin with a detachable front (left above); a wire frame with a plastic liner, perforated to let air through (left centre); and a plastic dustbin, also perforated (left below). A covering such as a plastic lid stops rain getting in, keeps the compost warm, and helps it rot more quickly.

5-7.5 cm (2-3 in) layer of coarse material such as pea and bean haulms, cabbage stems, and hedge trimmings.

10 cm (4 in) layer of soft vegetable waste such as kitchen vegetable trimmings or lawn mowings.

5 cm (2 in) layer of manure, or an organic fertilizer such as dried blood, and soil.

Soft vegetable waste.

5 cm (2 in) layer of soil and a sprinkling of ground chalk.

Soft vegetable waste.

Building up a compost heap in layers.

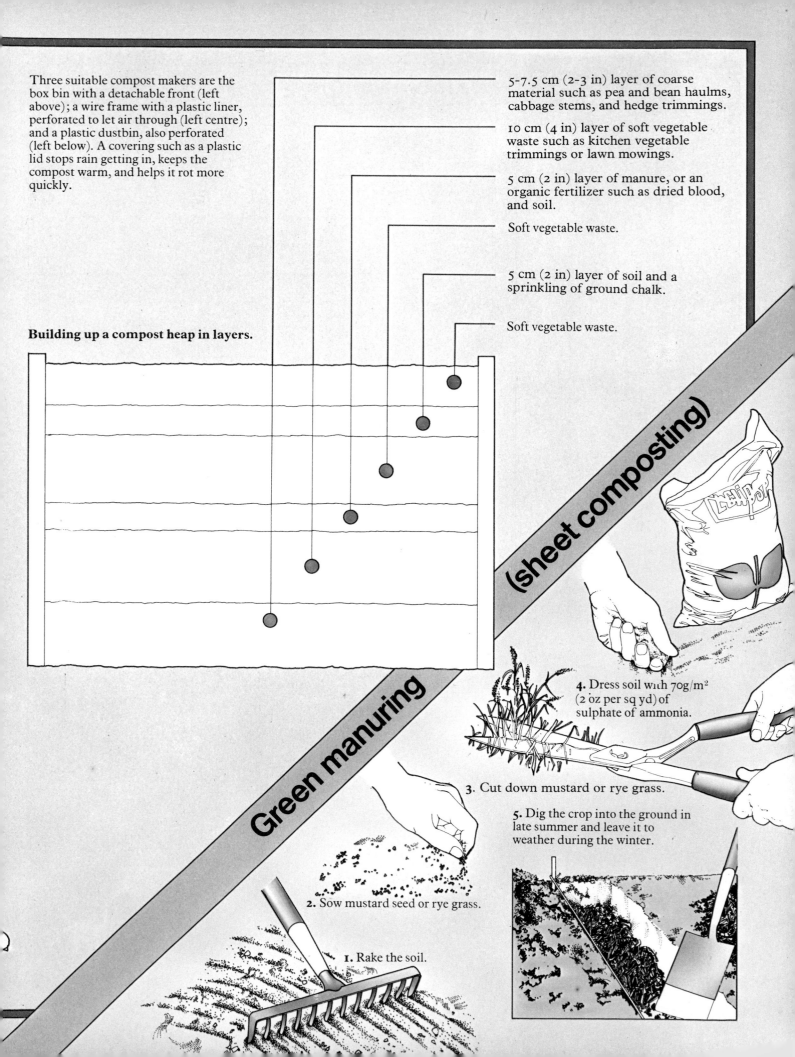

Green manuring

(sheet composting)

4. Dress soil with 70g/m² (2 oz per sq yd) of sulphate of ammonia.

3. Cut down mustard or rye grass.

5. Dig the crop into the ground in late summer and leave it to weather during the winter.

2. Sow mustard seed or rye grass.

1. Rake the soil.

Physical tests A trial dig of a hole to a spade's depth or more, will reveal a fair amount of information about a piece of ground.

Under wet conditions, clay soils will have puddles of water on the surface and be greasy to the touch. Clay will stick tenaciously to your spade and boots when digging. A sandy soil will be well drained and gritty in texture; feet and spade are easily cleaned, and the hole dug with comparative ease. Loams lie between the two extremes.

Under dry summer conditions clay soils become cracked, hard to cultivate, and lumpy. Conversely, sandy soil is easy to dig and is dry and dusty. If a bucket of water is thrown into the excavated hole, clay will not drain readily, but the water in sand will disappear rapidly. The loams will be intermediate in their response.

Digging chalk soils will reveal the tell-tale whitish subsoil of chalk or limestone, and whitish coloured lumps in the soil. Peat soils are usually dark, spongy and fibrous.

Observation Many plants are highly selective and, according to their presence or absence, you will be able to form a good idea of soil and climatic conditions. The following are a few well-established associations of plants and soils which can be seen in the wild and in cultivated areas.
Acid soils: heathers (calluna), rhododendrons, camellias, pine, Japanese maple, sheeps fescue (a fine-leaved type of grass), Scots pines and birches.
Wet soils: caltha (marsh marigold), forget-me-not, mimulus, astilbe, creeping buttercups, elders and willows.
Clay soils: similar to wet soils.
Medium loams: support vigorous mixed vegetation, roses, meadowsweet, brambles, bluebells, flowering thorns and hostas.
Sandy light soils: gorse, brooms, poppies, corydalis, tamarisk, helianthemum, geraniums.
Chalk soils: box and yew trees, viburnums, dogwoods, clematis and spindles, carnation, gypsophila and clovers in grass.

Soil type	Appearance	Physical qualities	Chemical status
Clay soil	Soil lies under water in wet weather. Sedges, rushes, buttercup, alder, willow in evidence.	Very slow to drain. Adhesive, greasy if wet or hard and lumpy when dry.	Naturally rich in plant food. Frequently neutral.
Heavy loam	Intermediate between clay and medium loam		
Medium loam	Strong-growing roses, shrubs and grasses.	Drains moderately quickly. Worked fairly readily.	Usually well supplied with plant food.
Light loam	Intermediate between medium and sandy soil		
Sandy soil	Light coloured soil. Gorse, broom and Scots pine. Heather in acid sands.	Quick draining. Easily worked in most conditions. Gritty to the touch.	Low level in nutrients. Often very acid. Needs regular feeding.
Chalk or Limestone soil	White or whitish subsoil. Dogwood, viburnum and clematis flourish.	Chalk is pasty when moist. Limestone is gritty to the touch.	Low in organic matter. Alkaline.
Peaty soil	Dark fibrous soil. Alder and willow trees often present.	Spongy and fibrous.	Low in phosphates. Often acid.
Stony soil	Often light-coloured. Many stones on surface. Sparse vegetation. Mountain ash present.	Shallow soils with large proportion of rock and stone	Low nutrient content. Needs regular and heavy feeding.
Acid soil	Heath grasses, heather, rhododendrons and fine-leaved fescue grasses abound.	Variable.	Variable.

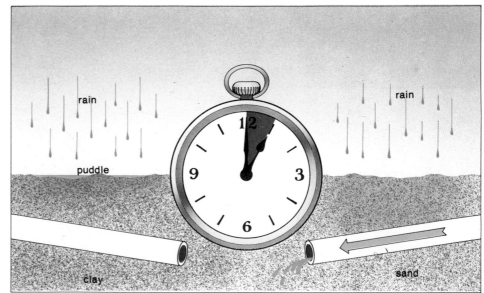

RIGHT Within an hour of heavy rain, clay soils (left) are noticeably slow to drain, sandy soils (right) drain quickly and evenly.

Manures, fertilizers and lime

If it is to produce good crops, the soil must have its reserves of various materials, such as humus, plant foods and lime, replenished at regular intervals. The organic matter is continuously being broken down, and without annual applications of fresh bulky manure, the crumb structure and the efficiency of aeration and drainage will rapidly deteriorate. Farmyard manure, compost and similar materials also supply certain foods, in addition to those gained from fertilizers.

Lime, which is continually being removed by crops and washed away by rain, is needed to neutralize the products of decay and to correct the pH of the soil. In conjunction with organic matter it creates and maintains land in good condition and by altering the structure of the soil, improves its drainage.

Manures

Improved soil conditions enable plant roots to forage more deeply for food and water, and the organic matter, when carefully used as a mulch or surface dressing, reduces moisture loss by acting like a sponge, and also provides trace elements and plant food. Dressings of manure are worked into the soil, usually in autumn and winter, or used as a surface dressing in spring and summer around fruit trees and bushes, roses and shrubs, to conserve soil moisture.

Types of manure There are two fairly distinct groups of manure: those which break down readily to release plant food; and those such as peat which are much slower to decompose, providing little by way of plant nutrients. The first group includes farmyard manure, composted straw or garden waste material, spent mushroom compost, and seaweed. Peat, pulverized tree bark, leaf mould, and spent hops belong in the second group.

Fertilizers

The new gardener may feel bewildered by the choice of currently available fertilizers. Very many materials are available, and there is often little to choose between the proprietary brands.

Some fertilizers are supplied as a base dressing *before* planting and others are supplied as a top dressing given while plants are growing. Base and top dressings usually provide the main plant requirements of nitrogen, phosphate and potash. They can be bought ready for use or mixed at home. Many gardeners use their own mixtures.

Base fertilizers are mostly available as ordinary or high potash types. The ordinary grades contain equal proportions of nitrogen, phosphate and potash, and are used for general feeding. The high-potash type are designed for fruit and flower crops and contain twice the amount of potash.

Top dressings can be applied dry or as a liquid feed. The many proprietary brands are sold as three grades: *high nitrogen*, used for celery and cucumbers; *ordinary grade*, for bringing on young plants; and *high potash*, for fruit and flowers, especially for exhibition purposes. The manufacturers' instructions should be followed carefully.

Lime

Lime is the common name for calcium, which is required by plants, beneficial bacteria and soil. In addition to helping to feed plants and bacteria, calcium in the soil under the action of manure, frost and wind, helps the soil to break up and become easier to cultivate. Lime is best applied during the winter months, some weeks after manure has been dug in, and two or three weeks before fertilizer dressings are applied. Unfortunately, calcium reacts with nitrogen in manures or fertilizers if they are applied at the same time, and causes a loss of nitrogen.

29

Popular fertilizers

Name	Analysis per cent			Fertilizer type
	N	P	K	
Bone meal	4	21	—	Base
Hoof and horn	13–14	—	—	Base
Potassium nitrate	15	—	45	Top
Nitro-chalk	15.5	—	—	Top
Sulphate of ammonia	21	—	—	Base and top
Sulphate of potash	—	—	48–50	Base and top
Superphosphate	—	16–18	—	Base and top

Home-made mixtures

Base fertilizer (1)

Hoof and horn–2 parts by weight
Superphosphate–2 parts by weight
Sulphate of potash–1 part by weight

Analysis per cent
5.6 N, 7.2 P, 10 K

Base fertilizer (2)

Superphosphate–2 parts by weight
Sulphate of ammonia–1 part by weight
Sulphate of potash–1 part by weight

Analysis per cent
5.2 N, 9 P, 12.5 K

Liquid feed

Potassium nitrate–1 part by weight

Sulphate of ammonia–1 part by weight

Analysis per cent
diluted to 28g/18 litres (1oz
per 4 gal)
17.5 N, 22.5 K

N = nitrogen, P = phosphorus, K = potassium

Soil acidity can be corrected by applying ground limestone or hydrated lime, according to the findings of a soil test (see p. 25). When hydrated lime is used, as distinct from ground limestone, 25 per cent less material is needed to produce the same effect.

Feeding your plants

Soils can be tested for acidity and for the major plant foods (see page 25), and this is important for basic crop nutrition. Nitrogen, phosphates and potash exert the greatest influence on plant growth, and with a little practice it is not too difficult to diagnose any imbalance during the growing season.

Nitrogen

Is necessary for growth of leaf and stem; too much causes dark, luxuriant, soft growth at the expense of fruiting. Nitrogen deficiency results in poor growth, pale small leaves and small but high-coloured fruits.

High nitrogen levels, warm wet weather and rich heavy soils, all encourage strong leafy growth at the expense of flower and some fruits. Such conditions are well suited to growing celery, and members of the cabbage family. Plums, blackcurrants and cooking apples will also thrive.

BELOW Mulching with compost.
ABOVE RIGHT Preparing the soil for planting by digging in manure.
BELOW RIGHT The variation between the lengths of growing season in north and south England.

Phosphate

(Its main chemical element is phosphorus) is required for root and seed development and early maturity. A deficiency results in poor, stunted growth. Phosphate is very rarely found in excess in soil since it is not particularly soluble.

Potash

(Its main chemical element is potassium) is vital to the efficient manufacture of starch in the leaves and the functioning of the chlorophyll complex, and to harden up soft growth caused by heavy nitrogen dressings. An excess can cause magnesium or iron deficiency, resulting in yellowing of the leaves and stunting. A deficiency causes the leaf margins to turn reddish-brown.

High potash levels in the soil, dry sunny conditions, and light well-drained soil, will tend to produce hard growth, early flowering and fruitfulness.

Dessert apples, fruits, flowers and seed crops are encouraged by these factors.

Plant preferences

Vegetables, generally speaking, need generous applications of manure, and heavy balanced dressings of nitrogen, phosphate and potash.

Fruits need adequate manure but the main nutrient emphasis is on fairly high dressings of phosphate and potash.

Flowers require phosphates and potash, with low nitrogen levels to promote flowering.

The feeding programme

Always spread manures or fertilizers evenly over the surface to be treated.
Autumn and winter: dig well-rotted manure into vacant ground and apply base dressings (slow-acting fertilizers) before planting new trees, shrubs and plants.

Lightly dig in manure around trees and shrubs, and apply a balanced top-dressing of fertilizer.

Spring and summer: apply fertilizer top-dressing to fruit bushes and roses, followed by a mulch to conserve moisture in summer. Liquid feeding with dissolved fertilizer can be carried out where growth is slow, but never feed plants that are dry; water them first.

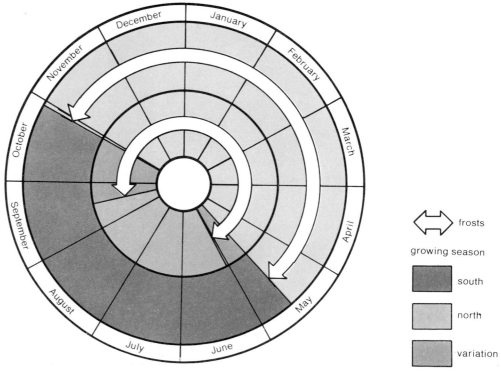

frosts

growing season

south

north

variation

31

Improving the soil

There are many soil-improving techniques, each beneficial in itself but providing the greatest impact when used in combination.

Cultivation Clay and other heavy soils can be improved simply by digging, but it is better to throw up the soil into ridges 60cm (2ft) wide in autumn, and allow frost, rain and wind to weather it and break up the lumps. A similar effect is achieved by digging trenches 60cm (2ft) wide to a spade's depth, and letting frost, rain and wind weather the ridges on each side of the trenches.

Forking

In spring when the land is dry enough to work, *lightly* fork over and level the land carefully to reap the benefit of winter weathering, especially on heavy soils.

Burning and ballasting

Burning is more suited to country districts, without smokeless zones. A layer of clay soil is placed over a slow-burning bonfire with air holes at the base and top. The granular burnt soil and the bonfire ash are afterwards scattered over the ground.

In ballasting, material such as clean sand or fine gravel is added to heavy soils to open them up. Over a few years they can be considerably improved by this process.

Sanding and marling

Occasionally, as in certain areas of Yorkshire, Kent, Hampshire, and Middlesex, the top soil rests on subsoil of a different nature. When a shallow layer of clay soil overlies a sand and gravel subsoil, if some of the sand or gravel is dug out, scattered over the heavy soil and mixed in, a considerable improvement can be made. Likewise, if a light sandy soil rests on clay, small

ABOVE A slow-burning bonfire covered with clay.
BELOW Ridging (left) and trenching (right) in winter.

quantities of the clay can be dug out and worked in a little at a time. This method has been practised for decades with some success, and is best carried out over a period of two of three years. Apart from the fact that clay or marl has to be weathered and is best worked in gradually, the energy and exertion involved in digging and cultivating is considerable.

Soil darkening

Soot improves the soil by darkening it, thereby helping it to keep warm since dark surfaces absorb heat while light surfaces reflect it, and provides small amounts of nitrogen and potash. Black or dark soil can be as much as $1\,°C\,(2\,°F)$ warmer than adjacent light-coloured soil under similar conditions. Where it can still be obtained household soot is an excellent soil conditioner, but avoid industrial substitutes. Soot is best allowed to weather for two or three months before coming into contact with plants. It can be spread over the land in winter to mellow, or weathered and worked in with the base fertilizer at about a spadeful per square metre (approximately $1\frac{1}{10}$ sq yd) before planting.

Green manuring

This consists of cultivating the land with a manure crop and making a seedbed for mustard seed or rye grass, which when part-grown is dug in. A scattering of sulphate of ammonia at the rate of 70g/m² (2oz per sq yd) is applied to the part-grown manure crop just before the crop is dug in (see page 27). This practice helps to overcome deficiencies in soil organic matter.

Drainage

All plants need some amount of air and water to grow and develop, but too much water or a prolonged build-up of cold air can be harmful. Even those soils which are naturally well-drained have produced better crops and suffered less from drought after improved drainage.

Land is made infertile by poor drainage or water-logging – a condition in which all the spaces between the soil particles are filled with water. Suffocation and death of plant roots are the direct consequence of stagnant water. The longer-term effects are an accumulation of soluble salts and products of decay. These harmful substances would be washed away by underground drains.

Wet soils are notoriously slow to warm up in spring, and also encourage the growth of weeds, such as sedges, rushes, thistles and docks. Such land is difficult to work, as crops can only use the soil layer above the water level.

Sandy soils, which feel gritty to the touch, drain more easily than clay, which resembles putty in texture.

When making a new garden or improving an established site, it is wise to check the drainage and this can be done by making a test dig. During the winter, dig out a hole 60cm (2ft) deep and cover it (with a dustbin lid for example) to prevent rain falling in. Inspect the hole daily, replacing the cover each time. If after 48 hours following heavy rain, less than 45cm (18in) of soil shows above the water table or water level, then attention to drainage is needed, especially if trees are to be planted.

Surplus moisture in gardens is usually best drained away by means of a soakaway or underground pipes or channels. Occasionally an existing drainage system becomes blocked through tree roots or ground subsidence, so it is advisable to check from time to time.

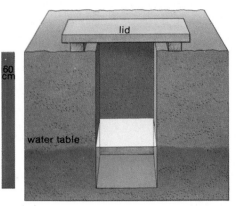

lid

60 cm

water table

gravel

drain

test hole

tile drain

ABOVE LEFT A test hole for checking drainage.
ABOVE RIGHT A land drain surrounded by gravel.

Land drains These are usually 10cm (4in) diameter porous pipes, laid near the bottom of trenches, surrounded in gravel and connected to a soakaway, main drain or ditch at the lowest point of the site. The pipes should have a rise or fall of not less than 2.5cm (1in) in a 2.5m (8ft 4in) run. The correct depth of trenches varies from about 75cm (2ft 6in) on clay soils to 105cm (3ft 6in) on sandy soils. The distance between pipe runs on heavy soils is 1.5m (5ft), and up to 4.5m (15ft) on lighter land.

Air drainage Wind frost can cause much damage but spring frosts on clear calm nights, when fruit trees are in full blossom, can be devastating. Under these conditions cold air, being heavier than warm air, settles in layers, filling up valleys and hollows known as frost pockets. Freezing air rolls down from higher ground and any obstruction across the current of the cold heavy wind causes the freezing air to build up like water behind a dam. Openings in a hedge or wall will allow the cold air to flow to lower ground. In gardens which are completely surrounded by walls or hedges, the layer of cold air builds up and cannot escape unless openings leading to lower land are made.

Screens and windbreaks vary in their effectiveness according to their permeability, that is, how well they filter and deflect the wind. Solid barriers like walls are less effective than trees, shrubs or hedges, which filter the air currents and protect a rather wider strip on the lee of the wind.

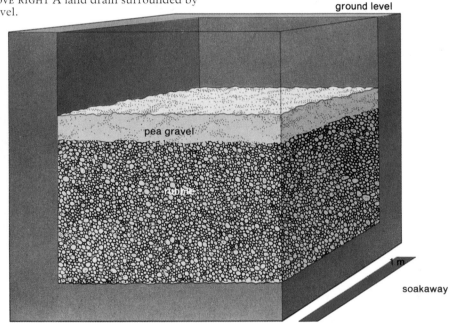

ground level

1.5 m

pea gravel

rubble

1 m

soakaway

The soakaway This method of drainage is suitable for small gardens (less than 6 × 9m (20 × 30ft) without a good outlet for water and is therefore particularly useful for town gardens. It consists of excavating a pit 1.5m (5ft) deep by 1m (3ft 4in) square, keeping the top soil and subsoil separate. (For those who are not used to digging, it is unwise to attempt too much at once.) Fill the soakaway, which should be sited in the lowest part of the plot, two-thirds deep with clean broken bricks

and rubble, covered with a 10cm (4in) layer of pea gravel (an aggregate of pea-sized bits of gravel), and finally cover with topsoil. If there is not enough topsoil, you will have to buy good quality soil: subsoil is not suitable as it hinders drainage.

ABOVE LEFT A soakaway – the best method of drainage for the small garden.
BELOW Freezing air rolls down from higher ground and obstructions will cause the freezing air to build up in frost pockets.

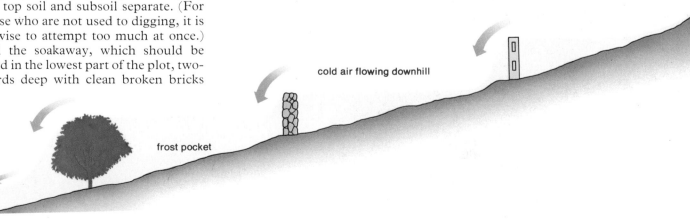

cold air flowing downhill

frost pocket

Plants for Different Soils

Note: The majority of cultivated plants will grow and thrive on neutral soils, which are neither acid nor alkaline.

In a similar manner soils which are medium loams, neither stiff clays nor sands, can be used without difficulty for most crops.

The following lists of plants are designed to meet the more difficult situations where special soil conditions exist.

Key to tables

Site requirements S = Sunny   Sh = Shade

Season and Nature of Interest

Y = All year   W = Winter   Sp = Spring
Su = Summer   A = Autumn   St = Stem
L = Leaves   Fl = Flowers   Fr = Fruits/berries

TOP Mountain ash
BOTTOM Laburnum

34

	Site Requirement	Season/Nature of interest
Trees suitable for Acid, Neutral or Chalk Soils		
Betula pendula Birch	S or Sh	Y/St Su/L
Cercis siliquastrum Judas tree	S	Sp, Su/Fl
Crataegus oxycantha Thorn	S	Sp/Fl A/Fr
Ilex aquifolium Holly	S or Sh	Y/L A,W/Fr
Laburnum anagyroides Laburnum	S	Sp, Su/Fl
Robinia pseudoacacia False Acacia	S	Su/L, Fl
Sorbus aria Whitebeam	S	Sp,A/L,Fl A/Fr, L
Sorbus aucuparia Mountain Ash	S	Sp/Fl A/Fr
Trees suitable for Heavy Soils		
Acer negundo variegatum Variegated Box Elder	S	Su, A/L
Betula pendula Birch	S or Sh	Y/St Su/L
Crataegus oxyacantha Thorn	S	Sp/Fl A/Fr
Ilex aquifolium Holly	S or Sh	Y/L A,W/Fr
Laburnum anagyroides Laburnum	S	Sp, Su/Fl
Malus baccata Siberian Crab	S	Sp/Fl A/Fr
Prunus cerasifera atropurpurea Purple-leaf Plum	S or Sh	Sp/Fl Su-A/L
Prunus serrulata various Flowering Cherries	S	Sp/Fl A/L
Sorbus aria Whitebeam	S	Sp, A/Fl, L A/Fr, L
Trees for Sands and Gravels		
Acer griseum Paperbark Maple	S	Y/St A/L
Betula pendula Birch	S or Sh	Y/St Su/L
Crataegus oxyacantha Thorn	S	Sp/Fl A/Fr
Ilex aquifolium Holly	S or Sh	Y/L A/Fr
Juniperus Juniper	S or Sh	Y/L
Pinus mugo Mountain Pine	S	Y/L
Shrubs requiring Acid Soils		
Andromeda polifolia Andromeda	S or Sh	Y/L Sp, Su/Fl
Azalea various Swamp Pink	S or Sh	Sp, Su/Fl

	Site Requirement	Season/Nature of interest
Calluna vulgaris Scotch heather	S	Y/L Su, A/Fl
Camellia japonica various Camellia	Sh	Sp/Fl
Erica various **Heath or Heather**	S	Y/L W, Sp, Su/Fl
Hamamelis mollis Chinese Witch Hazel	S	W/Fl
Rhododendron various Rhododendron	S or Sh	W, Sp, Su/Fl
Shrubs for Chalk Soils		
Aucuba japonica Spotted Laurel	S or Sh	Y/L A, W/Fr
Berberis various Barberry	S	Y/L Sp, Su/Fl A/Fr
Buddleia davidii Butterfly Bush	S	Su, A/Fl
Buxus sempervirens Box	S or Sh	Y/L
Euonymus fortunei variegata Creeping Evergreen Spindle	S or Sh	Y/L
Forsythia suspensa Golden Bell	S	Sp/Fl
Hypericum various St John's Wort	S or Sh	Su, A,/Fl A/Fr
Mahonia aquifolium Oregon Grape	S or Sh	Y/L Sp/Fl
Olearia various New Zealand Daisy Bush	S	Y/L Su/Fl
Philadelphus coronarius Mock Orange	S	Su/Fl
Rosa various Rose	S	Su, A/Fl A/Fr
Rosmarinus officinalis Rosemary	S	Y/L Sp/Fl
Spartium junceum Spanish Broom	S	Su, A/Fl
Symphoricarpos various Snowberry	S or Sh	A, W,/Fr
Syringa vulgaris Lilac	S	Sp, Su/Fl
Vinca various Periwinkle	S or Sh	Y/L Sp, Su/Fl
Weigela floribunda	S	Su/Fl
Shrubs for Heavy or Clay Soils		
Aucuba japonica Spotted Laurel	S or Sh	Y/L A, W,/Fr
Berberis various Barberry	S	Y/L Sp, Su,/Fl A/Fr
Chaenomeles speciosa various Flowering Quince	S	Sp, Su/Fl
Cornus various Dogwood	S or Sh	Y/St
Corylus maxima purpurea Hazel	S or Sh	Su/L

TOP Camellia
BOTTOM Hypericum

35

	Site Requirement	Season/Nature of interest
Cotoneaster various Cotoneaster	S or Sh	A, W,/Fr
Forsythia suspensa Golden Bell	S	Sp/Fl
Hamamelis mollis Chinese Witch Hazel	S	W/Fl
Hypericum various St John's Wort	S or Sh	Su,A/Fl A/Fr
Mahonia various Oregon Grape	S or Sh	Y/L Sp/Fl
Philadelphus coronarius Mock Orange	S	Su/Fl
Pyracantha atalantioides Firethorn	S or Sh	A, W/Fr
Ribes sanguineum Flowering Currant	S or Sh	Sp/Fl
Rosa various Rose	S	Su, A/Fl A/Fr
Skimmia japonica Skimmia	S or Sh	Y/L Sp/F W/Fr
Symphoricarpos albus Snowberry	S or Sh	A, W/Fr
Viburnum opulus various Guelda Rose	S	Su/F A/L A,W/Fr
Shrubs for Peaty Soils		
Andromeda polifolia Andromeda	S or Sh	Y/L Sp, Su/Fl
Azalea various Swamp Pink	S or Sh	Sp, Su,/Fl
Calluna vulgaris Scotch Heather	S	Y/L Su, A,/Fl
Cornus various Dogwood	S or Sh	Y/St
Daphne mezereum Mezereon	S or Sh	Sp/Fl
Eucryphia glutinosa Eucryphia	S	Su/Fl A/L
Magnolia soulangiana Magnolia	S	Sp, Su/Fl
Pernettya mucronata Pernettya	S or Sh	Y/L Sp/Fl A, W,/Fr
Pieris floribunda Pieris	S or Sh	Sp/L, Fl
Rhododendron various Rhododendron	S or Sh	W, Sp, Su,/Fl
Shrubs for Sandy Soils		
Berberis various Barberry	S	Y/L Sp, Su,/Fl A/Fr
Calluna vulgaris Scotch Heather	S	Y/L Su, A/Fl
Cistus cyprius Rock Rose	S	Su/Fl
Cytisus scoparius Broom	S	Su/Fl
Erica various Heather or Heath	S	Y/L W, Sp, Su/Fl

TOP Mahonia
BOTTOM Magnolia

	Site Requirement	Season/Nature of interest
Genista tinctoria Dyer's Greenwood	S	Su/Fl
Helianthemum alpestre Sun Rose	S	Su/Fl
Juniperus various Juniper	S or Sh	Y/L
Lavandula spica Lavender	S	Y/L Su/Fl
Rosmarinus officinalis Rosemary	S	Y/L Sp/Fl
Spartium junceum Spanish Broom	S	Su, A/Fl

The majority of herbaceous perennials and bedding plants prefer neutral soil conditions, but the following will thrive in chalk soils

Herbaceous Perennials for Chalk Soils

	Site Requirement	Season/Nature of interest
Achillea various Yarrow	S	Su/Fl
Brunnera macrophylla Anchusa	S or Sh	Sp, Su/Fl
Centranthus ruber Valerian	S	Su/Fl
Convallaria majalis Lily-of-the-Valley	S or Sh	Sp/Fl
Doronicum caucasicum Leopard's Bane	S	Sp/Fl
Erigeron hybridus Fleabane	S	Sp, Su/Fl
Geranium endressii Pink Cranesbill	S	Su/Fl
Gypsophila paniculata Gypsophila	S	Su/Fl
Iris various Iris	S	Su/Fl
Lavatera Mallow	S	Su/Fl
Tulipa Tulip	S	Sp/Fl

Bedding Plants and Rock Plants for Chalk Soils

	Site Requirement	Season/Nature of interest
Antirrhinum majus Snapdragon	S	Su/Fl
Arabis arendsii Wall cress	S	Sp, Su, /Fl
Aubrieta deltoidea Purple Rock-cress	S	Sp, Su/Fl
Bellis perennis Double Daisy	S or Sh	Sp, Su/Fl
Campanula various Bell flower	S	Su, A/Fl
Centaurea cyanus Cornflower	S	Su/Fl
Cheiranthus various Wallflower	S	Sp/Fl
Delphinium consolida Larkspur	S	Su/Fl
Viola wittrockiana Pansy	S	Sp, Su, A/Fl

Getting equipped

The buying of new tools merits careful forethought. The tool or appliance should be necessary and efficient, of well-tried design, reasonably priced and safe to operate (moving parts should be covered by guards), economical to maintain and easy to handle. One of the hallmarks of good design is simplicity – the greater the complexity, the greater the chance of breakdown. Assessing the construction, safety, economy, and ease of handling is very much a matter of comparing similar models.

Before buying tools and equipment, especially motorized appliances which deteriorate rapidly if left in the open, make sure that there is somewhere safe, dry and convenient to store them. Some tools may be used very infrequently, and it is better to hire these rather than spend a lot of money on items which will be on the toolshed rack far more frequently than in the gardener's hands.

Essential tools

The selection of tools you *need*, rather than those you would *like*, depends on your particular garden. Some implements are used for specific purposes, while others can have a variety of uses. The spade, for example, can be used for planting trees as well as preparing the ground for potatoes or other vegetables.

Identifying the appliances you need

There are four broad categories of necessary equipment: general purpose; flowers, vegetables and soft fruits; trees, shrubs and climbers; and lawns and hedges.

General-purpose items are used in most gardens and are the first priority. They include a spade, a digging fork, a good pocket knife, and a watering can with a rose. A medium-sized garden will need a sieve and wheelbarrow.

The growing of flowers, vegetables and soft fruits requires tools for working the soil and killing weeds, simple pruning, sowing and planting, spraying and watering. The most useful tools are an iron rake, one or more hoes, a cultivator, a trowel, a small handfork, a pair of secateurs, a sprayer, a measuring rod, a dibber, and a bucket.

A medium-sized plot will need a hosepipe and fittings. In wet districts, two short lengths of planking, 1.5m (5ft) long × 15cm (6in) wide, can be invaluable to work from and avoid churning up wet soil.

Trees, shrubs and climbers require extra pruning tools in addition to the foregoing items, and where there are fruit trees, spraying equipment will be required. Necessary items for this group include: steps or ladders, a pruning saw, a long-arm pruner, and a sprayer with lance for tall subjects.

Tools for lawns and hedges are fairly specialized and are mainly for cutting and trimming, but also include items to aerate and scarify turf. The basic requirements for the care of lawns and hedges are a wire rake, a pair of shears, a lawn mower, a pair of edging shears, a spade, a fork, a watering can, a wheelbarrow, a sprayer, a bucket and hosepipe. A sprinkler is useful in dry districts.

Equipment which is used less frequently – power cultivators or lawn aerators for instance – can usually be hired, as can smaller hand tools such as a pickaxe.

Choice of equipment

The most expensive gardening appliance is not always the best. When comparing makes, note the construction and materials as well as the design. Watch out for potential weak spots which can result in broken metal parts, handles coming adrift, or bent and unusable pieces. Poorly finished products will give you splinters and blisters, which are not only unpleasant, but make it difficult to carry on gardening. A useful test of sound metal in spades, forks, rakes and cultivators is to hold them off the ground by the handle and give the metal section a sharp tap with a coin; good metal produces a resonant ringing tone. The working parts of shears, saws, knives and pruning tools are generally best made from high quality carbon steel.

Stainless steel spades, trowels and forks, though more expensive, are easier to keep clean. The methods of fixing handles vary, but the socket or solid join is the most reliable. In the intermediate price range, the tang and ferrule method used for rakes, trowels,

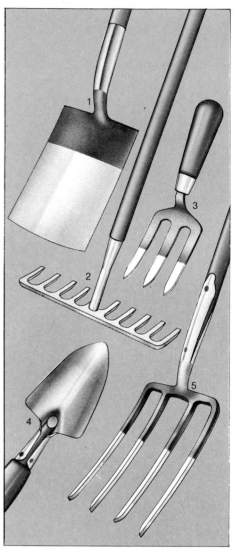

ABOVE Common garden tools with various joins between blade and handle:
1 Socket (solid)
2 and 3 Ferrule and tang
4 Pressed steel split ring
5 Rivets and straps

and small hand forks, is satisfactory. The pressed-steel tool can be reasonably satisfactory, but be wary of those with thin metal which may bend, and badly fitting handles secured by nails or small screws that can work loose. Strong, well-made handles can be constructed from wood, tubular metal or plastic. Wood and plastic tend to be warmer to the touch in winter and cooler in strong sunlight.

Sprayers, sprinklers, watering cans and other tools made of rust and corrosion resistant materials are preferable, if design and construction are satisfactory.

Basic equipment

To keep garden tools working efficiently and to prolong their useful life and reduce rust and corrosion to a minimum, it is important to clean them after use, and, in the case of cutting implements, to keep them suitably sharpened.

Before putting tools away, clean them and wipe the metal parts with an oily rag (a rag dipped in sump oil, for example). Replace badly worn moving parts as soon as possible before they wear out or break. In the interests of safety, equipment should never be left lying around.

When using any tools or equipment which require strenuous effort (such as spades, forks and saws) for the first time, do not attempt more than half an hour at a stretch.

Spade

There is little difference between a squared or rounded blade, but the tread or flange can cause heavy soil to stick, making for unsatisfactory work. The choice of a D- or a T-shaped handle is a matter of taste. Try it out for comfort before buying. The socket, or solid join, of shaft and blade is more reliable than the rivet and strap.

For deep digging, the blade should enter the ground almost vertically, putting weight on the foot to force the spade down. A trench in front of you is necessary for incorporating manure and double digging. A spade can do the work of many tools.

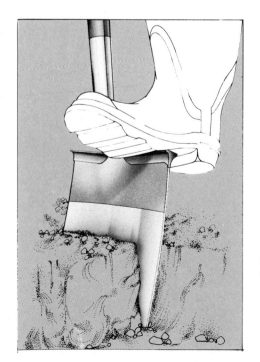

LEFT Garden spade with a squared blade and flange.

ABOVE The cyclical action of digging. Use the weight of the body to push the spade into the ground, lever the soil forward before lifting it, and turn the soil over as it is dropped in place.

39

General purpose border fork (left) and broad-pronged digging fork (right). Use the fork for lifting plants before transplanting (top).

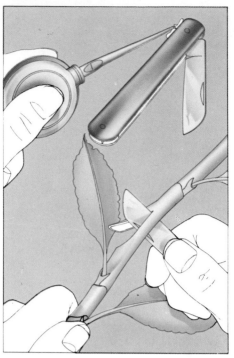

Oiling a pocket-knife (above) and cutting a shoot (below).

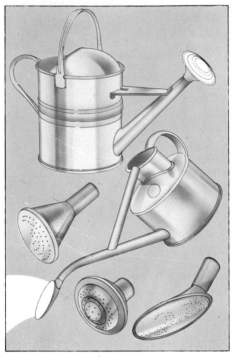

Watering cans and rose attachments. Oval-shaped roses provide a wider and more gentle distribution of water.

Garden fork

This tool is made in various patterns, but usually has four prongs, made of stainless or forged steel, which are of three types: rounded, squared, or flattened. The choice of handle, the method of securing the stem to prongs, and materials employed, are much the same as for spades.

Manure or compost handling; the pricking of fertilizers into the soil surface; breaking up, loosening and shattering lumps of earth; spiking or aerating turf; and gathering up tree and hedge prunings, are just a few uses of the fork. The broad-pronged version is not often seen, and apart from its use on heavier soils and for digging and lifting potatoes, it does not merit first priority status. Forks with narrow round or square prongs, however, are second only to the spade in importance.

Safety note A fork should be treated with great care. If you leave it in the garden even while you answer the telephone or have a cup of tea, make sure the prongs are pushed firmly into the ground. After use, store the fork out of reach of small children.

Pocket knife

A general purpose type which fits comfortably in the hand and has a good quality straight steel blade is the most useful knife to start with. A blunt knife is obviously useless, and straight blades are easier to sharpen than curved ones. A folding model is preferable to a fixed blade type as it can be carried about with safety.

In addition to cutting flowers, and string or twine, and trimming herbaceous or semi-hardwood shoots, a sharp knife is excellent for paring away saw wounds when pruning. When cutting any hard piece of wood, make the stroke of the blade away from and not towards you.

Keep the knife clean and sharp. An oilstone is excellent for sharpening blades.

Safety note Handle knives carefully; exercise caution when closing and opening blades, and make sure the cutting edge is protected when the knife is closed.

Watering can

Commonly available capacities are 4.5 and 9 litres (1 and 2 gal). Plastic cans are cheaper and lighter to carry than the japanned metal ones. A coarse oval and a fine round rose are useful, preferably made of brass that does not corrode.

When watering small seedlings and young plants it is better to use a rose, as a strong stream of water can knock the seedlings out of place in the drills. Avoid watering plants in strong sun unless shading can be placed over them for an hour or so. The water may evaporate quickly in the heat and dry out the tender roots.

Safety Note Always wash the can and roses immediately after applying any chemicals with mild detergent, and rinse thoroughly. Never use a can which has contained hormone weed killer for any other purpose.

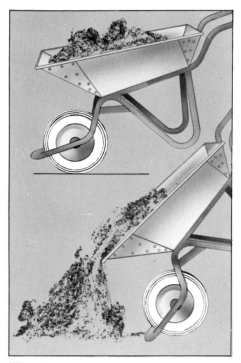

Wheelbarrow with weight over wheel.

Rakes: always push rake teeth into the soil when laying a rake down to avoid being hit by the upswinging handle.

Using draw hoe to make a V-shaped drill and for chopping weeds (above and right). 3-prong cultivator to loosen soil (below left). Dutch hoe push-pull action to kill weeds (below right).

Wheelbarrow

The user should be able to handle the wheelbarrow easily and without strain under most conditions.

Wooden barrows may look very nice, but they are heavy to handle, fairly costly, difficult to clean, and can rot. They are also less easy to sterilize for use when handling potting composts.

Metal barrows are made in different sizes, thicknesses and lengths.

The home gardener is not usually concerned with intensive use, so a well-designed and well-made lightweight galvanized barrow will serve most purposes. Where leaves have to be transported, extendable sections to increase the barrow capacity are handy.

Balance is important for easy use. The barrow body should be placed well over the wheel—thus ensuring that the weight is carried by the wheel and not the user. Wheels have pneumatic tyres or thin rubber rims. Pneumatic tyres are more suitable for models which will be used regularly over soil, rubber rims are more suitable for hard surfaces, such as paths. Wheel hubs with ball bearings are the easiest to manage.

Keep the barrow clean, and the hub well oiled or greased. With pneumatic models avoid running over broken glass or nails.

Iron rake

A 10- or 12-tooth steel head is a convenient size. A tang and ferrule connection is more satisfactory than a split socket and screw, and a 1.35m (4ft 6in) handle or shank is a convenient size.

The main functions of this tool are to create a fine tilth, that is, to reduce the surface soil to a fine crumbly consistency by pushing and pulling the teeth in comb fashion through the earth, to prepare seedbeds, rake up stones and rubbish, and level the top-soil.

Safety note Hang up the rake in the shed or storage area after use. When the rake is laid on the ground, place the head teeth down, to prevent anyone stepping or falling on the teeth or being knocked by an upswinging handle. A painful blow from the rake can black an eye or break a tooth.

Hoe

There are two basic types; the push or Dutch hoe, and the draw hoe. The former has a flat blade, which is used almost parallel with the ground. The draw hoe blade is at right angles to the handle. There are several variations of each type. Carbon steel heads are stronger, but more expensive than pressed steel. The carbon-steel hoes are constructed and fixed as the rakes are, whereas pressed steel ones usually have split ring fittings.

The Dutch hoe is used with a pushing action, to sever weeds and loosen the soil crust; walk backwards as you use it. The draw hoe is used with a chopping motion, with the operator moving forwards.

The draw hoe is also used to earth up, that is, to draw soil round plant stems, and to make shallow drills for seed sowing. It is more suitable for use on heavy soils than the Dutch hoe. Take similar safety precautions for the hoe as for the rake.

Cultivator

This consists of 3- or 5-prong tines, and is excellent for scarifying (breaking up) surface soil and weed killing.

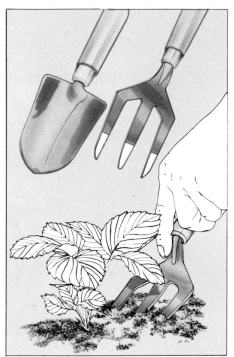

Trowel and handfork. The handfork can be used with a twisting action to loosen hard soil.

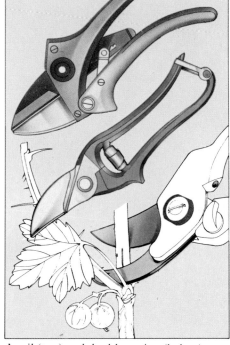

Anvil (top) and double-action (below) secateurs.

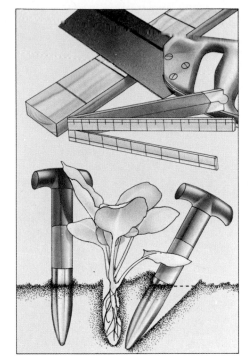

Measuring rod (above) marked off with saw cuts. Dibber (below) makes a hole for the plant and firms the soil around its roots.

Trowel

Where bedding plants and vegetables are grown in any numbers, a good trowel is indispensable. A carbon-steel scoop is preferable to pressed steel, giving harder wear but the stainless-steel type, although more expensive, is the most satisfactory as it is the easiest to use and keep clean.

The trowel is used for digging holes in which the roots of small subjects can be spread out when planting, and for covering the roots with fine soil and firming lightly.

Handfork

A short-handled, carbon-steel, three- or four-pronged fork, with a tanged, fixed handle, gives good service. Stainless-steel models are longer lasting and easier to clean, but they are more expensive.

Use the handfork to loosen the soil crust in confined spaces with delving and loosening action, which comes with practice.

Safety note Keep all forks away from very young children.

Secateurs

There are many variations of the two main types, the double cut and the anvil. The anvil is less elegant, but reliable and reasonably priced. Choose a size that suits your hand, and a model with a safety catch. The more expensive doublecut models, when sharp and in mint condition, tend to be favoured by exhibitors, but are not essential for general purposes.

Keep the blades sharp and the moving parts well oiled, and do not use secateurs for cutting any plant material more than 15mm ($\frac{3}{4}$in) thick. Avoid using a twisting action when severing tough pieces. Never use secateurs for cutting wire, metal or twine.

Safety note Avoid leaving secateurs where they can cause injury. Ensure that the cutting faces are closed and the safety catch is on when not in use.

Measuring rod and dibber

Although you can buy both these items, they can be easily made at home. For a measuring rod, use a 2m (6ft 6in) wood lath, suitably marked for measuring by shallow saw cuts at 15cm (6in) intervals. A dibber can be made from a 20cm long × 2.5cm diameter (8in × 1in) dowel, rounded at one end.

Use a measuring rod when planting to achieve the correct distance between plants. Use the dibber to plant small subjects such as small cabbage plants, and to sow large seeds such as broad beans. Make a hole with the dibber to the correct depth, and firm the soil round plant roots or seeds after planting.

Bucket and neatly stored hose-pipe with adjustable nozzle.

Portable steps, firmly placed on level ground.

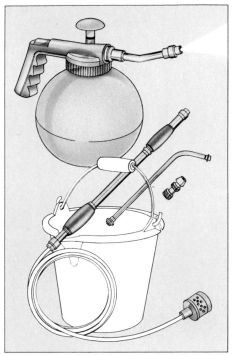

Pneumatic hand spray (above) and double-action sprayer with parts (below).

Bucket and hose pipe

For cheapness, ease and convenience, those made of plastic will serve their purposes well. A 9 litre (2 gal) bucket is a handy size. An 18m (60ft) length hose pipe is adequate for most small gardens, but up to twice that length may be needed for medium size plots, especially if they are long and narrow.

Keep buckets and pipes clean and store away from frost and strong sunlight when not in use.

Safety note Do not leave coils or stretches of hose-pipe lying about after use as they are easy to trip over.

Steps and ladders

Aluminium or alloy types are lightweight and easy to carry. All steps and ladders need to be kept in a good state of repair; wooden models deteriorate more quickly. You will need a ladder or steps for trimming tall hedges, tying climbing plants to their supports, and pruning trees. Put them away after use since as well as needing protection from the weather, steps left outside the house make life easy for burglars.

Safety note Never use broken or faulty steps or ladders, not even for one small job, and always make sure that they are firmly placed on level ground.

Sprayer

There are models of varying shape and size to suit most purposes. They usually work by compression or suction. The former type pumps air into an air-sealed canister, which forces the spray out when a valve is released. The suction types depend on the continuous action of a pump to deliver the spray. The main advantage of compression sprayers is that spraying can be continued without having to pump at the same time. The chief points to look for are construction from rust- or corrosion-resistant materials such as plastic or brass, adjustable nozzles for coarse or fine spraying, convenient size, and cost. If an extension lance can be fitted it will serve for spraying fruit trees.

Read the maker's instructions carefully before use.

Safety note Wash hands, sprayer and other items thoroughly after spraying. Use gloves and goggles if poisonous substances have to be used, but avoid poisons wherever possible. Keep people and pets away when spraying with poison. Store spray material, correctly labelled, in cool conditions, out of reach of pets and children and preferably under lock and key. Always follow manufacturer's instructions.

43

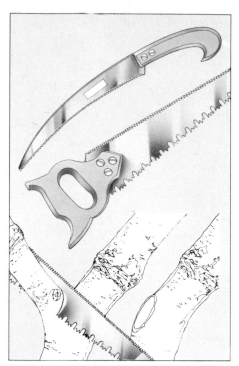

Grecian saw (top) and ordinary coarse-cut pruning saw (centre).
Lopping a branch, making an undercut first (below).

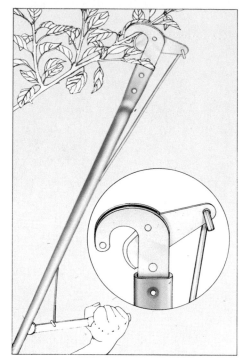

Long-arm pruner, blade action (above), handle operation (below).

Broad wire rake (above) for scarifying lawns, and fantail (below) for smaller areas.

Pruning saw

There are several types available: single- and double-edged, straight and curved, fixed and folding-bladed. The double-edged type with a rigid blade is best. The setting of the teeth should ensure that the saw groove is cleared with each stroke. A good blade will give a resonant ringing tone when slightly bent and released quickly. This tool is used to remove unwanted or surplus wood of 15mm ($\frac{3}{4}$in) thickness and over. To reduce the chance of splitting, undercut larger limbs to one-third of their diameter before overcutting. Examine branches for wire or nails before sawing, or the blade and teeth may be damaged. Clean and oil blades after use and ensure the teeth are sharp.

Safety note Before and during saw-work, make sure the area below is clear of people and pets. High (6m (20ft) plus) or heavy tree work is best left to the expert.

Long-arm pruner

These are made in various lengths; avoid those that are too heavy. The blades should be of good carbon steel, clean and sharp and have a smooth action.

Safety note Avoid balancing on the top of step ladders with these pruners. Keep the blade in the shut position when not in use.

Wire rakes

Wire or fan-tail rakes with 8 to 20 teeth are similar in most other respects to the iron rake and are needed for good lawn care.

Wire rakes are excellent for combing vigorously through turf to remove old dead grass, scattering worm casts, gathering up leaves and twigs, and for aeration.

Safety note Always hang up wire rakes when not in use. When placing them on the ground, make sure the teeth are face down, as you would with an iron rake.

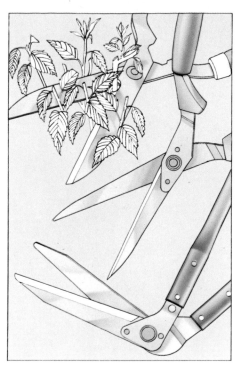

Hand shears, notched (top), straight (centre). Long handled edging shears (below).

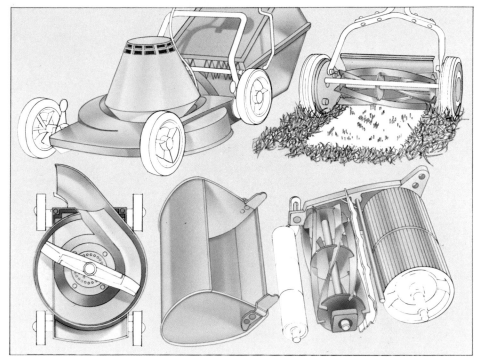

Rotary lawn mower (top left) and view of underside showing the propellor-like cutting blade.

Side wheel cylinder mower (top right) and rear roller mower (below). Parts (l to r): grassbox, front roller, cylinder, rear roller.

Shears – grass, hedge and edging

There are many models to choose from, so select one which is the right weight and balance for you. Shears should have a non-slip adjustable locking nut; buffers, to prevent fingers from being knocked together; hollow-ground, forged steel blades (nicked in the case of hedge shears); and securely fixed handles.

Grass cutting with shears is fairly straightforward, but hedge cutting can present problems. Use your measuring stick as a guide to ensure level cutting of the top and sides. Take care not to cut wire or the blades may be blunted and damaged. Use the nicked part to cut heavier hedge shoots.

Safety note Avoid leaving shears where they may fall and cause injury. After cleaning and oiling, place them safely away after use.

Lawn mower

There are two main classes of domestic mowers, the cylinder or reel, and the rotary cutters.

The first group, which can be manually or power-driven, are used on lawns which are kept well mown. There are side-wheel models, which are usually cheaper but cannot cut close to lawn edges, and rear-roller mowers, which not only cut close to the edges, but also roll the lawn and collect the mowings in a grassbox. A cylinder width of 30 to 35cm (12 to 14in) is adequate for most gardens. Electric models are quieter than the petrol-engined types.

Rotary cutters usually have petrol motors and are of the wheeled or the hover type. The hover model is very useful for cutting grass on steep slopes.

Before mowing, remove all hard objects from the lawn. Adjust the machine according to the maker's instructions and check that there are no loose nuts and bolts, and that the mower is in good working order. After mowing, clean and dry the machine, and oil all moving parts as advised by the manufacturer.

Safety note *Never* adjust a power mower while the engine is running even if you think the machine may have broken down. The cutter blades and other moving parts should have the necessary guards or covers on during use. Take care when oiling, mending and cleaning lawn mowers as the blades can spin.

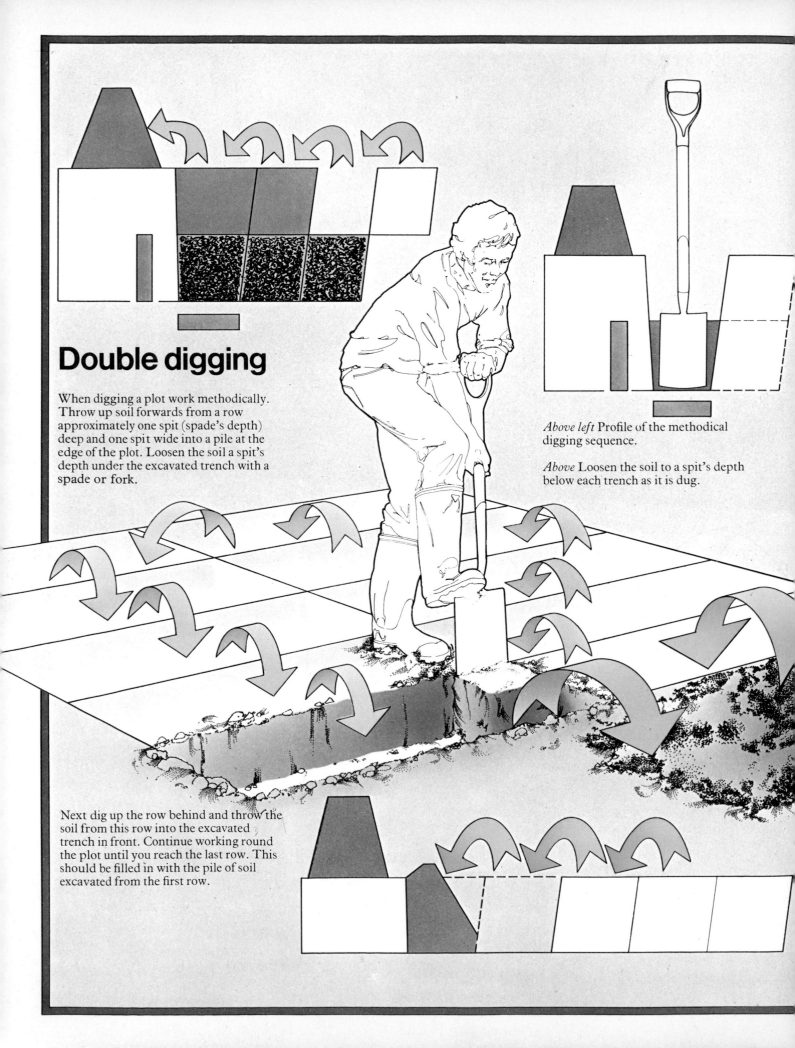

Double digging

When digging a plot work methodically. Throw up soil forwards from a row approximately one spit (spade's depth) deep and one spit wide into a pile at the edge of the plot. Loosen the soil a spit's depth under the excavated trench with a spade or fork.

Above left Profile of the methodical digging sequence.

Above Loosen the soil to a spit's depth below each trench as it is dug.

Next dig up the row behind and throw the soil from this row into the excavated trench in front. Continue working round the plot until you reach the last row. This should be filled in with the pile of soil excavated from the first row.

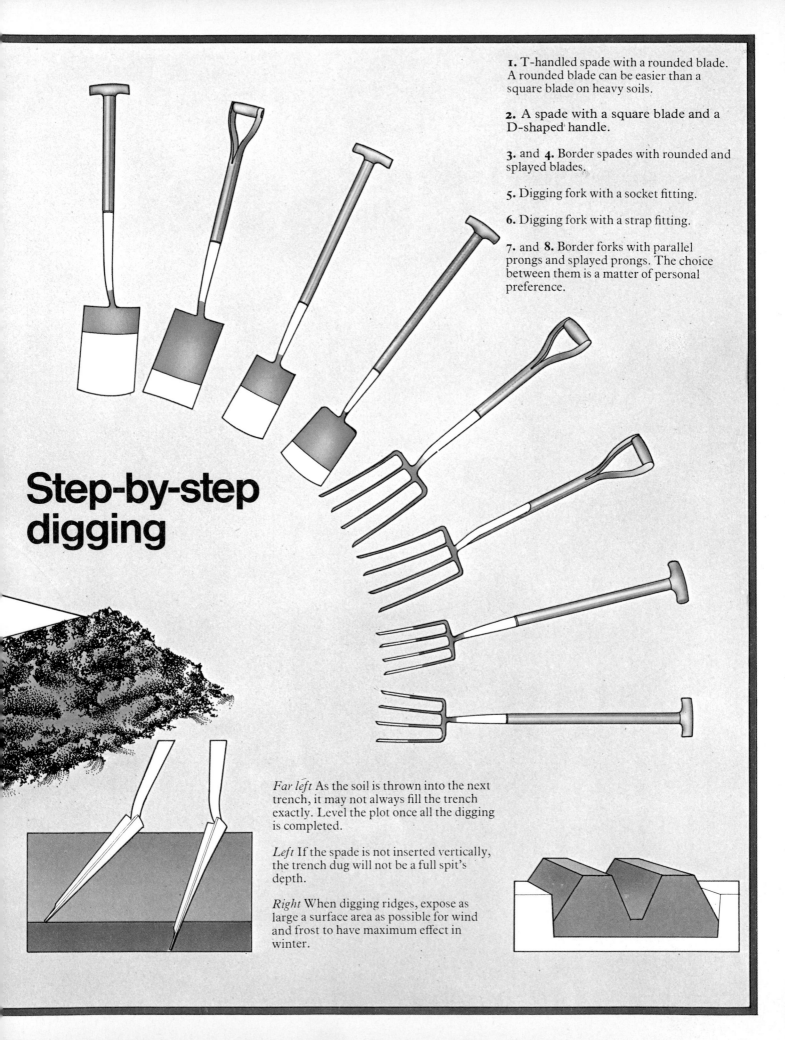

Step-by-step digging

1. T-handled spade with a rounded blade. A rounded blade can be easier than a square blade on heavy soils.

2. A spade with a square blade and a D-shaped handle.

3. and 4. Border spades with rounded and splayed blades.

5. Digging fork with a socket fitting.

6. Digging fork with a strap fitting.

7. and 8. Border forks with parallel prongs and splayed prongs. The choice between them is a matter of personal preference.

Far left As the soil is thrown into the next trench, it may not always fill the trench exactly. Level the plot once all the digging is completed.

Left If the spade is not inserted vertically, the trench dug will not be a full spit's depth.

Right When digging ridges, expose as large a surface area as possible for wind and frost to have maximum effect in winter.

PLANNING THE VEGETABLE GARDEN

There are many good reasons for growing vegetables. It is usually cheaper than buying them and the crop may be gathered fresh. The exercise is not only rewarding but, in these days of stress and strain, there is release of tension in working on the land and great satisfaction in watching crops develop.

Few of us are able to choose a perfect site for our garden; we have to use the ground adjoining our home. Even with an allotment, the position may not be ideal. That being so, we need to select with care the subjects most likely to succeed in the type of soil available.

A well-planned vegetable garden will yield crops throughout the year, especially if there is some form of glass protection. Insufficient or hasty soil preparation will be reflected in the quantity and quality of the crops harvested. Another advantage of making a definite plan is that the varieties to be grown and the amount of seeds required can be fairly accurately determined in advance. This will ensure that a lot of ground is not taken up by crops that are not so popular in the kitchen, as sometimes happens.

There is much pleasure to be gained by laying out a culinary herb garden. In the past, many elaborate and perhaps not very practical designs were planned, involving a great deal of work to keep them in shape. Annual herbs such as basil, chervil, dill, coriander and summer savory look best grown in clumps. Thyme, parsley and chives are useful for edgings. Since herbs vary greatly in height and spread, the larger growing species should be placed so that they do not shade the

The whole plot can then be kept in a fertile condition without the build-up of pests and diseases. Root crops such as parsnips, carrots and beetroot need a deep soil and can be followed by the brassicas – cabbages, cauliflowers, Brussels sprouts, broccoli, kales and so on. Peas and beans form the third group and are capable of storing nitrogen in their roots. This remains in the soil when the aerial parts are removed and, as the peas and beans are gradually rotated around the vegetable plot, the overall fertility increases.

However diligent one may be at controlling pests and diseases there is always a danger that some will remain in the soil in the form of eggs, larvae or spores. If the same crops are then grown again the next year the organisms are certain to attack even more severely. This is particularly obvious with the fungus causing club root which will attack all members of the cabbage family.

It is not always easy to arrange a planned rotation since household needs vary and there may be a demand for more peas, beans and salads rather than root crops. The area of each crop within a particular rotational plot may also vary according to individual needs. There may be a temptation – encouraged by tradition – to keep crops such as onions on the same site for year after year. This is dangerous since populations of stem eelworm can build up rapidly.

In very small gardens, plants have to be grown just where space is available. This sometimes means in odd corners and even boxes and other containers. Runner beans are often grown at the end of the plot, so that it is easier to gather the crop, while the plants can act as an attractive screen.

The simplest rotation extends for three years. For this purpose the vegetable garden is divided into three plots. Although by no means perfect, it does ensure crops are moved round methodically. The example shown opposite is based on the plan suggested by the Royal Horticultural Society. The Groups are (1) Peas, Beans, Salad Crops and Onions, (2) The Cabbage Family, and (3) Potatoes and Root Vegetables.

The usual size for an allotment is 27 metres (90 feet) by 9 metres (30 feet) which is sufficient for most families. It is best to measure and peg out the three plots on both sides of the allotment so that the position of the rows can easily be determined. Attempt to make three approximately equal-sized vegetable areas and rotate the crops as indicated on the plan even if you are using part of the garden.

A four-year rotation is more complex but may be better suited for your requirements. The extra plot is just for potatoes with the other root crops remaining on their own. The four groups would then be:

Group 1.
Early, main crop and late potatoes.
Group 2.
Peas, broad beans, dwarf and runner beans, celery, leeks, onions.
Group 3.
Root crops, carrots, beetroot, parsnips, salsify. Root crops should be grown on land manured the previous season, otherwise they may become forked and mis-shapen.
Group 4.
The cabbage family: cabbages, Brussels sprouts, broccoli, kale, cauliflower, turnips and swedes. This group will benefit if the ground is limed before sowing or planting.

Crops such as lettuce, radish and spinach have not been mentioned but these can be grown as catch crops and could follow early potatoes or early peas. Herbs, including parsley, chives and sage, can be fitted in at the sides of the beds.

Lettuces are a useful subject for intercropping.

Successional Sowing and Catch cropping

There is no need to make one large annual sowing of individual vegetables such as carrots and beetroot, many of which become old and tasteless before they can be used. It is far better to make small-scale repeated sowings throughout the season (successional sowings) and to practise catch cropping by sowing vegetables that mature quickly between rows of those that occupy land for a long time. The type of soil and the location of the site will have some influence on the varieties chosen, since the same variety will mature earlier on light loamy soil than it will on heavy clay ground.

Globe beet and shorthorn carrots can be sown at intervals up until the end of July. Peas can be put in until the third week in July, using the first early dwarf varieties such as 'Kelvedon Wonder'.

If a sowing of dwarf French beans is made about mid-July the crop will mature after the last of the runner beans. Ground can be cleared after the early peas have finished in July and sowings of early maturing cabbage can be made. Alternatively, 'All the Year Round' cauliflower or savoys make good follow-on crops.

Endive and lettuce are other crops to grow after earlier subjects have been cleared. Salad onions such as 'White Lisbon' can be sown from April until late August, while maincrop onions, including 'Ailsa Craig' and 'Bedfordshire Champion', if sown in August, will mature the following summer and will store much better than when in spring. The 'Japanese' onions, such as 'Express Yellow O-X', 'Senshyu Semi-globe Yellow', and 'Imai Early Yellow', are also sown in the autumn for lifting the following July.

Radishes can be sown in succession and can often be fitted in between other crops (intercropping) or in odd corners if there is full light and the soil is in good condition. Winter spinach and spinach beet may also be sown in summer.

Turnips can also be used for catch cropping and will be much more appreciated from early autumn onwards, when many vegetables are becoming scarce, than in summer. Bush marrows can be sown as late as mid-July, giving a crop which is often more tasty than that from

earlier sowings, as well as extending the season.

The secret of successful catch cropping is to prepare the soil well and ensure that it is fertile. The land should not be dug or moved deeply after the first crop has been cleared, and the soil should be brought to a very fine tilth so that the drills can be drawn out easily.

Food Crops in the Small Garden

The imaginative garden on the left has been designed to make the most varied use of an average-sized plot facing south-west. Assuming that it is attached to the house of a family who will want to relax and play in their garden as well as enjoy its visual appeal, only half has been given over totally to the cultivation of fruit and vegetables.

Immediately next to the house, a tiled terrace offers a convenient site for container-grown strawberries (in a barrel) and a bay tree (left), with chives and tarragon (right). In contrast to the neatly ordered vegetable patch, the decorative area is deliberately informal: the lawn circular, the edge of the terrace uneven and broken up by ground-cover plants. The flower beds are not all they seem, giving a home to some plants that are both attractive and edible. On the left, a peach tree is trained in fan-shape against the wall. Lettuces fringe the lawn, bush marrows grow plump in the centre of the bed, while globe artichokes occupy a permanent position in the corner. The trelliswork archway (placed *off*-centre) supports scarlet runner beans; more lettuces and marrows in the right-hand bed, plus tomatoes, sunflowers (for their seeds) and in the warmest corner of the terrace, a grape vine.

The greenhouse shelters houseplants as well as some unusual sun-loving vegetables: aubergines and green peppers in pots (they could stand on the terrace on really hot days).

A crop-rotation system is being practised in the vegetable garden proper. On the left, nearest the house, are rows of cabbages and cauliflowers; beyond them, onions, celery, leeks and peas with a catch crop of lettuce between. On the right of the path, root vegetables at the far end (carrots and beetroot) share the plot with celery and a block-planting of sweet corn behind the trellis.

Fruit trees are trained on both walls: apples are shown here, but pears or plums would do equally well. Two blackberry bushes are fan-trained against the far wall, with black and red currant bushes in front. This bed will be semi-permanent.

No tidy garden should lack a shed, and where better to put it than in the shade of your neighbour's great tree, where very little would grow successfully anyway. In time the ivy will trail over the shed and conceal its unlovely façade from view.

That other essential of the vegetable garden, the compost heap, is situated as far as possible from the house, but in a convenient corner for digging in the compost when it is ready.

Growing Vegetables Without A Garden

There are few situations in which it will not be possible to cultivate some vegetables, even if only salad sprouts on blotting paper or mustard and cress on a window sill. The best solution to growing in a limited space is to use growing bags, large pots, or barrels. You will have the advantage of being able to monitor very closely the condition of the growing medium. Suitable crops include tomatoes, peppers, runner beans (with support), many herbs, and strawberries.

A word of warning: soil-filled clay pots can be very heavy, so do not fill your balcony with them unless you are sure it can take the weight.

Above: Large pots and (below) growing bags save precious space. Container growing makes it easier to control soil pests and diseases.

Successional sowing

Successional sowing or planting of vegetables on a particular piece of ground will ensure a constant supply for the kitchen.

Such successional cropping can be achieved either by sowing or planting the follow-on crops.

FIRST CROP			FOLLOW-ON CROP		
Crop	Sown/Planted	Crop harvested by	Crop	Distance between rows	Distance between plants in rows
Sprouting broccoli (purple or white)	Planted June–July from an April–May sowing	April following year	**Dwarf French beans**	45 cm (18 in)	Thinned to 15 cm (6 in)
Early carrots (for pulling when young)	March sown	End May	**Dwarf French beans**	45 cm (18 in)	Thinned to 15 cm (6 in)
Kohl rabi or **Summer turnips**	March sown	Mid-June	**Main crop carrots** (for pulling young)	20–30 cm (8–12 in)	Thinned for use
Early peas	February–March sown	June–July	**Autumn lettuce**	30 cm (12 in)	Thinned to 30 cm (12 in)
Early broad beans or **Early summer cauliflower**	November sown Planted March from September sowing under glass	Beginning July Beginning July	**Winter turnips** or **Carrots** or **salad onions**	20–30 cm (8–12 in) 20–30 cm (8–12 in)	Thinned for use
Shallots	February planted	End July	**Winter turnips** or **Winter spinach**	38–45 cm (15–18 in)	Thinned to 20–30 cm (8–12 in) Thinned to 15 cm (6 in)
Second early potatoes	Late March planted	End August	**Salad onions**	20–30 cm (8–12 in)	0.5–1.0 cm ($\frac{1}{4}$–$\frac{1}{2}$ in)
Maincrop potatoes	End April planted	Beginning October	**Early broad beans** (November sown)	45–60 cm (18–24 in)	15–20 cm (6–8 in)

Successional planting

FIRST CROP			FOLLOW-ON CROP		
Crop	Sown/planted	Crop harvested by	Crop	Distance between rows	Distance between plants in rows
Summer spinach	Late March sown	Early June	**Sweet corn** or **Ridge cucumbers**	45–60 cm (18–24 in) 75 cm (30 in)	45–60 cm (18–24 in) 60 cm (24 in)
Early peas	February–March sown	June–July	**Leeks** or **Late savoys**	30–45 cm (12–18 in) 45–60 cm (18–24 in)	20–30 cm (8–12 in) 45–60 cm (18–24 in)
Early potatoes	Mid-March planted	June–July	**Autumn cauliflower** or **Late heading broccoli** (winter cauliflower)	60 cm (24 in) 75 cm (30 in)	60 cm (24 in) 75 cm (30 in)
Second early peas	March sown	Beginning July	**Leeks** or **Late savoys** or **Late heading broccoli**	30–45 cm (12–18 in) 45–60 cm (18–24 in) 75 cm (30 in)	20–30 cm (8–12 in) 45–60 cm (18–24 in) 75 cm (30 in)
Autumn-sown bulb onions or **Late broad beans** or **Shallots**	August sown March sown February planted	End July	**Savoys**	60 cm (24 in)	45 cm (18 in)
Second early potatoes or **Stump-rooted carrots**	Late March planted March–April sown	End August End August	**Savoys**	60 cm (24 in)	45 cm (18 in)
Spring sown bulb onions	March sown	Early September	**Spring cabbage**	45 cm (18 in)	30 cm (12 in)

A Succession of Greens

It is not possible to obtain regular supplies of greenstuff (brassicas) from a single sowing. Different varieties mature at different times and once ready they will not remain in good condition indefinitely.

A large seed bed is not necessary and one of approximately 1.8 m × 1.2 m (6 ft × 4 ft) will provide sufficient room for many sowings.

Seedlings should be transplanted when they have made four or five true leaves and are about 15 cm (6 ins) high.

Allow 75 cm (2½ ft) between Brussels sprouts, 45–60 cm (1½–2 ft) between cauliflowers, whilst 60 cm (2 ft) can be allowed between kales; the spacing distance for cabbages varying from 30–38 cm (12–15 ins).

Right: Good planning will ensure regular supplies

Harvesting Period	Crops and Varieties	Sown	Planted
January–March	**Late Brussels sprouts** 'Citadel', 'Achilles'	early April	late May
January–May	**Winter Cauliflower** 'St Buryan', 'English Winter', 'Snow White', 'Late Enterprise'	April–May	June–July
January–February	**White Sprouting Broccoli**	mid-April	June–July
March–April	**Spring Greens** 'Flower of Spring', 'Offenham', 'Wheeler's Imperial', 'April'	late July sown in final positions and thinned to 23 cm (9 in) apart in the rows after emergence	—
March–April	**Purple Sprouting Broccoli**	mid-April	June–July
March–April	**Curly Kale (Borecole)**	April–May	July–August
April–May	**Spring Cabbage** varieties as Spring Greens	July–August	September–October
May–June	**Rape Kale**	July (thin to 45–60 cm (18–24 in) apart in the rows after emergence)	—
May–June	**Early Summer Cabbage** 'Extra Earlihead', 'Golden Acre' 'Greyhound'	February	April
May–June	**Early Summer Cauliflower**	Late September (plants over-wintered under cold frames or cloches)	March
June–July	**Summer Cauliflower** 'All the Year Round'	January (under heat) March (outside)	March–May
July–August	**Summer Cabbage** 'Greyhound', 'Hispi'	mid-March	mid-May–mid-June
late July–September	**Green Sprouting Broccoli**	April–May	May–June
August–September	**Early Autumn Cabbage** 'Winnigstadt'	April–May	June–July
August–November	**Early/mid-season Brussels Sprouts** 'Early Half Tall', 'Peer Gynt', 'King Arthur'	late March	late May
August–December	**Autumn Cauliflower** 'Kangaroo', 'All the Year Round', 'South Pacific', 'Brisbane'	March–May	May–July
October–February	**Winter Cabbage** 'Ormskirk', 'January King', 'Christmas Drumhead', 'Winter Salad'	April–May	June–July

Planning and planting

Designing a garden

Garden design is based on certain fundamental principles and these should be considered before planning your first layout and work programme. As most modern gardens share an area of 160 to 320m² (200 to 400 sq yd) with a house and garage they will generally have to satisfy several requirements. When preparing the plan, write these down. As the scheme develops, fill in against each item alternative ways of dealing with it, and then decide on the best set of solutions for your site.

The *appearance* of the garden must please the eye; before rushing off to order trees and plant up flower beds, have a good look at your garden from all angles and aim to blend all its features into an harmonious whole. This is difficult to achieve and will inevitably take several seasons.

Paths, walls or hedges laid in straight lines that criss-cross and break up the plot will make a small garden appear smaller still. A curved line is more graceful and leads the eye more slowly to the focal point of the plot, giving an illusion of increased size. Meandering paths can provide a pleasanter walk – especially if flanked with fragrant and eye-catching planting schemes – than those that follow a straight line.

Path edges should either be well defined and kept clear of weeds or bordered with ground cover plants such as candytuft, to conceal the meeting of paving stone or path, and lawn or flower bed. For paths, walls and sheds choose building materials in keeping with the house and the region as a whole, using local stone where possible. Buildings and planting schemes should be related to each other. For example, it would be a mistake to surround a detached bungalow with trees that will eventually dwarf it and provide excessive shade. At the other end of the scale, a very low planting scheme with little colour will throw into unflattering relief a house that stands alone. Flowers, shrubs and small trees of different heights soften an outline and present a more restful view.

The second consideration is *cost*. It is essential from the start to plan your garden so that you can afford to maintain it, or you run the risk of being

forced to give up in despair after a couple of years and let nature take over. Give priority in the first year to work on any paths, drives and boundaries, as these give the garden a basic framework on which you can elaborate in succeeding years. Similarly, plants which will be permanent and take some time to reach maturity – such as hedges and decorative or fruiting trees – should be ordered and planted as soon as possible, otherwise more complicated schemes (or the laying of a lawn) will have to be disturbed to provide for them.

In the first year, buy only the basic tools and equipment for the necessary work. A spade for digging, a fork for lifting and turning, a rake and hoe. Make a measuring rod and use string and sticks for laying out individual plots. Choose the right tools for your height and strength; if you find gardening tiresome because you have the wrong implements, you will spend less time on the plot and the design will suffer. Leave the buying of major and specialized equipment such as lawn-

mowers and pruning shears until you have a lawn to mow and trees to train.

Any garden can be given an instant face-lift with the provision of colourful bedding plants – that is, annuals or perennials bought as young plants from a nursery and used for temporary display. However, this is a very expensive way of beautifying your garden and many bedding plants put in soil that has been neglected for some time die for lack of nourishment or from soil-borne diseases.

In subsequent years you will be able to cut the cost of bedding plants by growing your own from seed (see page 74), and by propagating from established plants. You will also find that most gardeners are only too happy to give cuttings and offsets to a fellow enthusiast. Weed and disease-free offerings are a splendid way of stocking up the garden, and it is likely that what thrives on your neighbour's soil will do equally well on yours.

A site which is being developed over a period of time does not have to look like a battlefield; any area which is to be

LEFT A carefully planned and immaculately maintained garden. The lawn and hard paths share a formal geometric look while the bedding plants have been chosen with particular attention to colour, shape and height.

BELOW An informal front garden in June.

BOTTOM A garden planted with heathers and conifers rather than bedding plants for year round interest.

BELOW A narrow town garden with effective use of a raised flower bed and climbing plants to cover the boundary wall.

left undeveloped can be seeded down to grass and mown, and the turf can be lifted and used again when the area is finally laid out. There will inevitably be a period, after the essential clearing and cleaning of the site has been completed, when the garden looks comparatively bare, but this is a useful time to observe the nature of the plot; to learn how light and shade strike it, what kind of soil you have to work, how heavy rain affects the land, and so on.

The last but most crucial question in the design is the *choice of plants*. This is a matter of personal taste, but for lasting satisfactory results the plants should also suit your site and soil. Avoid planting too closely or using over-vigorous trees or plants in con-fined spaces, as their demands on your time can be considerable. Plants of naturally tidy habit, such as heathers and dwarf conifers, need much less attention than roses, for example, but they grow more slowly. For advice on choosing the right plants for different soils and sites, see pages 34 to 37 and for trees and shrubs pages 96 and 104.

The model garden before transformation. This garden, abandoned for years, is about the worst state in which a small garden might be tackled by the amateur gardener. Very little of the existing site can be left as it is. The fence and shed are both in need of such extensive repair that they are probably better replaced. The boggy patch on the left indicates extremely poor drainage so a soakaway must be built. Fortunately, there may be some unpolluted rubble amongst the pile in the foreground which can be used for the soakaway. The rest must be cleared away. The attractive old birch tree at the far end of the garden (the south-west corner) will cast a lot of shade in summer, so careful thought must be given to how the shade area can be put to good use.

The first task is to make a plan of the existing garden, and a plan of this garden appears on page 60.

Making a plan

The first stage of the programme is to prepare a plan of your garden. However limited your artistic skills, it is worth making a scale drawing of the site. How much detail you include will depend on whether the aim is to improve an existing garden or to start from scratch. To make a plan you will need a tape measure, compass, spirit level, a ball of string, some wooden pegs, six 1.5m (5ft) canes, a 2m (6ft 8in) straight edge to check levels and for measuring, pencils, squared paper, a pen and a centimetre rule, and a flat surface to draw on.

Measure the length and width of the plot, noting any irregularities of outline. Where the aim is to improve an existing garden, you will need to note the size and position of existing beds and their present occupants. Reproduce all these outlines on graph paper. A suitable scale is 1:25 (4cm to represent one metre).

When starting from scratch it is essential to show the whole area including all buildings, boundaries, doorways and entrances, paths and any drives. Indicate proposed and existing features, compass bearings, and the position of trees, shrubs, and water courses. Details of drains, levels, prevailing wind, shaded areas, sunny spots, and any outstanding views should also be recorded on the plan. Use the pegs, straight edge and spirit level to obtain the levels, using the house as the main reference point. Stand the pegs firmly in the soil, so that the straight edge is exactly level (check with the spirit level) when resting on the pegs. Deal with any changes in level as described on page 10.

Ink in all details on the squared paper. If you have drawn up a list of the garden's functions use it in conjunction with the plan to arrive at a finished design. Make sketches of your proposals on tracing paper and place them over the site plan, trying out the various alternatives one by one. When you have decided upon a design, you can then make out a timetable for putting it into practice.

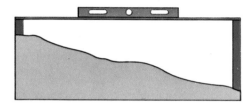

ABOVE Finding the level. Use the house as the main reference point.

BELOW A plan of the dilapidated model garden, see page 58.

BELOW RIGHT A plan of the proposed garden, see completed garden on page 64.

FAR RIGHT An alternative plan, adapted to accommodate a vegetable plot (brown area).

Key

1 Nepeta
2 Daphne
3 Forsythia
4 Potentilla
5 Pyracantha
6 Viburnum
7 Group of rose bushes (hybrid tea)
8 Rosa
9 Skimmia
10 Berberis
11 Aucuba
12 Buxus
13 Berberis
14 Elaeagnus
15 Symphoricarpos
16 Rhododendron
17-20 Dwarf conifers
21 Tubs of flowers
22 Hydrangea
23 Climbing roses
24 Clematis
25 Erica

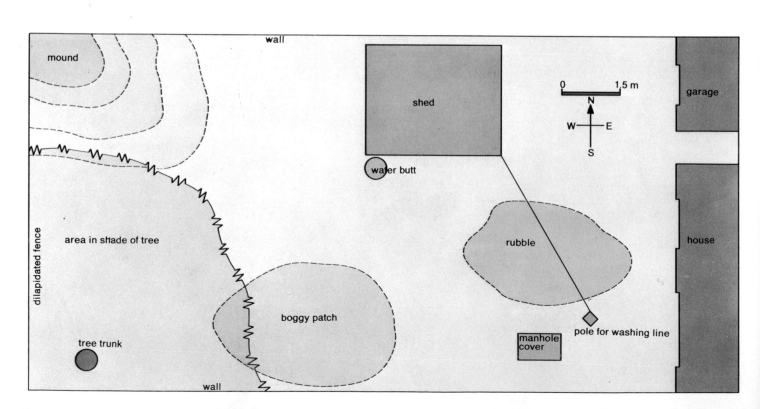

The model garden

Shown here is the site plan of the **imaginary garden drawn on page 58,** which includes most of the worst problems you are likely to encounter in a badly neglected site. The plot has been remodelled to provide a family garden. The pile of builder's rubble and washing line in full view of the back window are replaced with a spacious paved area brought to life with tubs of flowers (one of them hiding the manhole cover), climbing roses against trelliswork, and a clematis against the back wall of the house. The trellis provides a screen for the laundry area, still in easy reach of the house but in a corner where the proximity of the garage would make planting tricky.

The dilapidated fence at the west end of the plan has been replaced with a wall of patterned blocks, which provides a solid boundary but allows air and light to filter through.

The tumbledown shed is dismantled and a solid new one put up on the unpromising boggy patch, made firmer and well-drained by the rubble now buried beneath it. The new shed is centrally placed to serve the whole garden and is easily reached from the patio by stepping stones set into the lawn slightly lower than the level of the grass to facilitate mowing.

In the south-west corner of the garden an old birch tree casts a deep shadow, but provides an attractive view from the house. Little will grow under its branches but as it is distant from the house this a good spot for the composting area, hidden behind the shed. In the north-west corner, the mound is kept and planted with heathers.

In the new garden, the curving lawn is bordered by four main planting schemes. The most ambitious and demanding of these, the herbaceous border, is fully described on page 73. The other three are composed of shrubs and conifers which, after planting, require minimum attention and provide year-round colour and cover. Though energy and thought are needed to plan and plant such a garden, maintenance in subsequent seasons is confined to the lawn, a little pruning and training, and care of the herbaceous border.

The introduction of fruit and vegetables inevitably means more time working in the garden, but many people feel that home-grown produce is worth the effort. To prepare this particular site for vegetables, generous manuring would be necessary since the soil will have lost much nourishment over the years of neglect. The far end of the plot would be used for vegetables, and the south-facing part of the herbaceous border for fruit—cordon apples and pears or fan-trained blackberries against the wall and trellis, and black or red currant and gooseberry bushes in front.

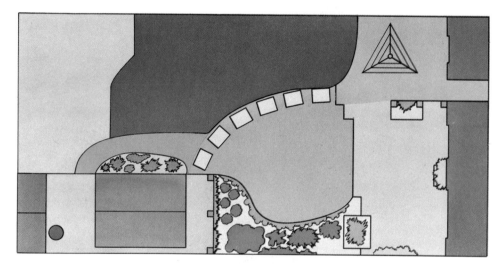

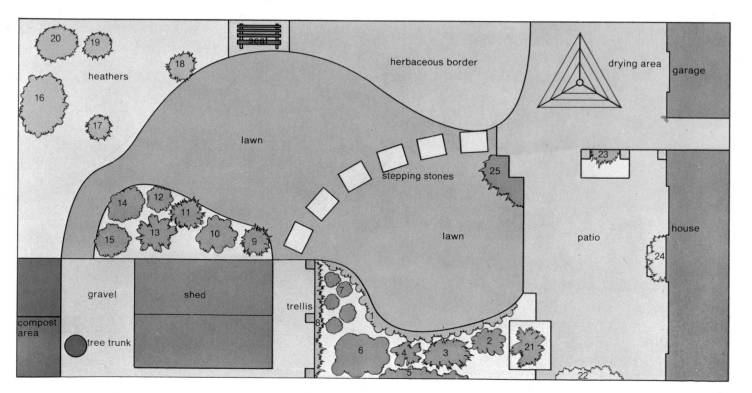

Programme of tasks

The work needed to turn a neglected site into a plot that deserves the name of garden can be covered in twelve steps. As there will be items on the timetable that do not apply to your site, it is certain that three or four hours a week devoted to gardening could bring your dream garden closer to reality within a year.

1. *Clearing the site.* The best time to start the basic groundwork is in early spring. Aim to remove all rubbish and to clear and dig out perennial weeds by the end of April. Difficult weeds can be cleared with a hormone weedkiller. Take care that no chemicals contaminate water and ponds and keep them away from children or pets.

2. *Excavate for, and lay paths and drives.* These jobs are much easier to do during the summer months. You may decide to have them laid professionally but it is still useful to understand the basic requirements.

The stability of a drive or path, particularly in winter, depends on a sufficient depth of hard dry foundation, covered with a waterproof capping. A serviceable drive to carry the average car might consist of a 15cm (6in) depth of 7.5cm (3in) hardcore covered with a 5cm (2in) layer of 18mm (¾in) gravel and topped with a 10cm (4in) layer of concrete mixed in the proportion 1 part concrete:2 parts sand:4 parts washed gravel. For paths use the same materials, but at half the depth of the above. As an alternative, a 5cm (2in) layer of black or coloured tarmacadam could be substituted for concrete for paths, but would be laid on top of the concrete for drives. Surfaces should not be completely level, but slope from

62

one side to the other or be raised in the centre. The fall should be 1:60, so that, for example, a 90cm (3ft) wide path would have a fall of 15mm ($\frac{5}{8}$in) from one side to the other, and if it were to be raised in the centre would have a 7mm ($\frac{5}{16}$in) fall from centre to edge.

3. *Lay drains.* Another major task probably requiring professional help, it is also best carried out in summer.

4. *Build sheds and walls, gates and fences.* Do as much as you can of this basic work in the first summer. When establishing boundaries, bear in mind that trees and hedges may grow to block drains, shed their leaves, and exclude light. To avoid contention go for hedges whose growth can be restricted, or fences or walls.

Badly built walls are dangerous. The foundations for a low wall should be at least twice as wide and the same depth as the thickness of the wall. Free-standing solid walls over 1.2m (4ft) high should be at least 23cm (9in) thick. Walls over 1.2m (4ft) high and

more than 3.6m (12ft) long should be professionally built.

Fence construction falls into the following categories: timber, steel, ironwork, wire mesh, plastic, and concrete.

Treat *timber* with a non-poisonous preservative, or the life of the fencing may be as little as three years. With care, timber can last at least 12–15 years. Concrete posts assist considerably in cutting maintenance costs. Heavy-gauge steel or iron railing, when regularly painted, can last indefinitely, but is very expensive.

Wire netting, though not exactly beautiful, is cheaper than many forms of fencing, but soon corrodes in coastal areas or in towns, unless protected with plastic coating.

Plastic mesh netting is one of the cheapest but also one of the most vulnerable barriers, as it is easily cut with a knife.

Concrete fencing is expensive but permanent, heavy and durable and requires no maintenance.

With all forms of fencing, strong supports are essential: common spacings are at 1.8m, 2.4m and 2.7m (6, 8 and 9ft), based on weight, type and height. Solid fencing, 1.8m (6ft) high is usually adequate for privacy. Corner and end posts require extra support to stop them being pulled in or over.

5. *Digging, levelling, manuring and liming.* These tasks need to be carried out in the autumn, before the ground becomes too wet or frozen to work, and to allow the winter to weather the soil in preparation for planting. Manuring and liming are discussed in more detail on page 29.

Changes of level can be achieved in various ways. Gardens on different levels offer wide scope for imaginative planting and provide architectural interest with varying widths and shapes. Steps can be used to link two areas of different levels (ramps should be no steeper than one-in-three). Lawns steeper than one-in-four will be difficult to mow.

Grassed or planted banks should be constructed carefully: where the ground level is being raised, keep back the topsoil to spread on the surface after levelling. Consolidate the earth as work proceeds, in layers no deeper than 15cm (6in) and make sure that the slope is no steeper than one-in-two. A rock garden is an excellent and decorative way to highlight variations in land form.

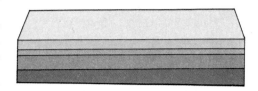
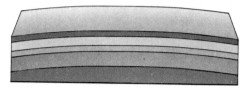

Laying a drive: surface sloping from one side to the other (top), and raised in the centre (bottom).

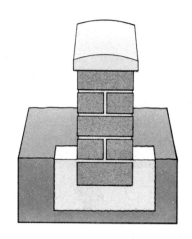

Foundations for a solid wall should be the same depth and twice as wide as the thickness of the wall.

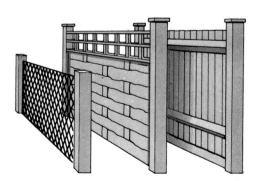

Solid timber fencing with strong supports.

LEFT The model garden in the making. The site has been cleared, paths and patio laid, a new wall erected and a soakaway built (under the foundations for the new shed where the boggy patch was). The soil has been dug and manured, and the flower borders pegged out.

6. *Ordering plants and materials* (this will vary from year to year). Most seedsmen issue catalogues towards the end of the year, and it is a good idea to place your order as soon as possible to be sure of getting the varieties you want.

7. *Planting and staking trees* is described on pages 98 and 99. Obtain and fix stakes and prepare the planting hole in advance to receive trees straight from the nursery.

8. *Planting hedges and shrubs.* It is a good idea to plant hedges and shrubs in your first year. They take several seasons to establish themselves and fill their allotted space, so the sooner you can get them going the better.

9. *Laying lawns and turfing* is best carried out in the autumn on a site well prepared the previous spring. If you are carrying out major clearance and building work, leave the lawn until your second year.

10. *Preparing for flowers, fruit and vegetables.* Site preparation for these specialized groups of plants is described in the relevant chapters, and can be started in the first autumn for sowing and planting the following year. For fruit bushes and particularly for trees which will occupy ground for long periods of time, soil preparation must be thorough. For the vegetable plot, follow a crop rotation plan from the start and prepare each site accordingly (see page 50).

11. *Sowing annuals, biennials and perennials from seed.* Early in the second spring, start sowing seed for summer and autumn bedding schemes.

12 *Prepare a maintenance plan* for the year, and try to tackle the job methodically. Routine maintenance is always a good idea.

The model garden completed. Care has been given to plant out in such a way that when the plants are established and grow bigger they will not overcrowd each other. This is why the new garden has a rather 'bare' look.

4. Firm the soil with the heel and toe method.

5. When turfing, always work standing on a board towards the unturfed area.

Step-by-ste

Whether turfing or laying a lawn from seed, the preparation of the area is the same (steps 1-3).

1. and 2. First level the area if it is undulating by adding more soil in the hollows and smoothing out the mounds. It is good for lawns to have a slight fall of 1 in 60 as this will help drainage and avoid pools of surface water.

6. Bond the turf like brickwork.

7. Peg the turf on a slope to stop it slipping.

10. Trim the edges of the lawn with a spade or half moon turfing iron, making a slanting cut.

8. Fill any gaps by sprinkling sandy soil between the pieces of turf.

9. Gently firm the turf in place.

Turfing

4. Firm the soil with the heel and toe method.

Mark the area for sowing into sections for correct seeding – 30-45 g/m² ($1-1\frac{1}{2}$ oz per sq yd).

aying a lawn

3. Rake over the ground to a fine tilth, removing stones and adding a general fertilizer if necessary. Do not let the area dry out.

5. Rake in the seeds and keep the area well watered, using a sprinkler attachment, as heavy watering would dislodge the seedlings.

Roll the lawn with a light roller after turfing or six weeks after sowing when the grass will be approximately 3 cm ($1\frac{1}{4}$ in) high.

Sowing

chamaecyparis

philadelphus

cytisus

Quick-growing shrubs and hedging plants

Key

Sh = Use as shrub
H = Hedging
E = Evergreen
T = Suitable for towns
S = Suitable for coast
A = Acid
N = Neutral
C = Chalk
Size – single measure is space to leave between hedging plants
All measurements are average and approximate at ultimate size

Name		Soil	Site	Size m or cm ht × wth	Size ft or in ht × wth	Season and nature of interest
Carpinus betulus Hornbeam	H	N C	Open	60cm	24in	Spring to autumn foliage, dry leaves in winter
Chamaecyparis lawsoniana Lawsons Cypress	H E	A N C	Sun	45cm	18in	All year round foliage blue green and gold
Cotoneaster simonsii Cotoneaster	Sh H	A N C	Sun or Shade	45cm 2·4 × 1·8	18in 8 × 6	Autumn scarlet berries
Crataegus oxyacantha Thorn or Quick	H	A N C	Open T	30cm	12in	Spring summer foliage and white flowers
Cupressocyparis leylandii Leyland Cypress	H E	N C	Sun S	90cm	36in	All year round foliage green and yellow
Cytisus scoparius Common Broom	Sh	N	Sun Open	2·4 × 2·1	8 × 7	Spring, whitish flowers
Elaeagnus ebbingei False Oleaster	Sh E	A N C	Open	3·6 × 2·4	12 × 8	All year round foliage grey green with silver undersides
Escallonia macrantha Chilean Gum Box	Sh H E	A N	Sun Mild	45cm 2·4 × 1·8	18in 8 × 6	All year round foliage, red flowers summer and autumn

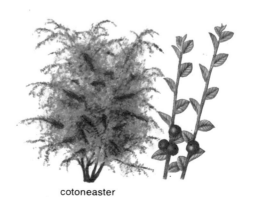

cotoneaster

ribes

spartium

elaeagnus

escallonia

forsythia

Name	Soil	Site	Size m or cm ht × wth	Size ft or in ht × wth	Season and nature of interest
Forsythia intermedia Hanging Golden Bell	Sh	A N C	T Open	2·4 × 1·8	8 × 6	Spring, yellow flowers
Ligustrum ovalifolium Privet	H	A N C	T Open	30cm	12in	Spring and summer foliage
Lonicera nitida Hedge Honeysuckle	H E	A N C	S Sun Mild	30cm	12in	All year round green foliage
Olearia haastii Daisy Bush	Sh H E	A N C	Sun or shade S	45cm 1·8 × 1·2	18in 6 × 4	All year round foliage Summer, scented white flowers
Philadelphus 'Sybille' Mock Orange	Sh	A N C	Open	2·4 × 1·5	8 × 5	Summer, scented, purple stained flowers
Potentilla friedrichsenii Shrubby Cinquefoil	Sh	A N C	Sun Open	1·2 × 0·9	4 × 3	Summer yellow flowers
Ribes sanguineum Flowering Currant	Sh	A N C	Sun or Shade	2·4 × 1·5	8 × 5	Spring, reddish pink flowers
Rosa various Rose	Sh H	A N	Sun	45cm 2·4 × 1.2	18in 8 × 4	Summer, autumn flowers, various colours, red hips
Spartium junceum Spanish Broom	Sh	A N C	Sun T and S	2·4 × 1·8	8 × 6	Summer yellow flowers
Symphoricarpus orbiculatus Snowberry	Sh	A N C	Sun or shade T	1·8 × 1·5	6 × 5	Summer, whitish flowers followed by pinkish-purple fruits in autumn
Tamarix tetrandra Tamarisk	Sh H	A N	Open S	45cm 3·0 × 2·4	18in 10 × 8	Spring, bright pink flowers
Weigela florida Diervilla	Sh	A N C	T Sun	2·4 × 1·8	8 × 6	Summer, red, crimson or pink flowers

symphoricarpos

tamarix

weigela

The flower garden

Flowers have various roles to play, whether it is to cover eyesores or provide material for the imaginative flower arranger. The key to success in a flower garden is the health and care of well-chosen plants, and although many modern aids for cultivating plants save time and trouble, they are no substitute for good garden practice and common sense.

The basic needs of plants are simple enough: a well-prepared soil and site; careful sowing and planting at the right time; adequate warmth, food and moisture; attention to training during the growing season, and pest, weed and disease control.

The guidelines set out in the following pages apply to flower growing in any size of garden both front and back and to containers.

UNDERSTANDING THOSE LATIN NAMES

Plant names can be confusing, and if you are not confident about coping with Latin, the pronunciation can seem alarming. If you depend on common names, however, you can be misled, so the approach taken in this book has been to steer a course between the extremes. Common names have been used where these are well known and not likely to lead to confusion, and the Latin names used are those under which you are likely to find the plants in a nursery or catalogue (even though these may not be botanically the most up-to-date).

Common names have the shortcoming of being vague – because there is no form of register several plants can have the same name. Star of Bethlehem can mean *Ornithogalum umbellatum* or *Campanula isophylla* – two very different plants. And, of course, neither name might mean much to someone in another country. A Latin name, on the other hand, is unique and international.

Fortunately most of the problem with Latin names is in the mind. Most of us will talk of forsythias, delphiniums, and antirrhinums without a second thought, and all these are Latin names.

All Latin names have at least two parts – the genus (which is equivalent to a surname or family name) and the species (which indicates the particular member of the 'family'). In *Cedrus atlantica glauca*:

Cedrus is the genus
atlantica is the species
glauca is the variety.

If the 'variety' has been raised in cultivation and not in the wild it is technically a 'cultivar' and should be given single quotation marks:

Cedrus atlantica 'Pendula'.

Because it makes no practical difference whether a good garden plant arose in cultivation or in the wild, the term 'variety' has been used for both types throughout this book.

What's in a name?

It is always important to be precise about names when you order plants. If you order *Forsythia × intermedia*, it will not be as good as the improved variety *F. × i.* 'Spectabilis'. And in the case of conifers – which can have particularly long and offputting names, missing a word like 'Nana' or 'Pygmaea' off the end can mean the difference between a forest tree and something for the rock garden!

Canterbury bell, forget-me-not and Brompton stocks are members of this class. Double daisy, sweet William, and wallflowers are best treated as biennials, although they are really perennials since their flowers in later years are poor in quality and quantity.

Half-hardy biennials are treated as for hardy biennials, but sown and overwintered indoors. This type of plant is not widely used outdoors and most half-hardy biennials – which are few in number anyway – are grown in a greenhouse. Some half-hardy perennials are treated as greenhouse biennials.

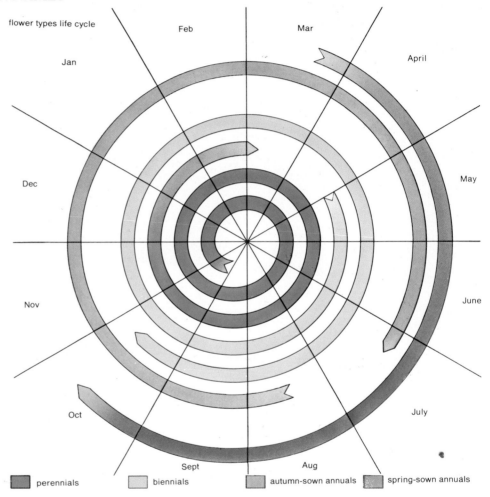

flower types life cycle

Jan, Feb, Mar, April, May, June, July, Aug, Sept, Oct, Nov, Dec

perennials   biennials   autumn-sown annuals   spring-sown annuals

Hardy perennials are plants which for practical considerations are planted from seed or division, flower for between one and five years according to type, and are then lifted, divided and replanted. Examples include golden rod, iris, and peony.

Half-hardy perennials are an important class of plants which are overwintered under cover or raised in greenhouses for outside planting. Begonia, dahlia, fuchsia and geraniums are members of this category.

Choosing the right flowers for your garden

A selection of plants which are well suited to your climate, soil, site and taste, will lay a sound foundation for your garden. The choice of a subject because of its colour or scent alone without due regard to the needs of the plant, can be disappointing and expensive. A visit to some local gardens, especially those where plants are labelled, can provide a fair amount of useful information. Make a note of those plants which flourish and you will learn something about the local soil and climate and the varieties likely to grow well, their habit, colour and flowering season. Observe your own garden at different times of the day and of the year, noting the sunny areas and the shaded or draughty spots, as well as the direction of the prevailing wind. While you may have limited control over climate, soil and site, in your choice of plants you can greatly influence the success of your garden.

Use this simple checklist to choose suitable flowering and other plants.

Site conditions
Sunny or shaded situation
Aspect – does it face N.S.E. or W.?
Exposed to wind or sheltered

Soil considerations
Acid or alkaline
Heavy or light
Fertile or poor

Plant habit
Height, spread and shape
Colour and flowering season
Expensive to buy or to maintain
Requires staking

Soil preparation

Most of the common flowering herbaceous plants, (which can include annuals, biennials and perennials), will grow and bloom satisfactorily on a wide range of soils. To get the soil into perfect condition, dig the ground to a spade's depth – 30cm (12in) – during autumn, and incorporate organic matter as you work, leaving the soil undisturbed until spring to be weathered by wind and frost. The organic matter can be in the form of well-rotted manure applied at the rate of 2.25kg/m² (5lb per sq yd) or as a 2.5cm (1in) layer of peat or pulverized bark. If you need the land for autumn planting, the soil should be prepared in summer and firmed before sowing or planting. Before setting out seeds or plants, the degree of soil acidity (the pH level) may need adjusting. Chalk-loving plants such as gypsophila or pinks will tolerate neutral soil, with a pH level of 7, but slightly above that figure is better. Additional lime is best applied two to three weeks before planting, at a rate based on the results of your soil test. Before planting or sowing, lightly fork in a proprietary base fertilizer dressing at the rate of 100 – 140g/m² (3-4oz per sq yd) which has an analysis of parts: nitrogen 5%, phosphate 5%, and potash 10%.

Spongy soil must be lightly firmed and raked again before plants or seeds are set out.

Before seeds are sown in their flowering positions, the beds need to be worked into a fine tilth to a depth of 7.5–10cm (3-4in).

BELOW A glorious herbaceous border.

Laying out a mixed flower border

The size, shape and levels of a mixed flower border will be largely influenced by the existing site. Depth and breadth of the bed should be taken into account as much as the proposed colour schemes and season of interest, and the height and character of the plants should relate to each other and their surroundings.

A simple plan for a border in front of a hedge could have tall plants placed at the back and shorter subjects to the fore. With large borders it is better to set plants in groups rather than individually, or a spotty effect can be created. Tall spiky plants like delphiniums and verbascum contrast well with round-headed flowers like achillea and phlox, or' with plants such as helenium that form a mounded clump.

The duration and times of the flowering season are quite important: borders close to the house need subjects that provide year-round colour although a traditional herbaceous border usually has a short but splendid season in summer. Small evergreen shrubs introduced in a mixed border provide a useful framework and give year-round interest.

Strong hues of red or yellow contrast well against shades of green and blue. White and cream blend harmoniously with most flower colours. Bronze, orange and pinks create a warm effect, compared with the coolness of blues and lavenders. Grey foliage blends or contrasts with red, cerise, pink and white shades.

Planting

Plant lifted plants in autumn or spring, and container grown subjects anytime except when in flower, or when ground is frozen or waterlogged. When the border has been dug, manured, limed and fertilized, the next stage is to measure out the planting positions with short sticks pushed into the ground. Measuring carefully saves future time and temper. Start planting at the back or at one end, and, working methodically, check soil level and plant positions occasionally, making sure plants are firm.

ABOVE Contrasting spiky heads of lupin (left) and foxglove (centre) with yarrow (back right) and phlox (front right).

BELOW Contrasting foliage of gladioli and phlox (back, left to right) and bergenia and hosta (front, left to right).

BELOW Marking out the border with sand and string.

RIGHT BELOW The completed mixed border (key right). This is the planting scheme used in the model garden.

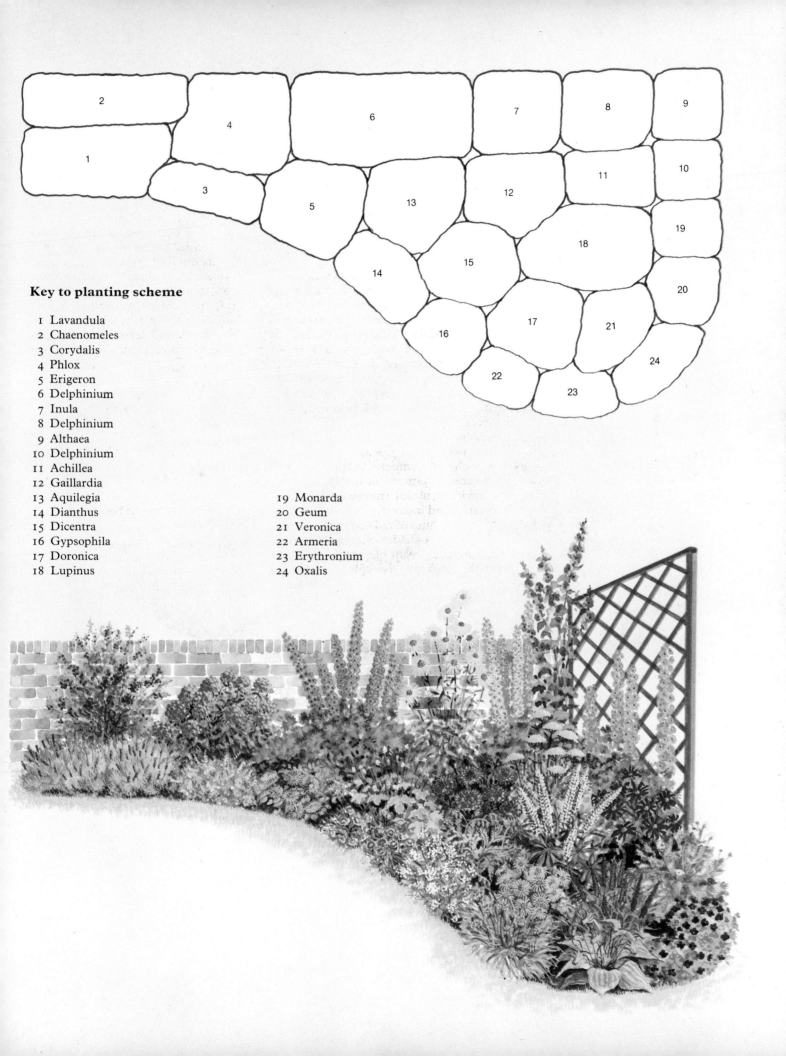

Key to planting scheme

1 Lavandula
2 Chaenomeles
3 Corydalis
4 Phlox
5 Erigeron
6 Delphinium
7 Inula
8 Delphinium
9 Althaea
10 Delphinium
11 Achillea
12 Gaillardia
13 Aquilegia
14 Dianthus
15 Dicentra
16 Gypsophila
17 Doronica
18 Lupinus

19 Monarda
20 Geum
21 Veronica
22 Armeria
23 Erythronium
24 Oxalis

SEED SOWING, THINNING AND TRANSPLANTING

A properly prepared seed bed is essential if maximum germination and growth are to be obtained. Seeds and seedlings need four things: moisture, warmth, air and, after germination, light.

The majority of seeds are small and need a fine crumbly bed which should be prepared well in advance of sowing time. If seeds are sown in lumpy soil they may lie in a pocket of air and when the tiny roots emerge these will soon dry out.

Never make the seed bed when the soil clings heavily to your boots and tools. Particularly where the land is heavy, it should be turned over and left rough in winter. After frosts, it will break down and produce the tilth which is almost impossible to secure even by much labour. Very heavy ground can be improved by the addition of sharp sand which will provide aeration, while finely ground peat will keep heavy soil open and prevent it drying out rapidly and cracking, which sometimes occurs on heavy land, to provide a suitable medium for growth.

Although dryness will not spoil germination before the process starts, once the seed coat opens, the young growth will soon die if the soil becomes dry. There are also seed-borne diseases which hinder germination, and insect pests and other hazards. This underlines the necessity of sowing seed in really good soil, containing humus matter which encourages even germination and a plentiful root system. Discourage soil-borne diseases by practising crop rotation.

Very shallow sowing is successful only if there is sufficient surface moisture present, from frequent showers, or irrigation. Deep sowing will only give good results if the weather remains dry enough to keep the surface soil open. The rule should be therefore, to sow rather more deeply on light, easily drained ground and more shallowly on soil which is heavy and holds moisture for a long period. For most crops, one should aim to have a seed bed which is firm at the base and fairly loose at the top.

There are various ways of sowing seeds, the most usual being to draw out drills and then to sprinkle seeds along them. Some gardeners mix very fine seed with sand, powdered peat or dry soil so as not to sow too thickly. Alternatively, a little lime may be added to the seed so that it will be easier to see where it falls into the drill.

Even sowing means less thinning, and stronger plants because they suffer less disturbance. Although careful sowing takes time, the effort reaps due reward.

There are various seed distributors on the market, some having a

number of holes like a pepper pot. It is usually possible to adjust a distributor to regulate the number and size of the holes. Seed shaken from the corner of the packet rarely falls out evenly.

Drills can be scratched into the soil with the point of a draw hoe or a stick. Flat-shaped drills are usually made for peas and beans, especially if sowing double rows. Care is needed to ensure that the base of such drills is level so that the seed does not become covered with varying depths of soil.

It is certainly wasteful to sow seed too thickly and then spend time thinning out. Apart from this, the scent that carrots and onions give off when handled, attracts carrot and onion flies. There is less trouble from these pests if thinning out is avoided.

Take out straight drills with a hoe against a taut line　　　　　*Sow large seeds from the packet, but use your fingers for very fine seed*

Once the seed is sown a covering of fine soil should be given. Using the rake deeply may disturb the newly sown seeds. Afterwards firm the soil, which can be done with the head of the rake, to help the tiny roots to gain a hold.

A further *very* light raking of the surface soil will ensure that moisture seeps through evenly and does not settle along the drills.

Should there be a prolonged spell of dry weather during which it is essential to sow the seeds, encourage germination by watering the opened drills generously before sowing the seeds. Runner beans and peas can be soaked for a few hours before sowing but this is not always satisfactory as some seeds may rot before growth starts. Another method some gardeners adopt is to place carrot seeds between layers of damp cloth or muslin. After a few days the germination process begins and the seeds can be sown in moist soil in the usual way. This does require care since wet seeds usually cling together and are difficult to separate. 'Fluid sowing' is a more satisfactory variation, and you can buy fluid sowing kits that come complete with instructions for use.

Many early sown seeds, including peas and beans, may be attacked by a soil fungus which disrupts growth. This pre-emergence damping off can be prevented by dusting the seeds with a fungicide.

Pelleted seeds enable you to sow them individually at the required distances apart. A drawback is that since the coating disintegrates slowly in dry soil, it is essential for the soil to be moist so that the material breaks up quickly and there is no delay in germination. Expensive F_1 hybrid seeds may be sold in pelleted form.

It is sometimes an advantage to sow vegetable seeds in containers and there are four main types to choose from. The seed box is particularly useful where a lot of seeds are to be sown and where they are expected to germinate freely. The standard seed boxes, measuring 20 cm × 36 cm × 6 cm (8 × 14½ × 2½ ins) deep, are a convenient size and can be placed closely together thus economizing in space. Wooden seed boxes have a comparatively limited life while plastic trays last longer and are easier to clean and sterilize.

The square earthenware seed pan is a useful container, although seldom used today. It is convenient where large quantities of slow germinating seed is being sown. Where a seed box would be too large, the 13–15 cm (5–6 ins) round seed pan is a good receptacle for small quantities of seeds. The 13 cm (5 ins) pot is not quite so good as the 13 cm (5 ins) pan, since it is deeper than is necessary. Pots and pans smaller than 13 cm (5 ins) in diameter dry out rather quickly and are less suitable.

Having chosen the container, the next thing is to provide drainage material. Crocks should be placed over drainage holes to prevent them clogging with soil, and it is a good plan to place a layer of fibrous peat or leaf mould or even rough loam, over the crocks before filling in with compost. As far as the crocking is concerned, one large piece should be placed concave side down over the drainage hole, and two or three smaller crocks around it. If a deep container is used, several layers of crocks are advisable.

John Innes seed compost is very suitable for sowing most seeds, although not essential, since a simple mixture of loam, a little peat or leaf mould and some sharp sand is sufficient for seeds to germinate evenly. Fill a pot or seed box by lightly pressing the soil in with the fingers, slightly over-filling the container, and then striking it off level with a straight-edged, tapping the receptacle several times before finally pressing level with a round or square presser or the base of an empty pot. This should leave the compost in the pot perfectly level and evenly firm but not compacted.

If the compost is nicely moist at sowing time, little water will be needed until germination takes place. The compost must never dry out but do not allow the surface to become caked from too frequent waterings. If it does, it may prevent the emerging seedlings from developing properly.

Thinning Seedlings

However carefully one may sow seed outdoors there is always some thinning out to be done. Do it when the seedlings are small, so there is a minimum of root disturbance to neighbouring plants. The best plants should remain in position, while weak and indifferent specimens should be removed.

Above: Sowing seeds in trays by hand. Never allow compost to dry out

Water the rows lightly some hours before thinning. Refirm the soil after thinning and if the weather is dry, water the rows. Do not do this unless really necessary or the roots will come to the surface and may be scorched by the sun.

With some crops, notably carrots and onions, thinning out is best done twice; the later thinnings being used in salads. Never delay the final thinning or the crop may be harmed by overcrowding.

Never leave unwanted seedlings lying on the ground, for disease spores may gain a hold and spread on to healthy plants. In the case of onions and carrots, flies may lay their eggs on the roots of the plants, attracted by the scent of the discarded seedlings.

1,2,3,5: Clay pots, saucers and seed tray 4,6,10: Plastic pots 7,8: Peat pots 9: Plastic seed trays 11: Strawberry pot 12: 'Jiffy' peat pots

Planting leek seedlings

Before planting, dip cabbage seedlings in calomel paste to deter club-root

Transplanting

Some crops including cabbages, cauliflowers and Brussels sprouts, peas and lettuce, transplant very easily, as do the flowers we raise as bedding plants. It is, however, vegetables that need most care.

If cauliflowers are planted too firmly, they may well show a tendency to become blind, producing robust leaves but no curds. The crown should always be clear of the ground, allowing no soil to lodge in the centre. When planting cauliflowers and other brassicas, dust the holes with calomel, or dip the seedlings in a paste of 4% calomel

dust mixed with water and flour, to lessen the risk of club root attacks.

Shallow drills can be drawn out and the plants set in them on high ground or where strong winds are frequently experienced. Cauliflowers need extra support by earthing up firmly round the stem. The drills will give protection from ground winds, help to prevent the roots from drying out in very dry weather, and aid watering since moisture will penetrate directly to the roots. When planting out in summer, some protection from strong sunshine must be given to newly moved seedlings, otherwise the young plants may wilt and die.

The planting can be done with a trowel or dibber. The advantage of

'Station' sowing. After germination, discard weaker seedlings

Prick out into pots holding seedling by its leaves

Above: The vegetable garden can be as beautiful as it is useful

Below: Harden off seedlings before planting out

using a trowel is that holes can be made to receive roots with a ball of soil, which means less disturbance to the finer roots and in turn, a less severe check to growth. The handle of the trowel can be used to press the soil firmly around the roots. If a slight depression is left around the stem, and should watering be necessary, it will ensure that moisture reaches the roots and is not dispersed around them. Once plants are growing well, the loose soil can be worked towards them, filling in the depressions to encourage sturdy growth.

A dibber is a useful little tool but it is advisable to make sure that air pockets are not left at the bottom of the hole. If this happens, water may drain into the hole and drown the roots. After withdrawing the dibber, make another hole at an angle to the first hole, levering soil against the stem to anchor it in position, and fill in any air pockets. The second hole can be left for watering the plant. Wherever possible, members of the cabbage family should always be planted with a dibber, excepting cauliflowers which do best in trowel holes. Cucumbers, sweet corn and tomatoes also do better when planted with a trowel.

When seeds have been sown in boxes or pots of John Innes compost or a peat-based mixture, they will have to be pricked out. Lift them carefully from the box – all of them – and replant them with more space into other receptacles or into their final positions in the garden. They must be lifted carefully by using a garden label, trowel or some other pointed implement. Transplant them immediately when the soil is nicely moist.

When moving seedlings take care to hold them by their leaves, never by the stem.

Seedlings raised under heated frames or in greenhouses must be gradually hardened off before being moved outdoors. Particularly in the case of brassica seedlings, a watch must be kept to ensure that flea beetles do not attack the young plants. As a precaution it is a good plan to dust the seedlings with flea beetle powder. This prevents attacks which can ruin a whole batch of plants.

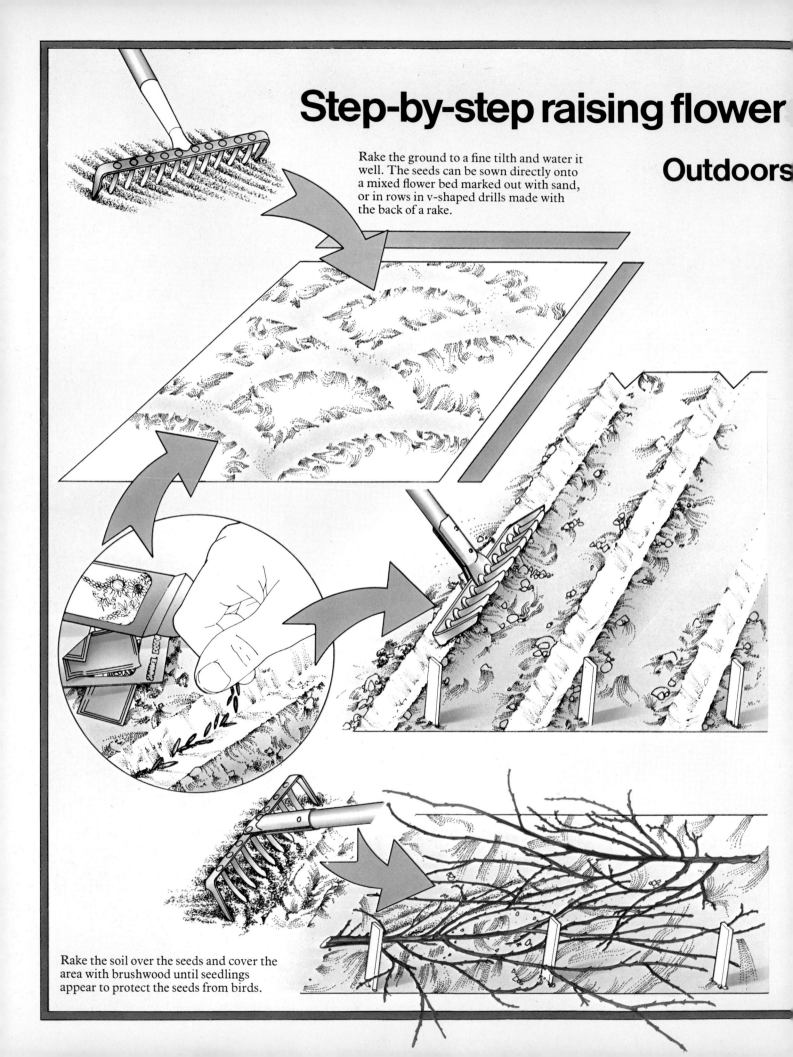

Step-by-step raising flower

Outdoors

Rake the ground to a fine tilth and water it well. The seeds can be sown directly onto a mixed flower bed marked out with sand, or in rows in v-shaped drills made with the back of a rake.

Rake the soil over the seeds and cover the area with brushwood until seedlings appear to protect the seeds from birds.

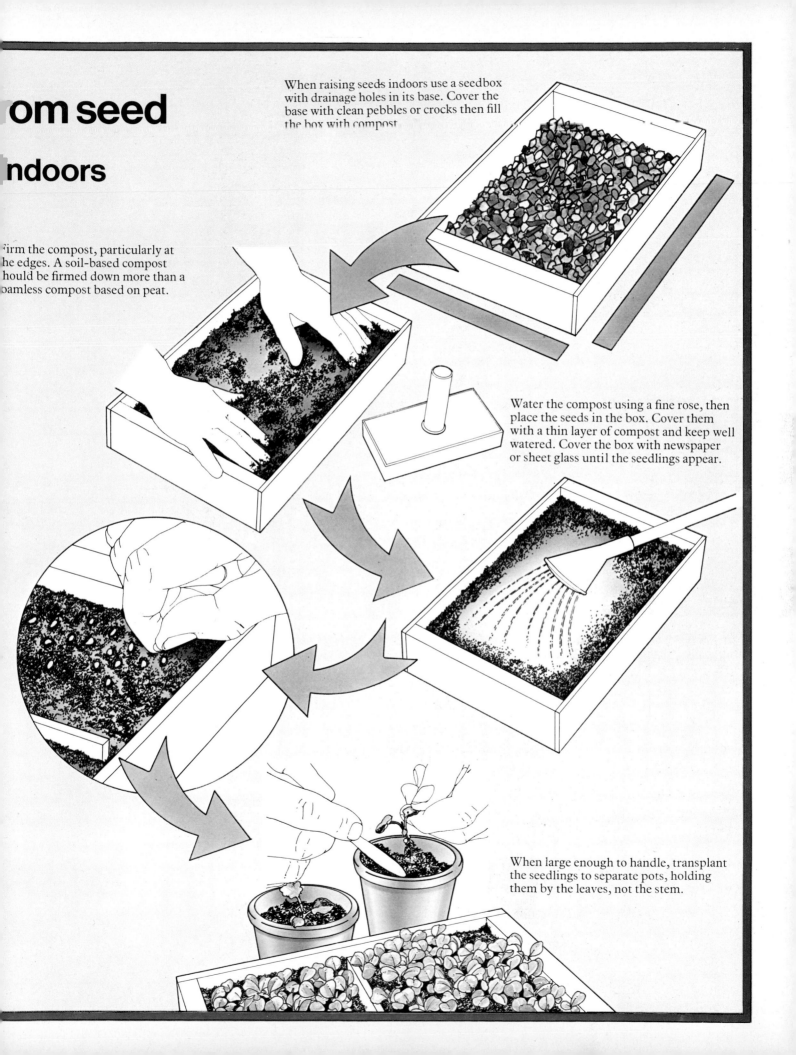

om seed

ndoors

When raising seeds indoors use a seedbox with drainage holes in its base. Cover the base with clean pebbles or crocks then fill the box with compost.

Firm the compost, particularly at the edges. A soil-based compost should be firmed down more than a loamless compost based on peat.

Water the compost using a fine rose, then place the seeds in the box. Cover them with a thin layer of compost and keep well watered. Cover the box with newspaper or sheet glass until the seedlings appear.

When large enough to handle, transplant the seedlings to separate pots, holding them by the leaves, not the stem.

50 Easy to Grow Colourful Flowers

Illustrated Guide

Key

The first of each entry is the botanical term followed by the popular name. The plants are grouped according to whether they are annual, biennial, or perennial.

Plant height is indicated by the following letters

T = 1·2m (4ft) or over
M = between 30cm (1ft) and 1·2m (4ft)
S = normally less than 30cm (1ft)

Flowering season is denoted by the following

Sp = spring
Su = summer
Au = autumn
Wi = winter

Flower colour range is grouped into shades and is indicated by letters

R = Reds
P = Pinks
Y = Yellows and Oranges
W = Whites or creams
B = Blues
L = Lilacs and purples

Name	Size	Colour	Season
Hardy Annuals The following can be grown in a variety of positions, but are usually better in a bed on their own than mixed with other types of plant			
Calendula officinalis Pot Marigold	M	Y	Su
Centaurea cyanus Cornflower	S or M	P W B L	Su
Clarkia elegans Clarkia	M	P R	Su
Coreopsis tinctoria Calliopsis	M	Y	Su
Delphinium consolida Larkspur	M	P W B	Su
Eschscholzia californica Californian Poppy	S or M	Y	Su
Godetia grandiflora Godetia	S or M	R P W	Su
Papaver nudicaule Iceland Poppy	M	R P Y	Su
Half Hardy Annuals These are suitable for use in flower beds where the plants are changed a minimum of twice a year			
Antirrhinum majus Snapdragon	S or M	R P Y W	Su
Callistephus chinensis China Aster	M	R P Y W L	Su or Au
Gazania hybrida Gazania	S	P Y	Su
Lobelia erinus Lobelia	S	P W B	Su
Matthiola incana Stock	M	R P Y W B L	Sp or Su
Nicotiana affinis Tobacco plant	M	R P Y W	Su
Petunia hybrida Petunia	S or M	R P Y W L	Su
Phlox drummondii Phlox	S or M	R P W L	Su

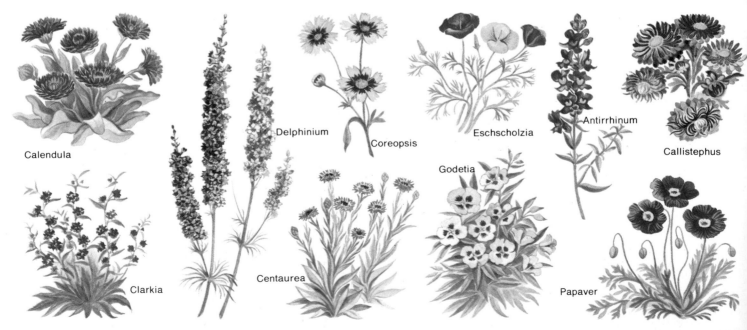

Calendula

Delphinium

Coreopsis

Eschscholzia

Antirrhinum

Callistephus

Clarkia

Centaurea

Godetia

Papaver

Name	Size	Colour	Season
Salvia splendens Salvia	S or M	R P	Su
Tagetes erecta African Marigold	M	Y	Su
Verbena hybrida Verbena	S or M	R P W L	Su
Hardy Biennials			
Cheiranthus cheiri Wallflower	M	R P Y L	Sp
Dianthus barbatus Sweet William	M	R P W	Su
Digitalis purpurea Foxglove	M or T	P R W L	Su
Matthiola incana Brompton Stocks	M	R P Y W L	Sp
Myosotis alpestris Forget-me-not	S	P W B	Sp or Su
Oenothera biennis Evening Primrose	M	Y	Su to Au
Half Hardy Perennials			
Begonia tuberhybrida Tuberous begonias	S or M	R P Y W L	Su to Au
Chrysanthemum morifolium Florists chrysanthemum	M or T	R P Y W L	Su to Au
Dahlia variabilis Dahlia	S M or T	R P Y W L	Su to Au
Fuchsia hybrids Fuchsia	S M or T	R P W L	Su to Au
Impatiens hybrids Busy Lizzie	S or M	R P W L	Su to Au
Pelargonium zonale Zonal pelargonium	S or M	R P W L	Su to Au
Penstemon hartwegii Penstemon	M	R P W	Su to Au
Viola wittrockiana Garden Pansy	S	R Y W B L	Sp, Su, Au

Viola

Penstemon

Pelargonium

Impatiens

Fuchsia

Chrysanthemum

Dahlia

Oenothera

Begonia

Nicotiana

Petunia

Matthiola

Tagetes

Cheiranthus

Matthiola incana

Gazania

Phlox

Verbena

Digitalis

Salvia

Dianthus

Lobelia

Myosotis

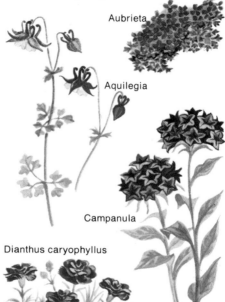

Name	Size	Colour	Season
Hardy Perennials The following list of herbaceous perennials includes plants which, with one or two exceptions, can be left undisturbed for 2 or 3 years. They can be used in herbaceous and shrub borders, rock gardens, and island beds.			
Achillea filipendulina Yarrow	M	Y	Su to Au
Alyssum saxatile Gold Dust	S	Y	Sp
Anchusa azurea Anchusa	M or T	B	Su
Aquilegia vulgaris Columbine	M	R P Y W B	Su
Aubrieta deltoidea **Purple Rock-cress**	S	P B L	Sp
Campanula glomerata Globe campanula	S or M	B L	Su or Au
Delphinium elatum hybrid **Delphinium or Perennial Larkspur**	M or T	W B	Su
Dianthus caryophyllus **Border Carnation**	S or M	R P Y W	Su
Dianthus plumarius Pinks	S or M	R P W L	Su
Erigeron speciosus Fleabane	S or M	P B L	Su
Gaillardia aristata **Blanket Flower**	M	R Y	Su to Au
Gladiolus hybrids Sword lily	M	R P Y W L	Su to Au
Kniphofia hybrids **Red Hot Pokers**	M or T	R Y W	Su
Lilium tigrinum **Tiger Lily**	M or T	O	Su
Lupinus polyphyllus Lupin	M or T	R P Y W B L	Su
Lychnis coronaria **Rose Campion**	M	P	Su
Primula vulgaris elatior Polyanthus	S	R P Y W B L	Sp

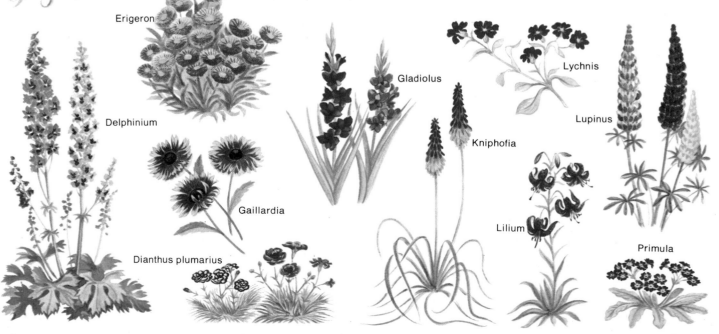

84

Maintenance of the flower garden

Weed control

Undisturbed weeds compete with garden plants for food and moisture and can be a source of pests and diseases. Among flowers, shrubs, fruit and vegetables, they can be prevented or controlled by cultivation or chemical means.

Cultivation is the most convenient method in the average garden. In summer, use the hoe regularly to chop off seedling weeds and leave them to wither in the sun. Do this job as early in the day as you can. In winter, dig in the weeds. Large weeds among flowers are best dug, cut off or pulled out, and the remaining small weeds hoed off or dug in as appropriate.

Chemical methods Use weed killer on paths or drives. Aminotriazole or simazine are suitable materials when used according to maker's instructions and are effective in most conditions.

Staking and tying

Flowers grown for display or cutting, such as dahlias or chrysanthemums, need to be staked and should be supported as unobtrusively as possible. Short pea sticks are useful and will be concealed by the supported plants. Push the sticks into the ground, and allow the flowers to grow between and above them. Large individual blooms for show purposes are best tied to separate canes. Support flowers which grow in clumps such as phlox, with a triangle of canes, using a loop of green twine to hold the stems. If you have an unobtrusive spot in which to grow flowers for cutting they can be held in place with horizontal nylon or wire mesh netting attached to posts. Young plants, especially those in pots, can be well supported by a split cane and tie or proprietary twist-grip.

1 and 2 twigs for plants to grow through; 3 and 4 horizontal netting; 5 large blooms supported by canes; 6 stopping; 7 and 8 deadheading; 9 thinning out surplus shoots; 10 disbudding.

Stopping and disbudding

Stopping means removing the growing point after four or six true leaves have formed. (The first two seedling leaves to appear do not count as 'true' leaves.) This causes the plant to make 'breaks' or shoots and to bear more blooms in a bushy rather than a tall form. Plants that respond well to this treatment include sweet peas, Brompton stocks, early-sown antirrhinums, chrysanthemums, dahlias, fuchsias and geraniums. Some varieties produce more shoots than can be supported and bloom to perfection, but by judicious thinning better quality, earlier flowers can be produced.

Disbudding Carnation, chrysanthemums, and dahlia blooms can be increased in size and quality by rubbing out the flower buds immediately below the terminal (or main) bloom bud.

Dead-heading

This term describes the cutting back of stems after they have flowered. The aim is to encourage another flush of flowers and improve appearance. Roses, delphinums, salvias, verbascums and bedding plants all benefit from dead-heading.

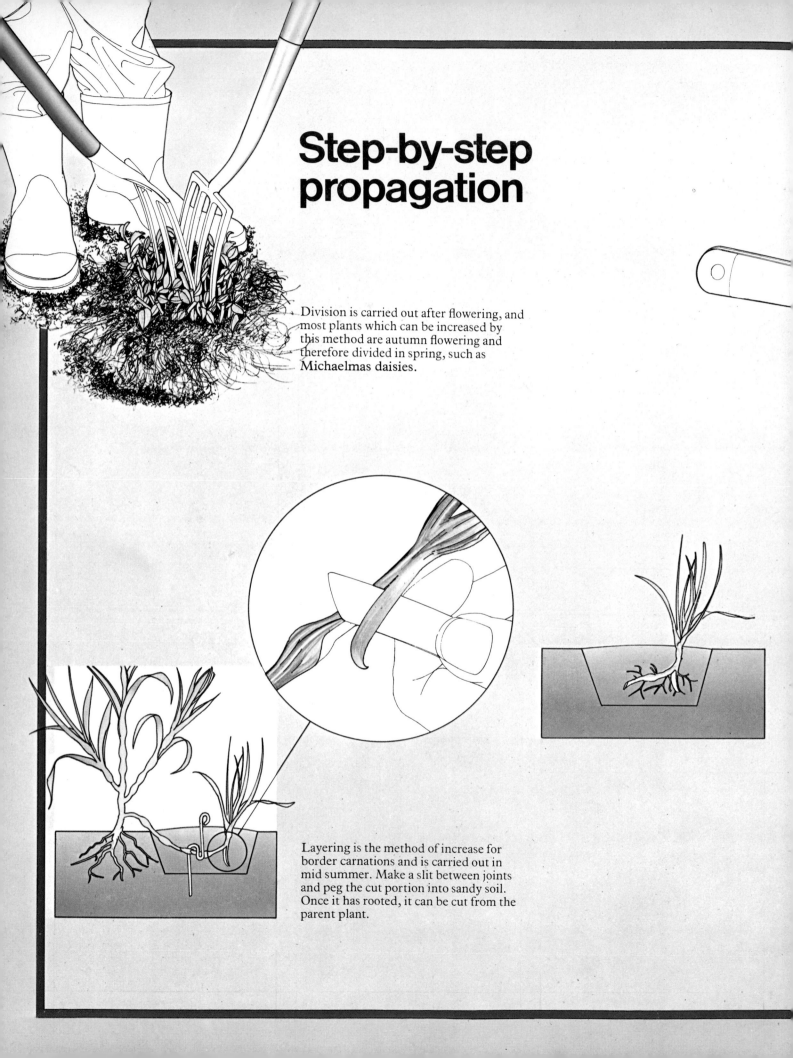

Step-by-step propagation

Division is carried out after flowering, and most plants which can be increased by this method are autumn flowering and therefore divided in spring, such as Michaelmas daisies.

Layering is the method of increase for border carnations and is carried out in mid summer. Make a slit between joints and peg the cut portion into sandy soil. Once it has rooted, it can be cut from the parent plant.

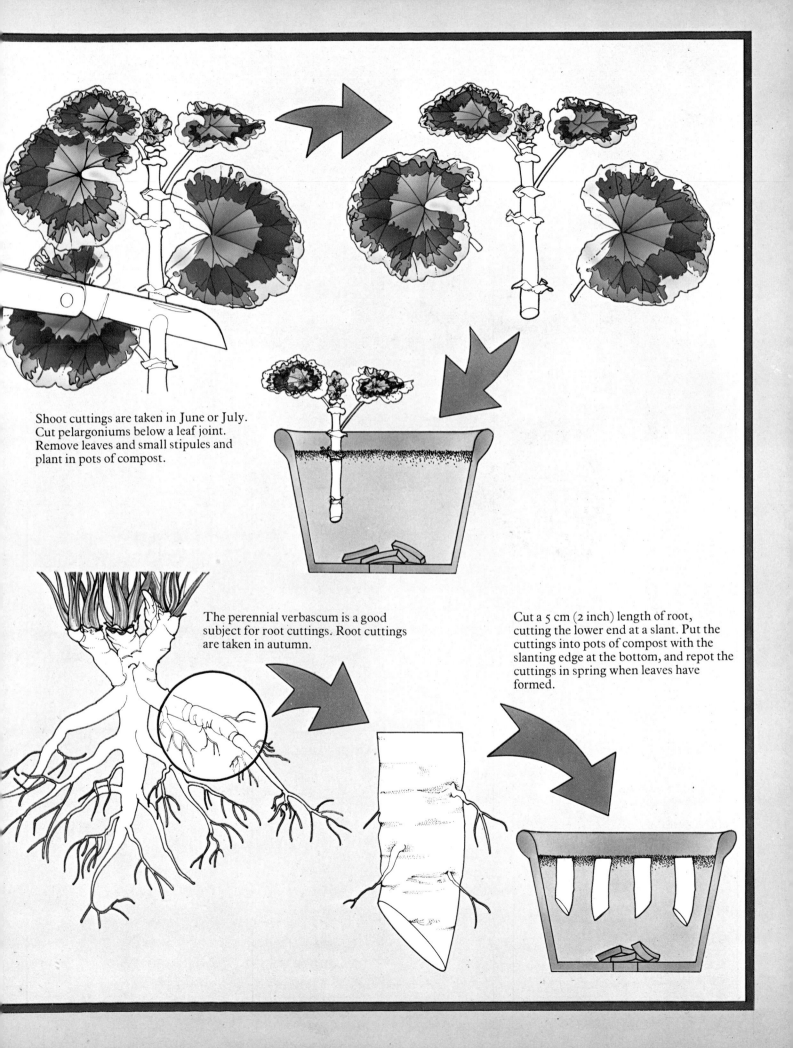

Shoot cuttings are taken in June or July.
Cut pelargoniums below a leaf joint.
Remove leaves and small stipules and
plant in pots of compost.

The perennial verbascum is a good
subject for root cuttings. Root cuttings
are taken in autumn.

Cut a 5 cm (2 inch) length of root,
cutting the lower end at a slant. Put the
cuttings into pots of compost with the
slanting edge at the bottom, and repot the
cuttings in spring when leaves have
formed.

Bulbs and corms

Bulbs and corms take their names from their form during the winter resting stage. These fattened or swollen parts of plants store plant food for the production of flowers and shoots until more favourable conditions return in spring. Bulbs and corms have a superficial resemblance to each other when viewed from the outside. However, if a bulb is cut cleanly in half from top to base, it will be seen to consist of layers of leaf scales. A corm cut in the same way reveals solid tissue. The significant difference from the growing viewpoint is that some bulbous plants (lilies, for example) can be increased by means of these leaf scales.

Tulips and daffodils are grown from bulbs; gladioli and crocus produce corms. Tubers occur in a number of forms, of which the two best known examples are the dahlia and the tuberous forms of begonia. Dahlias form a number of swollen finger-like roots radiating from the central stalk. With begonias, the tubers appear as flattened, rounded, hard tissue, slightly indented on one (mostly the upper) side. Tuberous plants are usually increased by means of cuttings, although the tubers can be divided.

Flowering season

There are very few weeks in the year when one or another member of this group is not in bloom and, aided by a cold frame and a window sill, they can provide year-round colour. Daffodils, hyacinths and tulips flower from December to May; begonias, gladioli and lilies continue the succession to late October, followed by crocus and cyclamen round to December again.

Colour and scent

The brilliant hues of this group include blues and pinks of hyacinths, reds and yellows of gladioli, and the peach,

ABOVE Underplanting of crocus.
ABOVE RIGHT A hyacinth bulb and a gladiolus corm. The cross-section of the bulb shows its leaf-scale formation.
RIGHT Daffodils make for easy spring gardening as they come up year after year.

Bulbs and Corms – species and colour

Note Catalogues of reliable suppliers are best consulted for named varieties because these change with great rapidity from season to season

Species or Kind	Common Name	Colours
Anemone apennina	Windflower	Blue, red, purple and white
Anemone De Caen hybrids	Single Poppy Anemone	Blue, red, purple and white
Anemone St Brigid hybrids	Double Poppy Anemone	Blue, red, purple and white
Anemone fulgens	Scarlet Windflower	Scarlet
Anemone hortensia	Garden Anemone	Blue, red, purple and white
Chionodoxa luciliae	Glory of the Snow	Blue and white
Colchicum autumnale	Autumn Crocus	Purple
Convallaria majalis	Lily of the Valley	White and pink
Crocosmia × *crocosmiiflora*	Montbretia	Orange-crimson
Crocus biflorus	Scotch crocus	Lavender
Crocus chrysanthus	Golden crocus	Orange-yellow
Crocus Large-flowered	Dutch crocus	Lilac, violet, white and yellow
Cyclamen coum	Spring Sowbread	Red
Cyclamen neapolitanum	Autumn Sowbread	Pink and white
Eranthis hyemalis	Winter Aconite	Yellow
Erythronium dens-canis	Dog's-tooth Violet	Rose
Fritillaria imperialis	Crown Imperial	Yellow
Fritillaria meleagris	Snake's head Fritillary	Chequered purple, yellow and white
Galanthus nivalis	Common Snowdrop	White
Gladiolus Dutch hybrids	Dutch or Garden Gladioli	Red, pink, yellow, white, scarlet
Gladiolus primulinus	Small Sword Lily	Red, pink, yellow, white, scarlet
Hyacinthus orientalis	Hyacinth	Red, pink, blue, white and purple
Iris reticulata	Reticulate Iris	Violet, purple and yellow
Iris xiphium Hybrids	Dutch, English and Spanish Iris	Blue, yellow, purple and white
Leucojum aestivum	Summer Snowflake	White and green
Lilium regale	Regal Lily	White, yellow throat, pink reverse
Muscari armeniacum	Grape Hyacinth	Blue
Narcissus poeticus	Poet's Narcissus	White
Narcissus pseudo-narcissus	Trumpet Daffodil	Yellow and white
Narcissus triandrus	Angel's Tears	Yellow
Oxalis adenophylla	Pink Sorrel	Rose-pink
Scilla siberica	Siberian squill	Blue and white
Tigridia pavonia	Tiger Flower	Red, yellow, purple and white
Tulipa various	Tulips	Red, white, yellow, scarlet, pink, orange, purple and some black throated

Planting bulbs and corms

Spring bedding Daffodils, hyacinths and tulips can be planted in beds in autumn, together with plants such as wallflowers and forget-me-not, to provide spring colour. Lift and replant them in an out-of-the-way bed after flowering to make room for other bedding plants.

Summer bedding Tuberous begonias and gladioli can be used to transform ordinary flower beds into scenes more reminiscent of hotter climates. To achieve this they should be started into growth in March by being placed in shallow boxes containing a mixture of equal parts sand and peat in frost-free frames or similar protection. Transplant outdoors when a small shoot (about 12mm (½in)) has developed.

Note: Catalogues of reliable suppliers are the best source for named varieties as these change with great rapidity from season to season.

Borders The colour and interest of herbaceous shrub borders can be enhanced by the use of day lilies, various types of true lilies, iris and crocosmia.

Grass planting Drifts of bulbs and corms naturalized in grass look very striking, but are best suited to little-used areas. Autumn and spring crocus, daffodils, narcissi and snowdrops are excellent for this purpose. To plant, lift an area of turf and fork up the soil beneath. Work in some peat and bonemeal before planting the bulbs or corms and then replace the turf.

BELOW *Crocosmia masonorum.*

crimson and orange shades of begonias. Jonquil, hyacinth and lilies are renowned for their scent.

Hardiness and ease of culture

Bulbs such as snowdrops, crocus, winter aconite and hyacinths are very hardy and provide a profusion of flowers when no other plants are in bloom.

With a minimum of care and attention crocus, daffodils, crocosmia and many lilies, once planted increase in number and strength, blooming year after year. Many bulbs and corms can be grown in confined spaces, such as town gardens and containers in places where it would be difficult or impossible to obtain colour from other kinds of plants.

Newly purchased bulbs and corms contain food reserves which have been built up over a number of years, and have the embryo flower already formed. They require a minimum of space, and adequate warmth, moisture and light for the flowers to emerge and open.

ABOVE *Eranthis tubergiana.*

Bowls and pans Winter or spring-flowering bulbs can be placed in containers of bulb fibre during September or October to flower the following spring. Water the bulbs and place them in a cool dark cupboard or cellar, or cover them with a 10cm (4in) layer of peat in a shaded spot out of doors. Keep the container moist. Bring the bulbs indoors and into the light about 10-12 weeks after potting, when roots have formed and the shoots are developing.

Rock garden There are several varieties of spring-flowering anemones and also chionodoxa, colchicums, crocus, iris, muscari and narcissus which can be placed in pockets of soil to extend the flowering season.

o denotes suitability
x denotes unsuitability

Bulbs and Corms – Planting

Name	Tulipa	Tigridia	Scilla	Oxalis	Muscari	Lilium	Leucojum	Iris	Hyacinthus	Gladiolus	Galanthus	Fritillaria	Erythronium	Eranthis	Cyclamen	Crocus	Crocosmia	Convallaria	Colchicum	Chionodoxa	Anemone
Height (cm)	10-75	30-60	7-45	3-15	15-20	45-240	10-30	15-60	15-30	30-120	15-30	30-90	15	7-10	7-10	10	15-120	20	20-25	15	15-45
Planting depth (cm)	10	7	7-10	2-7	5-10	10-12	10	7	12	10	5	10-15	7	5	4	7	7	7	7	7	7
Spacing (cm)	15	12-15	7-10	10-20	2-5	15-30	7	7-15	15	15	2	15-20	5	5	7	5	7	7	7	2	15
Flowering Season	Win-Spr	Sum	Spr	Spr-Sum	Spr	Sum-Aut	Spr-Aut	Spr-Sum	Win-Spr	Sum-Aut	Win-Spr	Spr	Spr	Spr	Aut-Spr	Aut-Spr	Sum	Spr	Aut	Spr	Spr-Aut
Bedding use	o	o	o	x	o	o	x	o	o	o	x	x	x	x	o	x	x	o	x	o	x
Border use	o	o	o	o	o	o	o	o	o	o	o	o	o	o	o	o	o	o	o	o	o
Cut flower use	o	o	o	x	o	o	x	o	o	o	o	o	x	o	o	x	o	o	x	o	o
Naturalizing in grass	x	x	x	x	x	x	x	x	x	x	o	x	x	x	o	x	x	o	x	x	x
Growing in container	o	x	o	o	o	o	x	o	o	o	o	x	x	x	o	o	x	o	x	o	o
Container size Minimum pots (in)	5	—	3	5	3	8	—	5-7	4	7	3	—	—	—	5	4	—	5	—	3	5
Planting season	Aut-Spr	Spr	Sum-Aut	Aut-Spr	Sum-Aut	Sum-Aut	Sum-Aut	Sum-Aut	Aut	Spr	Aut	Aut	Sum	Aut-Win	Sum	Aut-Win	Spr	Aut	Sum	Sum	Aut-Spr
Rock garden use	o	x	o	x	o	o	o	o	x	o	o	o	x	o	o	o	x	o	o	o	o

Trees, shrubs and climbers

sensitive to smoke and grime. In built-up areas, the only scope for greenery in many gardens is upwards, and climbing plants provide welcome relief. This group includes not only the familiar ivy and Virginia creeper, but also clematis, jasmine, cotoneaster, and pyracantha, all useful for covering walls.

Tree forms:
ABOVE Columnar
BELOW Weeping
ABOVE RIGHT Pyramid
RIGHT Round
FAR RIGHT Compact upright

The skilful disposition of trees, shrubs and climbers forms the backbone of many outstanding garden designs. Trees and shrubs heighten flat sites and give scale and character to any planting scheme. The play of light and shade, the movement and rustle of leaves in the wind, or the reflection on still water can be turned to great advantage.

The opportunities for planting large trees and shrubs in the small or medium-sized garden, are necessarily restricted and it is important that the plants are carefully chosen and maintained. The town-dweller's choice is further limited by the fact that many conifers and evergreens are particularly

One or two trees, with some well-placed, wisely-chosen shrubs and a climber, can be the making of a labour-saving and easily-managed garden. To this basic framework the enthusiastic gardener can add as much or as little as time and inclination allow.

There are trees, shrubs and climbers for all purposes and situations, ranging in size from a few centimetres to tens of metres in height and breadth. They can be columnar, pyramidal, rounded, compact, or open and spreading.

The variety of small trees and shrubs permits a planting scheme that will be in scale with any setting. A flowering cherry or magnolia gives an annual display of colour for a modest outlay, and heathers and dwarf conifers provide year-round colour and interest in a rock garden.

In all but the most severe climates, it is not only possible but practical to provide year-round colour with trees, shrubs and climbers.

Trees

Your choice of tree is governed by the conditions prevailing on the intended site – climate, soil type, and aspect – and also the habit (growth characteristics) of the tree itself. A limited space requires a columnar shape, whereas a bushy tree will suit a larger area. Trees

on page 96 lists a variety of trees which will be appropriate to most situations and are not too demanding to grow. Having decided which tree you would like, buy it from a reputable nurseryman or garden centre.

The correct naming of plants often puzzles the beginner and it is very frustrating to find out too late that you have bought the wrong variety. Ornamental deciduous trees (those which shed their leaves each year) are usually bought at stages classified as standards, half standards, bush forms and 'whips' or maidens. *Standard trees* have a clear stem for about 1.8m (6ft) below the branches. *Half-standards* have about

which is the grade most commonly available. In the measurement of standard and half-standard trees, the diameter of the stem is taken 1m (3ft 6in) above ground level.

Stock plants for transplanting are commonly available in one of four presentations:

Bare root plants have been lifted and all the soil removed from in and around the roots. This obviously puts a severe strain on the subject as the vital fibrous (very fine) roots can dry out irrevocably. Roses and some shrubs seem to recover but it exposes trees to severe shock.

Balled plants are trees which have been lifted from their growing position with a ball of earth holding together in and around the roots. This is satisfactory for small plants such as whips.

Balled and wrapped trees are balled plants with secure wrapping round the root and earth ball. This is necessary if the young tree has to travel any distance between lifting and planting.

Container grown trees are, as the name implies, those grown in some form of receptacle. These trees can be moved and planted at any time of year without disturbance provided the ground is not frozen or waterlogged. Trees planted during summer require substantial watering. Container-grown trees are more expensive than others.

LEFT Flowering trees give character to both town and country gardens and provide a glorious show of colour in spring.
BELOW Broom and flowering crab apple in a small town garden.

take nourishment from the soil appropriate to their size, and inevitably provide heavy shade, so it is unlikely that any other substantial planting will thrive in their presence. Vegetable and fruit plots should certainly be well away from large trees.

Choice of trees

This seemingly simple question triggers off others. What colour of foliage or flowers do you prefer? At what time of the year do you want the tree to be at its best? Do you want it to provide shelter from the wind and sun? Is there a rock garden or pool that you want the tree to blend with? The illustrated table

1m (3ft 6in) clear stem. *Bush trees* have a short leg of about 60-75cm (2-2ft 6in) before the stem divides. *Whips* or *maidens* are single unbranched shoots, and are the cheapest to buy but take longer to mature and train.

Grading for quality

Instant or semi-mature trees are the largest and most expensive and give an immediate effect but they require considerable attention and the chance of survival is not high.

Heavy nursery stock trees have better developed root systems, stems, and head or branch framework than the standard or ordinary nursery stock,

Feeding trees

This topic is usually given scant attention, because it is argued that if trees grow well in the wild without being pampered, why should they need special care in gardens? However, the conditions which trees have to contend with in most gardens are far removed from those in the wild. Starvation is one of the more common causes of failure among established specimens.

Trees need nourishment if they are to flourish, and this can be considered in three stages.

Before planting It is much harder to improve and to feed soil after planting. A base dressing of bonemeal at 140g/m² (4oz per sq yd) worked into the bottom spit (spade's depth) of the planting hole, with a similar quantity of a good balanced fertilizer well mixed up in the top spit of soil, is adequate pre-planting preparation for most garden trees.

Routine feeding can be given as an annual mulch of organic matter (peat or manure) plus 70g to 140g/m² (2oz to 4oz per sq yd) of balanced fertilizer dressing in spring. Give the heavier dressing where peat or pulverized bark is used. If there is excessive shoot growth (more than 45cm (15 to 18ins) per year) at the expense of flowers, reduce the mulch by half, and in the case of dwarf conifers, to one quarter.

Rejuvenation Starvation is a major cause of debility in old trees, but those making little or no growth can often be induced to make new shoots. Remove the turf covering the roots. Lightly fork the ground from the trunk to just beyond the drip line (tips of the longest branches) and apply a 7.5cm (3in) layer of fresh soil and rotted manure. Gently fork a top dressing of balanced fertilizer into the soil and manure mixture at the rate of 70g/m² (2oz per sq yd). This mulch is best carried out in the spring.

Pruning

The object of pruning is to create a shapely, balanced framework of branches that will admit adequate light and air evenly in young trees and subsequently to keep trees the desired size and shape; to regulate growth and check and prevent pests and diseases; and to rejuvenate old trees.

The principles of pruning can be expressed quite simply: prune hard for vigorous growth; prune lightly to encourage flowering and fruitfulness. If growth is excessive and lush through generous feeding, prune lightly. Poor growth resulting from under-feeding requires hard pruning to promote vigour.

Pruning in practice Buy trees with a basic framework of branches from a reliable supplier, and in most cases subsequent pruning will be only minimal.

If you prefer to establish the basic framework yourself you should buy a whip or maiden. In the first autumn, cut the stem of whips or maidens slightly higher than the point at which you want branches to form; cut or rub out any growths lower down. In the second year, three or more shoots should have formed; shorten these to one-quarter or one-third of their length. In the third year, if growth is only moderate, prune the branches again, this time to one-third their

length. For a pyramidal shape, allow a central leader (or shoot) to develop, and shorten or summer-prune any side-shoots.

Each autumn, remove inward-growing branches and shorten crossing branches which touch one another. Cut back dead or broken shoots to healthy wood. Trim trees to the desired shape and thin out any thickets of shoots as necessary.

Conifers need only the occasional trimming to shape. However, those which are to be transplanted should be root-pruned in the spring before the move. This is done by cutting the outside roots with a spade to encourage a ball of fibrous roots to develop. The distance of cut is a circle 15cm (6in) beyond the outmost shoots or drip line. The moving of large conifers about 1.5-2m (5ft-6ft) is best left to professionals.

Any cut over 2.5cm (1in) diameter must be painted either with lead-based paints or a proprietary plant-wound sealer.

The lopping of large tree branches is best carried out in autumn. Before starting, check to see that the branch will fall somewhere safely. First a cut is made on the underside, followed by a matching cut on the upper surface to avoid splitting the branches.

ABOVE LEFT Crown raising (left) – remove lower branches to show off bark or when underplanting. Crown thinning (right) – remove some branches to promote flowering.
ABOVE Root pruning a dwarf conifer.
LEFT *Malus floribunda elwesii*.
RIGHT Flowering trees and shrubs, contrasted with a columnar conifer.

Trees for small gardens

Name	Soil	Site	Size m ht × wth	Size ft ht × wth	Season and nature of interest
Acer palmatum Japanese Maple	Moist AN	T Sheltered	4·5 × 3·6	15 × 12	Spring to autumn Colourful foliage
Betula pendula Silver Birch	AN	T Open or shade	15·0 × 6·0	50 × 20	All year Graceful leaves and branches
Cercis siliquastrum Judas Tree	ANC	T Sun	7·5 × 4·5	25 × 15	Spring pink flowers Summer purplish seed pods
Crataegus coccinea plena Double Crimson Thorn	NC	T Sun, open	6·0 × 4·5	20 × 15	Spring crimson flowers
Laburnum vossii Laburnum	ANC	T Sun	6·0 × 4·5	20 × 15	Spring and early summer yellow flowers
Magnolia soulangiana alba Magnolia	AN Moist	Sun	6·0 × 4·5	20 × 15	Spring striking white flowers
Malus tschonoskii Flowering Crab Apple	NC Rich	T Sun	6·0 × 3·6	20 × 12	Spring pinkish white flowers. Autumn scarlet and yellow fruits
Populus alba White Poplar	N	S Sun open	15·0 × 7·5	50 × 25	Summer and autumn White undersides of leaves
Prunus cerasifera nigra Black-leaf Plum	NC	T Sun	6·0 × 4·5	20 × 15	Spring, pink flowers Summer and autumn dark leaves

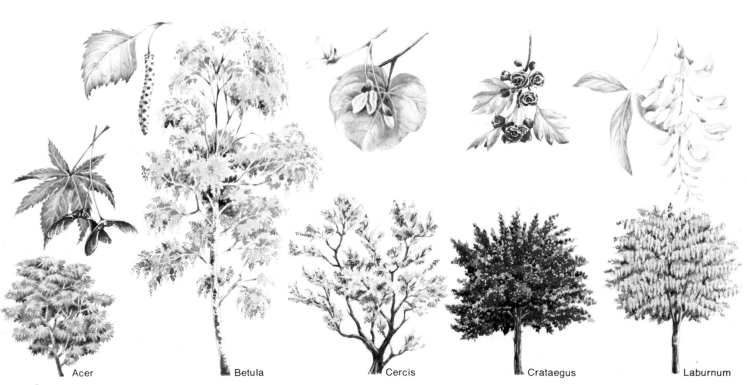

Acer   Betula   Cercis   Crataegus   Laburnum

Name		Soil	Site	Size m ht × wth	Size ft ht × wth	Season and nature of interest
Prunus serrulata 'Kanzan' Japanese Cherry		N C	T Sun	7·5 × 5·4	25 × 18	Spring, masses of pink flowers
Pyrus salicifolia pendula Willow-leaved Pear		N C	Sun	6·0 × 6·0	20 × 20	Spring, white flowers Summer and autumn, grey-white leaves
Rhus typhina Stag's Horn Sumach		N	Sun	6·0 × 4·5	20 × 15	Summer, large green leaves autumn leaf tints and brown fruits
Robinia pseudoacacia bessoniana False Acacia		A N C	Open T	15·0 × 6·0	50 × 20	Summer, whitish flowers delicate foliage
Sorbus aria Whitebeam		N C	Open T	9·0 × 7·5	30 × 25	Autumn red berries White underside to leaves
Sorbus aucuparia Rowan or Mountain Ash		A N Light Sandy	Sun Open T	6·0 × 4·5	20 × 15	Autumn clusters of red berries
Chamaecyparis lawsoniana pottenii Lawsons Cypress	E	N	Open	12·0 × 3·0	40 × 10	All year round blue green foliage
Cupressocyparis leylandii Leyland Cypress	E	A N C	Open Sun	12·0 × 3·6	40 × 12	All year round green finely divided foliage
Juniperus chinensis The Chinese Juniper	E	N C	Open Sunny	6·0 × 1·2	20 × 4	All year round green foliage
Juniperus communis The Common Juniper	E	N C	Sun	7·5 × 3·0	25 × 10	Year round grey green foliage
Pinus mugo Gnom Mountain Pine	E	A N C Light loam	Open Sun	0·75 × 0·75	2½ × 2½	All year green foliage
Thuya occidentalis homstrupii American Arbor-vitae	E	A N C	Sheltered Sun	3·0 × 1·5	10 × 5	Attractive bright green foliage all year round

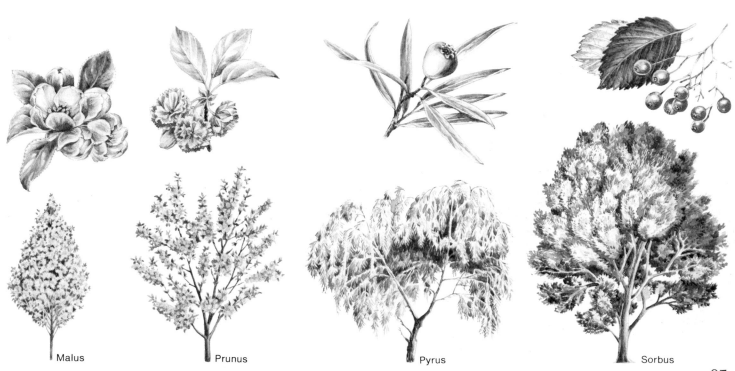

Malus   Prunus   Pyrus   Sorbus

Step-by-step planting a tree

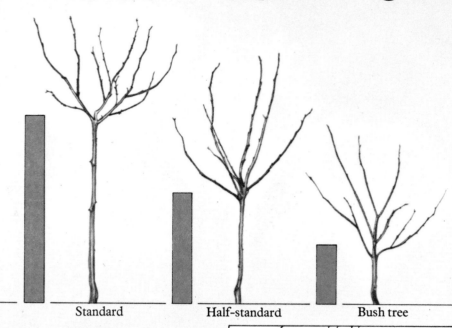

Standard   Half-standard   Bush tree

Above Tree forms, showing the height of the main stem which will need to be staked.

If trees are delivered in a dry condition, soak them for one or two hours in a bucket of water. If the trees cannot be planted soon after arrival, plant them temporarily at an oblique angle.

1. Dig a hole large enough and deep enough for the size of the roots of the tree. Break up the bottom of the hole and fork in peat and compost.

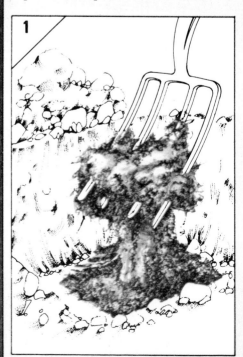

2. Insert a stake 4-5 cm (1½-2 inches) diameter and long enough to match the stem of the tree and reach 30 cm (12 inches) below the planting hole. The stake should be set to the windward side of the tree whenever possible.

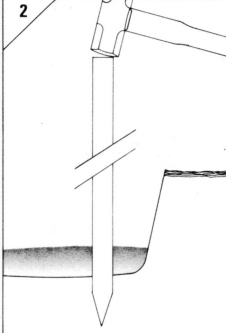

3. Put a layer of fine soil in the bottom of the hole. The tree will be placed directly onto this layer.

3a. The tree is placed on a layer of fine soil so that the soil mark on the stem aligns with the level of the surrounding ground. The soil dug from the hole is firmed around the roots as the hole is refilled.

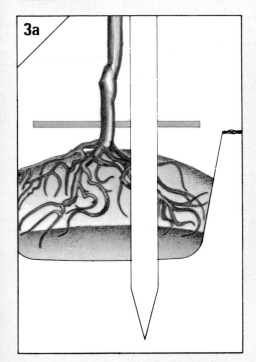

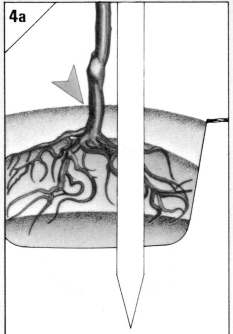

4a. Fill the remainder of the hole with topsoil, rounded above the soil mark. The soil will soon pack down to the surrounding ground level.

5. Fasten the tree to the stake with a tree tie and spacer and then prune back the branches to encourage vigorous growth.

4. Firm the soil around the roots with your feet as you fill in the hole until the roots are covered.

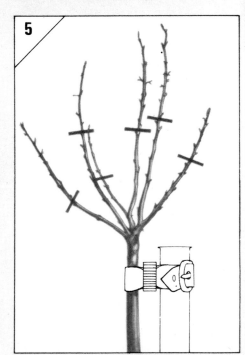

Shrubs, hedging plants and climbers

Shrubs, hedges and climbers also occupy the ground for a long time, so good soil preparation is necessary. Before planting you should provide adequate land drainage, dig over the planting spot, apply manure and fertilizer, establish a minimum depth (30cm (12in)) of weed-free soil, break up the sub-soil and check the soil acidity (pH) adding lime if necessary.

Select species which are suited to your district and soil, healthy, and of a manageable size, and varieties that will provide colour and interest at a suitable season. As with trees, wrapped-and-balled, container or pot-grown plants will suffer a minimum of check to growth. Hedging plants sold with bare roots can, however, soon become established. Suitable subjects are thorn and hornbeam, both of which will provide inexpensive functional barriers.

Planting season
Conifers and evergreens are best moved in September-October or April-May unless pot or container-grown, in which case planting can take place at any time, as long as the soil is not frozen or waterlogged. Deciduous plants can be safely set out between October and March, or at any time with containerized subjects, again in land that is not frozen or too wet.

Marking out and spacing
To save time and effort mark out plant positions with short sticks for indicators before digging out any holes. Spacing will vary according to the vigour of the variety and the method of planting. When plants of the same kind are grouped together, distances can be reduced to allow the branches of one plant to intertwine with another.

Measurements for individual shrubs and climbers are given in the illustrated tables on pages 104 and 105.

Planting
Wait for ground conditions to improve if the land is frozen or waterlogged. Plants which have dried out in transit should be stood in water for several hours before planting. Dig a hole wide and deep enough to take the spread-out roots. Place a moist peat layer 2.5cm (1in) deep in the base of the hole and fork this in. Position the plant, spread out the roots and cover them with fine soil, working this between the roots,

and firm the earth. The finished level of the soil surface should correspond to its nursery position and will be seen by the soil mark on the stem. Unless the land is very moist, water the plants to settle the surrounding soil.

With the possible exception of pot or container-grown subjects, plants which are moved invariably lose some roots. In order to restore the balance between root and shoot, some pruning is needed. With deciduous subjects shorten new growth by one half, but only trim conifers and evergreens lightly.

Some form of protection, especially with evergreen subjects, is helpful to plants placed in exposed situations. Choice conifers can be sheltered on the windward side with hessian or sacking supported on light posts. Chestnut paling secured to posts will shield hedges until they become established.

ABOVE Providing shelter for a conifer with a hessian windbreak.

Mulching In the spring following planting, a 5cm (2in) layer of compost or peat spread on the ground around the plants to cover the root area will reduce moisture loss. Water as necessary in a hot dry season, with a good soaking rather than frequent dribblings. Further mulching is advisable in subsequent years and it will also help to smother weed growth.

Feeding An application of 70g to 140g/m² (2oz to 4 oz per sq yd) of a good balanced fertilizer can be given

at the same time as mulching in the second and later years, unless growth is too vigorous.

Pruning shrubs
For pruning purposes, there are four main groups of shrubs, each needing different treatment.

Slow growing deciduous shrubs require little or no regular pruning, and are best left alone except for the occasional cutting back of untidy, weak or dead shoots. Examples include *Daphne mezereum,* (mezereon), *Hibiscus syriacus,* azaleas and lilacs.

ABOVE Part-pruned forsythia. Cut back the stems which have flowered to new growth.

Evergreen and coniferous shrubs require no pruning, but need an occasional trim to keep them neat and compact.

Spring and summer-flowering subjects which bloom on the previous season's growth should be pruned as soon as the flowers fall. Deutzias, forsythias, kerrias, philadelphus (mock orange) and weigelas are best treated in this way.

Cut the flowered stems back to new growth or plump buds.

Summer and autumn-flowering shrubs which carry their flowers on the current season's growth, usually during late summer and autumn, should be pruned during winter or spring by cutting out old flowered shoots annually. Where shrubs have reached the desired size and spread, cut the new growth back to within a bud or two of the older wood. Where a shrub is required to grow larger remove only half the length of new growth to build up a larger framework of shoot-bearing wood. Subjects pruned in this manner include: *Buddleia davidii*, fuchsias, hypericums and *Tamarix pentandra*.

Any plant with damaged, diseased or dead branches should be cut back to firm healthy wood or growth.

RIGHT Broom flowers on the previous season's growth. To prune, cut back flowered stems to new growth as soon as the flowers fall.

ABOVE Part-pruned tamarisk. Cut back hard in winter or spring.

Trimming hedges
Trim hedges early in life at the sides and top to encourage thick, bushy growth at the base. Clip hedges so that they narrow towards the top, never the reverse, to admit more light to the lower areas and prevent them becoming bare. There will also be less opportunity for snow to lodge on the hedge top and force the branches outwards, spoiling the shape. Cut rapid-growing subjects like privet and *Lonicera nitida* two or three times a year to keep them tidy. Cut beech and hornbeam in July.

Formal hedges of regular outline such as yew, box or *Lonicera* need cutting each time they make 15 to 20cm (6 to 8in) of growth. This promotes branching and makes a denser hedge.

Cut informal hedges of *Berberis stenophylla* and escallonia less frequently during the formative stage, lightly topping them at each 30cm (12in) increase in height to thicken them out. Thereafter an occasional clipping will keep them in shape.

Once any type of hedge has reached the desired size it will need only an occasional trim to prevent it getting out of hand.

Training climbers
The principles of shrub pruning also apply to climbing plants. These vary in their methods of support: twiners like clematis hang by tendrils, as do some vines; others, like ivy, cling with aerial roots, and virginia creeper (*Parthenocissus*) with small suction pads.

The two latter types of climber can be damaging to brickwork, unless kept severely under control. Most climbers are best trained against a lattice frame fixed to a wall, with a 5cm (2in) gap separating wall and frame. Wood or wire mesh lattice frames are cheaper than the cost of renovating stone or brick walls.

ABOVE Training a climber against a lattice frame.

Propagation
One of the easiest methods of increase is from seeds, but the range of good woody plants raised this way is limited as most shrubs, hedging plants and climbers are named varieties which do not come true from seed. Division, layers and cuttings are the methods generally used.

Some shrubs, such as some of the cotoneasters, plain-leaved hollies, and thorn used for hedging, can be raised from seed quite successfully, although they require a good deal of patience.

Raising shrubs from seed Shrub seeds usually ripen in autumn. They can be stored but are best sown straight away. Many kinds of woody plants do not germinate immediately they are sown, and need to be subjected to frost or cold to break their dormancy. This can be done by stratification: place freshly collected seed mixed with a small quantity of sand in pots or seed pans which have peat in the bottom, to prevent the mixture coming out at the base. Put the containers outside, sink them to the rims in sand and cover them with fine mesh netting to keep out birds and vermin, leaving the seeds to the action of frost and snow.

In spring, sow the seeds and sand in prepared pots or seedpans. Seeds of shrubs such as brooms and hypericum can be bought and sown without stratification.

The method of preparing seed containers and subsequent treatment is described in the section on flowers (see step-by-step guide on pages 80/81) and also applies to stratified seed. Prick out the seedlings into containers of potting compost as soon as they are big enough to handle.

BELOW *Clematis jackmanii*. The best method for increasing clematis is by half-ripe cuttings.

Division is a good method for beginners to increase plants, and is suitable for shrubs like kerria or euonymus, berberis, erica and spiraea.

Division is usually carried out in autumn or spring and consists of lifting the plant, teasing away and cutting off a rooted piece, which is replanted in prepared ground.

Layering is another easy method of multiplying plants and can also be used with success on many of the more difficult subjects such as quince.

The main requirement is that one or more branches can be pulled down to ground level. Select a healthy branch and make a slanting incision halfway through the stem. Peg this into prepared earth about 5cm (2in) deep at the cut area, and tie the tip in an upward position to a stick or cane. Lift the buried section when it has formed roots, about a year later; separate it from the parent plant, and replant. Rhododendrons, *chaenomeles* (Japanese quince) and many others can be raised in this way.

ABOVE LEFT Division of Aster.
LEFT Layering. The branch can be held down with a peg or a stone.

Cuttings Of the many ways of taking cuttings, four straightforward types will serve to increase the majority of garden shrubs and climbers.
Half-ripe cuttings consist of firm non-flowering new shoots, taken in summer and cut just below a leaf joint. The length of cutting varies from about 2.5cm (1in) in the case of heathers, to 10–15cm (4–6in) with buddleias.

Remove the lower leaves to half the length of the cutting. Dip the cut end in hormone rooting powder, insert the cutting to one third its length at the edge of a pot filled with cutting compost and firm it. Water and cover with a polythene bag and place in the shade or in a propagator. If a quantity of cuttings are needed, a garden frame can be used with a 7.5cm (3in) layer of cutting compost, well firmed, levelled and watered. 10cm (4in) pots can take four to six cuttings: cover the drainage holes with clean crock or gravel; fill the pot with cutting compost; firm with a presser to leave the surface 1cm (½in) below the rim of the pot for watering and finally dust the surface with sharp sand.

Hardwood cuttings can be taken in two ways: with a heel – a portion of stem attached – or as node cuttings which are cut just below a leaf joint or scar. Take 25 to 35cm (10 to 14in) lengths of firm new growth in autumn, removing any remaining leaves on deciduous subjects. Cut cleanly below a leaf scar, or trim the heel; and cut the top end above a bud to leave the finished cutting about 20 to 30cm (8 to 12in) long.

In a sheltered spot make a narrow trench about 15cm (6in) deep and 5cm (2in) wide. Fill this with sandy cutting compost and insert the cuttings about 15cm (6in) deep and about 10cm (4in) apart. Tread the soil down to press it against the cuttings. Never let cuttings dry out. They can usually be transplanted a year from the time they were taken. Forsythia, weigela and escallonias are raised successfully from hardwood cuttings.

Root cuttings A few fickle subjects such as *Rhus typhina* (the stag's horn sumach) and *Daphne genkwa* can be raised from root cuttings, usually taken in winter or spring. Root cuttings from shrubs are taken in the same way as for flowering plants, see page 87.

BELOW LEFT AND RIGHT Taking heel cuttings.

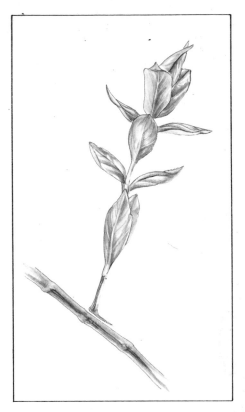

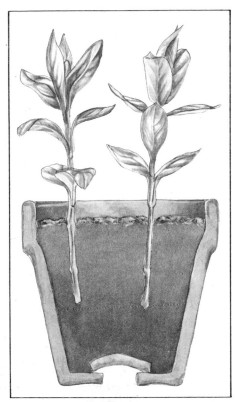

LEFT Taking a node cutting.

ABOVE Shrubs and climbers in a small garden.
Ceanothus (blue flowers), *Eccremocarpus* (orange flowers) and *Philadelphus* (white flowers).

103

Colourful Shrubs

Name	Soil	Site	Size m ht × wth	Size ft ht × wth	Season and nature of interest
Azalea Swamp Pink	Moist A	Light shade	wide range		Spring and summer, flowers colours various including scarlets, reds and flame
Berberis thunbergii Barberry	A N C	Sun	1·2 × 0·9	4 × 3	Spring, yellow flowers, summer and autumn red berries Flame, red and yellow foliage
Buddleia davidii Butterfly Flower	A N C	Sun Open	3·0 × 2·4	10 × 8	Summer and autumn, flowers shades of purple, mauve, pink and wine
Calluna vulgaris Ling or Heather	A N	Open Full sun	0·6 × 0·6	2 × 2	All year foliage, golds, greys, greens and rusts. Summer and autumn flowers, shades pink, purple, wine, white, lavender
Camellia williamsii 'Donation' Camellia	A N	West facing sheltered	3·0 × 2·4	10 × 8	All year gloss green foliage spring, pale pink semi-double flowers
Caryopteris clandonensis Blue Spiraea	A N C	Sun	0·9 × 0·6	3 × 2	Summer and autumn, lavender blue flowers
Cornus alba sibirica Red-barked Dogwood	Moist A N C	Sun light shade	2·4 × 1·8	8 × 6	Autumn and winter, red coloured young shoots
Cytisus scoparius Broom	N	Open sun	1·8 × 1·2	6 × 4	Spring and early summer gold, cream, buff, yellow and reddish flowers
Daphne mezereum Mezereon	A N C	Light shade sun	1·2 × 0·6	4 × 2	Winter, early spring, fragrant, pink, mauve and white flowers
Deutzia scabra Deutzia	A N C	Open sunny	2·4 × 1·5	8 × 5	Summer, white or white-tinged purple flowers
Erica carnea Heaths	A N C	Open sun	0·3 × 0·3	1 × 1	Year round foliage-various. Winter and spring flowers, pink, carmine, white and wine
Fuchsia magellanica Lady's Ear-drops	A N C	Light shade or sun	1·5 × 0·9	5 × 3	Summer and autumn flowers, purple and scarlet
Hibiscus syriacus Tree Hollyhock or Shrubby Mallow	A N C	Open sun	2·4 × 1·5	8 × 5	Summer and autumn flowers, blue, maroon, pink rose-purple and white
Hydrangea macrophylla Hydrangea	A N C	Sun	1·8 × 1·2	6 × 4	Summer and autumn flowers, pink, red, carmine, white and blue
Hypericum patulum St Johns Wort	A N C	Light shade or sun	0·9 × 0·9	3 × 3	Summer and autumn Golden-yellow flowers
Philadelphus hybridus Mock Orange	A N C	Sun Open	1·8 × 1·2	6 × 4	Summer, white, cream or whitish flowers

Key

1	Azalea	9 Hypericum
2	Buddleia	10 Caryopteris
3	Camellia	11 Lonicera
4	Hibiscus	12 Erica
5	Hydrangea	13 Cotoneaster
6	Clematis	14 Wistaria
7	Fuchsia	15 Chaenomeles
8	Spiraea	16 Pyracantha

1   2   3   4   5   6   7   8

Name	Soil	Site	Size m ht × wth	Size ft ht × wth	Season and nature of interest
Potentilla fruiticosa Shrubby Cinquefoil	A N C	Sun	1·2 × 0·9	4 × 3	Summer and autumn flowers, yellow and orange shades
Rhododendron hybrids Flame Flower	A	West aspect light shade	Various	Various	Year round foliage, winter spring and summer flowers pink, flame, scarlet, purple
Spiraea bumalda Garden Meadowsweet	A N C	Sun or light shade	0·9 × 0·2	3 × 2	Summer flowers, pink
Syringa vulgaris Lilac	A N C	Open sun	3·0 × 2·1	10 × 7	Summer, fragrant flowers, white, pink, violet, crimson, purple, lilac
Viburnum tinus Portugal Laurel or Laurustinus	A N C	Sun Light shade sheltered	3·0 × 1·8	10 × 6	All year foliage, winter and spring flowers, pinkish buds scented white flowers
Weigela florida Diervilla	A N C	Open sunny	2·4 × 1·8	10 × 6	Spring and summer flowers, creamy white, pink and crimson shades

Key A = Acid
N = Neutral
C = Chalk

Climbers

Name	Soil	Site	Size m ht × wth	Size ft ht × wth	Season and nature of interest
Chaenomeles speciosa Japonica	A N C	Sunny Southern aspect Sheltered	2·4 × 1·8	8 × 6	Spring flowers, shades of pink, red and scarlet
Clematis 'Lasurstern' and 'Nelly Moser' Clematis large-flowered hybrids	N C	Sunny South or West aspect	Various	Various	Summer and autumn flowers, tones of pink, purple, red, carmine, white and violet
Cotoneaster horizontalis Herring-bone Cotoneaster	A N C	Sun or shade Open	1·8 × 1·8	6 × 6	Summer flowers, pink Autumn and winter red berries
Lonicera caprifolium Honeysuckle	A N C	Sun or light shade	4·5 × indefinite	15 × indefinite	Summer, creamy white or pinkish scented flowers
Pyracantha atalantioides Firethorn	A N C	Sun or shade	4·5 × 3·0	15 × 10	Summer flowers, white. Autumn berries red or yellow
Wistaria sinensis Wistaria	A N C	Sun. South aspect Sheltered	indefinite	indefinite	Summer flowers, scented, mauve or white

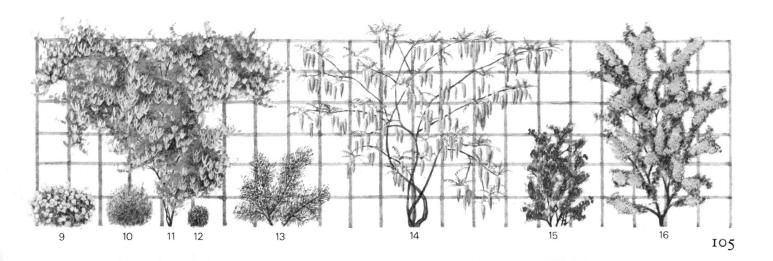

9   10   11   12   13   14   15   16

Roses

The uses and range of rose species and varieties are very wide. Roses are popular in formal beds, and for less-regimented planting, in borders or shrub beds. Climbing and rambling species can be used to disguise hard walls, to screen undesirable views, to cover pergolas and to scent the air. Roses can be used in rock gardens to cover the ground with colour, or to climb through trees. They are good for cutting and floral arrangements. Such diversity of function and such a wealth of species in the rose family provide a bewildering choice.

Varieties of roses:
1 Shrub rose
2 Miniature rose
3 Hybrid tea
4 Floribunda
5 Climbing rose

Classification of roses

The old hybrid tea roses are now classified as large-flowered, and floribundas as cluster-flowered. But as the traditional names are still widely used, we have retained them here.

Shrub roses include many types, most of which flower less profusely than the hybrid teas and floribundas. The blooms are usually single or semi-double, and are attractive not only for their flowers, but also for the hips, or seed cases. These roses are mostly used in shrub borders, hedging and informal situations.

Miniatures These diminutive roses can be used in rock gardens, pots and even window boxes. They grow to a height of about 22 to 37cm (9 to 15in) and have double or semi-double flowers, ranging in size from about 1 to 4cm ($\frac{1}{2}$ to $1\frac{1}{2}$in) across.

Hybrid tea roses are the most popular for the majority of purposes and include those with large, well-formed fully double flowers having one main flower per stem. These are found in most colours, are highly fragrant, and are excellent as cut flowers for floral arrangements. Members of this group bloom more or less continuously in summer.

Floribunda roses are of more recent origin than hybrid teas and of a rather more vigorous habit than the former. They carry clusters of flowers, double, semi-double and single and are very popular.

Climbers and ramblers are invaluable for providing necessary cover. Climbers have a permanent framework from which side shoots develop, while ramblers have their main growth from the base of the plant. Ramblers have only one annual flowering period. Flower shape and form can be of the hybrid tea, floribunda, or shrub type. There are climbing forms of just about every kind of garden rose.

Acquiring roses

It is a good idea for the new grower to look at the catalogues of two or three leading rose-growers and select varieties common to each. If two or three producers sell the same variety, it is likely to be reliable. A collection of good, named varieties can be obtained from top growers early in the planting season, as these are unlikely to be available in end-of-season clearance offers. To get the best quality it is necessary to go to the actual grower.

Budded or grafted plants provide better rootstock. Some rootstocks produce many suckers which are undesirable shoots of the root variety and they should be removed with secateurs. The fault often lies not in the rootstock itself but in its preparation in the nursery.

Form Roses can be obtained in various shapes and sizes according to their purpose. Standards have a bushy head on a tall stem of 1.2m (4ft), the crown of which may be upright or weeping in habit. Half-standards are similar to the above, but have a shorter leg with about 75cm (2ft 6in) of clear stem.

The other forms are the bush and climbing roses.

Pest and disease resistance Where possible, it is helpful to see the varieties of your choice actually growing, and note if they suffer from blackspot or mildew, as both diseases can be difficult to control in bad years. The former occurs as dark spots on the leaves, the latter as a white powdery covering on leaves and flower buds.

The Care of Roses

Firming and mulching In the spring following planting and subsequent springs, firm the soil round the roots if winter winds and frost have loosened them. Lightly prick up the soil between plants with a fork after pruning the roses, removing any weeds as you go.

In well-prepared soil feeding will not be necessary until the second year, when 100g/m² (3oz per sq yd) of a high potash balanced fertilizer should be applied before lightly forking the soil. After feeding, spread a 2.5 to 5cm (1 to 2in) thick covering of compost, peat or similar mulch around the plants, to conserve moisture in summer and smother seedling weeds. This improves the soil and produces better flowers as a result.

Cultivation and weed control If the soil has been mulched all over, little cultivation will be required until autumn when a light forking-over should be given. Remove any weed growth. Keep the hoe moving to kill weeds and create a dust mulch where there is no mulch cover. Water occasionally during any prolonged drought after planting. Climbers and ramblers need tying in as they grow, which requires regular attention during the growing season, as plants can be loosened and damaged in strong winds.

ABOVE Dead-heading roses.

Disbudding and dead-heading The practice of disbudding is used mainly for exhibition blooms. Where large single blooms are required, one flower bud on a stem is selected and the remainder removed. If a cluster of flowers is required, the central bud only is removed, causing a number of flowers to open simultaneously.

Dead-heading involves the removal of old flower heads and should be done as soon as blooming finishes. Where hips are required, as in the case of shrub roses, dead-heading is not carried out. Cut back the old flower head and half the length of the flower stem to a good bud or leaf and reduce this to one quarter as the season progresses. In flower clusters, the dead heads only are removed, until all the flowers in a group have finished blooming. The cluster is then cut out in its entirety. Cut back dead or seriously diseased stems and shoots to healthy tissue.

Carry out routine measures of pest and disease control, especially at the first sign of trouble. Insecticide and fungicide sprays are usually needed for aphids, blackspot and mildew.

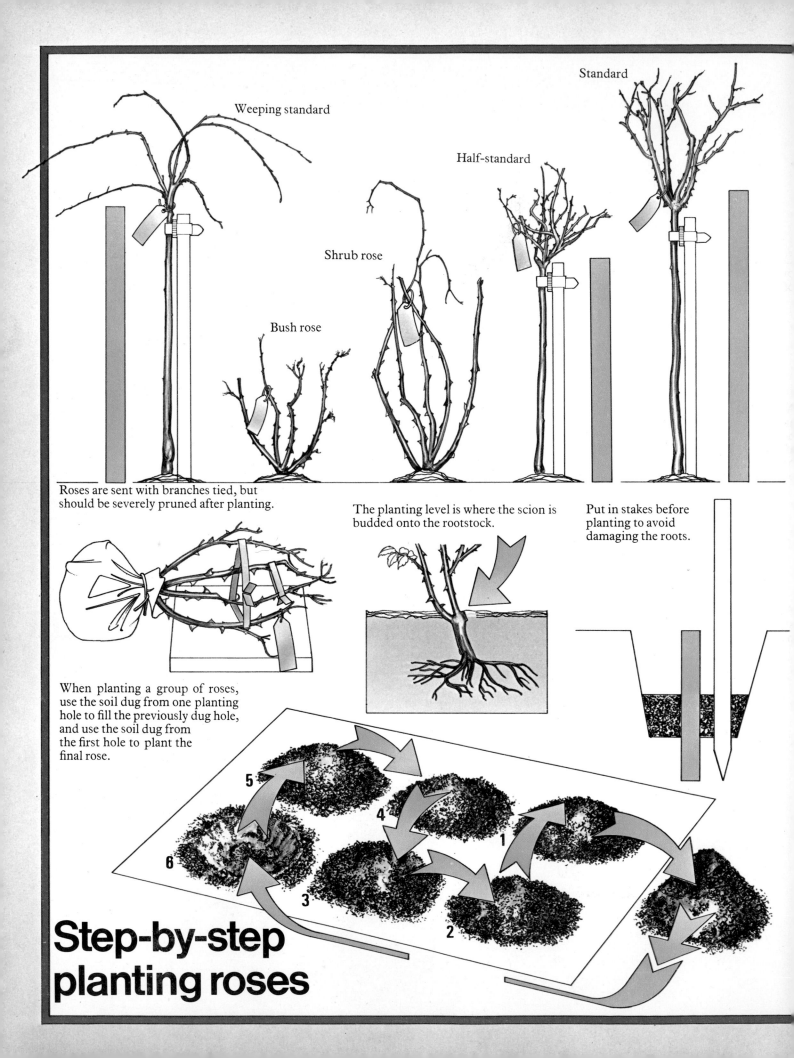

Weeping standard

Standard

Half-standard

Shrub rose

Bush rose

Roses are sent with branches tied, but should be severely pruned after planting.

The planting level is where the scion is budded onto the rootstock.

Put in stakes before planting to avoid damaging the roots.

When planting a group of roses, use the soil dug from one planting hole to fill the previously dug hole, and use the soil dug from the first hole to plant the final rose.

5

4

6

1

3

2

Step-by-step planting roses

Step-by-step pruning roses

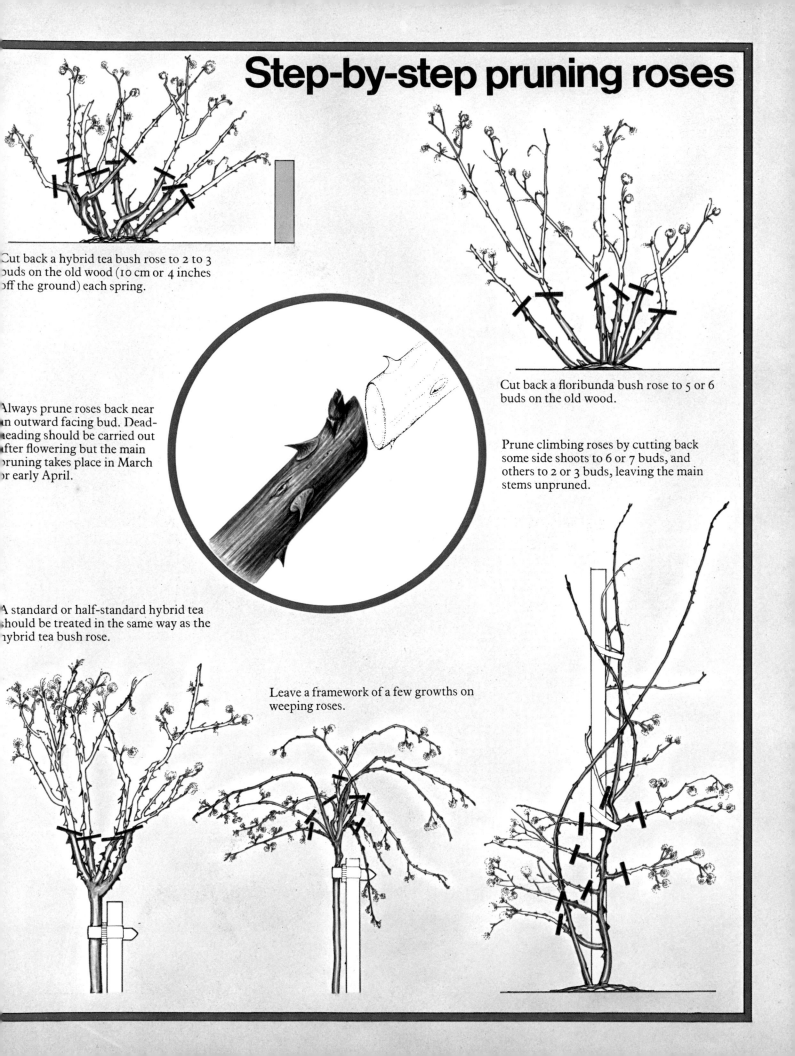

Cut back a hybrid tea bush rose to 2 to 3 buds on the old wood (10 cm or 4 inches off the ground) each spring.

Always prune roses back near an outward facing bud. Dead-heading should be carried out after flowering but the main pruning takes place in March or early April.

A standard or half-standard hybrid tea should be treated in the same way as the hybrid tea bush rose.

Cut back a floribunda bush rose to 5 or 6 buds on the old wood.

Prune climbing roses by cutting back some side shoots to 6 or 7 buds, and others to 2 or 3 buds, leaving the main stems unpruned.

Leave a framework of a few growths on weeping roses.

VEGETABLES UNDER GLASS

There are many advantages to growing vegetables under glass and the use of cloches in the cultivation of vegetables and salad crops is in no way difficult.

Since cloche culture can bring forward by several weeks the date of maturity, it is a great help in successional sowing. So often the supply of salad plants falls off in the autumn and no more home grown produce is available until early spring.

It was French market gardeners who first used handlights or cloches to bring on early crops, particularly lettuces. The continuous cloches now so much in use are a great improvement, as they can be placed in continuous lines, the ends of which can be sealed with a sheet of glass or plastic, to prevent draughts. The tent type is ideal for lettuce and various catch crops, but the larger barn type makes it possible to grow taller plants successfully. Ventilation is provided by openings at the top of the cloches.

There is no difficulty in raising globe beetroot such as 'Boltardy' and 'Detroit' under tent cloches. Seed should be sown in a crumbly fertile soil, first working in a balanced fertilizer at 112 g (4 oz) per sq yd. Make the drills 10 cm (4 ins) apart and 2.5 cm (1 in) deep. Sow one row under tent cloches and three rows, 20 cm (8 ins) apart, under the low barn type. This tasty crop adds colour to any salad.

For first-class produce, fairly rich moist soil is of prime importance. Ground manured for a previous crop is suitable for all cloche and frame varieties. Rake the surface soil finely, or put down a 5 cm (2 ins) layer of compost in which to sow seed. Carrot 'Early Horn' can be grown similarly and young raw grated roots are excellent in the salad bowl.

'Golden Self Blanching' celery can be sown broadcast under barn cloches. Thin the seedlings so that they stand 20 cm (8 ins) apart, or plant at the same distance under cloches. Close planting encourages natural blanching, which can be helped by placing straw between the plants when they are growing well.

Celtuce is a two-in-one vegetable, for the leaves which have a high vitamin content, are used as lettuce, although the delicacy is in the heart of the stem, which is crisp and crunchy with a nutty celery-like flavour.

Dandelions are plants we usually regard as weeds, but the leaves are first-class used in salads. Sow under cloches in rows 25–30 cm (10–12 ins) apart. Plants must not be allowed to flower. For blanching cloches must be darkened, or inverted pots placed over the leaves, otherwise they are bitter. Roots can also be lifted in November and packed in boxes and kept in the dark for blanching like chicory.

Lettuce remains the base of most salads. Thin sowing pays as plants have room to develop; eat the early thinnings. 'Tom Thumb', excellent under cloches, and the newer 'Hilde' form compact hearts. 'Little Gem' is a superb cos variety of medium size and unbeatable for crispness and flavour. Always plant firmly but not deeply.

Salad onions are fast growers so long as the soil does not dry out. Sow in drills 20 cm (8 ins) apart and keep the cloches closed until growth is seen. 'White Lisbon' is one of the best for pulling young for salads, although the thinnings of the bulb varieties can be used.

Radishes bring colour to salads. They may be grown alone, six or seven rows to a cloche, or as an intercrop with lettuce. Here again moisture is necessary for quick, succulent growth. 'French Breakfast' is half red and half white, while 'Cherry Belle' is a fine scarlet globe variety with crisp, white flesh. Both are reliable croppers. 'China Rose' and 'Black Spanish' are autumn and winter-maturing varieties.

Garden Frames

There are four standard patterns of garden frames, determined by the size of the glass or light. The English frame is 2 m (6 ft) long by 1.20 m (4 ft) wide, usually glazed with 16 sheets of glass each measuring 45 cm (18 ins) by 30 cm (12 ins). A smaller one, often known as the Lady's Light, measures 1.20 m (4 ft) by 1 m (3 ft), and is easier to handle. The Dutch light measures 1.50 m (59 in) by 78 cm (31¾ ins) and is glazed with a single pane of glass, which means it is expensive to replace the glass if it is broken. The French frame is easily made and measures 1.25 m (4 ft 4 ins) by 1.26 m (4 ft 5 ins).

Sectional frames of cast aluminium or steel are on the market, while many satisfactory portable frames are available with single or span roof. These have sliding tops, easily removable for access.

The size of frame you buy or make will depend on the purpose for which it is to be used, although the aim should be to have one as large as space and pocket allow. Many frames are made with 1.20 m (4 ft) extensions, so that any length of run can be achieved.

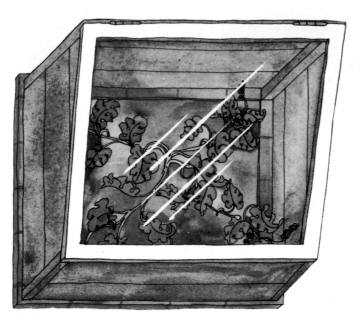

structure, or it will become muddy making it difficult to attend to plants in winter or wet weather.

Keep the glass clean. Carefully seal any cracks with putty so that rain drips cannot penetrate. Make sure that it will open and shut properly without water getting between the panes or hinge joints. Give water with care to avoid excess moisture in the frame. An old-fashioned remedy for keeping out dampness is to place a lump of quicklime under each light. This takes up air moisture in winter, lasting for several weeks.

Heat escapes through the bottom of the frame into the surrounding soil. A 5–7.5 cm (2–3 ins) deep bed of cinders placed at the base of the frame area before soil is added, greatly reduces the loss.

Many small frames are available, but none less than 1.20 m (4 ft) by 1 m (3 ft) gives much scope. A lot can be done with two or three of the 2 m (6 ft) by 1.20 m (4 ft) size. These yield worthwhile quantities, instead of handfuls, of edible crops. An ideal soil depth is up to 60 cm (2 ft) at the front and 75 cm (2½ ft) or more at the back.

Provided the main electricity supply is nearby, you can heat your frame by soil cables which should be laid on 5 cm (2 ins) of sand and covered with another 5 cm (2 ins) before 60 cm (2 ft) loamy soil is put on. Make sure there is no crossing or touching by different sections of the same heating elements. Cables must be totally insulated against damp. Always buy cables specially made for greenhouse work, and carry out regular safety inspections of any electrical equipment.

Damp and draughts cannot be kept out just by keeping the top closed. Without air, mildew and rotting will occur. Ventilation is needed daily, except in very cold or frosty weather. Never let cold winds blow into a frame. For this reason the sliding light is better than the hinged type, for it can always be kept open away from the wind by using little blocks. Frost-resisting mats are valuable during severe cold, but should not be used when they are wet. It is an advantage to have duplicate mats so that the wet ones can be dried.

With heat you can force chicory, rhubarb and seakale in January,

Melons need protection all their growing life. For frame cultivation prepare the planting hole towards the back of the frame by filling it with good compost and replacing the soil in a mound on top. Plant the young plant firmly on top and train it to fill all 4 corners of the frame

Where possible, place the frame due south and not under or too near trees. If backed on to the greenhouse or other building giving protection from north winds, so much the better. Avoid hollows or ground liable to become waterlogged.

The body of the frame can be of tongued and grooved timber, brick, breeze blocks or metal. Frames must be constructed on a proper draught- and damp-proof base. Provide a firm footwalk round the

Left to right: Glass barn cloche, rigid plastic cloche, tent cloche, polythene tunnel

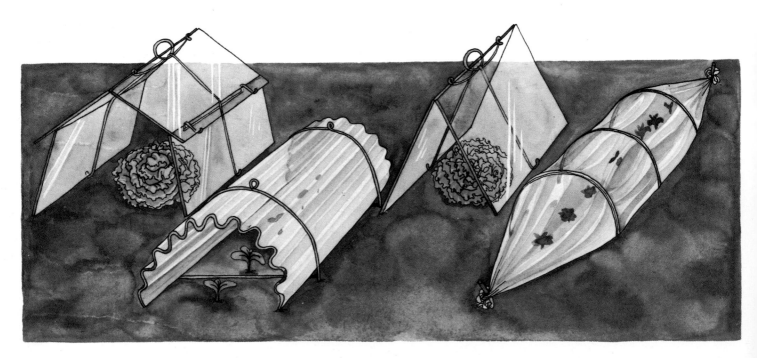

and plant early potatoes like 'Maris Bard' and 'Arran Pilot'. Lettuce sown in September will heart by Christmas, while partially-grown lettuce, cauliflower and endive plants can be placed in frames to mature. Parsley transferred to frames in October will give winter pickings. Continuous supplies of mustard and cress may be harvested by sowing on canvas stretched over the soil.

Dutch Net or Cantaloupe melons can be grown in frames. For each plant, prepare a trench a foot deep and wide. Fill this with fermenting manure, topped with a mound of soil on which to plant the melon. Apply water and keep the frame closed for four or five days. Shade from hot sun and avoid excess moisture. Wait for four or five female flowers to open simultaneously, then hand pollinate them, so the fruits develop evenly. Spray the flowers with water in early mornings. Give liquid manure each week. Cut the fruit when a circular crack appears at the base of stem.

Greenhouses

What can be grown in a greenhouse depends largely on the temperature that can be maintained. Instead of having an empty greenhouse after the autumn crops are over, use it for growing tasty winter salads. The best place for these is in the border and in many cases it is possible to move the staging to make more room. Since light is important, a house with glass almost to ground level is particularly suitable. Good ventilation is essential especially during periods of mild weather.

In smaller houses with a brick or wood base, it is better to make a bed on the staging. If this is slatted, asbestos or slates can be placed on the staging before putting on the compost. Bricks or something similar will be required for the front of the staging to prevent the compost from falling off the edge. Some crops will grow well in pots or boxes of good fertile, rather porous soil.

Lettuces are always wanted. Sowings made towards the end of October will be ready for cutting from late January onwards. Sow the seed in pans or boxes and prick off as soon as the seedlings can be handled. After 2 or 3 weeks they will be ready for their final quarters. Space them 18—20 cm (7—8 ins) apart. Sometimes one can buy strong young seedlings but only do so from a reliable source. Good varieties are: 'Cheshunt Early Giant' and 'Kloek'. The Dutch variety 'Kwiek' is specially suitable for the cold greenhouse. Plant them 20 cm (8 ins) apart each way, spraying with derris if aphids appear.

Dwarf French beans can be sown in pots (25 cm (10 ins) diameter being the best). These should be well crocked, and three parts filled with a good compost. Then place 5 or 6 beans 4 cm (1½ ins) deep around the edge of the pots. The soil should be just moist and no water given until the plants are growing nicely. Moisture encourages damping off. As the plants develop more compost is added until it comes to within 25 mm (1 in) of the top of the pots. When the flowers open, syringings of water twice a day should be given to encourage a good set.

Delicious young carrots can be enjoyed in winter if a short horn variety is sown. Boxes can be used but the border is best. Good, but not over rich soil is recommended. Sow in drills 13 mm (½ in) deep and 13—15 cm (6 ins) apart. Dibble in pelleted seed at 7.5 cm (3 ins) apart to avoid wasteful thinning. Keep the soil uniformly moist but not wet. Good varieties for this purpose are 'Early Gem' and 'Amsterdam Forcing'.

Turnips can be treated similarly and are best used while small. Radishes are no trouble and can be grown on the staging or in the border. Sow thinly 13 mm (½ in) deep, firming the soil after sowing.

Melons are a rewarding and delicious greenhouse crop

Keep the compost moist to encourage quick growth. 'French Breakfast' and 'Sparkler' are particularly suitable.

Mustard and cress call for a temperature of around 13°C (55°F). Boxes or pots can be used, or the staging or border where larger quantities are needed. Well firm and water the compost and when most of the moisture has drained away, sow the seed rather thinly, but do not cover it with soil. Sheets of brown paper or hessian laid over the soil help to draw up the seedlings. When they are about 4 cm (1½ ins) high, remove the covers. So that they mature together, cress should be sown four days before mustard.

Mint can be grown in pots. Once growth is seen, give mist-sprays of water to provide the right atmospheric conditions.

To obtain an early crop, cauliflower 'All the Year Round' can also be sown in the greenhouse. Alternatively, plants from earlier outdoor sowings can be brought in and potted up. If they are to mature under glass, space them 45 cm (18 ins) apart about the middle of January. Keep the temperature around 18°C (65°F) during the daytime.

Where a temperature of not less than 18°C (65°F) can be maintained, a sowing of tomatoes made during the last week in November or early December, will with proper management, produce plants from which you can start picking from late March onwards. Sow in trays or pans and prick out and pot on in the usual way.

From seed sown in late November, plants will be ready for their fruiting quarters in January. Between these months, water with care to prevent roots rotting. It will usually be convenient to plant a row of tomatoes beside the cucumber bed just before the cucumber plants are set out. But it will only be possible to obtain two or three trusses of fruit, which will not be so weighty or the quality so good, as the later crops. Their value, however, will more than make up for the reduced crop.

Chicory is another useful winter vegetable. From seed sown in May, the roots are ready for lifting from October onwards, and will produce chicons in January.

Greenhouses are usually categorized by the amount of heat that can be provided. The cold greenhouse is one that is never heated by anything but the sun and it is pleasant to realize that good crops can be had without any artificial heat. In extra cold weather some protection can be given by providing blinds or similar covering which can be used as necessary.

The main problem with a cold greenhouse is that the air may become damp, which is why some ventilation should be given whenever weather conditions are reasonable.

The cool greenhouse is one where a minimum night temperature of 4–7°C (40–45°F) can be maintained. This must be controlled, which means adequate ventilation. It is perhaps plants in smaller greenhouses that suffer most when air conditioning is wrong, especially if sufficient ventilators have not been provided. Fresh air is important and though when the air vents are opened this naturally lowers the temperature, it moves the stagnant, dank air, leading to the buoyant atmosphere so vital for plant health.

The intermediate or warm house provides a winter night temperature above 8–9°C (48°F). This allows for a wide range of plants to be cultivated. Such houses are usually very strongly built on firm foundations and sited where they benefit most from the sun's heat.

Here again ventilation plays an important part in keeping the plants healthy. It pays to install automatic ventilation which is governed by the weather conditions and greenhouse temperature. Automatic ventilators cost nothing to run and are easily fitted. They comprise a narrow cylinder filled with a mineral substance which expands or contracts at the smallest change in temperature to operate a ventilator push rod.

In a hot house the winter temperature never falls below 16°C (61°F). Few amateur gardeners can afford this degree of heat.

There are various methods of heating greenhouses, including the hot water system, using solid fuel, a boiler and pipes; electricity, gas or paraffin. The hot water method is satisfactory for warmth is distributed evenly without creating a dry atmosphere. It is doubtful whether a solid fuel boiler is best for the owner who is away all day, since it needs stoking at least twice a day and regular cleaning. This applies even though solid fuel boilers have been modernized and can be kept going longer without attention.

Electrical heating is time and labour-saving and requires no boiler

Extend the season for lettuce by using a frame

Get French beans off to a good start with cloche protection

or fuel storage. With thermostatic control, a pre-determined temperature can be maintained so long as the right heaters have been chosen and there are no power cuts! There are various ways of using electricity for heating:

1 By a wire grid over which air is blown by a fan.
2 By a convector heater exuding warm air. Rapid warmth is produced although distribution is not so even.
3 By radiant tubes, plates or strips.
4 By immersion heater used for hot water pipes.

Soil warmth can also be provided by electric cables. This is used to provide bottom heat for propagating seeds or growing cuttings and does not substantially increase air temperature.

Oil heaters are popular but call for special vigilance with safety measures. Use high-quality paraffin or heating oil that will not give off poisonous fumes. Always keep the burners clean so that incomplete combustion does not release harmful gases, and stand the heater itself in a place where it cannot be knocked over or where severe draughts might catch the flame. For large greenhouses, heaters with outside chimneys should be used but for small houses, several portable models are available. These need little attention other than re-filling. Choose one producing a blue flame which results from complete combustion of the oil. A yellow flame indicates the formation of carbon particles but does not necessarily indicate that harmful fumes are being emitted.

Manufacturers usually indicate how long a heater will burn with one filling. More important is how much heat is produced. Heat is lost through ventilation, but stagnant air encourages fungoid and other disorders, and particularly with paraffin heating a degree of ventilation is always needed, except during the most severe weather.

Growing Fruit Under Glass

At one time it was customary in large gardens to maintain an orchard house. This was usually a structure in which fruit trees were grown either with or without heat. The trees were planted out in borders or grown in pots, in fact they were often grown by both methods since then every part of the orchard house could be fully occupied in the production of fruit.

Vegetables Under Glass in Winter

Vegetable	When and How to Start	Where to Grow	Growing Instructions	Ready for Use
Asparagus	October–November – dig up roots after the foliage has died down	Heated greenhouse (21°C/70°F) or in a frame over a hot bed	Use 3 or 4 year old roots. Pack roots tightly together in boxes or the ground. Cover with 8–15 cm (3–6 in) of soil	Cutting begins 3–4 weeks after the start of forcing
Bean – dwarf French	January–February – sow seeds	Heated greenhouse (13°C/55°F) or warm frame	Sow 6 seeds round the edge of a 25 cm (10 in) pot	March onwards
Bean – climbing French	January–February – sow seeds	Heated greenhouse (13°C/55°F)	Sow seeds in double rows 30 cm (12 in) apart with 75 cm (30 in) between double rows. Thin plants to 20 cm (8 in) apart in the rows	March onwards
Carrot	January–February – sow seeds	Warm or cold frame	Sow short-rooted cultivars. Broadcast seed to give each plant 4 sq cm (1 sq in) of space. Rake in lightly	Early May
Cauliflower	September – sow seeds and then plant into pots/frames in March	Cold greenhouse or cold frames	Space sow seed in frame at 5 cm (2 in) square. Transplant into 25 cm (10 in) pots or into frames at 45 cm (18 in) square	May–June
Chicory	November onwards – lift roots before frosts. Store in frost-free place and force successionally	Heated greenhouse (15.5°C/60°F) or warm cellar/shed	Pack roots tightly together in pots or boxes. Cover with straw or stable manure	Hearts or 'chicons' are ready 4–5 weeks after the start of forcing
Chives	January – lift plants from outside	Heated (13°C/55°F) or cold greenhouse/frame	Pot up plants into 9 cm (3½ in) pots	As soon as new shoots are produced
Endive	July – sow seed outside and lift plants in October	Cold frame	Grow plants at 30 cm (12 in) square. Replant into frames at 30 cm (12 in) square. Blanch heads as required	1 week after start of blanching
Lettuce	September onwards – sow seeds and transplant young plants	Heated (13°C/55°F) or cold greenhouse or frame	Plant successionally in heated structures throughout winter. Plant in either November or February in cold houses/frames. Set out plants at 25–30 cm (10–12 in) square	December onwards from heated houses. March–May from cold greenhouses/frames
Mint	November – lift roots from outside after the foliage has died down	Heated greenhouse (15.5°C/60°F) or frame	Pack roots tightly together in pots or boxes. Cover with 5 cm (2 in) of soil	January onwards
Mustard and cress	September onwards – sow seeds	Heated greenhouse (15.5°C/60°F) or frame	Sow thinly in pots, boxes or on moistened tissue paper. Sow cress 3–4 days before mustard	2–3 weeks after sowing
Peas	December–January – sow seeds	Heated greenhouse (13°C/55°F) or frame	Use dwarf cultivars. Sow 6 seeds round the edge of a 25 cm (10 in) pot or sow thinly in narrow drills	April onwards
Potatoes	December – plant tubers	Slightly heated (7°C/45°F) or cold greenhouses or frames	Plant 2 or 3 'chitted' tubers in a 25 cm (10 in) pot. Alternatively plant tubers 30 cm (12 in) apart in the ground and grow as for outdoor crops	April onwards
Radish	January onwards – sow seeds	Slightly heated (7°C/45°F) or cold greenhouses or frames	Use short-topped cultivars. Broadcast seed at 8 g per m² (¼ oz per sq yd) and lightly rake in	March
Rhubarb	November onwards – lift roots from outside	Heated greenhouse (13°C/55°F) or warm cellar/shed	Pack roots loosely in boxes or on the ground. Cover with soil and maintain complete darkness during forcing	4–5 weeks after start of forcing
Seakale	November onwards – lift roots from outside	Heated greenhouses (13°C/55°F) or warm cellar/shed	As for Rhubarb	5–6 weeks after start of forcing
Tomato	December onwards – sow seeds and subsequently plant into pots or the soil	Heated (17°C/65°F) or cold greenhouse	Raise plants in 9 cm (3½ in) pots. Transplant into 25 cm (10 in) pots or glasshouse soil with plants 35–45 cm (14–18 in) apart	Picking of heated crops begins in April. Cold crops are ready from June onwards

Today things are different and apart from grape vines, it is doubtful whether any gardener would buy a greenhouse solely for the purpose of growing fruit. Not the least advantage of growing any kind of fruit in the greenhouse is that it can be brought to perfection before those growing in the open air. This is especially so if it is possible to heat the house sufficiently to exclude frost during the flowering period and for a few weeks afterwards.

Pot grown trees can be plunged outdoors after the fruit has been gathered and this helps the wood to ripen and form fruit buds for the following year.

The span roofed house with a low brick wall forming the base is best for this purpose. Ideally, it should be sheltered from the north and east and should be capable of receiving full measure of uninterrupted sunshine. Staging is not required, for the pots can stand on beds of gravel.

Grapes are grown on their own roots, being raised from 'eyes' while figs are propagated from cuttings. Other fruit trees grown in pots should be on dwarfing stocks. For apples, the East Malling IX or M27 are reliable and for pears Quince or Quince 'A' are suitable. Peach stocks too are favoured by some growers. Peaches themselves are best on Mussel stocks which can also be used for plums.

So long as one is prepared to wait for fruiting, well-grown one-year-old trees can be considered ideal for starting in the 45 cm (18 ins) size pots. Compost on the lines of the John Innes No 2 mixture is quite suitable. Sometimes these young trees have thickish roots and these are best trimmed back with a sharp knife sufficiently to enable the root system to be placed in the pot without cramping. It is important to retain undamaged all the fibrous roots which of course, arise from the thicker roots.

Three- to four-year-old trees, planted very early in November are most suitable. Sometimes they can be bought already in pots from the nurserymen although they cost a little extra. Alternatively, they are sold removed from the pots in which they were started, so they can be easily repotted.

With these older trees some root pruning will be necessary to enable the roots to fit easily in the pots. Although some of the longer top growths can be shortened at the time of potting, any necessary pruning should be done in February when the roots are beginning to grow again.

Plenty of crocks should be placed in the bottom of the pot in the usual way for good drainage and after putting in some of the compost the young tree is placed in the pot and the soil carefully worked among the roots. If, as the soil is added, the base of the pot is tapped sharply on the bench, it will ensure that the soil and roots are in close contact and expel any air pockets. A potting stick is very useful for firming the soil, although care must be taken not to knock off or bruise any of the fibrous roots.

With the one year or maiden trees, it is best to plunge (sink) them in a bed of weathered coal ashes or something similar, leaving them in the open air for one year to become established. After the second year the pots can be taken into the greenhouse each January, where sufficient water with overhead mist sprays should be given from January onwards to encourage early growth.

Older trees can be taken straight into the greenhouse after being potted, and if 60 cm (2 ft) is allowed between them it will permit air to circulate freely. Excepting during frosts, the ventilators should be left wide open until the end of January.

During the early part of the year the soil should be allowed to become almost dry, subsequently give it a good soaking. About the second week in February the ventilators can be kept closed at night and opened just a little on dull days.

It is important not to allow the temperature to attain more than 8°C (46°F) at night, or 12°C (54°F) by day. From this stage onwards, as the flowers begin to open, more heat will be required while regular ventilation will help to set the fruit.

The trees should be encouraged to develop properly by disbudding which takes the place of summer pruning and they are repotted every second year.

During summer frequent watering is necessary, often as much as twice daily. Some liquid feeding will be beneficial from the time the fruits begin to swell, liquid organic manure being ideal for this purpose. Routine spraying with insecticides and fungicides is carried out in the same way as for outdoor trees.

Apples, pears, plums and cherries are not forced but grown under cooler conditions. Plums perhaps, appreciate a little more warmth than the others. Apples and pears can be placed outdoors in a warm sunny spot once the fruit begins to colour and mature.

Peaches can be forced to ripen their fruits in May, and if it is possible to have some trees plunged outdoors these can be brought into the greenhouse once the earlier batch of trees has fruited. Peaches and nectarines are frequently grown as fan trained specimens placed directly into the greenhouse border.

The following varieties are reliable.

Dessert apples: 'Ellison's Orange', 'Ribston Pippin', 'Cox's Orange Pippin' and 'James Grieve'. Cooking apples: 'Annie Elizabeth', 'Newton Wonder' and 'Monarch'.

Pears: 'Doyenné du Comice', 'Louise Bonne of Jersey', 'William's Bon Chrétien'.

Plums: 'Early Transparent' Greengage, 'Victoria' and 'Czar'.

Figs grow well in pots especially 'Brown Turkey' and 'White Marseilles'. Leading shoots must be pinched back when they have made up to 30 cm (1 ft) of new growth and all side shoots stopped two leaves beyond the fruits.

Cherries need selecting with care because of pollination requirements. 'Early Rivers', 'Governor Wood', 'Frogmore Early' and 'Bigarreau Napoleon' are suitable for growing together and two or more variaties should ensure fruit. 'Stella', however, is self-fertile.

The best varieties of grapes for indoor culture include:

'Black Hamburgh', well known for producing good crops with or without heat. It is excellent for growing in pots or very early forcing and also as a pollinator for some shy fruiting varieties. The fruits are large, round and blackish, with a sweet flavour and tender flesh.

'Buckland Sweetwater', is an early sweet variety requiring similar treatment to 'Black Hamburgh'. The large round berries have a bright green, transparent skin which often shows as amber.

'Gros Maroc' is a large thick-skinned grape of a rich reddish-purple colour darkening with age. The tender flesh is sweet and juicy and this is really a first class variety for growing in warmth.

'Madresfield Court' is an early muscat, producing medium sized, tapering bunches of dark purple firm fleshed berries which are tender, juicy and rich. A free setting variety, it likes just a little warmth. The foliage is an attractive reddish-crimson when it fades.

'Royal Muscadine', synonymous with 'Chasselas de Fontainebleau' is an early variety, with medium-sized bunches of small golden-yellow berries which turn a cinnamon shade when exposed to bright sunlight. It is excellent for growing in a sheltered garden or cold greenhouse.

Opposite: Amateur growers of greenhouse grapes will get best results from 'Black Hamburgh' which is easiest to pollinate

A-Z GUIDE TO VEGETABLES OUTDOORS

The health of a nation or individual is its greatest attribute and a knowledge of food values is of primary importance. Although on reflection it may seem obvious that we ought to eat foods that make us fit and keep us well, we do often ignore this fact.

Well documented experiments tell us that a very large proportion of a healthy diet should consist of fruit and vegetables, both raw and cooked. When cooking vegetables, more of the vitamin content will be retained if the cooking time is as brief as possible. If boiling in water, use very little liquid; or

better still, use a steamer. This has the added benefits of retaining food colour and texture.

To obtain the maximum value from ground used for vegetable growing, cultivate those crops most suited to the soil available. Some vegetables are easier to grow than others but there should be no problems with beans, beetroot, carrots, cabbages, lettuce or peas. It is advisable to concentrate on crops which are expensive to buy, those which mature in autumn and winter and those which are scarce in the

shops when required.

Successional sowings of many crops during spring and summer ensures a long harvesting period, while intercropping and catch cropping means that the ground is always fully occupied.

Vegetable gardening may seem less glamorous than growing colourful flowers but with the rapid increase in prices many gardeners are now growing their own vegetables to save money. In so doing they are getting their vegetables fresher and provided varieties are selected carefully, they

will enjoy the best in flavour and quality. There is a great deal of pleasure and satisfaction to be gained from growing your own vegetables well and trying out unusual species along with the old favourites.

The regular eating of salads in which green stuffs predominate will provide vitamins and valuable salts which are usually lost in cooking. All too often what are served up as salads are limp lettuce leaves, hard beetroot and tough skinned pieces of tomatoes. There are literally dozens of other items which are easy to grow and which enliven any salad with colour and taste. These we shall refer to in detail later but they include corn salad, endive, dandelion, beet tops, nasturtiums, chinese mustard and asparagus peas. Then there are many flowers which help to make salads more interesting: bergamot, calendula, rosemary and rose petals. Yellow and striped tomatoes also attract attention, while the very small fruiting varieties of various shapes are a little out of the ordinary but certainly tasty.

From the small patch given over to the herb garden there will always be supplies which can make so much difference to the taste and appearance of many dishes prepared in the kitchen.

It pays to buy seeds and plants from a reliable source and to depend on varieties known to be of high quality and yield.

Vegetable growing

The tending of a skilfully managed vegetable garden contributes to the household economy and is a source of satisfying exercise.

Basic requirements for vegetables

Essential tools for the average plot are fully described on pages 38 to 45. They should include a spade, fork, rake, hoe, trowel, a measuring stick and garden line. A medium-sized plot for three people requires an average of 3-4 hours weekly work. This will however depend on many factors: the size of the plot, the kind of crops grown, the type of soil and the method of cultivation.

Poor feeding and general neglect of the soil will be reflected in the performance of the vegetables. Keep vegetables sufficiently warm, well-fed and watered and carry out tasks as they arise. Follow the rules and reap the results.

Cost

The cost of seeds, manures, fertilizers, tools, pesticides and weedkillers varies widely. Compare prices before making purchases and you will avoid much needless expenditure. Savings can also be made on purchases of manures, sundries and seeds by several gardeners joining together to buy in bulk.

Once your land is in full production, keep the weeds down. Good husbandry and crop rotation reduce bills for weed-killers and pesticides to a minimum. Crop failure is due as much to the ravages of pests and diseases as any other cause.

Size of site needed

This is determined by the number of people there are to feed, their tastes, and whether the aim is to meet all or only part of those requirements from the garden. The following table gives a guide to the approximate area required to feed three people.

Crop	Row length (m)	Row width (cm)
Group A (Seed and stem crops)		
Beans– Broad	d4.5	67
Beans– French	s6.0	40
Beans– Runner	d4.5	60
Cucumber	s2.25	60
Celery	d3.0	40
Leek	s9.0	30
Lettuce intercrop	s9.0	30
Marrow	s2.25	60
Onions	s22.5	30
Pea	s9.0	80
Shallots	s4.5	30
Spinach	s4.5	30
Spinach Beet	s4.5	40
Sweet Corn	d2.7	90
Tomato	s2.7	45
Group B (Root Crops)		
Beetroots	s9.0	30
Carrots	s13.5	30
Parsnips	s4.5	45
Potatoes early	s9.0	60
Potatoes maincrop	s27.0	67
Swede garden	s9.0	45
Group C (Greens)		
Broccoli, sprouting	s4.5	60
Brussels Sprouts	s13.5	67
Cabbage, Autumn planted	s13.5	45
Cabbage, Spring sown	s9.0	50
Cabbage, Savoy	s9.0	60
Cauliflower, Autumn use	s4.5	60
Cauliflower, Winter use	s4.5	60
Kale	s4.5	45
Turnip intercrop	s4.5	45

s = single, d = double

LEFT A small vegetable garden. Flowers for cutting are also grown here.

The area of groups A, B and C should be equal in the interest of good cultivation with a regular rotation of crops to prevent a build-up of disease in the soil.

Supposing in Group A that the family prefer French beans to peas. The area of beans can be increased at the expense of peas.

Revised areas

Crop	Original	Revised
French beans	6.0m × 40cm	13.5m × 40cm
Peas	9.0m × 50cm	4.5m × 80cm

BELOW Preparing the vegetable plot for next season's crop.

Similar adjustments can be made between other crops, but any re-arrangements should be made between crops within the same group, otherwise the rotation benefits may be lost.

The area of land required to feed one person under poor conditions may be 90m² (100 sq yd), but in good circumstances the requirement can be half that figure.

Until the capabilities of your soil, the climate, and the appetites of your family are known, start off with the lower figure, which is based on a plot size of 13.5 × 9m (45 × 30ft). In very small gardens, the problem will be to reduce the area still further and cut out plants that need a lot of space, such as maincrop potatoes, peas and Brussels sprouts.

Preparation of the plot

Vegetables need richer soil than any other group of garden plants. They are also vulnerable to many pests, diseases and weeds. Vegetable crops are usually considered in three categories for the purpose of soil treatment:

Group A the seed and stem crops such as peas, beans, onions and leeks.

Group B the root crops, potatoes and parsnips.

Group C the brassicas (greens) such as cabbages and Brussels sprouts.

Divide the vegetable garden into three plots of equal size, using pegs or markers for permanent reference. Label these plots A, B and C, and treat each one to a basic programme of autumn and winter cultivation, following the advice on crop rotation given on pages 50 and 51.

Artichokes

There are at least three very different plants known as artichokes and which are of value both as vegetables and as attractive features of the general garden.

GLOBE ARTICHOKE *Cynara scolymus*

This is the species of which the buds are eaten. The flower is spectacular and the foliage ideal for floral arrangements. It is perennial and provides good ground cover. There are few plants which are so versatile.

In the past some confusion has existed concerning the origin of this plant. It was introduced into Britain from southern Europe about 1548 but is still not as popular here as on the Continent.

Of upright habit, the globe artichoke grows to a height of 1.20–1.80 m (4–6 ft). The well cut leaves are 60–90 cm (2–3 ft) long, greyish-green covered with white down on the undersides. The purple flowers produced in autumn are surrounded by an involucre of fleshy scales which with the central heart are the edible portion of the plant and are considered a great delicacy eaten hot with melted butter or cold with vinaigrette sauce. The flower heads should be cut with a short piece of stem, when young and tender, before opening, otherwise they become coarse.

Globe artichokes grow best in warmer districts. Weathered ashes, strawy manure and bracken are all useful for covering the crowns during late autumn and winter.

Move the ground deeply during the early winter, working in plenty of dung or good compost. Roots or suckers are planted from March to May. These will give a succession of heads from June to early October, especially if strong suckers are used. Plant firmly 75 cm (2½ ft) apart with 1.20 m (4 ft) between the rows. It is possible to intercrop with lettuce, carrots and turnips during the first season.

In good soil globe artichokes will remain productive for 5 or 6 years. An annual winter dressing of decayed farmyard manure will encourage good quality heads. Top dressings of an organic fertilizer in the spring are beneficial.

Always gather the heads at the bud stage. If it is not possible to use them immediately, the stems can be placed in water where they will keep fresh for some days. After the largest central heads have been cut, the side buds will develop. If plants due to be grubbed out are cut down to within a few inches of the ground early in July, new growths will form. The strongest of these can be blanched to provide chards. To do this draw the stems together and tie with raffia, putting straw or hay around the plants and earth them up. Blanching takes 5 or 6 weeks.

Varieties include 'Green Globe' and 'Purple Globe', the former being hardier and having fewer prickles. A particularly good well-flavoured French Variety is 'Gros Vert de Laon'.

JERUSALEM ARTICHOKE
Helianthus tuberosus

The word Jerusalem is believed to be a corruption of an Italian word *girasole* for *Helianthus annuus*, the sunflower to which this plant is related. The name artichoke was given to denote the similarity in the flavour of this root to the globe artichoke scales.

Although a hardy perennial plant, it is better to replant each year. The plants can be used as windbreaks, as a division or screen in the garden or for protecting tender crops, since they grow 1.80–2.10 m (6–7 ft) high.

They do best in enriched deeply dug, medium to light soil. Fish manure, well worked in, is most beneficial. On heavy ground the tubers are difficult to harvest and slugs may be attracted to them. A surface dressing of weathered ashes or sharp sand helps keep pests away.

Sometimes soil conditions make it possible to plant in February but March and early April are the usual times. Place tubers about the size of a pullet's egg 25–30 cm (10–12 ins) apart in drills or furrows about 15 cm (6 ins) deep. Cover lightly, and work in some fish manure or other organic fertilizer.

Allow 90 cm (3 ft) between rows. Once growth starts, draw up soil towards the plants. In exposed windy places, a stake at the end of each row connected with 2 or 3 strands of wire will keep the plants upright.

If the plants show signs of flowering, remove the buds so the plant's energy is devoted to the production of tubers. Towards the end of October cut off top growth within 30 cm (12 ins) of the soil.

The tubers are hardy and can be left in the ground and lifted as required. They have a better flavour freshly dug than stored, although it is possible to store the tubers in boxes of sand or soil or in clamps outdoors. When harvesting remove every tuber from the soil otherwise 'odd' plants become a nuisance the following season.

To prepare Jerusalem artichokes, scrub clean with a stiff vegetable-cleaning brush and drop each one into water to which a little lemon juice has been added to prevent discoloration. Cook by boiling in their skins. Drain and peel after 7 minutes.

RECOMMENDED VARIETIES: 'New White' is of excellent flavour and better than the purple-skinned sort. 'Fuseau' has smooth tubers which are easier to deal with in the kitchen.

Globe artichokes ready for cutting

CHINESE ARTICHOKE *Stachys affinis* (syn. *tubifera*)

Similar in appearance to the Jerusalem artichoke and in flavour to the true artichoke, this is not an artichoke at all. The spirally twisted tubers vary in length from 2.5–7.5 cm (1–3 ins). At their widest part they are about 2.5 cm (1 in) thick. It is a member of the family *Labiatae*; most *stachys* are grown for their attractive flowers.

It flourishes on a well cultivated light soil where the situation is sunny. On poor ground work in compost or organic fertilizer before planting in March and April. Place the tubers 10 cm (4 ins) deep and 23 cm (9 ins) apart with 38–45 cm (15–18 ins) between rows.

Use tubers of Jerusalem artichokes quickly after harvesting

During dry weather the rows should be watered to encourage even development. The tubers mature from November onwards and should be dug as required. Use them as soon as lifted. Never expose them to light or they will turn green and be inedible. If stored under cover for any length of time they may grow again and become flavourless.

ASPARAGUS *Asparagus officinalis*

The wild species grows in sandy coastal regions, which suggests that the plant has a preference for sand and salt, yet large quantities of cultivated asparagus grow in peaty or loamy soils. But whatever soil is used, it must be well-drained. Medium loam enriched with humus matter is ideal; heavy ground by itself is usually too cold for good growth. Applications of manure and other organic material not only assist drainage but make the soil warmer, and a warm soil and favourable aspect encourage an earlier crop. Frost pockets and low lying areas are not suitable for asparagus growing, because the young buds may be damaged by spring frosts.

Since this crop remains in position for many years – up to 20 years is not unusual – soil preparation must be thorough. To grow asparagus on dirty, weed-laden land means constant work in cleaning the site. Early soil preparation and enrichment is essential, and although planting is not done until the spring, manuring must be done in autumn.

There are two ways of obtaining a crop from seeds or plants. Obviously the latter will produce results before plants raised from seed. In a good seed bed, which should be firm and brought to a fine tilth, seed can be sown thinly from the end of April onwards, making the rows 38–45 cm (15–18 ins) apart. The drills should be made 2 cm ($\frac{3}{4}$ in) deep. Germination is always slow and it is a help to mix a little radish seed to mark the rows and facilitate early hoeing, since the radish germinates so quickly. Soaking the seed in water speeds germination. Firm the drills after sowing.

One-year-old crowns can be moved without much damage, but whatever their age at least a year, preferably three, are needed for

Left: Chinese artichokes. Right: Spears of asparagus 'Regal Select'

them to become established. Planting is best done towards the end of March or in early April when the soil is fit to work and warmed by the sun. Rake in a dusting of fish meal, 100 g per m² (3 oz per sq yd), before opening the trenches. It is important to spread out the roots at planting time. This applies whether the crowns are being grown on the ridge system, or on a flat bed. The central bud should be at least 8 cm (3 ins) below the surface. Never let the crowns dry out before being planted.

The plants should be set out in rows 60 cm (2 ft) apart, with 1.05 m ($3\frac{1}{2}$ ft) between rows. It is unwise to cut the spears until the plants are three years old, and even then, harvesting should cease quite early in June. Subsequently, the cutting season will be prolonged to the end of that month.

RECOMMENDED VARIETIES:

The question of strains and varieties is important and many specialist growers have their own selection. 'Argenteuil Early' is an old but widely grown variety, most valuable because it is the earliest open ground sort. 'Connover's Colossal' is the best known and always popular. 'Kidner's Variety' produces very large spears. Two lesser known American sorts 'Mary Washington' and 'Martha Washington' are resistant to rust disease, although not as heavy cropping as the English varieties.

Male plants are preferable as they not only yield more heavily than the female, but

there are no infuriating seedlings appearing in spring, as there would be if females were grown and allowed to seed. Use special knives for cutting the crowns, severing them cleanly 8 cm (3 ins) below soil level.

Always leave some fern to develop to help build up the following season's crowns. Cut the fern down to about 15 cm (6 ins) above the soil surface in the autumn; do not allow the berries to ripen, since unwanted seedlings will result.

AUBERGINE *Solanum melongena* var *Ovigerum*

Often known as egg plants, aubergines are worth growing in a small way. Ideal for cultivating in the warm greenhouse, in warm districts they are often successful outdoors, once risk of frost has passed. Frames and cloches may also be used.

The soil, which must be prepared early, should be enriched with old manure and plenty of compost. Sow seed in late February or early March, using pots or boxes of sandy soil in a temperature of 15°C (60°F).

When they can be handled, the seedlings should be pricked out into 7.5 cm (3 ins) pots, or into soil blocks, using fairly rich compost. By the end of April they should be ready for 13 cm (5 in) pots. This will prevent any check from starvation. Spray with water daily to prevent red spider damage.

Towards the end of May, the plants can be put under frames or cloches, which should be kept closed for a few days, so the plants settle down quickly. When the plants are 15 cm (6 ins) high, take out the growing point.

When the resultant laterals have grown 10 cm (4 ins), they too should be stopped. Allow up to six fruits to develop on each plant removing all others which attempt to form. Keep on with the overhead sprayings to ensure that red spider does not gain a hold. Later crops can be sown directly into prepared sites under cloches.

The fruits are ready to gather from July to October. They should be handled with care since they bruise easily. To cook, the skins may be removed or left on. Slice and leave for 30 minutes after a dusting with salt. Pat dry and fry or bake in a casserole.

RECOMMENDED VARIETIES: 'Burpee Hybrid' is a fine dark violet sort, 'Black Prince' has large purple-black fruits and is very early, while 'Moneymaker' is an outstanding early variety with dark purple skin.

Aubergines are best grown in pots or growing bags under glass

Beans

There are several different vegetables of varying habits falling into this broad category.

BROAD BEAN *Vicia faba*

One of the oldest of cultivated vegetables having been grown in Britain for centuries, it is an annual with stiff quadrangular, hollow stems. The large seeds are white or green, according to variety. Broad beans will grow on almost any soil and while they like moisture, avoid badly drained ground liable to become waterlogged in winter and that which dries out in early summer.

A cool, deep, fertile soil, manured for previous crops is ideal and there should be no lack of humus. Lime too is necessary, although it should not be applied at the same time as farmyard manure. It is better to give a dusting of lime when the final surface preparations are being carried out. Broad beans like an open, but not exposed position, with plenty of light and spring sunshine, without being exposed to winds.

Sowings can be made outdoors in November or from mid-February to April, or under cloches from January onwards. Sowings after mid-April crop poorly and are subject to blackfly. Even for the November sowings some kind of glass covering is useful, since severe frosts will sometimes damage the plants. The plants will need uncovering in April, by which time they will be nearing the top of the glass. It is not worth making an autumn sowing in cold districts or where the soil is naturally very heavy and badly drained. Should weather conditions prevent an early outdoor sowing, sow the seed in February in boxes in a heated greenhouse for planting outdoors in April.

For the earliest sowings, the Longpod varieties should be used, since they are

Longpod broad beans at harvesting stage

good flavour; 'Red Epicure', a strong grower notable for its rich chestnut-crimson coloured beans of delicious flavour and 'Dreadnought', large pods of excellent quality.

WINDSOR VARIETIES: 'The Sutton', growing about 30 cm (1 ft) high and branching freely, can be sown at close spacing and is very reliable; 'Green Windsor', excellent flavour; 'Imperial White Windsor', long pods with large beans and 'Promotion' a high yielding variety.

HARICOT BEANS *Phaseolus vulgaris*

Very useful for winter eating, these are varieties of dwarf French beans specially grown for their dried seeds, not fresh pods. It is a pity haricot beans are not more widely cultivated. Sowing and culture are the same as for other French beans but the pods are left on the plants until they are ripe and are turning yellow. To give the plants an early start they can be sown under cloches at the beginning of April.

They can be gathered individually as they reach ripeness but it is easier to pull up the complete plants and hang them in bunches or in a sack in any airy place to allow them to become really dry.

When the pods are brittle the beans can be shelled or where large quantities are concerned, the pods can be carefully beaten with a stick which will knock out the seeds. These should be spread on paper or sacking in a cool greenhouse or other airy place, to complete drying, when the seed should be really hard and free from mildew. It is important that the seeds should be quite dry before they are stored in jars, tins or sacks. The storage place must always remain dry or the beans will be affected with mildew and will taste unpleasant.

RECOMMENDED VARIETIES: Varieties are now available which ripen satisfactorily in temperate climates. 'Chevrier Vert' is a vigorous and productive variety also suitable for eating green. 'Comtesse de Chambord' strong growing variety, smallish white round seeds.

CLIMBING FRENCH BEANS
Phaseolus vulgaris

These varieties can be cultivated outdoors in warm districts but they are particularly

hardier and heavier yielding than the Windsor. The latter, however, are of better flavour. Sow the seed 5 cm (2 ins) deep with about 45–60 cm (1½–2 ft) between the drills.

Place the seeds zig-zag, 15 cm (6 ins) apart in double rows. Dwarf varieties can have rather closer spacing. Whether you use a single or double row is not crucial.

Particularly with autumn sowings, extra seeds should be sown at the end of the rows for filling up gaps. As the seedlings begin to push through the soil they should be slightly earthed up. This will give added protection as well as anchoring the plants better. The earliest sown plants can be protected with bracken, straw or cloches during severe weather. This covering should be removed when it is mild.

Keep down weeds by regular hoeing along the rows, which will also benefit the plants. Frequent inspection of the plants is advisable so that blackfly can be dealt with by spraying derris or a similar insecticide before the pests gain a hold.

Pinch out the top growth once the first trusses of flowers are in full bloom. This not only helps the pods to develop well, but discourages blackfly which like to settle there.

Broad beans should be gathered while they are young and before the skins become tough. Early picking will not only mean good flavoured tender beans, but a heavier and more prolonged cropping season. Side shoots should be removed too, although sometimes when the main growth has finished cropping, a secondary basal growth develops and will yield quite well. The top growth of finished plants can be cut off and the roots dug in.

LONGPOD VARIETIES: 'Express', early, producing long pods of white beans. 'Aquadulce Claudia', very early, excellent for autumn sowings; 'Meteor' is a heavy cropper of

suitable for growing in the greenhouse during the winter and early spring. For the earliest crops, the seeds should be sown during the first days of August.

A deep well drained soil containing a fair supply of organic matter is needed. Avoid the over use of nitrogen or the plants will become leafy at the expense of beans. Put one bean in each position where a plant is wanted, with a few extra seeds at the end of each row to gap up with or pull out as the case may be. For healthy growth before sowing or planting, a soil temperature of 12°C (55°F) is necessary.

Climbing French beans can be grown in greenhouses which are wired overhead for tomatoes and the rows can be the same distance apart as the tomato plants, that is, a double row 45 cm (18 ins) apart, then a space of 68 cm (27 ins) and then another double row 45 cm (18 ins) apart. The distance between the plants in the rows is 45 cm (18 ins). For supports, a stout peg to which is attached a T piece, is driven in at the end of the rows to carry a wire 10 cm (4 ins) from ground level exactly over the rows.

A single strand of soft stout string is tied to this wire and to the top tomato wire and the plants are trained up it. Never tie the string to the collar of the bean plant as is frequently done with tomatoes. A night temperature of 15°C (60°F) is required at all times for an early crop of beans. This can be increased by several degrees during the day.

A well-ventilated house is necessary and frequent overhead sprayings of water are desirable to keep down red spider and encourage quick growth.

Once the plants are climbing well and beginning to flower less overhead spraying is required. Careful feeding is needed, should it be decided upon at all, and it is best to use organic based liquid fertilizer. It is advisable to stop the laterals otherwise growth tends to become too crowded.

The cultivation of a spring crop of climbing beans can be gained by sowing seed in the middle of February, when the soil is warm. If the light is very poor bean plants will not climb.

For this sowing, it is best to use 20.5−23 cm (8−9 in) pots into which 6 seeds are sown when the compost is nicely moist so that watering is not needed again until after germination. Cover the pots with glass and paper, removing both when the seedlings appear.

The beans should be picked while young and tender and to ensure a continuous supply of fine-flavoured crops.

Once the crop is finished and the plants are removed, they can be followed by a planting of late tomatoes.

RECOMMENDED VARIETIES: 'Veitch's Climbing' also known as 'Guernsey Climbing' has flat 15 cm (6 ins) pods. 'Kentucky Wonder' forms clusters of round fleshy pods. 'Violet Podded Stringless' is of good flavour and has violet pods which turn deep green when cooked.

DWARF FRENCH BEANS
Phaseolus vulgaris

Although usually referred to as French beans, there is reason to believe they came from South America. They are sometimes known as kidney beans because of the shape of the seeds which can be eaten green or dried. In the United States stringless beans are referred to as snap beans or shell beans if grown for their seeds.

Dwarf French beans will grow on most soils that are reasonably warm and well drained. Early soil preparation is advisable, working in well-rotted manure or compost and raking the soil down fine. These beans make a good follow-on crop for ground that grew brassicas, including Brussels sprouts, for which the ground was well enriched with old manure. Bone meal or fish manure at 100 g per m² (3 oz per sq yd) provides phosphates, and 140 g per m² (4 oz per sq yd) of lime should be given if the soil is sour.

In warm districts it is possible to sow seed at the end of April but usually it is best to

Dwarf French bean 'Remus'

wait until May. Take out drills 5 cm (2 ins) deep and 45 cm (1½ ft) apart.

Sow 12−15 cm (5−6 ins) apart. To allow for possible failures, sow extra seeds at the end of the row.

Gluts can be avoided by sowing small quantities at two or three weekly intervals until mid-July.

Bushy sticks placed at intervals along the rows will keep the plants upright and prevent the beans from trailing on the ground where they will be nibbled by slugs.

Pick the beans before they grow old and stringy. This not only ensures good, tender pods, but encourages the plants to keep on cropping. Under good cultivation one may reckon that a double row a metre (yard) long will produce about 2 kg (4 lbs) of pods.

Flageolet beans are the seeds of dwarf French beans, culled from pods gathered before they are fully ripe. The pods are discarded. Flageolet beans are widely used in France but as yet unfamiliar in English cookery. They have a deliciously delicate flavour, however, well worth trying, and are best prepared by steaming or minimal boiling in water before serving with butter and a sprinkling of herbs.

RECOMMENDED VARIETIES: 'Black Prince' of medium habit, pods up to 16 cm (6½ ins) long; 'Canadian Wonder', an old variety still good if a selected strain is sown; 'Masterpiece', excellent flavour, useful for cloche culture; 'Mont d'or', a golden podded or wax bean of dwarf, leafy habit; 'Pencil Pod Black Wax', bushy plants slightly curved medium sized pods; 'Tendergreen', stringless beans 15 cm (6 ins) long; 'The Prince', fleshy pods of splendid flavour.

RUNNER BEANS *Phaseolus multiflorus*

Usually treated as an annual, the runner bean is actually a perennial, forming tuberous roots which can be lifted in the autumn and stored for replanting the following spring. Excepting during times of seed shortages, there is no advantage in doing this, for the seeds sown in early spring give an abundant crop the same year. That most varieties produce scarlet flowers originally gave rise to the common name of Scarlet Runner, although some varieties have white, pink or red and white flowers.

Runner beans can be used effectively as attractive climbing plants as well as producing a heavy crop over a long period. They should be given a deep, cool root run, if possible, where the ground has been double dug with decayed manure, compost or other bulky material worked in. Apply a surface dressing of lime just before the seed is sown.

It is not advisable to sow outdoors until danger of frosts has passed. To make sure of an early crop, where a frame or a green-house is available, seed can be sown early in boxes about 13 cm (5 ins) deep, the seedlings being planted out after the frosts. Cloches can be used for standing over ground where the rows are to be made.

For kitchen use it is not the length of the beans that matters so much as straight brittle pods. For exhibition purposes it is a different matter for there is keen competition to secure really long, clean pods and good cultivation will bring rewards.

For the growing position a deep rich soil is best. On light, sandy soils it is helpful to take out trenches up to 20 cm (8 ins) deep and to place in them a really thick layer of compost, peat and other moisture retentive material with the addition of fish meal. Finish off the trench so there is a depression, for this will help to prevent the roots drying out during summer. On heavy land it is best not to make a trench but to dig the entire plot, otherwise the trench may become a sump for draining water.

Double rows 23–30 cm (9–12 ins) apart in the trenches makes it easy for staking and where a quantity of beans are being sown, the double rows should be 1.50–1.80 m (5–6 ft) apart. If possible, supports should be in position before the seed is sown 23 cm (9 ins) apart in the rows.

Hazel and ash poles are very suitable and

A white-flowered variety of runner beans with stringless pods

they can be placed upright or at an angle so the tops cross. Other poles placed through the tops of the crossed poles and fastened together, form a strong structure. Alternatively, string or bushy hazel sticks can be used or a group of poles or strings can be placed in a circle and connected to one central pole to form a tent-like structure. Alternatively, use proprietary bean support frameworks, or stout netting.

Once they begin to climb, the seedlings need some directing so they do not grow into each other. It is possible to grow runner beans without any support and for this purpose the growing points are pinched out when the plants are 25–30 cm (10–12 ins) high. The resultant shoots are also stopped and this leads to bushy growth, but heavier, more shapely beans and a cleaner crop undamaged by slugs are produced when supports are provided.

Frequent summer hoeings will keep down weeds and a mulch of leaf mould, peat or strawy manure in early summer will act as a weed smotherer and prevent the soil from drying out. Harvest the pods regularly,

Support systems: left, battens and strings; centre, rows of poles; right, netting stretched between posts

otherwise the production of pods will slow down. If the beans cannot be used fairly quickly after being picked the stem ends can be placed in shallow water where they will remain fresh for several days if kept cool.

Frequent overhead sprayings of water during summer will keep the foliage in good condition and encourage a good set. The dropping of buds and flowers before the pods develop is often due to a dry atmosphere and the absence of pollinating insects. Overhead sprayings help to distribute the pollen.

VARIETIES: Many varieties are available, including 'Achievement', 'Crusader', 'Enorma', 'Prizewinner', 'Scarlet Emperor', 'Streamline' and 'White Achievement'.

'Hammond's Dwarf' and its white form, are dwarf non-trailing 'runner' beans growing about 40 cm (16 ins) high. Extra early

'Streamline' is a reliable runner bean

and excellent for growing under cloches, they do not need staking and produce 20–23 cm (8–9 ins) pods continuously over a period of ten weeks or more if gathered regularly. Seed is sometimes difficult to obtain.

SOYA BEANS *Glycine hispida*

Although many rather extravagant claims have been made for the virtue of this bean, there is no doubt that it is a most valuable food crop which can be grown under widely varying conditions. Under ordinary good culture it produces a sizeable yield and since it has a high protein level, which is above that of other vegetables, as well as various vitamins, it is well worth growing. Even when the size of crop is limited because of adverse summer weather conditions, the

protein and vitamins content makes it a crop to grow. These beans have many uses in the kitchen and are sometimes used as a substitute for meat.

Growing 45–50 cm (18–20 ins) high, seeds can be sown in boxes in the same way as dwarf French beans, the seedlings being moved to their cropping sites in early June. Alternatively, seed can be sown in prepared positions in a sunny spot in the open ground at the end of May or early June. Growth is sometimes slow at first and the flowers are somewhat insignificant, but subsequently there is much vigour.

A soil containing plenty of humus matter and not lacking in moisture will provide the plants with the conditions they like.

BEETROOT *Beta vulgaris* var *esculenta*

A native of N. Africa and W. Asia, this crop is now widely distributed throughout the world. It is in great demand for salads although it can also be served hot. The roots should be used while young and tender before they become coarse and stringy.

A light deep soil is best for this crop, preferably one that was heavily manured with old compost or some other organic manure the previous season. A dusting of fish manure forked into the surface soil before seed is sown will do much good. The earliest sowings of globe varieties can be made in late April or early May according to soil conditions, with further globe sowings until late June. Maincrop varieties should be sown during the last half of May.

Space the rows 38 cm (15 ins) apart and 2.5 cm (1 in) deep. Each beetroot capsule is really a cluster of seeds so that sowing must be done very thinly. If two capsules are dropped in at stations 15 cm (6 ins) apart they can finally be thinned to the strongest plant per station. The second thinnings will be large enough to use.

Weeds should be kept down by careful hoeing which also aerates the soil surface. When pulling or lifting the roots for use, twist off the tops of red or crimson varieties – do not cut them or they may 'bleed' and lose colour.

Left in the ground too long, beetroot may be damaged by wet and frost, therefore lift and store early in November. Handle with care to avoid bruisings and store the roots in boxes of sandy soil or in clamps of small size to prevent heating. Heaps 1.20–1.50 m (4–5 ft) high and 1.20 m (4 ft) wide are

large enough. Provide a ventilation shaft of straw, or a drain pipe can be used to allow sufficient air to keep the roots firm. When dry, place the roots pointing inwards, in an orderly manner to form a compact heap.

RECOMMENDED VARIETIES: round or globe-shaped: 'Beethoven', 'Boltardy' and 'Detroit'; intermediate or oval; 'Formanova'; long; 'Cheltenham Green Top'.

A new variety known as 'Burpees Golden' 'Golden Beet' produces globe-shaped roots with golden skin and yellow flesh. It does not 'bleed' and can be cooked in the usual way while the leaves can be served like spinach.

BROCCOLI, SPROUTING
Brassica oleracea var *italica*

This is a hardy vegetable of good flavour which makes a pleasant change, especially as it matures when other green vegetables

are becoming scarce. The same soil preparation and cultural methods are required as for cauliflowers. Since the plants are fairly tall growing, they should not be placed where they are exposed to strong winds.

Seed need not be sown until April, but early soil preparation is necessary. Sow thinly and transplant early so the seedlings do not become drawn. Farmyard manure or a good substitute should be worked in. Alternatively choose a position well manured for a previous crop. Give a surface dusting of lime before planting out, if the soil is acid. Very rich soil leads to soft, sappy growth, liable to winter damage. Allow 75 cm (2½ ft) between the plants.

Sprouting broccoli is gathered when the flower heads are just beginning to form. If cut about two thirds of their length, more shoots will be produced from the base of the

Above: Round beet 'Detroit'; above right: 'Calabrese' green sprouting broccoli; below: the purple-sprouting variety

stems. Do not cut off the leaves since these afford some protection to the sprouts, although they can eventually be used. As with other members of the brassica family, sprouting broccoli is much more palatable steamed than boiled.

RECOMMENDED VARIETIES: 'Early Purple Sprouting', at its best from February onwards; 'Late Purple Sprouting' matures from March onwards; 'White Sprouting' is hardy and ready from early March onwards.

'Calabrese' (green sprouting broccoli) is an excellent vegetable for late summer and autumn use which differs from the ordinary sprouting broccoli in that it first produces a good sized central head 15 cm (6 ins) or more in diameter. When this is cut, the plant produces from each joint, shoots or sprouts which should be gathered when they have a 10–12 cm (4–5 ins) stem.

Under good growing conditions 'Cala-

brese' is very productive, more so than the purple and white forms, probably because it makes most of its growth during the better weather conditions.

Apart from farmyard and other bulky manures added when the soil is being prepared, a good dressing of fish manure or bone meal, say 100–140 g per m² (3–4 oz per sq yd) will encourage the production of the heads each year.

Sow seeds in April, first pricking out the seedlings to another bed so that they form plenty of roots and become sturdy specimens for planting 75 cm (2½ ft) apart each way. Cut the heads from late July until September.

A dressing of fish manure each spring is helpful and the plants should be replaced every three years.

RECOMMENDED VARIETIES: There are now several strains including 'Atlantic', ready for cutting in the autumn from a spring sowing: 'Gem', F_1 hybrid, 'Corvet', is a F_1 hybrid which is particularly useful for deep freezing; 'Green Comet' is a F_1 hybrid giving a really large head, and 'Late Corona' a F_1 hybrid which is late maturing.

'Nine Star Perennial' provides heads rather like small cauliflowers. Since it is a perennial, the ground must be in really good condition at planting time.

BRUSSELS SPROUTS
Brassica oleracea var *bullata*

This most valuable and popular member of the large brassica family was derived through selection from the wild cabbage. Although it was not until towards the end of the last century that Brussels sprouts became widely grown in most European countries, they were known and cultivated in Belgium, particularly in areas around Brussels, more than 750 years ago. The sprouts are produced in the axils of the leaves in the first year of this biennial plant.

It is successfully cultivated in all soils, excepting those which are badly drained or very loose. The soil should be highly fertile. For best results the aim should be to provide an open, airy situation, with wide spacing to ensure good sprout development. A long season of growth is required.

Deep, early cultivation should be carried out, not only to allow the soil to become sweetened and well-weathered, but to give it time to settle. Good sized, tight sprouts cannot be obtained from hastily prepared, loose

Brussels sprouts 'Early Half Tall' will be ready from October

cessional sowings of the right varieties have been made and it should be possible to gather sprouts well into April.

Apart from frost and wet damage which sometimes occur, one occasionally finds when cutting open a sprout that there is a dark streak of tissue in the middle. This is usually due to the plants growing in poor, wet, badly drained soils. Brussels sprouts are subject to the same diseases and pests as other members of the cabbage family but should not suffer unduly except from attacks of mealy cabbage aphid. Malathion may help but the pests are difficult to control.

RECOMMENDED VARIETIES: many improved cultivars have been introduced and among the best are the following F_1 hybrids. 'Achilles', producing long lasting tight sprouts; 'Citadel', maincrop; 'Peer Gynt', early; 'King Arthur', prolific; and 'Focus', extra good flavour. Other reliable varieties include 'Irish Elegance', 'Roodnerf Stiekema Early' and 'Roodnerf Stabilo', late cropping.

CABBAGE *Brassica oleracea* var *capitata*

Wild cabbages can still be found growing in many Mediterranean regions and parts of England and Ireland. Breeding over many years has given us the varieties we now know so well.

Cabbages contain a fair amount of vita-

'Hispi' is a reliable summer cabbage

soil. There is no hard and fast rule regarding the place in crop rotation of sprouts, although they follow potatoes or early turnips very well.

Sprouts do best where they follow a well manured and deeply cultivated crop, where the soil does not lack lime. Where such a position cannot be provided, farmyard manure and well-rotted compost, say a bucketful to a square metre, should be worked into the ground in late autumn or winter. A dressing of a good organic fertilizer such as fish manure, hoof and horn or bone meal is beneficial, and hoof and horn in particular supplies slow acting nitrogen. Alternatively, use a balanced compound fertilizer. Also give an occasional top dressing of organic based fertilizer when plants are in full growth, but not after the end of June, otherwise leafy growth will develop and the sprouts will be loose and of poor quality. Make sure there is potash in the soil for this encourages firmness.

Sowings can be made under cloches or in the cold frame during February. The resultant seedlings should be pricked out 8 cm (3 ins) apart in prepared beds under other cloches or frames but must not be coddled. Subsequently they can be moved to prepared open ground sites.

The main outdoor sowings for succession should not be attempted before April, following good weather in March. It is also possible to make open ground sowings in August or early September. In normal seasons, these plants stand the weather well. Sowing at various times ensures a crop of sprouts over an extended period, although improved modern strains make autumn sowings unnecessary so long as early spring sowings are made. All outdoor sowings must be thinned out early, to ensure sturdy growth followed by firm sprouts.

Once the seedlings are 10–12 cm (4–5 ins) tall, which will usually be from early May onwards, they should be moved to their final positions. Choose a showery period for the job or water the plants in. Space the dwarf sorts 75 cm ($2\frac{1}{2}$ ft) apart and the tall, strong growing varieties 90 cm (3 ft) apart. This spacing allows for an early catch crop of lettuce, radish or spinach to be grown between the rows. Where a large number of plants are being grown, the growing points of some specimens can be pinched out when the buttons are beginning to form, to ensure that all the plants do not mature together. It also helps the buttons to develop firmly.

Since Brussels sprouts like firm root conditions, tread the soil if it is puffy, before planting. Weeds must be kept down and decayed leaves on the Brussels' stems removed to prevent grey mould from developing. Always use up loose, blown buttons first, but do not cut off the top of the plants until all the buttons have been picked. The head of the plant gives protection and helps in the growth of the buttons.

Picking will normally commence from late October onwards and provided suc-

min C, with smaller quantities of vitamins A and B and also calcium and iron. They are usually divided or classified as 1 spring cabbage, 2 summer and autumn cabbages, 3 winter varieties, including savoys. Botanically the savoy is *Brassica oleracea* var *bullata* and originated in Savoy, France; they are described below.

Sow cabbages in prepared seed beds in drills about 18 mm ($\frac{1}{2}$ ins) deep and 15 cm (6 ins) apart. As a precaution against club root, sprinkle calomel dust along each drill. Where cabbage rootfly has been a problem use Bromophos insecticide. This applies to all the cabbage family. Lightly firm the soil after sowing to assist germination. Do not leave the plants too long in the seed bed or they may become thin and drawn, with a poor root system.

Where possible spring maturing sorts should be given light ground, since this warms up quickly and encourages rapid development. If cabbages follow a well manured crop such as peas or beans there will be sufficient bulk in the soil. If humus is not present it will pay to work in decayed manure, compost or similar material. In the absence of any of these bulky types of manures peat or leaf mould can be used, plus a good dressing of fish manure. Lime is needed by all brassicas and if the soil is acid a dusting of garden lime should be applied as a top dressing before planting out.

To provide cabbages throughout the year means sowing seeds at different times. Cabbages to mature in late spring or early

Round-headed cabbages of the Dutch type mature from October to February

summer should be sown in late July, when they can follow early potatoes or peas. Transplant in September or October making the rows 45 cm (18 ins) apart with 22—30 cm (9—12 ins) between the plants. If, in April, the plants are growing slowly, an application of Nitro-chalk 35—50 g per m² (1—1$\frac{1}{2}$ oz per sq yd) will encourage growth.

Summer and autumn maturing cabbages are sown from February onwards under glass and outdoors from March onwards. Sow these little and often to ensure that all the plants do not mature together.

A sowing of the summer sorts can also be made in January or February in the cool greenhouse or frame. Plants from these sowings are planted outdoors in April.

Sow winter cabbages from the end of April to late May, the seedlings being planted out when the soil is moist. They need wider spacing than the earlier sorts. Make the rows up to 60 cm (2 ft) apart with 38—45 cm (15—18 ins) between plants. As soon as they can be handled thin the seedlings 5 cm (2 ins) apart. When they are about 15 cm (6 ins) transfer them to their final quarters.

Late cabbages may need extra phosphate and more potash to enable them to stand winter weather. Spring cabbages can be helped by applying a dusting of Nitro-chalk along the rows. Any spring cabbages which fail to heart may be used as spring greens.

Red cabbages are usually grown for pickling, but are very useful as an unusual

winter vegetable cooked with onions, apple and a little spice, or chopped raw as a colourful variation on coleslaw. Sow in March, eventually spacing the plants 45 cm (18 ins) apart. They are better after they have been touched by frost. A distinct type of very hardy winter cabbage, it will stand quite severe frosts without harm. Savoys have deeply crinkled leaves and this seems to be the reason why some people do not grow them, preferring, instead, the smooth leaves of the cabbage. Properly cooked, savoys are tasty and especially valuable in northern areas and other cold districts.

They grow in ordinary soil which has been well cultivated and can be used to follow early potatoes or peas. The ground will probably have been manured for these crops, so that all that needs doing is to fork over the surface and, if the soil is acid, give a dusting of lime. On poor land compost or fish manure can be worked in. Make the ground firm before planting.

Seed is sown in April, the plants being moved to their final positions in July, preferably during showery weather, otherwise the ground should be watered. Allow 60 cm (2 ft) each way for the bigger-growing sorts and 45 cm (18 ins) for the smaller kinds.

RECOMMENDED VARIETIES: spring maturing varieties: 'April', 'Durham Early', 'Hispi', 'Offenham Flower of Spring', 'Wheeler's Imperial'; summer maturing: 'Extra Earlihead', 'Greyhound', 'Golden Acre', 'Hidena',

Cardoons tied up for blanching

'Derby Day' is a good summer cabbage

'Vienna', 'Winnigstadt'; autumn and winter maturing: 'Christmas Drumhead', 'Winter White'. Savoys: in order of maturing, from October to April: 'Dwarf Green Curled', 'Best of All', 'January King', 'Ormskirk Late', and 'Alexander's No. 1'. Red cabbage: 'Niggerhead', 'Ruby Ball'.

Savoy cabbages like 'Best of All' are very hardy

CARDOON *Cynara cardunculus*

A near relative of the globe artichoke, this handsome plant has silvery, fern-like foliage. It is grown for its blanched stalks, which are not unlike the chards produced by globe artichokes. These are used in the same way as celery, both subjects requiring similar culture.

Cardoons like a rich, moist soil and succeed in trenches about 30 cm (1 ft) deep and 20 cm (8 ins) wide, where there is rotted manure or decayed compost at the bottom.

Plants can sometimes be bought but usually, they are raised from seed sown from March onwards, keeping the roots moist throughout summer. Occasional applications of liquid manure will encourage good, tender growth.

From mid-September the plants will be ready for blanching. One method is to tie all the leaves together and then earth up as for celery, or corrugated tubes can be placed over the plants. Alternatively, bracken or straw can be used for a covering. The blanching process takes eight or nine weeks. The stems should be dry before starting the blanching, or they may rot when earthed up. The balanced stalks and inner leaves that are used in salads, soups and stews.

RECOMMENDED VARIETIES: there are two types – the French cardoon, often listed as Tours, has long stems with prickles which makes it difficult to work with. The spineless Spanish cardoon has less flavour and the plants apt to run to seed.

CARROT *Daucus carota* var *sativus*

The carrot is probably unequalled by any other vegetable as a source of vitamin A, and the roots also contain quantities of vitamin B and C.

Although there are white and yellow carrots, it is the orange and orange-red varieties which are usually grown. Colour is important, since it is directly related to the carotin content, which is found in the outer layer of the root. Heavy foliage indicates a thick core, although it is necessary for the foliage to be strong enough to allow for easy pulling.

This crop likes a deep soil where the moisture content can be maintained at a good level. Drought conditions affect the size and texture of the roots. Plenty of organic matter should be in the soil, but where manure is not well rotted, the roots become forked.

Sowing time extends over a long period, and in favourable seasons drilling can start in February, using a stump-rooted variety such as 'Nantes'. Cloches can be used to secure a very early crop. To facilitate even,

thin sowing, seed should be mixed with sand and some gardeners make this moist, to encourage quick germination. The drills should be about 6–13 mm ($\frac{1}{4}$–$\frac{1}{2}$ in) deep and about 30 cm (12 ins) apart, the surface being lightly firmed after sowing.

Carrotfly can be a menace, and is best controlled by thin sowing and disturbing the foliage as little as possible, and dusting drills with Bromophos.

Late sowings can be made in July, with early or quick maturing varieties. These will provide tender young roots in autumn and early winter. These normally escape the carrotfly.

Although shorthorn varieties are excellent for growing under cloches or early outdoor sowings, they do not produce the weight of crop yielded by the intermediate and long rooted type.

The intermediate varieties are best for most soils, since they do not need such a great depth of soil and there is less difficulty in storing than the long varieties.

RECOMMENDED VARIETIES: earlies 'Early Horn', 'Nantes', 'Early French Frame'; intermediate: 'Ormskirk Market', 'Chantenay', 'James Scarlet', 'Amsterdam Forcing'; long: 'St Valery', 'Vita Longa'.

CAULIFLOWER (winter type)
Brassica oleracea var botrytis

Once known as heading broccoli winter cauliflower. Most winter varieties fold their leaves protectively over the curd. Summer cauliflower leaves tend to grow upright.

Winter cauliflowers grow on many types of soil so long as they are fertile. An open, but not exposed position is needed, and one not likely to become a frost pocket. Freshly manured ground is not required. Winter cauliflowers are best planted after early potatoes, beans, peas or lettuce. An application of lime is recommended. A dusting of superphosphate and sulphate of potash worked into the seed bed provides the phosphates young cauliflowers need. Avoid fertilizers rich in nitrogen for these encourage quick growth of plants that are easily damaged by frosts.

Bring the seed bed to a fine tilth for even germination and lumpy soil gives cover to flea-beetles. Sowing time is from early April onwards according to soil, weather and variety. Make the drills 13 mm ($\frac{1}{2}$ in) deep and 23 cm (9 in) apart. Sow thinly and after dusting the drills with calomel powder as a

Early carrot 'Nantes' is of French origin

precaution against club root lightly firm the soil after covering the seed. Keep the bed weed-free by frequent light hoeings or hand pullings. Ground reserved for cauliflowers should be well-cultivated making the surface firm but not hard. Do not leave the plants in the seed bed too long or they will

'St Valery' is one of the most popular long carrots

become thin and lanky and never produce good heads.

Discard coarse, poorly shaped, badly coloured plants and any without growing points. Ideal seedlings have short sturdy stems, plenty of fibrous roots and four or five good coloured leaves. This should be the size if you have to buy plants. Dull, showery weather is the best time to move the plants but if it becomes necessary to transplant during dry periods water the seedlings in. The old practice was to 'puddle' the plants. It consists of mixing soil, cow dung and water in a bucket and putting the roots in it. This mixture clings to the roots and supplies moisture for some time.

Do not plant cauliflowers too closely. Smaller growing sorts, which include the increasingly popular Australian varieties, should be placed 45 cm (18 ins) apart with 60 cm (2 ft) between the rows, but most varieties need to be 60 cm (2 ft) apart with 67–75 cm (27–30 ins) from row to row. Close spacing prevents plants from developing fully and makes it easy for disease to

gain a hold. Plant firmly and keep the hoe moving, particularly until the plants are established. Draw the soil towards the plant stems for this anchors the plants more firmly, giving protection and preventing moisture settling round the stems.

Cut the heads as they mature. Left too long they continue to grow and the good tight head of curds will open out and turn a poor colour and become 'ricey'. Early morning sun can damage the curds. To prevent this, heel over the plants in November so that the heads face the north. This is done by taking some soil away from the north side of the plants and pulling them over, then place the soil on the opposite side from where it was taken, making it nicely firm.

If heads mature faster than needed, they can be kept back a bit by bending a leaf or two over the centre of the plants, which also gives protection from frost. If the entire plant is pulled up and hung in a dry, airy place the curds will remain in a good condition for seven to fourteen days.

RECOMMENDED VARIETIES: autumn and winter use: 'Veitch's Self Protecting' (August, September); 'Snow's Superb Winter White' (November onwards); 'St Agnes' (December—January). Australian varieties include: 'Boomerang Bondi' (September); 'Kangaroo' (August—October); 'Barrier Reef' (late October); 'Canberra' (October—November) and 'Snowcap' (November—December).

For spring use: 'Leamington' (March—April); 'Markanta' (April—May).

For summer use: 'Royal Oak' (May—June); 'Asmer June' and 'Asmer Midsummer' (June).

CELERIAC *Apium graveolens* var *rapaceum*

This is the delicious turnip-rooted or knob celery with a nutty flavour not found in other vegetables. Splendid for winter use, it can be grown where celery has proved difficult to cultivate. It is at its best from mid-October onwards. The roots can be peeled and boiled or grated and used in salads.

Since celeriac is planted on the flat it means less work than is needed for celery. Best results come where an open sunny position is provided. Dig the ground deeply during the winter adding farmyard manure

or compost. Leave the surface rough for the weather to break down, and apply a dusting of lime.

Sow the seeds in a pot or box of light compost in March in a cool greenhouse or closed frame where the temperature is not less than 15°C (60°F). Keep the compost moist to prevent a check to growth. Harden off the seedlings in a cold frame before planting out in May.

It is helpful if mature compost or peat is worked into the bed. Alternatively balanced fertilizer at 100–140 g per m² (3–4 oz per sq yd) will be beneficial. Space the plants 30–38 cm (12–15 ins) apart with 45 cm (18 ins) between rows. Plant so that the little bulbous-like roots just rest on the top of the soil. Remove all side-shoots and make sure there is no shortage of moisture.

Excepting in cold districts where the roots should be stored in boxes of sand in a shed, lift roots as required. During the winter a covering of straw or bracken will be helpful. At the end of October, lightly earth up the plants as a protection against frosts.

RECOMMENDED VARIETIES: 'Giant Prague', hardy; 'Early Erfurt', a smaller, earlier variety and 'Globus' of good flavour and cooking qualities.

CELERY *Apium graveolens*

Celery was originally cultivated for its medicinal qualities, but is now widely grown as a vegetable. It was derived from the wild plant sometimes known as 'smallage' which grows in moist places in many parts of the world. A biennial plant, it is eaten raw or cooked, while considerable quantities are now canned for use.

Moisture loving, celery does best in peaty or similar soils where there is a high water-table, but this does not mean a water-logged position. Acid soil suits this plant better than chalky soil.

Celery is often grown on the 'flat', blanching being done by covering the stems with 'collars' or even drainpipes. For finest results trenches are best. Make them 38 cm (15 ins) wide for single rows and 45 cm (18 ins) or more where double rows are being grown. Dig them 45–60 cm (12–18 ins) deep and throw the soil equally on both sides of the trench, where it can, if required, be used to grow a catch crop such as lettuce or radishes. When growing a double row, the plants should be placed side by side and not zig-zag as is usually done with a double row. This makes it easier for blanching. If more

than one double row is grown, allow at least 90 cm (3 ft) between them. Better plants are secured from single rows. Should side shoots develop, pull them off.

For the earliest sticks, sow seed from the third week in February into early March. Make the main sowings during March and April. The later sowings are less likely to produce plants which 'bolt' — especially likely with self-blanching types sown too early. Sow very thinly in boxes or pots of seed compost. Give a light covering of seed compost, firm the surface and apply a sprinkling of water. Cover with glass and paper and keep in a temperature of 15°C (60°F) until growth is seen. Then remove the covering and when the seedlings can be handled easily, prick them off into other boxes. After ten days or so, remove them to a frame or cloches for hardening off. As far as possible, lift the plants from the seed box with plenty of soil on their roots. This will lessen the check. Unless it is showery, give the soil a good watering after planting firmly during late May. Frequent sprayings of clear water will prove beneficial during spells of dry weather. Once established, the plants revel in plenty of moisture, while good growth can be encouraged by applying a dried blood solution or a well balanced fertilizer. Keep side shoots and decayed leaves removed. A sprinkling of weathered soot over the leaves deters celery fly.

Blanching is done by earthing up, a process which must be carried out gradually. It is usually possible to add at least 15 cm (6 ins) of soil at each operation, which will have to be repeated at least three times at 14 day intervals. The roots should be moist and the leaves dry when this job is done. Tie the stems with raffia or the corrugated paper round them so that the soil does not enter the centre of the plants. The leaves should be left exposed and the soil made smooth and steep, so that rain is deflected.

The blanching process takes seven or eight weeks. During severe frosts celery plants should be protected by straw, bracken or similar material, removing it when mild conditions return. Blanching can also be achieved by wrapping brown or corrugated paper around the plants, tying it with raffia so that water does not remain inside.

RECOMMENDED VARIETIES: white: 'Giant White', 'Invincible', and 'Wareings Dwarf White'; Pink or red: 'Giant Red'.

Celery grown in trenches is generally superior in flavour

Celery, Self Blanching. Most useful where space is limited or where the gardener does not wish to make trenches. It is not difficult to cultivate this crop, which requires soil rich in organic matter. Farmyard manure worked into the ground some months before planting will be beneficial. Failing manure, use bulky organic material such as ripe compost, peat or leaf mould with a good sprinkling of bone meal.

Apart from open ground culture, self-blanching celery can be grown where a modified form of French gardening is practiced. On suitable, well-manured soils hot bed frames can be used effectively for this celery which can follow early carrots or globe beet. All that is needed is to dig and clean the ground, adding a good sprinkling of balanced organic fertilizer, or hoof and horn meal.

Of the white and cream varieties, 'Golden Self Blanching' is the most popular, while 'American Green' is crisp and tender. The fine seeds should not be sown until early March, earlier sowings being liable to run to seed. It is a mistake to sow deeply and the lightest possible covering of finely sifted soil is sufficient. Afterwards, water with a fine rosed can. Germination is often slow, largely depending on the temperature.

Once growth is seen, ventilation should be given and early pricking out 5—8 cm (2—3 ins) apart is essential. Later move them to the open ground or frames allowing 23 cm (9 ins) each way.

The basic cultural operations are hoeing, weeding, watering, and leafspot control. The close planting suggested leads to blanched stems but additional help can be given by placing clean, dry straw between the rows ten days before the crop is gathered, which it must be prior to severe frosts.

Self-blanching celery is available from the end of August onwards, before ordinary celery is ready. Generally speaking the flavour of self-blanching celery is not as good as trenched celery.

RECOMMENDED VARIETIES: 'American Green' selections include 'Greensnap' and 'Utah Green'; 'Golden Self Blanching' selections, include 'Golden Elite' and 'Monarch Self Blanching'; 'Lathom Self Blanching'.

CELTUCE *Lactuca sativa*

Coming from China, this unusual vegetable is quite easy to grow, although it has never become really popular. It should be sown

'Solid-White' celery is an old favourite

Right: Forcing chicory in pots. Cut off top of roots above crown. Trim ends if necessary. Place 5 roots to a 22.5-cm (9-in) pot and cover completely with another pot to exclude light. Keep in a warm place (10°C/50°F min) for 4 weeks before harvesting blanched chicons with sharp knife

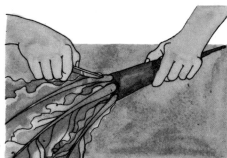

from the end of April onwards, covering the seeds with 12 mm (½ in) of fine soil and allowing 30 cm (12 ins) between the rows. It is advisable to sow little and often and to thin the plants so they finally stand 23—25 cm (9—10 ins) apart.

Celtuce is sometimes referred to as the 'two in one' vegetable, since the leaves, which have a high vitamin content, can be used as lettuce, whilst the heart or crisp central stem is often eaten raw in salads or cooked in the same way as celery.

CHICORY *Cichorium intybus*

This crop is grown for the thick stalks and ribs of its leaves which, when blanched, are eaten in salads or boiled. The Brussels Witloof chicory particularly, should be grown for providing a delicious salading in winter and spring. This becomes available when lettuce and endive are usually scarce and expensive to buy. It can also be eaten like celery, with cheese, and can be stewed and served with melted butter in the same way as seakale. It is the Magdeburg chicory which, after drying, roasting and grinding the roots, is used for mixing with coffee.

Sow seed from late May onwards, in rows 45 cm (18 ins) apart, thinning the seedlings to 30 cm (1 ft) apart. Select a well-worked soil, plentifully supplied with organic matter which does not dry out. A dressing of fish manure 100 g per m² (3 oz per sq yd) will be helpful.

In October, forcing begins in succession when roots are lifted from the open ground. The best roots for forcing are about 5 cm (2 ins) in diameter. Chicory can be forced in sheds, but a cool or cold greenhouse is better. A forcing pit with a temperature of not less than 10°C (50°F) is ideal for growing chicory or a special place can be reserved at one end of the greenhouse.

The procedure is simple. Make a trench 30 cm (1 ft) deep and 60 cm (2 ft) wide, fork the bottom and place the roots upright and close together. Water in when the trench is full of roots. Soil from the second trench can be used to cover the roots in the first trench and watered to wash the soil around the roots. Then place the remainder of the soil over the roots to a depth of 23–25 cm (9–10 ins). The last soil covering must be dry to ensure clean, healthy heads. Chicory is ready for cutting when the sprouting shoots, known as chicons, show through the soil. Keep them out of the light or they will turn green and become bitter and useless.

Another method is to cut off the leaves to within an inch of the crown at the end of September. Then earth up as for celery. Supplies of delicious heads will then be available from December onwards.

RECOMMENDED VARIETIES: A fairly new variety, 'Sugar Loaf' (Pain de Sucre) can be strongly recommended. This has the appearance of a well grown cos lettuce with a long standing solid head, most useful for salading. 'Red Verona', is another good variety which when forced, produces a compact red head. Both these varieties should be cultivated as for endive and are excellent salad vegetables.

CHINESE CABBAGE (Chinese Leaves) *Brassica cernua*

More like a cos lettuce than a cabbage, with green leaves forming an oval or oblong head. This crop has for many centuries been widely used in China. It is only in this century that it has attracted attention elsewhere, firstly in the United States. Chinese cabbage is now becoming increasingly popular, since it has many uses and, after picking, keeps in the refrigerator more satisfactorily than lettuce.

The plants are rapid growing and must be used immediately they mature otherwise they throw up flower heads and become useless. Frosts will spoil the plants. If the soil becomes dry in hot weather the leaves are inclined to wilt badly and lose their freshness.

Sow at intervals from mid-June to early August, making the drills 60 cm (2 ft) apart and 2 cm ($\frac{1}{2}$ in) deep, thinning the seedlings

Chinese cabbage is easy to grow and can be cooked or used in salads

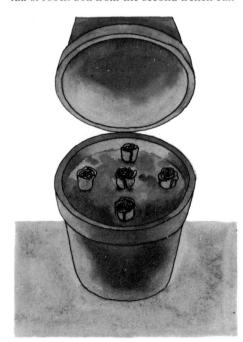

so there is 23 cm (9 in) between them. Chinese cabbages do not transplant well and are at their best during a damp season. They should be watered generously during dry spells.

As the elongated heads develop, a tie or two of raffia should be placed around the outer leaves to ensure the formation of a good blanched head. The heads are cut complete as with cabbage. The leaves can be used as a substitute for lettuce or steamed or boiled. They should be cooked very quickly. There is no unpleasant cabbage smell when they are cooked.

RECOMMENDED VARIETIES: 'Chili', tender, crisp, spicy flavour; 'Pe tsai', pure white, cos lettuce-like heads when blanched; 'Michili', growing 38–45 cm (15–18 ins) tall, and up to 7–10 cm (3–4 ins) in diameter; 'Wong Bok', large, tender juicy heads; 'Sampan', large squat heads.

CHINESE MUSTARD *Brassica juncea*

Widely used in the United States and parts of North America and sometimes in tins or cans in this country, Chinese mustard is not unlike the better known Chinese cabbage, with its loose distinctive, rather open habit of growth. It is hardy and can resist hot, dry weather when many other forms of green stuff fail to grow well and are in short supply.

Growing about 60 cm (2 ft) high, it has several common names including mustard greens, mustard spinach and tender greens, and it is sometimes used as a substitute for spinach. The flavour is quite strong.

Seed can be sown from April to August. Make the rows 38 cm (15 ins) apart and thin the seedlings so there is about 15 cm (6 ins) between them. In fairly rich, moist soil, growth is rapid and it is often possible to gather a useful picking of leaves within seven or eight weeks of sowing. If the ground is on the poor side, it should be enriched before planting and when in growth, the plants can be encouraged to make more leaves by applying a nitrogenous fertilizer.

Plants left unused will quickly run to seed, so it is advisable to cut down the entire plant at ground level rather than picking off individual leaves as is done with spinach or with leaf lettuce.

The succulent leaves of Chinese Mustard 'Pak-Choi' grow up to 50 cm (20 in) long

CORN SALAD *Valerianella locusta*

This is also known as Lamb's Lettuce and there are several good forms. Eat the leaves raw or cooked. Easily grown, it is a useful substitute for lettuce during the winter. This crop can follow early potatoes, peas or broccoli. Make the drills 19 mm ($\frac{3}{4}$ in) deep and 30 cm (1 ft) apart.

Sowings can be made at intervals from the end of July until the end of September

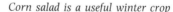

Corn salad is a useful winter crop

to provide supplies from autumn until spring. The young plants should be thinned out so there is 15 cm (6 ins) between them. They make an excellent cloche crop.

Cress

Several distinct plants fall into this group, but all are eaten raw in salads.

CRESS *Ledpidium sativum*

This is the plain leaved or common cress which is easy to grow in trays or pots or on the greenhouse bench in beds of finely sifted soil. The curled or double cress is preferred by some gardeners although there is no difference in flavour. Known in Britain for over 400 years, cress was at one time valued for the medicinal properties in the seed. It is useful for its food value since it contains vitamins C and B1 while it is beneficial when used for green manuring.

White mustard is a member of the cabbage family and best known for its part in 'mustard and cress'. An annual plant, it is a native of Britain, and other European countries. Black or brown mustard is not really suitable for salad purposes since the leaves are so hot and unpalatable. *Brassica napus* or agricultural rape is often used instead of white mustard for salad purposes. Its leaves maintain their colour well and do not decay as quickly as mustard.

Seed can be sown under glass during the autumn and winter, when it will provide valuable salad material. It is also in demand throughout the spring and summer. If both crops are to mature together sow cress four days before mustard. A minimum temperature of 10°C (50°F) is suitable and a fine, fairly rich, nicely moist compost should be used. The seeds need only be pressed in and not covered with soil. After sowing place damp paper or hessian over the receptacles or seed beds, removing it as soon as growth is seen. This prevents the surface soil from drying out and encourages germination.

Bulb bowls filled with bulb fibre will grow excellent crops and where small quantities are required seeds can be sown directly into small punnets or pots. Keep them in the dark for a few days until long stems have been made; then bring them into light so the leaves become green.

Seed can also be sown outdoors on slightly raised beds.

Sufficient moisture must always be available. If the compost is nicely damp at sowing time no further watering need be carried out until the seedlings have established themselves and are growing well.

LAND CRESS (American Cress)

In spite of its name this plant is hardly known in America. An excellent substitute for watercress, the tender young leafy shoots are used in salads. It does not require water in the same way as the normal watercress and is much easier to manage. The plants appreciate semi-shade and do well in a north border, succeeding in town gardens and in damp situations that other crops will not tolerate.

Make the first sowings in late March to give pickings from late June onwards. Prepare a seed bed with plenty of organic material. Bring the surface to a fine tilth and sow in drills 20—23 cm (8—9 ins) apart and 13 mm ($\frac{1}{2}$ in) deep. Alternatively, broadcast the seed thinly and rake it into the surface. Cloches or frames encourage quicker growth. Do not thin the seedlings; leave them to grow like well-spaced mustard and cress. The soil should be kept moist for continued production.

Seed of American or Belle Isle perennial cress can also be sown in August and wintered under a well-ventilated frame for early spring pickings. Protection may be necessary during severe weather. Keep the soil just moist or the plants may rot. There is a less common variety known as Australian cress, which has pointed leaves of a mild agreeable flavour.

Mustard and cress are easy to grow

Land Cress, a hybrid form, is less susceptible to frost than other cresses

WATERCRESS *Nasturtium officinale*

This nutritious crop is available over a long period when other salad ingredients are scarce. It has a higher mineral content than lettuce and salad onions, and contains useful quantities of vitamins C and B1.

One reason why some people say they dislike watercress is that they so often see it sold as a bundle of discoloured, wizened, leafy stalks.

Henslow, in his book on 'The Use of British Plants' says the Latin name is derived from *nasus* – the nose, and *tortus* – twisted, from the pungent sensation. It was familiar to the Ancient Greeks as *kardomon*, and was used in salads. It was also valued for its medicinal virtues. Its nutritive value is attributed to its aromatic oil and exceptionally high mineral content.

Watercress is divided into two main groups, the green which is available in summer, and the more popular brown or winter strains. The green form produces long shoots which do not always branch well. This is a drawback if the growing area is limited. In addition, the plants seem only to flourish where the temperature of the water rises appreciably during spring and summer. This has the advantage of making them suitable for growing in streams and other shallow water. The depth of colour seems to depend on both climatic conditions and water temperature.

Phillip Miller in 1754 records 'that many people preferred these herbs for their

Clear streams are the natural habitat of watercress

agreeable warm, bitter taste; and being accounted an excellent remedy for the scurvy and to cleanse the blood'.

Watercress can be propagated from seed or cuttings. With the former, sow from mid-June to mid-August on an almost dry seed bed.

Sprinkle the seed thinly over the soil, then water lightly to encourage germination which normally takes a week. The little plants soon form a tap root. The seed bed should then be pressed down to firm the soil to encourage a mat of roots to form at the bottom of the bed.

Anyone who has a constant supply of water can grow cress in specially constructed beds. Water from natural springs is warmer in winter than that of streams.

While running water is ideal for growing watercress, a crop can be grown without it. Select a shaded position where the soil is rich and moist in summer. If the site is naturally on the dry side make trenches up to 20 cm (8 ins) deep and filled with vegetable compost, covering this with 5 cm (2 ins) of soil, so the surface is a little below the surrounding soil.

If you already have watercress plants it will be easy to strike cuttings from the sturdy shoots. Do this in May and June for autumn and winter cropping, and in September and October for spring and summer cutting; the brown variety is best for later cutting.

Watercress is rarely, if ever, attacked by diseases, and if the beds are kept free from rubbish, slugs will not be a nuisance.

CUCUMBER & GHERKIN *Cucumis sativus*

Indoor Good greenhouse or frame grown cucumbers cannot be bettered for flavour, but they do require rather more care in their cultivation than many other less fussy vegetables.

Preparation of the growing area is important, and there is nothing better than good clean straw, horse manure and turfy loam which has not been stacked too long. Old loam will have lost a good deal of its fibre and will be inclined to dry out frequently. Tests have shown that two parts of loam to one of strawy manure is about right. Bone meal and hoof and horn can be mixed either separately with the loam or when it has been mixed with the manure. An 8 cm (3 in) potful of chalk to each barrow load of loam will boost sturdy growth.

Sow seed in standard 35 × 23 cm (14 × 9 ins) seed boxes or in pans, filling them with compost made from good clean fibrous loam and well-rotted horse manure, to within 13 mm ($\frac{1}{2}$ in) of the top. Use a fairly gritty, not too fine a soil mixture.

Cover the boxes with glass and paper and place them on the staging in a temperature of at least 18°C (65°F). Rapid germination is required and this usually takes place within three days. The glass is then removed.

From this time on a moist atmosphere is needed. Take care not to damage the roots of the seedlings when they are being moved. (Some gardeners prefer to sow directly into small pots to avoid this transplanting). The seedlings will need more root room within a fortnight of sowing and as further growth proceeds repot into 13 cm (5 in) and then into 15 cm (6 in) pots. Maintain night temperature of at least 18°C (65°F). A continuous humid atmosphere is necessary but the roots must not lie wet.

When the plants are well-established (about a month after sowing) they will be ready for their final positions. Make the holes in the bed large enough to drop in the ball of soil and roots, and carefully firm the soil around the little stems. Allow at least 60 cm (2 ft) between the plants each way. Place a stake near each plant so they can climb up to the horizontal wires.

Keep on training the growths up the wires and regularly take out the growing points. Allow the main stem to grow to the top of the wire, when it should be stopped.

Two cucumber plants in a greenhouse will be enough for a family's needs

This encourages fruiting and the development of side shoots which in turn will need to be stopped at the second joint and tied in. Developing sub-laterals must be stopped at the first joint, this process continuing until growth slows down and energy concentrated on the remaining shoots.

Most plants have male and female flowers and the males should be removed, as they are not needed for fertilization. The female flowers are easily distinguished by the swollen 'bulb' (embryonic fruit) behind the petals. You will find that if the flowers are fertilized, not only is the cropping capacity of the plants lessened, but also that the fruits have a bitter taste.

Several varieties producing all female flowers are available, such as 'Fertila' and 'Femdan', which crop heavily and produce fruit free from bitterness.

Cutting must be done regularly once the plants come into bearing. The time taken for fruit to develop depends on the season. January sowings do not usually mature until late March, but from spring sowings cutting should be possible in about seven or eight weeks.

Some years ago, as a result of various trials, cordon training systems were developed. Such plants are exceptional for the sustained vigour and first class fruits which are produced within six weeks of sowing. The individual fruits are straight and attractive in appearance. The weight and quality of the crop depends entirely upon the skill of the individual grower. It is customary to wind the plants up strings as is done with tomatoes.

Sow the seeds in trays or pots covering them with a 6 mm ($\frac{1}{4}$ in) layer of moist soil. Once germination occurs, gradually bring the seedlings to full light and pot them on about the third day, before they straighten up. From then on, keep the compost moist. The first stopping of the growing point causes shoots to break out rapidly from the base. These should be rubbed out the moment they are seen.

Fruits begin to appear in clusters of five to seven at the base of the rough leaves, and provided the plants are in good condition all should be allowed to mature; they are soon ready for cutting. Care is needed with the first fruits. If possible they should be spaced equally around the stem and should not touch the soil, otherwise they will become mis-shapen. Following the pinching at the second rough leaf, shoots are nipped back again at the next leaf and this stopping at the leaf joints continues as long as there is vigorous upward growth.

Fruit clusters result from each stopping.

After the first fruits have matured and are harvested, a second crop of larger clusters will emerge from the joints, and these usually need thinning to get good shaped high quality fruits.

An oddity I have grown is the so-called Serpent Cucumber, the fruit of which curl round like a snake, and are 90—120 cm (3—4 ft) long. Grow it in the same way as ordinary cucumbers.

Outdoor or ridge These cucumbers should be grown in fairly rich soil, avoiding fresh manure. Plant them on little mounds, with well rotted manure being placed at the bottom of the hole. Seed is sown in the warm greenhouse or frame in April and once the first leaves have developed, pot plants singly into 7 cm ($2\frac{1}{2}$ ins) pots, where they can remain until planted outdoors at the end of May. Alternatively, sow outdoors in early May, placing two seeds at each station.

Allow 45–60 cm ($1\frac{1}{2}$–2 ft) between the plants, spacing the rows 60–75 cm (2–$2\frac{1}{2}$ ft) apart. It is wise to nip out the growing point when the stems are about 38 cm (15 ins) long. This encourages branching and each lateral shoot is then stopped one leaf beyond the first fruit. Plenty of moisture is needed during dry weather.

RECOMMENDED VARIETIES: 'Bedfordshire Prize' and 'Nadir' an F_1 hybrid producing long fruit of outstanding quality. Less common is 'Crystal Apple' producing round creamy-white fruit the shape of a good sized apple.

There are several F_1 Burpless hybrids, all of which are valuable since they are not indigestible. Remarkable long-fruited Japanese varieties include 'Chinese Long Green', smooth skinned fruits up to 60 cm (2 ft) in length and 38 mm ($1\frac{1}{2}$ ins) in diameter. 'Ladora' is a good 'all female' greenhouse cucumber.

'Patio-Pik' is a compact grower which crops heavily, while 'Fembaby' is a vigorous F_1 hybrid producing only female flowers, and has shapely green fruits up to 20 cm (8 ins) long.

Above: 'Kyoto' is a Japanese variety of cucumber that can be grown outdoors. Below: Gherkins are ridge cucumbers picked at 10 cm (4 in) long

Gherkin The gherkin proper, *C. anguria*, is a weed, native to the U.S.A., whose immature fruits are used for pickling. In Europe the vegetable used in this way is the immature fruit of the ridge cucumber. If grown for pickling, the aim should be to produce succulent fruits up to 10 cm (4 ins) long. To ensure this, gather them before they become large and coarse.

General culture is the same as for cucumbers, the main difference being that plants rarely transplant satisfactorily. It is therefore best to sow seeds where they are to remain. Do this in early summer on well prepared and enriched sites. Bulky manure or compost encourages a good root system. Place the seeds 2.5 cm (1 in) deep and if two are put in stations 60 cm (2 ft) apart the weakest seedling can be removed when the plants are growing well.

RECOMMENDED VARIETIES: 'Boston Pickling' is one of the finest, producing good coloured juicy fruit. 'Parisian Pickling' and the American 'Ohio' are reliable.

ENDIVE *Cichorium endivia*

This salad plant is not grown as much as it deserves. An annual, belonging to the chicory family, it has been cultivated in Britain since the sixteenth century. Endive resembles lettuce, although the plants have to be blanched before use, otherwise they will have a bitter taste. Now that lettuces are expensive in winter, there is good reason for growing endive, which is in season from November to April.

This crop prefers a well drained, sandy loam with a dry sub-soil. The ground need not be freshly manured or very rich, but the plants do best in soils with a high humus

Blanching improves the flavour of endive

content. Work in a good general fertilizer, preferably of organic origin, such as fish meal at 100 g per m² (3 oz per sq yd) before sowing seed.

The earliest sowings should be made in March on a hot bed, in heated frames or under cloches. Plant out the resultant seedlings from mid-May onwards. Outdoors, successional sowings may be made from late May until late August. Space the drills 38 cm (15 ins) apart, and gradually thin out the seedlings, so that there is about 30 cm (1 ft) between them.

The plants will be ready for blanching about 12 weeks after sowing. This can be done by tying them with raffia or covering with slates, boards, inverted flower pots with the drainage holes blocked, or with rough hay or litter. Blanching takes six or seven days and it is best to cover a few plants at a time. Make sure they are dry at the time, or the leaves will rot. Excepting in warm, south-western districts, move the later sowings to frames or cloches for blanching to be carried out.

RECOMMENDED VARIETIES: There are two distinct types of endive, curled and plain leaved. Of the former, 'Ruffec' and 'Meaux' are first class. The plain leaved sort, such as 'Batavian Green', is best for winter work, being hardier than the curled types.

FLORENCE FENNEL *Foeniculum vulgare* var *dulce*

Though related to the herb common fennel, Florence fennel differs in that it is grown as an annual, is smaller, and is cultivated for the bulbous stem rather than the foliage.

Raw sliced fennel goes well in salads. Cooked, it goes well with pork and chicken or in fish dishes. The flavour is anise-like.

Florence fennel needs a warm summer to do well. Sow seeds outside in April after working a light dressing of all-purpose fertilizer into the soil. Sow in shallow drills 45 cm (18 ins) apart, thinning the seedlings to 23–30 cm (9–12 ins) apart in the rows. Keep adequately watered. Earth the bulbs up as they begin to swell in order to blanch them. Harvest ripe bulbs as required from September. The leaves may be used as those of common fennel for flavouring. There are no named varieties of Florence fennel.

Both the bulbs and foliage of fennel can be used in cooking

142

GOOD KING HENRY
Chenopodium bonus—henricus

Sometimes known as Mercury or All Good. While dormant, this hardy plant carries a number of crowns which in early spring open to produce small green leaves, followed by light green fleshy shoots which bear clusters of green leaves at their growing points. These should be gathered and eaten in the same way as spinach which they resemble in flavour and for which they can be used as a substitute.

Good King Henry is an old-fashioned plant worth reviving

When young, these shoots are useful for including raw in salads. The more mature leaves should be cooked and eaten as spinach. Six or twelve shoots can be tied in bundles and gently cooked with just enough water to cover. The thick fleshy roots can be cooked and served with hot melted butter.

Seed is sown in the spring, the plants being finally spaced about 30 cm (1 ft) apart. Unlike asparagus, the plants can be cut the first year after planting. This subject is valued because it is rich in iron and other health giving properties.

These plants respond to an early spring mulching of decayed manure or compost. The top growth must not be covered.

HAMBURG PARSLEY *Petroselinum crispum* var *tuberosum*

This is a dual-purpose vegetable, the roots being used like parsnips or carrots and the tops as parsley. Perhaps this is not so surprising when it is remembered that parsley belongs to the same family as the carrot. As the name suggests, this crop is much used in Germany.

The soil should be prepared as is done for parsnips and seed is sown in deeply culti-vated ground from late March onwards. Make the drills 6 mm ($\frac{1}{4}$ ins) deep and 38 cm (15 ins) apart. Thin out the plants so that there is 15—20 cm (6—8 ins) between them. They like plenty of moisture during the growing season and should be kept free from weeds.

The foliage usually remains abundant in winter and can be used for flavouring. The roots can be used from early October on-wards. They are hardy and can be lifted as required, or taken up and stored in boxes of moist sand. Well grown, the roots will be 15—17 cm (6—7 ins) long and about 7—8 cm (3 ins) thick, and look much like parsnips.

KALE *Brassica oleracea* var *acephala*

This is a member of the large cabbage family and is sometimes known as borecole. One particular variety of kale was once eaten by Dutch peasants or Boers and became known as Boer's kale. Plain-leaved kales have the strongest flavour and are generally grown for feeding livestock though perfectly edible. The curly-leaved varieties are best for human consumption.

Kales are hardy and withstand severe weather conditions. Since they mature from February to April, they are valuable when there is little other greenstuff about. Soil containing organic matter leads to the heaviest yields. Lime should be present and badly drained positions and frost pockets avoided.

This is a crop which can follow early potatoes, peas or broad beans for which the

Kale is one of the hardiest cabbage plants

Roots and leaves of Hamburg Parsley

land was well-prepared. Where this is being done, it is not necessary to re-dig the ground, simply remove weeds and debris. Sow seed from late April onwards, a little earlier in northern districts. Most kales can be sown in beds for transplanting in the usual way, but 'Hungry Gap' is best sown where it is to grow.

Planting distances vary according to habit of growth. For the majority, allow 45 cm (18 ins) between plants with rows 60 cm (2 ft) apart. For 'Hungry Gap' allow 38 cm (15 ins) each way. If the central or growing point is removed in January it will encourage the side shoots. Kale should not be used too early but kept until spring when greenstuff is scarce.

RECOMMENDED VARIETIES include: 'Aspara-gus' kale which is now difficult to obtain. It produces in spring long thin shoots re-sembling asparagus which can be cooked in bundles in the same way.

'Cottagers' 75 cm (2$\frac{1}{2}$ ft) high has crinkled leaves on strong stems and is not particularly good flavoured. The 'Dwarf Green Curled' and 'Tall Green Curled' are hardy; the top part of the plant is first out to provide 'greens' and then the stem produces short shoots which are gathered in the same way as sprouting broccoli.

'Hungry Gap' is a hybrid sown in sum-mer for cropping the following spring when greenstuff is scarce. It is extremely hardy and withstands drought, wet and frost.

'Pentland Brig' is a fairly new kale bred in Scotland. Very hardy, it produces an abundant crop of shoots from February to April.

Ornamental kales with purple or silver-variegated leaves are very decorative. The leaves turn green when cooked.

Despite its name, kohl rabi 'Purple Vienna' has white flesh

KOHL RABI *Brassica oleracea* var *gongyloides*

This is a crop which must be grown quickly, otherwise it becomes tough. It should be used when the 'bulbs' are the size of a cricket ball. On light soils it is a good substitute for turnips which are liable to fail, and it has a distinct nutty flavour.

Sown from early March onwards, either broadcast or in drills 38 cm (15 ins) apart, the 'bulbs' will be ready from mid June. Thin the seedlings so there is 15–17 cm (6–7 ins) between them.

Kohl rabi is not particular as to soil so long as it contains plenty of humus matter and is well-drained. This hardy plant will usually come through the winter without harm but the roots will not keep for any length of time when stored.

Kohl rabi is not particularly susceptible to attacks by pests. The only disease likely to cause problems is club root. This is a member of the cabbage family, which is prone to this disease. Crop rotations will prevent a build-up.

RECOMMENDED VARIETIES: Although seedsmen normally offer the seeds simply as kohl rabi, there are several forms, including 'White Vienna' and 'Purple Vienna'.

LEEKS *Allium porrum*

Provided the ground has been deeply worked, leeks will grow in almost all moisture-retentive soils that drain well. The best position is one well-manured for a previous crop such as early cabbages or peas, which will be cleared from the ground in time to make room for leeks. Make sure the site selected does not lack lime.

Although the crop can be cultivated on the flat, the best method is to grow the plants in trenches. These should be taken out 25–30 cm (10–12 ins) deep, and 30 cm (1 ft) wide, for a single row, or 45 cm (18 ins) wide where a double row is being grown. Work decayed manure, compost or other organic matter into the bottom of the trench, on top of which place a layer of fine soil, to bring the depth of the trench to 15 cm (6 ins). Where bulky manure is not available, fish manure or bone meal can be used at 70–100 g per m² (2–3 oz per sq yd).

For the earliest crop a sowing can be made in January under glass in a temperature of 15–18°C (60–65°F) using trays or pans of seed compost. As soon as the seedlings can be handled prick them out into other boxes keeping them in full light near the glass in a temperature of around 12°C (54°F). Toward the end of March, move the plants to the cold frame for hardening off before planting outdoors in April and May.

Alternatively leeks can be raised under cloches from the end of February onwards. Make the rows 23 cm (9 ins) apart, and by the end of March or early April, the young plants can be left uncovered. Once they are 20–23 cm (8–9 ins) high they should be moved to their final positions.

When growing leeks on the flat make 15 cm (6 ins) deep dibber holes 20–30 cm (8–12 ins) apart, and drop the seedlings into them. Do not fill the holes with soil, instead, pour a little water into each hole. This will wash some soil over the roots which can be filled up as growth develops, although they often become full naturally. If the foliage droops or the tips of the leaves wilt or lie on the soil the plants should be cut back or worms may pull these drooping leaves and upset the plants. In prolonged dry weather the leeks should have their roots and leaves trimmed before planting. All leeks should be in their final positions by early July.

Once the plants are growing well they can be helped by dusting a good organic fertilizer along the rows at 50–70 g per m² (1½–2 oz per sq yd) run. An application of liquid manure at 14-day intervals from mid-August to the end of October, will help further in producing really thick stems. Keep down weeds and remove any flower stems that appear.

When grown in trenches the earthing up process will normally begin about a month after planting, soil being drawn up at intervals of 3 to 4 weeks. The soil used should be fine so that the plant stems are covered evenly. Some gardeners place rings of corrugated paper around the stems before earthing up. This stops the soil from falling between the leaves and prevents grittiness when the leeks are cooked.

Leeks can be lifted as required throughout the autumn and winter. Any left in the ground at the end of April should be moved and heeled in near a north wall or hedge in order to release the ground for another crop.

For exhibition purposes, leeks will require extra cultural attention. Special leek shows are still held, particularly in the northern parts of the country. The standard there is very high and 14 cm (5½ ins) or more should be the length of the perfectly straight blanched portion of stem. Measurement tables are often used and competition is keen.

Leeks should be thoroughly cleaned under cold running water before cooking to make sure they are completely free of grit.

An excellent main crop variety of leek is 'Royal Favourite'

RECOMMENDED VARIETIES: 'Winter Reuzen', a winter hardy variety producing well-blanched white stems. 'Musselburgh', an old hardy, reliable variety with long thick stems; 'Lyon', also old, large growing and good for late lifting; 'Prizetaker', hardy and splendid for exhibition; 'King Richard', a fairly new sort producing solid white stems usually much longer than other varieties; 'Walton Mammoth', one of the best varieties with medium green foliage and long thick, solid stems, valuable for exhibition; 'Malabar', a quick growing variety for autumn use and 'Winter Crop', a really winter hardy sort.

LETTUCE *Lactuca sativa*

Lettuce is the most popular salad plant, valued as much for its green leaves as the blanched heart.

Lettuce are classified in several ways. There are two main divisions between the cabbage (crisphead or butterhead) types, and cos: they may be classified further as summer and winter varieties, and those suitable for frame or greenhouse cultivation.

The cabbage section is the largest group, taking in varieties which are quite small, such as 'Tom Thumb', and the really large so-called butterheads which have soft, smooth light green leaves. There are others having quite brittle leaves. These are not often obtainable in shops since they do not market or travel well but they are first class for the gardener who can use them straight from the garden.

Summer lettuce should be sown in March, where they are to mature, although it is best to delay sowings in very cold districts or when the soil is wet. To ensure succession it is better to sow a little seed at frequent intervals, say, once a fortnight, rather than large quantities at once.

'Webb's Wonderful' is the best-known crisphead lettuce

Make the drills about 13 mm ($\frac{1}{2}$ in) deep, and 30 cm (12 ins) apart and cover the seed with fine soil. Thin sowing should be practised, so that there is little necessity for thinning the rows. Use some of the plants before they grow too large for this prevents overcrowding, which, because of root competition can sometimes lead to bolting.

Winter lettuce can be sown in light well-drained soil. If the plants follow a crop which was well-manured this should encourage steady growth. Here again, if some good organic fertilizer is worked into the surface soil at the rate of 100 g per m² (3 oz per sq yd) it will be helpful.

Winter lettuce should be sown about the second week in September, making the rows 30 cm (1 ft) apart, and thinning the plants so early so that there is about 15 cm (6 ins) between them. Thin the rows, later removing alternate plants. Although these thinnings have no hearts they can still be used in the kitchen. Winter lettuce can also be sown in pots or boxes and this may be necessary in cold and northern districts. Seedlings raised in this way will be ready for planting out from the third week in October onwards, according to soil, situation and district. It is possible to leave the plants in the seed bed to over-winter, then planting them out in March. They will be ready for use from the middle of May onwards.

Where heat is available lettuce is a really rewarding crop. Certain varieties have been bred for production under glass in winter. With these, plenty of light is essential and this is one reason why it is necessary to keep the glass clean. Use John Innes compost No 1 to avoid trouble from botrytis infection.

Sow the seed in standard-size seed boxes. If carefully done, 150 seeds will be sufficient for each box. Move the seedlings into their final cropping places as soon as the first pair of true leaves are showing well.

They should not be left to become large before being transplanted. Final spacing varies according to variety, some sorts growing larger than others. Even the largest varieties should not need more than 23 cm (9 ins) each way, and many are placed in rows 18–20 cm (7–8 ins) apart, with 18 cm (7 ins) between plants.

Once the greenhouse or frames are planted it is a good plan to water the seedlings well straight away, and to maintain a temperature of just over 15°C (60°F). After about ten days the temperature can be lowered to 10°C (50°F) or so. Little more

Cos lettuce 'Lobjoit's Green' is firm and flavourful

water will be necessary until January after which time it will need to be given more frequently.

When planting out seedlings, whether in the open ground or in greenhouses, make sure the tap root goes straight down and is not turned up in the hole.

Lettuces sometimes bolt or run to seed prematurely. This condition is caused by high temperatures and long days. With summer transplanting, especially during a dry spell, seedlings will often throw up a seed head even when the roots are moist. The flavour will then be impaired by an unpleasant bitterness and the plants should be consigned to the compost heap.

Leaf lettuce 'Salad Bowl' is a good choice for growing-bag cultivation

Lettuce are ready for cutting as soon as the heart is nicely firm. Once growth begins to push up from the centre it is a sign that the plants are beginning to run to seed and they should therefore be eaten as soon as possible. If it is not possible to use them immediately they can be pulled up complete with roots and placed in a cool shaded position in vessels of very shallow water. A special watch must be kept for aphis attacks.

The majority of the best modern varieties of cos lettuces are self-folding and need no help by tying. Even so, during spells of dry weather they may not heart up well, and it is therefore a good plan to give a light tying with raffia or soft string.

There are some varieties of lettuces, chiefly of American origin, which do not heart, and in these cases individual leaves can be pulled off and used as required. Notable among these is 'Salad Bowl', which is shaped like a rosette, about 30 cm (1 ft) across, with curled and lobed leaves.

RECOMMENDED VARIETIES: Although as a result of comparison trials the number of lettuce varieties in cultivation has recently been reduced, there are still many sorts offered in seedsmen's catalogues. It is possible to obtain a mixture of cos and cabbage varieties which mature at different dates, thus extending the cutting period. Too high a temperature at seed sowing time will inhibit germination, however, especially with butterhead types. Lettuce are usually grouped under separate headings which give some indication of their type. They include the following:

Cabbage Crisphead: 'Pennlake', 'Avoncrisp', 'Great Lakes', 'Iceberg', 'Webb's Wonderful'.
Butterhead: 'Avondefiance', 'Buttercrunch', 'Tom Thumb', 'All the Year Round', 'Hilde'.
Loosehead or leaf varieties: 'Grand Rapids', 'Salad Bowl'.
Cos: 'Little Gem', 'Paris White', 'Lobjoit's Green Cos'.
Hardy winter lettuce for sowing in the open ground in autumn: 'Arctic King', 'Imperial Winter', 'Valdor', 'Winter Density'.
Forcing varieties: 'Kordaat', 'Kloek', 'Kwiek', 'May King', 'Blondine' – all are excellent for sowing under glass from September onwards.

MARROW & COURGETTE
Cucurbita pepo ovifera

The marrow, more properly known as the vegetable marrow, and the courgette, which is a baby marrow, belong to the same family as cucumbers and melons. All have a high water content, and some vitamin A, and all have either a trailing or climbing habit of growth.

Cultivation Sow seeds into pots in April. Allow two seeds for each pot and when the seedlings have established themselves discard the weaker one and transfer the healthy seedling to a permanent growing position in a frame. To ensure germination, lay the required number of seeds on a sheet of damp blotting paper in a warm place for 2 days before planting. Make up beds by digging sites of 30 cm (1 ft) or more deep, and filling them with well-rotted manure which should be trodden in and covered with soil. Make a small planting hole with a trowel and put the plants in firmly. Water as necessary and keep the frame lights closed until danger of frost has passed. Toward the end of May remove the glass and give a boost to growth by watering in a dressing of dried blood. Outdoor crops are fertilized by bees and other insects but for early fruits it is advisable to pollinate the female flowers on each plant by hand using a camel hair brush. This is best done about mid-day, preferably when it is sunny and the flowers are dry. The female flower is easily recognized by the embryo fruit present at the back of the petals. Once the flowers have set and the fruit is developing, regular watering and occasional feeds of

Courgettes are small, sweet tender marrows and are easy to grow

liquid manure are essential. The earliest fruit may be ready for cutting by mid-June.

The first outdoor sowings should not be made until the middle of May into prepared planting sites. These outdoor plants will produce fruit from July until the end of September. Planting distances for bush types is 1.20 m (4 ft) square and for trailing varieties 1.80 m (6 ft) square.

RECOMMENDED VARIETIES: 'Long Green Bush' and 'Long Green Trailing'; 'Marco', F_1 green courgettes, bush; 'Tender and True', round marrow fruits, bush; 'Table Dainty', short striped fruits, trailing; 'Zucchini', F_1 prolific green courgettes, bush.

MELON *Cucumis melo*

These plants, which can be cultivated in a similar manner to cucumbers, have been grown for centuries. They are easy to manage when grown in favourable positions and where they have the maximum amount of sunshine.

Seed can be sown in a propagator in April, or on hotbeds of about 22°C (72°F)

in pots or boxes. Use a mixture of loam and peat to which a little wood ash and old mortar rubble has been added, or a proprietary loam- or peat-based seed compost.

Place the seed edgeways 13 mm ($\frac{1}{2}$ in) deep, and keep the propagator closed until germination occurs. Then give ventilation and water as necessary. When the seedlings have two leaves, move them to the frame or Dutch light, where a bed has been prepared by incorporating plenty of well-rotted manure. Handle them with care and give some shade until they are established.

Plant on slightly raised soil to prevent moisture collecting round the base of the stem at soil level, to avoid collar rot. Shade from direct sunshine and regular ventilation are important factors.

Frequent syringings of water will help in providing a moist atmosphere. When the plants have formed three leaves pinch out the leading shoot, preferably when it is sunny for quick healing of the wound, to encourage laterals to form. Once the laterals have formed four leaves, they too are stopped above the third leaf and it is on the sub-laterals that the fruit is borne.

Male and female flowers are produced,

the latter being larger and recognized by a small swelling at the base. Pollen is usually transferred to the female flower by bees and other insects but early in the season and with frame plants, it is advisable to hand pollinate. This is done by picking the male flowers and lightly rubbing the pollen on to the stigma in the centre of the female flower. Wait until four or five flowers are open together, so the fruits develop evenly.

If possible, do this job between 12 noon and 2 pm, preferably when it is sunny and the flowers fully open and dry. After a few days, the swelling at the back of each female flower will begin to enlarge.

Plants can also be placed in the cold frame or under cloches from the middle to the end of April. Prepare a good hole for each plant, filling it with well-rotted manure. Plant the melon on a little ridge to avoid the roots becoming waterlogged. Cutting begins in August. Signs of ripening are a crack on

'Ogen' melons ripening in the greenhouse

the fruit near the stalk, deep colour and a rich honey smell.

Water melons can be grown where a little heat is available. Sow the seeds in April in pots of peaty compost standing them in the cold frame. When the seedlings are ready for their fruiting positions select sandy soil, well-mulched with good compost. Set the plants on little mounds about 75 cm ($2\frac{1}{2}$ ft) apart remembering that the plants will not be bushy specimens but will be kept to one main stem growing 1.50 m (5 ft) or more. Make sure water does not settle round the plants or stem rot will develop.

Shallow furrows can be made both sides of the plants as necessary during the summer or clay pots can be sunk in the soil near the plants and these can be frequently filled with water. After the fruits have set, carefully place them on pieces of wood or slate to prevent slug or other pest damage.

RECOMMENDED VARIETIES. The group known as Canteloupe melons are the easiest to manage and include 'Dutch Net' and 'No Name'. For growing with little or no heat, also the F$_1$ 'Burpee Hybrid', which has rounded golden, netted fruit and thick juicy, orange flesh. 'Sweetheart' is another splendid hybrid with salmon-pink flesh. It does well in frames or under cloches. 'Charentais' is a small delicious variety with scented flesh. Of the varieties of melons needing heated or warm greenhouse treatment, 'Hero of Lockinge', 'Blenheim Orange' and the green fleshed 'Emerald Gem' are most reliable. Water melon 'Florida Favourite' produces oval fruits of 2.7 kg (6 lb) or more with green skin and pink flesh.

MUSHROOM *Psalliota campestris*

Mushrooms require a precisely controlled environment in cellars or in boxes under the staging of a greenhouse. Wherever you choose to grow mushrooms, the site must be clean, draught-free but well-ventilated, dimly lit or dark, and capable of maintaining a temperature between 10 and 13°C (50−55°F). Mushroom spawn needs a particular compost in which to thrive. Readymade mushroom compost is available and should be used if you are unable to prepare suitable compost in your own garden. To do this, use only wheat-straw-based horse manure. Make a broad heap and leave for a week or ten days to generate heat. Turn the outside of the heap to the inside three or four times over the following month, watering it as necessary; the process is complete when no smell is given off and the texture of the compost is friable. Pack the compost firmly into the chosen growing site about

30 cm (1 ft) deep. The temperature will rise and then fall to 24°C (75°F), at which point put lumps of spawn about the size of a golf ball 1 cm ($\frac{1}{2}$ in) below the surface 30 cm (1 ft) apart each way. Ten days later cover the compost with a damp layer of 'casing' (50:50 peat and chalk). About a month later the mushrooms will appear. Harvest regularly to maintain productivity and mushrooms will keep coming through for up to two months. Never use spent compost for a second crop of mushrooms.

ONION *Allium cepa*

One of the most widely grown and valued of all vegetables, the onion has been known and grown for thousands of years. There are numerous varieties, some suitable for Autumn sowing, some best sown in Spring, others which are valued as salad or spring onions, while a number are useful for producing small bulbs for pickling.

Onions are a crop which responds well to generous cultural treatment and it is advisable to select a good site.

Both the bulb and salad or spring onions prefer a medium to light soil. Onions used to be grown on the same patch year after year, but this is not generally recommended because of the possibility of disease building up. Good drainage is important although the soil must not dry out. The best crop is produced on medium loams which have been deeply cultivated and enriched with compost or generous amounts of farmyard manure. The site should be free from perennial weeds and away from buildings or trees which would cast shadows and one where there is free air circulation and exposure to full sun.

'Button' mushrooms appear about a month after spawning

Many gardeners have their own ways of making an onion bed. Some prefer to prepare the ground by digging deeply and placing a layer of decayed vegetable matter at the bottom of the trench, following this with a layer of soil then a generous sprinkling of sulphate of potash and bone meal. More soil is then applied covering the bed, with wood ash lightly pricked into the surface soil. Do this as early as possible — October is not too soon. Then before sowing the seed, apply a dusting of hydrated lime to ensure that the soil is not acid.

If the ground is inclined to be loose it should be firmed by treading lightly or a light roller can be used. For the earliest and largest bulb onions, seed should be sown in the open in late August or early September. Sow thinly in rows 30–38 cm (12–15 ins) apart. The seedlings should be transplanted in March and April 15 cm (6 ins) apart in rows 30 cm (1 ft) apart. One disadvantage with autumn sowing is that if the winter is very mild the seedlings may make too much soft growth and some may run to seed prematurely.

When transplanting the seedlings take care not to break the roots. Use a fork to prise up the soil along the rows. Plant firmly so that the bases of the seedlings are just settled in the soil. They must not be buried deeply but be well embedded in the soil.

According to soil and weather conditions spring sowings can be made from early March onwards, although the bed should have been prepared well before that time. Never attempt to sow while the soil is sticky. Sow shallowly in rows 25–30 cm (10–12 ins) apart after making the soil firm. A 7 g (¼ oz) packet of seed will sow a row about 15 m (50 ft). Thin the seedlings gradually using the thinnings in salads, leaving the plants finally to stand at least 10 cm (4 ins) apart. Take care not to bruise the seedlings otherwise the scent emitted may attract the onion fly. Always firm the soil along the rows after thinning out has been done.

Seed of salad onions is usually sown early in September. This will supply pullings from early March onwards. A second sowing should be made in late February or March as soon as soil conditions are suitable. Make further successional sowings until June.

Make the rows 20–30 cm (8–12 ins) apart and sow fairly sparingly. There is no need to thin the seedlings which can be used as needed. 'White Lisbon' is the most widely grown and easily obtained variety.

The so-called Welsh or 'ever-ready' onion, A. *fistulosum*, is a hardy perennial

Onions have the same soil requirements as beans and peas

producing spring onion-like growths quite closely together. Available throughout the year they are a reliable standby when the usual spring onions are not available.

They can be propagated by division of the clumps in early spring or autumn; any good well drained soil is suitable. Seed is occasionally available and can be sown in June or July.

If you want to grow large exhibition onions seed should be sown under glass early in January. Use trays of John Innes seed compost making it firm before sowing thinly. Cover the seed with compost, make the surface firm and level. Then give a sprinkling of water and place the trays on the greenhouse staging where the temperature is around 18°C (65°F) and cover with a sheet of glass and brown paper. Once germination is seen remove glass and paper and keep the trays on the staging in the

light. After three or four weeks the seedlings can be moved to the frame for hardening off preparatory to planting outdoors in April.

RECOMMENDED VARIETIES: Many varieties are available and among the best are the following: 'Ailsa Craig', one of the most useful of all purpose varieties which can be sown in spring or autumn. 'Bedfordshire Champion' makes large globular bulbs much like 'Ailsa Craig' and is excellent for exhibiting. 'Reliance', an extra fine vigorous growing variety and a wonderful cropper; best results come from autumn sowing. 'White Spanish', very large bulbs which keep sound a long time.

'Barletta Barla' is probably the best for pickling having pure white globe-shaped bulbs. 'The Queen' is another particularly good pickler with silver skin, while 'Giant Zittau' has long been used for this purpose.

'Amber Express' is one of the new Japanese onions and should be sown in October

The Welsh onion is a useful perennial

For spring onions 'White Lisbon' is wholly dependable. slender-shaped with white skin.

A new race known as Japanese onions has been developed to give early maturity. Seed must be sown in the autumn, the bulbs maturing and being ready for lifting in July. They are heavy croppers. Varieties include 'Express Yellow' and 'Extra Early Kaizuka' making flattish bulbs while 'Imai Early Yellow' forms globe shaped bulbs.

Onion sets These are favoured by gardeners who have had trouble from onion fly or who do not wish to make a seed bed or plant out seedlings in spring. Sets are small onions which have been arrested in their development and dried off and stored during the winter. They are generally sold by weight, 225 g (8 oz) being enough for the average garden.

Culture is simple: treat the soil as advised for seed sowing. Plant the sets shallowly from early March onwards according to soil conditions. Allow 10–15 cm (4–6 ins) between the bulbs with 30–40 cm (12–15 ins) from row to row. Check the rows in the weeks following planting to make sure the small onions are still in place.

Several varieties are available and 'Sturon' is a distinct type making large solid keeping onions which very rarely bolt. It is of attractive appearance with rich golden-yellow skin and keeps well. 'Stuttgart Giant' is semi-flat with a clear amber skin.

There is also a strain of 'Ailsa Craig' sets which are prepared for exhibition by special heat process. Start the bulbs in pots during March and April or plant in the open ground towards the end of April.

ORACHE *Atriplex hortensis*

Sometimes known as Mountain Spinach, there are three forms of this annual: green, white or red, all growing about 1.20 m (4 ft) high. The red variety is not out of place in the ornamental garden, but it should not be allowed to flower there, since it seeds itself freely and can become a nuisance.

The young leaves are excellent in salads, while the older ones are cooked like spinach.

Orache is an ornamental food plant

People who find ordinary spinach indigestible can eat this type without discomfort. Seed can be sown thinly in moisture-retentive ground from the end of March to the end of July. Plant rows 45 cm (18 ins) apart and thin the seedlings early so that there is 38 cm (15 ins) between them. It is best to gather some leaves from each plant rather than stripping individual plants.

PARSNIP *Pastinaca sativa*

A native of Great Britain, the parsnip is a nutritious vegetable containing vitamin C with traces of B1 and A, iron and calcium. A useful vegetable, it may well be that the reason it is not used more widely is because it is not always cooked properly. Parsnips steamed or baked are delicious.

It is one of the easiest vegetables to grow and thrives in a deep, light to medium soil

'Avonresister' is a reliable variety of parsnip

where there are few or no stones. Parsnips can also be grown on shallow ground so long as the fairly new stumprooted varieties are used. On thin, gravelly, chalky soil the roots tend to fork. It is best to select a site which was generously manured for a previous crop. If soil is very poor and it is not possible to obtain bulky organic manure, a complete fertilizer can be used at the rate of

140 g per m² (4 oz per sq yd).

This crop occupies the ground for a long time, which is one reason why it is not popular in small gardens. It is one of the first crops to be sown, usually at the end of February or early in March. Seed is sown in drills in the usual way, or a few seeds can be placed at stations 15 cm (6 ins) apart, or if extra large roots are required an even wider spacing can be allowed.

Individual holes can be made up to 60 cm (2 ft) deep with 7.5–10 cm (3–4 ins) diameter at the top. These holes can be filled with a compost of three parts clean garden soil and one part of good compost or rotted manure. Pass this through a 6 mm (¼ in) sieve. Sow three seeds in each hole and thin the seedlings down to the strongest one. The rows should be 30 cm (12 ins) apart.

Seed is liable to be slow in germinating and it is quite a good plan to sow radish or lettuce seed along the rows. The quick germination of these will show where the rows are, and prevent loss when the ground is being cultivated. Thinning must be done early, the best time being when the first two true leaves have developed. After this, cultivation consists of keeping down weeds.

Parsnips are hardy and can be left in the soil throughout the winter and dug as required. Since the roots are needed when the soil is liable to become frozen hard, it is a good plan to use straw or other protective material for placing around some roots, making it easier to lift them. Alternatively, some roots can be lifted and stored in sand, although this is not recommended since the roots tend to go soft.

There are very few diseases or pests likely to attack parsnips, except canker fungus which may be troublesome. This may be seen as cracks and brown areas chiefly around the top, and other places. Fungi and a physiological disorder are the culprits and often appear in badly drained soil; if too much nitrogen was given; or if the roots were damaged by the hoe.

RECOMMENDED VARIETIES: 'Avonresister', needs less space than other varieties and it is most resistant to canker; 'Hollow Crown Improved' heavy cropping, well shaped, broad shoulders; 'Offenham', intermediate size with broad shoulders, useful for shallow soils; 'Tender and True', medium size, extra tender flesh; 'The Student', well shaped roots of fine flavour; 'White Gem', a medium sized broad shouldered variety with smooth skin; 'Lisbonnais', one of the largest and longest varieties.

PEA *Pisum sativum*

The garden pea has been cultivated for centuries. Its food value is good, for among other properties it contains vitamins A, B and C and calcium and iron in small quantities. Peas are grouped as either round or wrinkled. The former are hardier and are widely used for autumn sowing. Wrinkled peas are generally of superior flavour since they have more sugar than starch.

The average family of four requires about 1 kg (2¼ lb) of shelled peas to make a decent dish. Good medium soil is necessary. Peas occupy the ground for a long time so it is important that the land should be in good condition. Move the soil fairly deeply working in good compost or rotted manure, while a dusting of fish manure at 100–140 g per m² (3–4 oz per sq yd) well raked in before sowing, will provide all the feeding

Above: 'Onward', the most popular second-early pea. Below: Ripe pods of 'Kelvedon Wonder', a first-early variety

matter the plants will need. Once the soil has been worked into a fine, friable condition, it will be ready for sowing. Flat bottomed or V shaped drills should be drawn out 8 cm (3 ins) deep. The distance apart of the drills depends on variety, but as a guide, the dwarf sorts growing 30 cm (1 ft) high, should be spaced 38 cm (15 ins) apart. Those growing 60–90 cm (2–3 ft) high should be allowed 60–90 cm (2–3 ft) between rows and for the taller sorts allow about the same distance between the rows as the height of the variety.

Autumn sowings can be made from the end of October onwards using the round seeded varieties. Spring sowings can commence in mid-March, these being made more thickly, and 43 cc (¾ pint) of seed will sow a row 15 m (16 yds) long. For the later sowings 28 cc ($\frac{1}{2}$ pint) is sufficient for the same length row. It is best to go back to the earliest wrinkled varieties for the latest July sowings.

Birds often attack pea seedlings as they come through the ground. It is a good plan to place pea guards or to stretch strands of black cotton along the rows. Twiggy sticks should be inserted as soon as the seedlings can be seen, as they keep them from blowing about and from falling on the ground where they become a prey to soil pests. Use pea sticks or netting for the final supports. A mulch of peat drawn towards the plants will prevent the soil drying out and ensure an even supply of moisture to the roots.

The earliest varieties will be ready from June onwards and successional sowings will give pickings into late September.

RECOMMENDED VARIETIES: good first early round seeded varieties include: 'Meteor', 45 cm ($1\frac{1}{2}$ ft); 'Superb' 60 cm (2 ft), and 'Pilot', 45 cm ($1\frac{1}{2}$ ft).

First early wrinkle-seeded: 'Hurst Beagle', 45 cm ($1\frac{1}{2}$ ft); 'Kelvedon Wonder', 45 cm ($1\frac{1}{2}$ ft) and 'Early Onward', 60 cm (2 ft).

Second early and main crop wrinkle-seeded: 'Histon Kingsize', 1.05 m ($3\frac{1}{2}$ ft); 'Hurst Green Shaft', 75 cm ($2\frac{1}{2}$ ft); 'Onward', 75 cm ($2\frac{1}{2}$ ft) and 'Miracle' 1.35 m ($4\frac{1}{2}$ ft).

Late wrinkle-seeded varieties: 'Lord Chancellor', 90 cm (3 ft); 'Senator', 90 cm (3 ft); 'Victory Freezer', 75 cm ($2\frac{1}{2}$ ft);

'Winkossa' is an interesting variety, producing small 'petit pois' peas. If sown in October it will crop in June.

Sugar or Mangetout peas Provided they are gathered when young these peas are a real delicacy. The entire pods are eaten, and all the preparation they need is topping and tailing, as required for French beans. Seed is sown in the ordinary way. Since birds find the young pods attractive, it is wise to cotton the rows. Slugs too, may attack the plants and young pods if they are allowed to fall

Above: 'Mangetout'. Below: asparagus peas are delicacies with a fine flavour

over and touch the ground. This is why they should be given supports at an early stage. 'Carouby de Maussane' and 'Dwarf Sweet Green' are recommended varieties. A fairly new sugar pea known as 'Sweetpod', bears light green, succulent pods of sweet flavour.

The Carlin pea These are peas grown chiefly in the north of England, being used especially on mid-Lent Sunday, which was once widely known as Carlin Sunday. The seeds, now seldom offered by seedsmen, are very distinct, being darker than any other variety and resembling lentils.

The cultivation for the Carlin pea is the same as for the ordinary types, the seed being sown in April. Choose a well-limed patch of soil and work 100 g per m² (3 oz per sq yd) of fish manure into the site before sowing.

Plants grow more than 2 m (6 ft) high, and must be provided with suitable supports. Neither birds nor mice are interested in these peas, which are rarely if ever, attacked by mildews, and other troubles associated with the normal sorts.

The plants produce a prolific crop of short pods, particularly during July and August. They should be left until fully ripe when the entire plants can be pulled up and the pods shelled. It is essential to allow the seeds to dry well, after which store them in a cool, dry place for winter and spring use. The dried seeds should be soaked for some hours before being cooked until tender. If sprinkled with sugar and rum, the flavour is superb.

Asparagus pea *Tetragonolobus purpureus* In spite of its common name this is not an ordinary garden pea and it is only because of its flavour that asparagus comes into the name at all. It has deep brownish-red flowers.

Not fully hardy, it is best to raise plants in gentle heat, sowing in April, gradually hardening the seedlings for planting out towards the end of May onwards. A sunny situation should be provided and the soil should be on the light side. Pick the pods while small — not more than an inch long and cook them whole. Left to grow large they become stringy.

Petit Pois This is reckoned by epicures to be the best of all. Very popular in France, it has a delicious sugary flavour. Seed should be sown in April, making the drills 25 mm (1 in) deep. Allow 10–15 cm (4–6 ins) between the seeds, with the rows about 1.06 m

(3½ ft) apart. Because these plants grow 90 cm—1.20 m (3—4 ft) high it is an advantage to provide supports.

Gather the pods immediately they are filled, and if they are steamed without delay, the peas will readily fall out of the pods and the full flavour will be there too! 'Gullivert' is the variety most usually grown.

The Purple Podded pea This is a little grown type of pea, which has deep green foliage but flowers and pods of a purple colour. It needs normal culture for peas and is hardy. Growing about 1.35 m (4½ ft) high or more and it succeeds in most soils. The peas which are green, may be used fresh in the ordinary way or can be dried for winter use. In either case they have a most pleasing flavour.

PEPPER *Capsicum annuum*

Sweet Peppers are not cultivated as much as they deserve. This is probably because they are often thought to be hot. If they are properly grown and cooked, they are a real delicacy. Some success is being achieved in breeding self stopping (those which branch freely) varieties which have a more compact habit.

Plants can be raised in exactly the same way as aubergines, spacing the seeds 2.5 cm (1 in) apart in pots or trays of seed compost. Do this in February or March in a temperature of about 15°C (60°F). Prick off seedlings as soon as they are big enough to handle moving them to small pots when they reach 15—18 cm (6—7 ins). Keep them in full light and spray with water frequently to keep off red spider.

If the plants are to be grown in a sunny, sheltered position outdoors, they can be pricked off into soil blocks or peat pots of John Innes No. 1 compost. Plants are also grown under cloches or frames. It is best to plant in shallow trenches and to raise the glass when necessary keeping the plants covered throughout growth.

The plants grow 60—75 cm (2—2½ ft) tall, and bear white flowers that are followed by fruit which colours according to variety. If plants fail to produce side shoots, pinch out the growing points. Once the fruit begins to swell, liquid fertilizer will prove beneficial.

Capsicums vary in length from 10—13 cm (4—5 ins) although in the case of the bull-nosed types, they are only 5—8 cm (2—3 in) long but much thicker and irregularly shaped. Chilli peppers are very hot and only used for flavouring and pickles.

RECOMMENDED VARIETIES: Green peppers are the red and yellow sorts before they turn colour. Good varieties include: 'Canape' with sweet mild flesh; 'Bell Boy' F_1, 'Burpee Hybrid' and 'New Ace', a heavy cropper for glass culture.

POTATO *Solanum tuberosum*

We eat more potatoes than any other vegetable. This crop is grown where ground needs to be cleared of weeds before other crops are planted. Potatoes will grow on all types of soil, although a deep, well-drained medium loam is best. Soil has a great influence on flavour. Plenty of light and air are required, for under stagnant, close conditions blight may spoil the crop. Heavy clay and peaty soils are said to produce 'waxy' or 'soapy' tubers, but this is not always so.

Early soil preparation is helpful. Farm-yard manure, seaweed or compost can be worked in when digging the ground during the winter. Then leave the surface ridged if the land is heavy, so that it breaks down easily at planting time. At planting time, rotted manure or compost spread along the rows underneath the tubers, makes the roots more active. For the maincrop and even the second early sorts, manure can be supplemented with a good fertilizer such as bone meal or hoof and horn.

Medium sized tubers the size of a hen's egg and weighing about 56 g (2 oz) are best, the most usual size being those which have passed through a 6 cm (2¼ ins) riddle but will remain on a 3 cm (1¼ ins) one.

Buy fresh, certified seed every year to be sure of a healthy crop. Very large tubers can be cut. This should be done lengthways, so each portion has at least two strong sprouts. Cover the cut portions with a damp cloth until they can be planted.

Green peppers are best grown in the greenhouse

'Desiree' is a popular potato variety

Harvest potatoes carefully to avoid damaging the tubers

When planting, take out flat bottomed trenches about 15 cm (6 ins) deep, deeper on light land. A layer of leaf mould or peat sprinkled along the opened trench helps to ensure that the tubers retain good skins.

The earliest tubers can be spaced 25–30 cm (10–12 ins) apart with 45–60 cm (18–24 ins) between rows. Second earlies can be spaced 30 cm (12 ins) apart with 60 cm (2 ft) between rows. Maincrops need to be 45 cm (18 ins) apart with the rows 75 cm (2½ ft) apart.

The earthing up of potatoes keeps the haulm upright, and prevents the new tubers from becoming exposed and turning green, when they become useless for eating. The extra covering of soil also protects the tubers from blight.

Earthing up is done gradually and can be started when the stems are 20–23 cm (8–9 ins) high. The ridges made should have fairly sharp, sloping sides. This allows

Rows of potatoes earthed up

heavy rains to drain off.

Potatoes can be grown successfully under black polythene without earthing up. The ground is prepared in the usual way, the tubers being pressed lightly into the surface. A sheet of polythene is then laid over the rows, a cross cut about 8 cm (3 ins) long, like a plus sign being made over each tuber. Fix the edges of the polythene by taking out a little furrow 5–8 cm (2–3 ins) deep. Cover the edges with soil, making it firm by treading.

This leads to quick growth, supression of weeds, and the retention of moisture. Scatter slug bait over the ground, under the polythene, for the dark, cool shelter this cover gives makes an ideal hiding and breeding place for slugs.

Early potatoes are ready for lifting when the flowers begin to wither; main crops when the leaves turn yellow. The earliest crop is usually ready at the beginning of July. To ensure that tubers are really ready for lifting, it is a good plan to scrape away the soil and remove one or two tubers. Then light rub the skins. If they remain firm the tubers are ready for harvesting.

New potatoes in the autumn can be obtained by following on with another planting of early potatoes, on ground from which the first crop has just been lifted. From the first lifting, select sound shapely tubers about the size of a Victoria plum, weighing between 42–57 g (1½–2 oz).

Expose the chosen tubers to the light and sun for two or three days and then replant. Choose a favourable sheltered site. Turn over the soil fairly deeply, working in a good dressing of an organic fertilizer. Then make a trench 13–15 cm (5–6 ins) deep and place the tubers 25–30 cm (10–12 ins) apart with 52 cm (21 ins) between rows.

RECOMMENDED VARIETIES: *First earlies:* 'Arran Pilot', white kidney, floury, heavy cropper; 'Home Guard', medium sized, oval; 'Ulster Chieftain', white, oval; 'Ulster Prince', white, kidney, crops well under dry conditions; 'Epicure', a good cropping variety, white, round; 'Stormont Dawn', white, floury, good flavoured.
Second earlies: 'Craig's Alliance', white flesh; 'Craig's Royal', creamy fleshed kidney; 'Dunbar Rover', white fleshed, floury; 'Great Scot', white round. 'Maris Peer', white oval, shows some resistance to scab.
Maincrop: 'Arran Peak', white flesh, keeps well; 'Dr. McIntosh', white kidney, grand for exhibition; 'Majestic', white kidney, waxy, irregular shape. 'King Edward', large tubers, heavy cropper; 'Maris Piper', white.

PUMPKIN & SQUASH *Cucurbita maxima, C. moschata*

Pumpkins and squashes are two more members of the interesting family *Cucur-*

'Hundredweight' Pumpkin grows to proportions worthy of a harvest festival

'Golf Nugget' squash is highly decorative

bitaceae, which includes vegetable marrows and courgettes, cucumbers and melons. Cultivation techniques are similar to those described for marrows (q.v.). The planting site should be prepared by digging in a generous quantity of farmyard manure at 30 cm (1 ft) deep and covering with soil to make a mound on which the plant can be generously watered without becoming waterlogged. All members of this family are composed of about 90 per cent water and must be kept well supplied with water throughout their season of growth. Construct a 'moat' around the growing mound and keep this full of water rather than watering the plants directly.

The culinary uses of pumpkin are few: pumpkin pie is a great American favourite, and slices of pumpkin roasted with pork to soak up the flavoursome juices is an idea worth experimenting with.

Squashes are divided somewhat confusingly into two groups, summer and winter: in fact cultivars from each group can be grown at various times of the year. The proper winter squashes, known in America as Hubbard squashes, are eaten when they are ripe (unlike vegetable marrows, which are eaten when they are immature) and in fact keep in store for up to 4 months in a cool but frost-free place. They contain considerably more nutrients than marrows, cooked cabbage, or summer squash, and far less water.

Vegetable spaghetti is a very unusual variety which is grown in the same way, harvested when about 20 cm (8 ins) long and then cooked whole. When cut in half the flesh is eaten in strands just like spaghetti and is very good with butter and freshly ground black pepper.

All the members of this family have attractive bright orange flowers which can be eaten if dipped in batter and quick fried.

The custard marrow, or scalloped summer squash, has not been very widely grown in this country, although it has been known for about 400 years.

Perhaps one of the most popular reasons for growing members of this family is that, as well as being edible, they are very decorative plants, both in their trailing or climbing habit of growth and in their beautifully coloured fruits. One plant can occupy a surprising amount of ground and cover it generously with its broad-leaved foliage.

RECOMMENDED VARIETIES: 'Baby Crookneck', yellow squash, with a neck like an umbrella handle, bush; 'Custard White', flat white with scalloped edge, bush; 'Gold Nugget', round yellow fruit, bush, winter keeping; 'Golden Delicious', top-shaped orange fruit, trailing, winter keeping; 'Hubbard's Golden Squash', orange-yellow pumpkin, trailing, winter keeping; 'Little Gem', orange-sized, round squash, trailing, winter keeping; 'Mammoth', ' probably the best-known

pumpkin, trailing, winter keeping; 'Sweet Dumpling', delicious squash, looks like a melon, trailing, winter keeping; 'Vegetable Spaghetti', yellow strings of flesh when cooked, trailing.

PURSLANE *Portulaca oleracea*

This is a plant which is much valued in Eastern countries, although it has also been grown for centuries in Europe. An annual with succulent foliage, it thrives in light soil, and likes the sun. The young leaves can be cooked or used raw in salads and sandwiches and give a delicious flavour to soups. To ensure succession, sow the seeds in small batches from April onwards. The rows should be 23 cm (9 ins) apart and the seedlings are thinned to 15 cm (6 ins) in the row. They transplant well but should never lack moisture.

Purslane is an attractive addition to salads

RADISH *Raphanus sativus*

This easy crop can be cultivated in the open ground, the cold frame and the cool greenhouse. An excellent catch crop, it can be grown on the sides of celery or leek trenches or between rows of lettuce or other salad plants. There are red, white and red and white varieties, varying in shape from round or globe to half-long and fully long with a broad top. The newer varieties have dispelled

Quick-growing radish 'French Breakfast'

the belief that radishes are hot and cause indigestion.

Although radishes do not need deep soil, the ground should be well prepared and stay moist, for quick growth is required for crisp, succulent roots. Soil containing plenty of organic manure is ideal. Dry soil induces leafy growth with little or no bulb development.

Do not sow too thickly. While it is quite usual to spread (broadcast) the seed, it is best to sow in drills 15 cm (6 ins) apart and about 13 mm ($\frac{1}{2}$ in) deep. Make the soil firm after sowing for loose soil rarely produces firm roots. A half ounce of seed will sow two rows 4.50 m (15 ft) long. Thin the seedlings early so that all have an opportunity to develop properly and if flea beetles are troublesome dust the drills with carbaryl or HCH powder before the seed is sown. Pull the roots as soon as they are usable.

RECOMMENDED VARIETIES for early maturing outdoors: 'Flamenco', 'French Breakfast', 'Cherry Belle', 'Saxa', also known as 'Red Forcing', 'Red Prince', 'Icicle' white, 'Wood's Frame' a long variety deep pink in colour, and 'Sparkler' half-red and half-white.

Winter radishes These can be sown from July onwards, although in warmer areas, wait until August. Make the drills 23 cm (9 ins) apart, thinning the plants to 15 cm (6 ins) in the rows. The roots can be left in the ground to be dug as required or they can be lifted in November or December and stored in boxes of sand, sandy soil or peat. Winter radishes can also be grown in boxes although these should be at least 20—23 cm (8—9 ins) deep. For good results the roots require plenty of moisture in the growing season, otherwise they become stringy and very hot.

RECOMMENDED VARIETIES of winter radish: The variety 'China Rose' is one of the best, being similar to a very large 'French Breakfast'. The skin is cerise-red, the flesh white and crisp. 'Black Spanish' has black skin and white flesh and comes in round or long rooted forms. 'Mino Early' is a fat sausage-shaped variety with a very mild flavour. All need slicing and are not eaten whole.

The Bavarian radish is a most unusual variety, forming roots the size of large turnips, the top growth reaching 75—90 cm ($2\frac{1}{2}$—3 ft). This is a variety which is served in Bavarian beer halls where it is cut into spiral pieces or grated and served in salads. The decorative seed pods are an added attraction especially since they make a useful sandwich filling if cut and used while green.

Although an easy crop to grow, gardeners often find there is plenty of top growth but the roots are small and stringy. This is usually because the soil is 'thin' and lacking in phosphates vital for good root development. Overcome it by dressing the soil with 140 g per m² (4 oz per sq yd) of superphosphate before sowing.

RHUBARB *Rheum rhaponticum*

An easy plant to grow, rhubarb will remain productive for many years. Sadly it is often grown in positions which are badly drained or where the soil is poor.

Although its food value is not great, rhubarb is much appreciated early in the year before fresh fruit becomes available. This ancient plant has medicinal value and was originally used solely for this purpose. The leaves are poisonous since they contain oxalic acid.

Dig the soil deeply since the plants make thick branching roots. If stable, farmyard

Tender shoots of forced rhubarb. Bins or boxes can replace the traditional terra-cotta pots

manure or compost is worked in it will provide feeding material over a long period. Bone meal and wood ashes are also beneficial. For earliest outdoor rhubarb, a fairly sheltered position is required.

Plant in November, or February and March, when the soil is workable. Allow 90 cm (3 ft) between the crowns, for they increase in size and need ample room. Spread the roots fully, planting firmly, covering the crowns with 5 cm (2 ins) of soil. Do not pull any stalks the first season and in subsequent years always leave some stalks on each plant.

It is best not to pull after early July excepting in the case of stalks needed for jam or wine making. Rhubarb should not be cut but gripped at the base of the stem and pulled with a jerking movement. Flower heads should always be removed. To keep the plants productive, give a dressing of manure annually. Inverted pots or boxes placed over some of the plants will provide earlier outdoor pullings.

Rhubarb is generally trouble free. If plants show signs of rotting at the crown, dig them up and burn them.

raised to 10°C (50°F) and after a further eight to ten days to 15–18°C (60–65°F).

RECOMMENDED VARIETIES include: 'Prince Albert', 'Linnaeus' and 'Victoria'. If one or more of these are grown it will provide a natural succession of sticks for pulling from April onwards. For forcing, 'Champagne' and 'Dawes Champion' are good. It is possible to raise rhubarb from seed. 'Glaskin's Perpetual' and 'Holstein Bloodred' which mature quickly are the best for this purpose.

SALAD SPROUTS

For centuries the Chinese and Japanese have eaten sprouted seeds, knowing that they contain valuable proteins as well as other health promoting qualities. Seeds for sprouting are now offered by several seed firms and apart from Alfalfa and Mung beans, Adzuki, Fenugreek and Triticale are now available, as well as a mixture of Salad Sprouts.

The simplest way of growing them is to place the seeds in a jam jar indoors and fix muslin over the top with an elastic band. Fill the jar with water and shake well. Do this morning and evening until sprouting occurs. The time will vary from three to seven days and the sprouted seed can be eaten raw or cooked.

The Mung Bean, *Phaseolus aureus* is now becoming popular because of its high food value. It has a high protein content and contains vitamin E. The tasty sprouts are served in Chinese restaurants, frequently being added to rice dishes. All they need is to be cooked for a few minutes in boiling water containing a little salt.

They are as easy to grow as mustard and cress and are most useful for persons living in a flat or otherwise without a garden. Simply sow the beans on the surface of damp peat or flannel in a dish or bowl, cover the containers with polythene and place them in a cupboard or other dark moderately warm place. They will soon germinate and produce their succulent blanched top growth which will be ready for use within a few days. Cut the shoots when about 5 cm (2 ins) long and cook as soon as possible, when they will be crisp and nutty. Remember to keep the material moist at all times. It is best to sow small quantities at frequent intervals, rather than fewer large sowings. These beans cannot be grown outdoors.

Forcing rhubarb While it is usual to force three year old plants, rather younger specimens can be used, provided they are strong and healthy. Plants to be forced should not be pulled during the summer. This means that the energy of the plants will have been directed entirely to building up strong crowns for producing a good crop when forced.

The simplest way to force rhubarb is in boxed soil under the heated greenhouse staging. If sacks or hessian are draped in front of the staging this will provide the necessary darkness. Should hot water pipes be under the staging, it is best to stand a sheet of asbestos or some boards in front, to screen plants from the heat.

Timing is important. If the aim is to produce sticks for Christmas, forcing should commence in mid-November. To maintain a succession, bring in batches of crowns at fourteen-day intervals. Make sure that the soil is nicely moist before planting.

Pack the crowns closely together, filling in the spaces between them with sandy loam, fine peat or leaf mould so that there are no air pockets. Once planted, the crowns should be given a good soaking with water. To begin with, a temperature of 8°C (45°F) is adequate, but a week later it should be

Salad sprouts are ready within a few days of germinating

SALSIFY *Tragopogon porrifolius*

This is a biennial plant, often known as the vegetable oyster because of its flavour. It is not widely grown in this country, but is much used as a winter vegetable in France and Italy. It likes a deep, light, moisture retentive soil, preferably enriched with decayed manure or compost the previous season.

Sow seed in mid-April in drills 25 mm (1 in) deep and 30 cm (1 ft) apart, and thin the seedlings to 15–18 cm (6–7 ins) apart. The roots are ready for use from October onwards and may be lifted as required, being treated like parsnips. Take care not to damage them or they will 'bleed' and loose their nutty flavour.

If some plants are left in the ground during winter young top growth, which has an asparagus flavour, can be cut and cooked in spring. The cream coloured roots should be 15–23 cm (6–9 ins) long, and 5 cm (2 ins) thick. They can be steamed or boiled in their skins, which are rubbed off, before being served with white sauce. The variety usually grown is 'Sandwich Island'.

SCORZONERA *Scorzonera hispanica*

Very similar to salsify, this is preferred by many because of its flavour and its help in various forms of indigestion. Fertile soil, free from clods or stones, ensures straight roots. Sow seed from April onwards in drills 25 mm (1 in) deep and 38 cm (15 ins) apart. Thin the seedlings early, leaving strong plants 15 cm (6 ins) apart. The plants are perfectly hardy and while roots can be stored in boxes of sand, it is better to lift as required and cook without delay.

Boil or steam the roots before peeling. The black skin is not easy to remove, the best way being to rub them in a cloth while the roots are hot.

Left in the ground for the second year the plants often produce flowers. In ancient cookery books, we read that if flower buds are gathered, washed and dried, they can be cooked in butter until they are brown and then mixed with eggs for making omelettes.

'Russian Giant' is the variety usually offered.

Left: Salsify and (below) scorzonera

SEAKALE *Crambe maritima*

This native of Britain and other European countries may be found growing wild in coastal districts. Best results come from good sandy loam which holds moisture without becoming waterlogged. Cultivate the ground in autumn, working in bulky manure. When final soil preparations are being carried out in the spring, fork in a light dressing of an organic fertilizer such as fish manure at 70–100 g per m² (2–3 oz per sq yd).

Seakale stalks have a delicate nutty taste

Plants can be raised from seed, although a couple of years elapse before forcing crowns are produced. Sow seed in prepared beds early in April, the rows being 38–45 cm (15–18 ins) apart and 25 mm (1 in) deep. Thin the seedlings early so that they stand 13–15 cm (5–6 ins) apart, and take out any flower heads that develop.

A quicker method of propagation is by root cuttings, usually known as thongs. They should be straight and clean, 15 cm (6 ins) long and pencil thick. Cut them horizontally at the top and sloping at the bottom.

These cuttings are prepared when lifting plants for forcing. Tie them in bundles and bury in sandy soil, either in the frame or a sheltered position outdoors until planting time in spring. While they are buried each root normally produces several buds, but only the strongest one should be retained. The best time for planting is during March when the soil is workable. Make the rows 45 cm (18 ins) apart, with 30 cm (1 ft) between the plants.

Seakale needs forcing, and this can be done in the open by covering the plants with pots or boxes, around which old manure should be heaped. It is also possible to blanch seakale where it is growing, by earthing up the plants, using soil that is dry, fine and friable. Best results come when the roots are taken into cellars, frames or are placed under the greenhouse staging. Stand to encourage plenty of young tender leaves to develop. This crop will go on until the winter when some roots can be forced indoors to extend the supply.

Seakale is prepared in the same way as asparagus, by boiling or steaming and served with melted butter.

SHALLOTS *Allium cepa* var *ascalonicum*

Shallots are easy to cultivate and require much the same growing conditions as onions. Largely used for pickling, they are also useful for grating into salads. In addition, some of the fresh young shoots can be cut and used as spring onions.

They will grow in a wide variety of soils, although they dislike heavy clay. Freshly manured land is best avoided but well rotted compost or manure dug in during the autumn is beneficial, particularly where exhibition bulbs are required. Fish manure 70–100 g per m² (2–3 oz per sq yd) will also be helpful.

It is possible to raise shallots from seed but the resultant plants are liable to bolt. Normally, small bulbs are planted from early February onwards. At one time gardeners reckoned to plant shallots on the shortest day and harvest them on the longest day, but this is neither necessary nor practical, because of bad weather usually experienced at that time of the year.

The soil should be nicely firm at planting time. Loose skins and dead tops should be taken off before the bulbs are pressed into the soil about half their depth. Space them 12–15 cm (5–6 ins) apart with 30 cm (1 ft) between rows. Birds sometimes force them up. It is advisable to inspect the rows from time to time after planting, so that the bulbs can be pushed back into position again, although they do not like to be buried deeply. Take care not to damage the growing plants when hoeing or otherwise cleaning the ground.

Once the leaves begin to yellow during the summer, draw the soil away from the bulbs to encourage ripening, then lift and dry thoroughly before storing in a cool dry, airy place. The red or common shallot is the most widely grown although some gardeners like the yellow variety. For exhibition purposes, 'Hative de Noir' is greatly favoured.

Shallots have a wide range of culinary uses

Make successional sowings of summer spinach for a constant supply

SPINACH *Spinacea oleracea*

Of Persian origin, this plant was once grown almost solely for medical purposes. There are various kinds, and by sowing successively it is possible to have spinach available throughout the year. While not everyone's favourite green vegetable, it is undoubtedly full of goodness. Flavour will be better if little water is used in cooking.

Summer spinach tends to run to seed quickly on light soils so it is advisable to work into the ground, bulky moisture holding material such as decayed manure or compost. Quick growth is needed and it is beneficial if liquid manure is applied along the rows once the plants are growing well.

Summer spinach should be sown in early March, in drills 20 mm (¾ in) deep and 30 cm (1 ft) apart. Cover and firm in the seeds with the head of a rake. Thin the seedlings early using the thinnings for salads. Further sowings can be made at fourteen day intervals and if the weather is very dry, first soak the seed in water for about twelve hours. If plants begin to run to seed they are best pulled up.

Winter spinach should be sown from mid-August to mid-September, preferably on beds raised about 8 cm (3 ins) to provide good drainage. Thin the plants early so they stand 13–15 cm (5–6 ins) apart. If left too close they are liable to bolt.

While summer spinach can be picked quite hard, winter spinach must not be overworked. Pick the outer leaves only, rather than stripping individual specimens.

This will ensure a regular supply of fresh, young tender leaves. In colder areas the plants should be protected by continuous cloches or straw, bracken, etc. placed between the rows.

RECOMMENDED VARIETIES:
Summer: 'Viroflay' is a fine round seeded variety with smooth round leaves. 'Long Standing Round' has thick, dark green foliage; 'Nobel' is a heavy cropper with large, fleshy leaves. *Winter:* 'Broad leaved Prickly', a hardy abundant cropper and its selection 'Standwell' produce hardy, large succulent leaves over a long period; 'Greenmarket' is slow to run to seed and resistant to disease.

Spinach, Perpetual; Spinach Beet *Beta vulgaris* var *cycla* This is a perennial beet, and an excellent substitute for the true spinach. It produces green leaves but no typical beet root. The leaves are larger and more fleshy than those of summer spinach and are easier to gather and cook. One sowing in April and another in late August will usually ensure a year-round supply. On fairly rich soil, make the drills 13 mm (½ in) deep and 38 cm (15 ins) apart and thin the seedlings so there is 15–20 cm (6–8 ins) between them. Make sure the roots do not dry out in summer. Always keep the young leaves picked even if you cannot use them immediately. Left to grow old, production slows down with loss of quality. Remove the flower heads too.

Spinach, New Zealand *Tetragona expansa* While not a true spinach this plant has similar leaves and can be used as a substitute for summer spinach. It grows well on light, dryish soils, tolerates heat and does not run to seed like the ordinary spinach.

It has a different habit of growth too, since it grows rather flat and spreads rapidly over the ground. The plants do not bolt and if the growing tips are pinched out, an abundance of leaves will be produced forming a ground cover, stifling almost all weeds.

Sow seed under glass in March, first soaking it in water overnight. Move the plants to their final positions in mid-May. Open ground sowings should not be made until towards the end of May. Space the plants 60 cm (2 ft) apart with 75–90 cm (2½–3 ft) between rows and do not allow them to become overcrowded. While this spinach will grow well in dry soils, the leaves will be all the more succulent if plenty of water is given during dry weather. Alternatively, sow under cloches *in situ* in April. Harvesting normally continues from early July until frost kills the plants.

SWEDE *Brassica rutabaga*

Giant turnips, which are known as swedes, originated in Sweden more than 180 years ago. They are hybrids between a turnip and wild cabbage. Purple, white or yellow varieties are available, all with yellow flesh. Hardier than turnips, garden swedes are sweeter but slower growing. They rarely become woody. Sowing time is early May for northern districts and mid-May or early June elsewhere.

Swedes prefer well-drained soil, rich in organic matter and early preparation is advisable, working in farmyard manure or compost. Sow the seed in 25 mm (1 in) deep drills, 45 cm (18 ins) apart, and subsequently thin the seedlings so that there is 30 cm (1 ft) between them. Roots can be left in the ground for use as required in winter. They are very rarely damaged by frost. If a few roots are lifted and packed in boxes of soil, taken into the cool greenhouse and kept in the dark, blanched top growth will develop. This can be cut and boiled, providing a tasty winter dish.

Above left: Spinach beet is very hardy while New Zealand spinach (above right) resists drought.

Below: 'Jubilee' is a bronze-top swede

SWEET CORN *Zea mays*

This is a distinct type of maize with a sugary fruit reserve. It is used as a vegetable and should not be confused with starchy types of maize used for fodder.

Plant sweet corn in blocks to aid wind-pollination

This crop is unsuited to high altitudes and places exposed to sea winds. Medium and light soils are best, ideally manured for a previous crop. When growing in really light soil, work in manure before the crop goes in, while a general fertilizer can be raked in before sowing.

Where small quantities of seed are involved, they can be sown in 7 cm (3 in) pots from the second week in May. Don't sow earlier or the roots may become pot bound and growth will be stunted. Sowing in boxes cannot be recommended because of damage to the roots when transplanting.

Seed can be sown in cold frames where the plants can be left to mature, or cloches are useful for covering direct outdoor sowings.

For uncovered sowings from the third week in May onwards, 5 cm (2 ins) deep furrows are drawn out in a fine tilth. Two seeds are dropped in at 45–60 cm (18–24 ins) intervals and later thinned to one seedling. Make the rows 45–60 cm (18–24 ins) apart, the greater distance for the varieties which mature later.

Thinning is done at the five leaf stage discarding all unhealthy or insect damaged plants. Sweet corn is wind and insect pollinated and carries male and female flowers on the same plant. The best crops are secured where the plants are grown in blocks, because the pollen can easily reach other plants instead of being lost which nearly always happens when the plants are grown in single rows.

The grains set after fertilization and become the edible 'cob'. Proper harvesting influences the yield and it is necessary to gather them carefully so that only fully developed cobs are cut or picked. Once the green husks are pulled aside, the way is open for earwigs to enter. It is therefore, most unwise to strip off the husk to find out if the 'corn' is ready.

According to season, picking begins about the third week of August. If a creamy solution springs from the grains when pressed with a finger nail, they are ripe. The cobs are trimmed by removing untidy 'silks' or broken outer husks. Keep the cobs in the cool until they are used.

RECOMMENDED VARIETIES: 'Golden Bantam', early sweet and tender; 'Prima', fourteen days earlier than 'Golden Bantam'; 'Golden Standard', tall, heavy cropper; 'Kelvedon Glory' and 'Northern Belle', two reliable F_1 hybrids of good flavour.

TOMATOES *Solanum lycopersicum*

Records show that the tomato has been known for many centuries. Natives of South America, these plants came to Britain in the sixteenth century when they were cultivated as ornamental subjects under the name of Love Apples.

The fruit contains vitamin C, although less than that found in the juice of black currants, strawberries or oranges. Vitamin B1 is also present, but it is their vitamin A content that makes tomatoes so valuable.

Whether grown outdoors or under glass, the plants are raised the same way. Since the seeds are large and can be handled individually, they should be spaced 13 mm ($\frac{1}{2}$ in), 6 mm ($\frac{1}{4}$ in) deep, apart in boxes or pans of a clean seed sowing compost. Cover the seeds, then place glass and paper over the boxes to exclude light.

For quickest results, keep the receptacles in a temperature of 18–20°C (65–68°F). After a few days growth will be seen and the covering can be removed. Once the seed leaves open, transfer each seedling separately into a small pot or soil blocks.

When they have settled in the pots, the temperature can be reduced a little with free ventilation. Pot up only first class seedlings. Plants with fern-like leaves are known as rogues or 'jacks' and should be discarded.

Really strong plants can be produced by maintaining a fairly even temperature. When the heat varies, growth is irregular. Sturdy, short jointed plants of a deep green colour are likely to be the most fruitful. Avoid long-jointed, wiry-stemmed plants.

The majority of gardeners sow seed in a heated greenhouse from early February onwards in order to obtain fruit throughout the summer and autumn.

Tomatoes thrive in the warm greenhouse where there is an absence of draughts, good ventilation and a minimum night temperature of around 12°C (55°F). For preference, use a greenhouse glazed to ground level if the plants are to be grown in the 'floor' or border. Otherwise, the beds will have to be raised or made up on the staging. Alternatively, grow the plants in large pots or deep boxes, or growing bags.

It is unwise to put tomatoes outdoors until danger of cold weather has passed. Allow 38–45 cm (15–18 ins) between the plants. If more than one row is planted have rows 90 cm (3 ft) apart. Bush types need wide spacing, say 60 cm (2 ft) between the plants and 90 cm (3 ft) between rows. Stake and tie immediately after planting, further ties being made as growth proceeds.

Disturb the roots as little as possible. Pot grown plants are easy to knock out. Those raised in boxes should be carefully removed, with plenty of soil adhering to the roots. Transplant them firmly so there is 13 mm ($\frac{1}{2}$ in) of soil above the roots.

Standard varieties are usually grown on a single stem, all side shoots being removed while they are small. They can also be grown on double or treble stems depending on their strength. It is rarely worthwhile allowing outdoor plants to carry more than four trusses of fruit for there is insufficient time for more fruit to ripen. Pinch out growing points in late summer, even if they have only formed three trusses.

When buying plants choose a named variety from a known source. Plants from street barrows or other draughty places have often suffered a check from which they may never fully recover. Well grown specimens, ready for planting, should be 18–20 cm (7–8 ins) high, stocky, short jointed with dark green foliage.

Whether outdoors or indoors, tomatoes like fairly rich root conditions. Strawy horse manure is ideal but difficult to obtain. Among good substitutes used by growers are moist wheat straw, well dusted with hoof

'Kirdford Cross' is a disease-resistant variety

and horn manure, ripe compost, well decayed seaweed or spent hops. Peat or leaf mould helps to increase the humus content and provide bulk which encourages plenty of roots. Add lime if the soil is acid and sour.

At planting time, make sure the sub-soil is moist. Beds on the greenhouse staging can be made up with the same soil mixture. First place asbestos or a similar covering over the slats, followed by drainage material. Boards 23–25 cm (9–10 ins) wide, should be fixed to the front and back of the staging, to get the proper root depth when the compost is added. This need only be 13 cm (5 ins) deep at first. Add more compost as growth proceeds, so the soil level comes to within 25 mm (1 in) of the top of the board.

Liquid manure should be given at ten day intervals once the first truss of fruit has set. For plants in pots or boxes, a simple soil mixture on the basis of the John Innes No 2 can be used.

Side shoots should be removed cleanly and as early as possible, and if the dwarf or bush varieties make too many stems, it is best to reduce their number.

Tomatoes can be grown successfully in frames of various kinds, and barn cloches are also suitable. Place these structures in a fairly open, yet sheltered position, preferably running north and south, to encourage

Pinching out side shoots from tomato plants

good growth.

Planting is usually done about mid-April. A bed of fairly rich soil should be made up, adding moist peat to encourage a good root system. Good supports will be needed. Keep the glass on the frames until June, ventilating freely whenever the weather is favourable. Plants under tall frames can be supported by wire or string and canes.

Cloches should be placed on a sunny site sheltered from winds. Take out a trench 20 cm (8 ins) deep and 30 cm (12 ins) wide at the top, tapering to the bottom. Apply a good organic fertilizer and plenty of peat at the base of the trench, to provide proper growing conditions.

Planting outdoors Tomatoes are most accommodating plants but it is essential to make a good start for complete success.

Since plants are frost tender, weather conditions and the state of the soil must be such that growth continues unchecked once **very early in June. But be guided by the season and local conditions.**

Many gardeners now use hormone setting sprays when atmospheric conditions are unsuitable for natural fertilization, or where growth is rank and flowers fail to set fruit. With good culture these aids should not be necessary, but it is important to get the bottom truss of fruit to set, for this encourages even, healthy growth and improves both the quality and setting tendency of later trusses.

Intermittent drying out and heavy watering lead to irregular growth as well as cracked fruit. A surface mulch of peat, leaf mould, or similar material will help to maintain a cool root run enjoyed by the plants, as well as preventing the surface from drying out.

On deep well-prepared land, artificial

'Gardener's Delight' is a sweet-flavoured tomato

watering should be less necessary. If it can be avoided so much the better, for continued light watering in hot weather tends to bring the roots near the surface, where they suffer from dryness much more than when they are deep in the soil.

If the soil has been well prepared and enriched, it should be unnecessary to give extra feeding. Should growth become luxuriant and rank, a dressing of seaweed manure scattered round the plants and watered in, will help to steady growth.

Outdoors, it should easily be possible to bring three trusses of fruit to maturity. If the position is warm and sheltered and the weather good, a fourth truss can sometimes be allowed. There is no point in allowing plants to waste their strength on growth and flowers from which it is impossible to secure fruit. When the chosen number of trusses has been selected, the plants should be stopped at one leaf beyond the top truss and from that time, one or two side shoots can be allowed to develop.

This will keep the sap flowing and discourage fruit splitting which sometimes occurs once the plants have been stopped. The excess of sap is absorbed by the fruit which cannot expand fast enough and the skin cracks, particularly if heavy rains follow a period of dry weather. Old and discoloured leaves should be removed to improve air circulation as well as lessen the possibility of blight infection.

Gather the fruit as soon as it is well coloured. In some districts birds will peck the fruit once it begins to colour. Often they are only seeking moisture, so it is helpful to place shallow containers of water near the plants. This applies to other crops, both vegetables and flowers, which birds sometimes attack, particularly during spells of hot, dry weather.

If in autumn, some fruit is still unripe, complete trusses should be cut off and hung up in the warm greenhouse or living room. Alternatively, fruits can be gathered individually and wrapped in paper and placed in a drawer or box, where they will ripen in the warmth and darkness. Ripening fruit will be available over a period of weeks.

Autumn and winter fruiting By careful planning, ripe fruit will be available from the greenhouse from autumn onwards – a time when fresh fruit is appreciated. For autumn fruiting, seed should be sown towards the end of May using boxes of good compost, with a layer of peat at the bottom. For a winter crop, sow in the greenhouse in summer. Space the seed at least 5 cm (2 ins) apart and cover the boxes with paper to prevent them drying out. Remove the covering once germination occurs. This spacing results in the minimum root disturbance at pricking off time.

It also means that seedlings can be moved straight from the seed boxes to small 60 size pots, 7 cm (2¾ ins). Repot into larger pots as growth develops. By the time 20–30 cm (8–9 ins) pots are reached the plants should be sturdy and in full growth. Keep them in the cool for a week or two. Then stand outdoors in a sheltered place for a

A plum-shaped Italian tomato – 'Roma'

couple of months.

For the final potting, provide a good layer of drainage crocks and use a soil mixture of four parts turfy loam, one part strawy horse manure, and a good sprinkling of hoof and horn meal, or wood ash. Alternatively, use John Innes potting compost No. 3. While outside, feed the plants with liquid manure. This encourages short, stocky growth and strong fruit trusses. Fish meal can be lightly worked into the soil in the pots and watered in. Take the plants into the greenhouse towards the end of summer. Air and light are essential, with a night temperature of 10°C (50°F). The ripening process will be slow, but the fruit colours up evenly.

RECOMMENDED VARIETIES: Although some tomato varieties have been in cultivation for many years, new varieties are introduced annually. This does not mean that all of them are better than the older kinds. The following are among the leading sorts and can be relied upon to crop and grow well:
'Ailsa Craig', good shape, heavy cropper, splendid flavour;
'Alicante', for outdoor and indoor cultivation, free from greenback;
'Big Boy', an F_1 hybrid for greenhouse cultivation, producing extremely large fruits with meaty flesh and fine flavour;

'Eurocross BB', an outstanding variety of excellent quality;

'French Cross', of superb flavour, producing round fruits of uniform shape;

'Gardener's Delight', an outdoor variety with small fruits of sweet flavour;

'Growers Pride', a heavy cropping, reliable indoor variety;

'Kirdford Cross', a compact growing, leafmould disease resistant variety;

'Marmande', large, irregularly shaped fruit, an outdoor variety;

'Moneymaker', a popular, heavy cropping variety, medium sized fruits;

'Outdoor Girl', a heavy cropping outdoor sort;

'Ronaclave', an early outdoor hybrid with large, non-greenback fruit;

'Supercross', a variety tolerant to virus and cladosporium (leaf-mould disease);

'Super Marmande' produces large ribbed fleshy fruit with a good flavour. Ideal for slicing. Suitable for growing outdoors or under glass.

'Tangella', similar to 'Ailsa Craig' but an intense tangerine colour;

'The Amateur'; 'Sleaford Abundance'; two of the most popular bush tomatoes, heavy cropping.

There are one or two yellow fruiting varieties, such as:

'Golden Sunrise' and 'Golden Boy' which have thin skins and excellent flavour.

'Tigerella' has fruit striped yellow and red. Flavour is the same as red varieties.

Tomatoes are ideal subjects for growing-bags

Ring Culture The culture of tomatoes in bottomless rings is a method which provides controlled conditions of nourishment and water supply.

Rings of different materials can be used. Stand the rings on weathered ashes, small grade clinkers, sand, crushed ballast or peat. Gravel or stone chippings can be used but are not so moisture retentive. The depth of the aggregate should not be less than 10 cm (4 ins). About 15 cm (6 ins) deep is suitable.

While it is not essential to lay polythene before putting down the aggregate it is an effective way of isolating the aggregate layer from the greenhouse soil if in the past there has been trouble from disease or eelworm. In this case some provision must be made for the escape of surplus water. The aggregate must be kept constantly moist so that the roots probing it stay nicely damp.

Where there is sufficient height, tomatoes can be grown in rings on greenhouse benches and provided shade is given the plants can be trained to the roof. There is no problem in growing tomatoes in rings in the open ground. Select a south facing site, and raise the aggregate layer a little above the surrounding soil to prevent compost washing into or over the aggregate. John Innes No 3 compost is suitable for ring culture.

It is possible to buy bituminized cardboard rings for this method of culture. A good size is 20 cm (8 ins) deep with a top diameter of 23 cm (9 ins). Having made a 5–7.5 cm (2½–3 ins) layer of compost firm on the bottom of the ring, over the aggre-

Ring culture of greenhouse tomatoes

gate, the tomato plants should be planted firmly. Top up the soil to within 4 cm (1½ ins) of the top of the ring. Leave this space for initial waterings and for feeding.

Give a good watering so the roots settle and after ten days, apply water close to the plant stem (ball watering). Keep the aggregate wet at all times. About a month later the roots will penetrate the aggregate and ball watering should cease, all moisture will then be drawn through the secondary root system in the aggregate, and feeding can start into the rings at 7 day intervals.

Do not water into the rings after feeding until it is evident the compost is becoming dry. It is best to use a diluted liquid fertilizer, since this will be carried to the fibrous roots more quickly.

The fertilizer first used on tomatoes grown in rings was known as 667 from the analysis of 6% each of nitrogen and phosphoric acid and 7% potash. It also provides the necessary magnesium for good colour. Several good proprietary tomato fertilizers made to a similar analysis are readily available. Once the first truss has set, give liquid fertilizer at 7-day intervals.

Plants in rings require more feeding than those in the border in order to give quantities of good fruit. The removal of side shoots and general attention for tomatoes in rings is the same as that required by conventionally grown plants.

Outdoors, ring culture is carried out in the same way as with the greenhouse plants, although it is helpful if the side of the aggregate layer is protected by boards of bricks to keep it in position. Supports should be given at planting stage.

nd transplanting vegetables

10. Cover seeds with fine soil if the ground is rough and cloddy. Otherwise rake them in to give them a good covering.

11. Thin out seedlings by chopping, using a narrow draw hoe 10-15 cm (4-6 inches) wide, or pull them out by hand.

12. Lift cabbages and sprouts with a fork for transplanting after thoroughly watering them.

13. Seedlings for transplanting: lettuce with round-balled roots (left); cauliflower grown in pots overwintered in cloches (centre); trench or self-blanching celery (right).

14. Transplant seedlings with a dibber, levering the dibber to firm the soil against the roots.

15. Transplant trench celery into a wide flat-bottomed trench, and earth up with a trowel.

16. Trim the leaves of leeks and transplant into dibber holes. Do not firm soil, but water in so the growing plant can swell more easily.

17. When transplanting cauliflower, make a hole with a trowel and test it for size before knocking the plant out of the pot.

18. Test cabbage to see that it is firmly planted – a small portion of the leaf should tear away without shifting the plant.

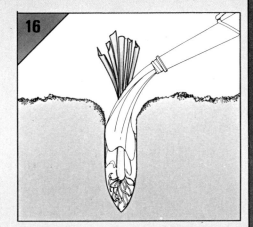

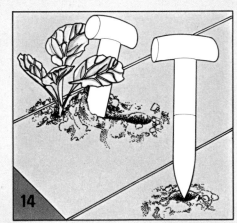

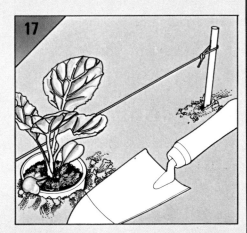

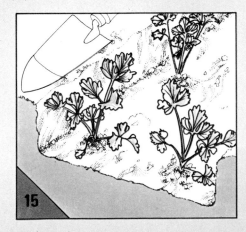

Growing vegetables in containers

Contrary to expectations, container grown vegetables can and do out-yield some crops grown in the ground. Container cultivation enables the owner of a small or town garden to grow plants on patios, in porches, on window sills, balconies, roof tops and other difficult places.

The range of vegetables which can be grown easily and successfully depends largely on the size of receptacle, type of compost, and the subsequent care and attention. When choosing suitable containers, the main points to bear in mind are the needs of the plant, ease and convenience of cultivation and appearance.

The principal needs of a plant are: space and depth to develop, adequate food and moisture, suitable anchorage and support, avoidance of extremes of temperature, and freedom from poisons, pests and diseases.

Watering should not be messy nor should containers dry out too rapidly, and training the growing plants should be a fairly easy task.

Appearance is important in conspicuous places: there are many types of container to choose from and they should be reasonably accessible. Plastic pots and troughs are clean, lightweight, and easy to handle and the more ornate ones look quite attractive. Growing bags are very convenient out-of-the-way places or for use in place of diseased soils. Timber tubs and window boxes are made in various sizes and though pleasing to look at, they have two possible defects: their weight, and the fact that, unless treated with preservatives, they will rot. Glazed earthenware containers are the best but very expensive. Unfortunately the porous type stain.

Although loam-based or soilless potting composts suit most subjects, those of the all-peat type are less satisfactory for beetroot and carrots, where a preparation containing a fair proportion of sand or 25% or more gravel aggregate is better.

Unless you have the facilities to raise them from seed, tomatoes, cucumbers, courgettes and marrows are best bought in young plant form. Other vegetables can be sown directly into their final pots and thinned out as necessary, or raised in seed pans on the window sill, as with lettuce. Water carefully and give developing plants a balanced diluted liquid feed. Spray plants with derris or malathion if aphids appear. Pick off and burn any dead, dying or diseased foliage.

Train climbing beans, courgettes or marrows in tubs, over a wigwam of canes, tying in new growth as necessary with soft string. Pinch out the plants when they reach the top of the supports.

Grow potatoes, dwarf beans and carrots in deep containers, supporting potatoes and dwarf beans with twigs to prevent them falling over. Container growing requires careful choice of varieties. Choose dwarf, compact, early-maturing types from the following list:

Dwarf bean–Masterpiece
Beetroot–Boltardy
Carrot–Parisian Rondo, a round type, or Early Nantes, stump-rooted
Courgette–Zucchini
Cucumber–Patio-Pak F1 Hybrid
Lettuce–Tom Thumb
Marrow–Smallpak
Onion–White Lisbon
Peas–Mangetout Dwarf de Grace
Potato–Foremost
Radish–French Breakfast
Shallots–Dutch Yellow
Tomato–Tiny Tim, or Sub-arctic Plenty

ABOVE Lettuce in a proprietary growing bag.
LEFT Tomatoes in pots on a balcony.
RIGHT Vegetables in the flower garden.

Vegetables in the flower garden

In small gardens, where a lack of space prevents the allocation of an area exclusively to vegetables, the idea of growing flowers and food together is attractive. It is particularly important in these circumstances to prepare the ground well and look after the crop attentively.

Observe rotation requirements as in an ordinary vegetable garden: Wallflowers and arabis also suffer from the club root that affects cabbages. Control pest or diseases as soon as any signs of trouble appear, by spraying or dusting.

Display vegetable plants so that their decorative qualities are shown to advantage and their utilitarian nature masked by the overall effect. Do not separate flowers from vegetables, interplant them: carrots, for example, among gladioli.

Not all vegetables will thrive in the flower garden, but the following combinations have proved successful.

Display the red-flowered runner bean (Scarlet Emperor) as a screen or backing to a flower bed, or grow them in clumps, stopping them at 1.5m (5 ft) and using a cane wigwam of that height for support. They are then less over-powering among other flowers.

The dark red leaves of beetroot 'Globe' or the 'Ruby' Swiss chard make a useful contrast of foliage texture and colour dotted among geraniums or begonias in summer bedding. Leeks with their strap-like foliage make a quite useful substitute for ornamental sweet corn when dotted among African marigolds, antirrhinums and French marigolds. Lift the leeks when the summer bedding is pulled out. 'Musselburgh' is a good choice for this situation.

Parsley ('Imperial Curled') can be grown as an edging round flower beds.

The salad onion 'White Lisbon' makes a delicate division between different groups or blocks of low-growing plants such as *Phlox drummondii*, or *Begonia semperflorens* instead of the more common blue-green fescue grass.

Sow carrots of the 'Concord' variety among summer-flowering anemones – both have similar foliage – and interplant with gladioli to give height, each complementing the other.

Chives make useful edging or dot plants and produce an attractive crop of pink flowers. Plant various thymes in a sunny position in a window box or in a rockery in association with other plants. Sow a clump or two of the purple-podded peas among herbaceous border plants for contrast. Dwarf kales, either coloured for summer use or curled green used as dot plants among early flowering daffodils and forget-me-not can be effective, but it is important that dead or discoloured leaves are removed as soon as possible.

Nasturtiums provide a good display of summer colour and the leaves add piquancy to any salad. When their fruits have set, pot-grown sweet peppers can be planted among bedding plants to provide colour and interest especially when decorative plants such as nemesia have finished flowering. Some of the small bush types of tomato can be grown among flowers. The variety Sub-arctic Cherry grows happily even in hanging baskets, producing a profusion of small bright red fruits. Harvest the various crops of plants, pods, or roots gradually, so that the decorative effect or general appearance is not ruined by the sudden gaps or loss of colour.

Harvesting and storing vegetables

The time and cost of producing good wholesome home-grown food can be wasted unless crops are gathered in the right conditions and properly kept until they are required for the table.

When to pick crops

Vegetables have to be harvested at the right stage of development before they become too tough for eating, and the maturing process must be slowed down by storing the crop until it is required.

The swollen roots of root crops are organs for storing plant energy and unless growth is arrested will continue to develop, form fibre and be tough to eat. To be tender and succulent, salads like lettuce should be used as soon as they are ready; their storage life cannot be extended beyond a few days. Stem and leaf crops like celery and spinach also have a limited life once picked, but will stand on the plant for a few weeks

Storing in boxes or clamps

In autumn, before the severe frosts arrive, lift and trim crops such as turnips, carrots and beetroot and place them in a frost-free shed between layers of dry sand or peat in boxes. Store larger quantities in clamps outside. Place the roots on beds of clean straw and cover them with straw 10cm (4in) thick. Finally, cover with a layer of soil 15cm (6in) thick, leaving a straw plug for ventilation to prevent sweating and rotting.

Harvesting individual crops

Broad beans: Pick the pods before the beans harden, and use fresh or freeze for future needs.

French and runner beans: Pods are ready for picking if they snap when bent and before the seeds swell. Use fresh and freeze the surplus.

Cauliflower: Protect curds by bending a leaf or two over the developing head to avoid sun or frost damage.

Celery: Use self-blanching types when ready and before the frosts. Dig trench celery as required. When blanched, from about October, they can be left standing in the ground until February.

Kale: Pick over each plant removing a few leaves each time, starting at the centre and working down. Since it is very hardy, this crop will usually stand outside for weeks in winter.

Leeks: Lift carefully as required, leaving the remainder in the ground.

Lettuce: Begin cutting when young to avoid a glut. In summer, lift plants with roots and stand two or three in a shallow bowl of clean water in a cool airy place to give an extra few days' life.

ABOVE Potato clamp.

ABOVE Twisting leaves of beet.

ABOVE Carrots stored in sand.

in cold winter weather if protected from severe frosts.

Seed and pod crops can be used when tender, green and fresh, or they can be frozen or dried. Peas, beans and sweet corn can be preserved for quite a long time in excellent condition when quick-frozen, as can cauliflowers and broccoli. Their life in the fresh state cannot be easily extended beyond a week or so. Hearted cabbages and mature marrows will last for several weeks if they are hung up in nets in a cool airy place.

During the coldest months of the year hardy vegetables like leeks, parsnips, Savoy cabbage and kale can remain in or on the ground without coming to much harm, provided pigeons and other birds are prevented from eating them.

Beetroot: Pull small roots for immediate use, twisting off the leaves. Do not cut them off or the beet will 'bleed' and be useless. In autumn lift large roots, twist off the leaves, and store in boxes or clamps.

Brussels sprouts: Start picking sprouts from the base when firm and solid, but before they begin to open. Midseason and late varieties will keep on the plants for several weeks in cold weather. Freeze surplus buttons.

Cabbage: Hearting types will stand for a week or two in summer or several weeks in autumn or winter. Cut solid heads and store in airy nets hung up in a cool place out of direct sunlight.

Carrots: As for beetroot.

Marrows and Courgettes: Start cutting when small. Allow marrows to mature at the season's end, cut and store in suspended nets in a cool airy place.

Onions: As the bulbing onions mature and the stems fall over, bend the remainder down, lift, and dry off three weeks later on slatted or wire mesh trays. To store, tie up in ropes or spread thinly on trays for drying in a cool airy place. Use thick-necked bulbs first. Lift salad onions as needed.

Parsnips: Lift roots as required when the leaves begin to die down, leaving the crop in the ground. In February, dig up the remainder and store in layers of sand or peat in boxes.

Peas: Pick when the pods are almost filled and before they change colour or turn pale. Freeze surplus peas.

Potatoes: Dig and use early or new varieties when the flowers die. Lift maincrops when the foliage dies off. Dry for an hour or two after lifting. Store in boxes in a dark airy frost-free place or in a clamp.

Shallots: Lift, divide and dry on wire trays as for onions when the foliage dies down in summer.

BELOW Well stocked and attractive small herb garden.

Spinach (all types): Pick regularly as soon as leaves are large enough to use.

Swedes: Leave in the soil and dig up as required.

Sweet corn: Test seed between finger-nail and thumb when the silks or tassels turn brown. Pull cobs with seeds of a creamy consistency. Leave ones with watery sap for a few days. Freeze surplus cobs.

Tomatoes: Pick fully ripe fruit with green calyx attached. Remove trusses of green tomatoes at the end of the season and ripen indoors in a warm dark place.

Turnips: Lift early types young when about golf ball size. Dig up maincrop, twist off leaves, store in boxes in layers of peat or sand protected from frosts or in clamps.

Herbs for the winter

On the next 14 pages you can read about the wide range of culinary herbs that you can grow – and on page 173 there are instructions on how to dry and prepare many of them for dry storing. Not all herbs are suitable for this treatment, however, and it may be worth looking at some of the alternatives.

Many herbs can be frozen, and you will have the benefit of better colour even if there is a loss of texture. Many herbs can be kept in good condition for at least six months. Do not blanch them, but wash and chop them before freezing, which is best done in small batches.

Do not overlook the possibility of *fresh* herbs in winter. Put a cloche over a late sowing of parsley, or sow some seeds of chives or parsley in mid or late summer, and grow in pots to take indoors for the winter.

171

A-Z GUIDE TO HERBS AND SPICES

Herbs cannot be omitted from any plans drawn up for growing vegetables. Apart from their aroma, they possess undeniable health giving properties. Spices too, can be used with herbs in tasty meals and snacks.

Many people obtain their herbs dried in jars or packets. Although in an average sized garden it is not possible to grow all the herbs needed for the kitchen, it should not be difficult to find a place for a useful selection. While parsley, mint, sage and thyme are indispensable, others of great culinary worth are just as easy to cultivate.

The herb garden may be considered an adjunct to the vegetable garden and a minimum of labour is needed for its upkeep. Keep a watchful eye on rampant growers and cut them back or divide them before they smother less vigorous kinds.

If a choice of site is available select one which faces west and slopes slightly, to receive maximum sunshine. Since the garden will be more or less permanent, the

ground should be deeply trenched and enriched with a generous supply of manure or compost and a scattering of bone meal. Sharp sand, bonfire ash or leaf mould will lighten heavy, clingy soils.

With perennial and biennial herbs, a top dressing of loamy soil applied each spring as growth commences, will promote steady growth. Keep the bed in a healthy vigorous condition by lifting, dividing and replanting young portions of the perennial kinds about every four years.

Spices have been grown and used for centuries and although there is rarely any shortage of these, how many of these will grow if seeds or roots are planted in pots or in the open ground? Unfortunately, many are treated and dried so throughly that all life has gone from them when you buy them in the shops.

Capsicums or chillies are grown chiefly for their edible pods, but they are also very colourful, and make attractive greenhouse and living room plants. Culture is simple in this country, even though these plants are natives of East Africa, the West Indies and India. Seed is readily available and is sown in trays or pots in February or March, in light, rich soil, in a temperature of 15°C (60°F). Move the seedlings singly into small pots and give them more room as they increase in size. The first move can be avoided if seed is sown individually in the small thumb pots. By the time the plants reach 50—60 cm (20—24 ins) high, they are usually laden with fruit.

To ensure herbs are available throughout winter they need to be dried. This is best done just before the plants come into flower for the flavour is then at its peak. Ideally gather the leaves when the dew has just dried and before strong sun reaches them, but do not pick them when they are limp through being in strong sunshine or windblown. It is best to tie the cut stems into small bunches, for it is difficult for air to circulate around a large bunch and this could lead to lack of flavour and mildew.

While you can hang small bunches in a cool airy shed or outhouse the ideal place is a dry warm room where the air is moving slightly. Another method is to spread the herbs on a bench or table in a cool dry place. In very wet seasons, small quantities can be dried gently in a very cool oven. They can also be dried in paper bags but holes should be punched in them to let air in and moisture out.

Herbs to dry in trays include chervil, lovage, parsley, thyme and rosemary. When dry, it is easy to rub the leaves of many herbs into a powder which can be put into jars or other containers and sealed tightly to use as required. Keep them in a cool dark place and use within six months.

Herb and spice seeds to dry, include coriander, cumin, caraway, dill and fennel. For these, cut the whole plant and place it head down in paper bags to catch the seeds as they fall.

The herbs in the list starting on page 176 are among the most useful to grow.

Shopping for herb plants

When buying herb plants it is as well to be perfectly clear in your own mind what you are buying; for instance, whether you are shopping for pot marjoram, winter marjoram, or wild marjoram (which is the same as oregano). Without this working knowledge of herbs you will need a fair degree of luck, as herb suppliers occasionally get the naming of certain varieties wrong – yes, there can be genuine confusion even among experts!

Whether this matters very much depends on how seriously you take your herb growing. The wrong thyme may make little difference to your cooking, even though some types are superior for culinary use, but if you are sold Russian tarragon as French tarragon, there is no comparison in flavour. One taste and you will know the difference immediately.

The following notes on the 15 popular herbs illustrated highlight some of the possible confusions, together with buying hints.

Angelica

This giant among herbs is easily raised from *fresh* seed – indeed, it will happily self-seed if allowed to flower, but it will also die off afterwards and you will have to wait two years for new plants to reach maturity. So, you may prefer to buy a plant, making sure that it is not showing signs of premature flowers.

Balm, lemon

If you plant your herbs among the flower borders, it is worth trying the variegated form, but the pale green one is best for culinary use.

Basil, sweet

This popular herb is normally treated as a half-hardy annual; you will need to provide protection for plants bought before, say, early June. The quality of bought plants tends to be variable, but basil is not particularly easy to raise from seed.

Bay

A ready-trained standard 'bay tree' is expensive – so, unless you want a tree-sized specimen, look for your bay among the small herbs at the garden centre. A small rooted cutting, up to say 25 cm (10 in) high will be inexpensive and perfectly adequate for culinary purposes.

Chervil

This is easily raised from seed, but if you prefer to buy a plant make sure it is not flowering prematurely – as it soon runs to seed. A good plant should have delicate, well-formed pale green leaves, deeply segmented, and a slightly hairy stem – rather like parsley, but finer.

Chives

In garden centres, the label often just says 'chives'. Elsewhere you may have the option of 'giant' or 'ordinary' or 'dwarf' chives. Most authorities say that the 'giant' chives do not have such a good flavour, but others suggest that these are not in fact distinct plants. So buy 'dwarf' chives if you can, but don't be too surprised if they grow larger and become less flavoursome.

Dill

This hardy annual with feathery leaves off a shiny main stem, is raised from seed, but germination can be erratic so you may prefer to buy a plant. Choose one that is growing strongly but not flowering.

Fennel

Fennel is easily grown from seed but, again, for a single specimen you are better off buying a plant. It is not impossible that you will be sold Florence fennel (a vegetable) by mistake – it has a more bulbous base – but even if this happens the leaves can still be used for flavouring.

Marjoram

Most marjorams can be used for culinary flavourings, but pot marjoram (*Origanum onites*), also known as French marjoram or English marjoram in some catalogues, is one of the best. For the most subtle flavour try sweet marjoram (*O. marjorana*).

Mint, apple

With this variety, confusion sometimes arises – you may be sold Bowles mint instead since both have woolly leaves. There is also a variegated form of apple mint.

Mint, spearmint

You are unlikely to have any problems identifying this mint – thanks to its distinctive aroma.

Parsley

The parsley most commonly grown has dark green, curly leaves, but you may be offered French parsley, which has broader, plain leaves and a stronger flavour.

Sage

The grey-green, hairy leaved form of *Salvia officinalis*, is the one most often used in the kitchen, but if you grow your herbs in the flower border, you may prefer one of the coloured or variegated forms. Unless you want it for such ornamental purposes, a small specimen will suffice.

Tarragon

French tarragon which has a stronger aniseed aftertaste is the one you want for flavour. It needs winter protection, but it is well worth the trouble – the hardier Russian type is a poor substitute; indeed, many people actually find its flavour unpleasant. The two are often confused, but easily distinguished by the taste once you know the difference.

Thyme

Ordinary broad-leaved thyme or the common type – is all you need for culinary use. Although you may also like to try *lemon thyme* (*T. citriodorus*) with its delicious citrus flavour and aroma. Unless you want thyme solely for decorative purposes, don't be distracted by the many other varieties.

Key
1 Balm
2 Parsley
3 Marjoram
4 Thyme
5 Chervil
6 Dill
7 Angelica
8 Fennel
9 Sage
10 Tarragon
11 Chives
12 Apple Mint
13 Spearmint
14 Sweet Basil
15 Bay

ALECOST (Costmary) *Balsamita major*

This is a pleasant herb with a scent of mint. The roundish leaves are greyish-green, the button-like flowers are yellow. Growing 45–120 cm (1½–4 ft) the plants flourish in a sunny position in rich soil. Finely chopped leaves add zest to salads, soups and stuffings. At one time an ointment was made from the leaves and used for soothing burns and bruises.

ANGELICA *Angelica archangelica*

Angelica leaf and flowerhead

There are several forms of this plant to be found growing wild in Britain. The true angelica of confectionery is a native of parts of Russia and Germany, although it grows in most European countries.

Growing 90 cm–1.50 m (3–5 ft) high, it is either a biennial, dying after flowering, or a short lived perennial. It prefers partial shade and a cool moist, but not wet, root run. The broad umbels of white flowers appear in May and June and if they are removed before they develop, the plant is more likely to survive the winter.

It is best to sow seed in spring, although it can also be sown in early autumn. Angelica has sculptured foliage of stately appearance and this makes it valuable as a feature plant. The thick hollow stems possess an aromatic scent which is retained when they are candied. The young stems are greatly valued when cut up and used in tarts with rhubarb, as well as in jams. A leaf added to salads imparts a pleasing taste, while both foliage and roots have certain medicinal qualities. A tale connected with this plant says that it holds powers against evil spirits.

BALM (Lemon Balm) *Melissa officinalis*

Growing in any soil, this plant reaches 90 cm–1.2 m (3–4 ft) high, has lemon scented leaves and small white flowers in summer. Propagation is easy: by division of roots in spring or autumn or seed sown in boxes in May. Thin the seedlings early and finally move them to their permanent places 60 cm (2 ft) apart. Although of little commercial value, the dried leaves retain the refreshing lemon flavour which makes them useful for stuffing poultry. A leaf or two placed in the tea pot with the tea provides a pleasant drink. A useful bee plant, it was also once used to soothe the nerves and 'drive away melancholy'.

Above: Alecost in flower
Below: Balm is a perennial herb

Above: Basil has many culinary uses
Below: A bay tree enhances any garden

BASIL *Ocimum basilicum*

Widely grown in Britain and treated as a half-hardy annual, basil is a perennial in warm countries. Seed is sown under glass in late March/early April in a temperature of 15°C (60°F) and the plants are moved to the garden in early June. Alternatively, sow outdoors in sandy soil in May. Germination is usually erratic. The irregularly shaped leaves have a pleasant clove-like flavour, useful to adding either fresh to tomato salad or dried to soups and stews. Flowers are white or purple-tinged. Basil has been cultivated for centuries and is said to 'procure a merrie heart'. At one time it was infused with water used for washing.

BAY *Laurus nobilis*

This evergreen laurel-like shrub should be grown either in the open ground or in tubs in a sunny sheltered place. It is valued for its leaves, either fresh or dried. The flavour is potent so use the leaves sparingly. The yellow flowers in May are often followed by purplish berries. It is best to buy new plants in pots since transplanting from the open ground is not always successful.

RED BERGAMOT *Monarda didyma*

Summer blooms of bergamot

Known also as bee balm and oswego tea, this is a perennial growing up to 90 cm (3 ft) high. The plants like a cool root run and should never lack moisture in summer. Both leaves and flowers can be included in salads and the leaves may be used fresh or dry to impart an aromatic flavour to the usual Indian or China tea. A few leaves chopped fine are delicious in salads and fragrant in pot pourris.

BORAGE *Borago officinalis*

This most decorative plant is worthy of a place in any garden. It was Gerard who said that borage can be used 'for the comfort of the heart, to make the mind glad, and drive away sorrow'.

It is an excellent bee-plant, while the leaves and stalks are frequently used by herbalists to remedy chest and throat complaints. The leaves and flowers are useful in pot pourri while the blue flowers brighten a salad dish. The leaves and peeled stalk should be used sparingly, since they impart

177

Borage is an attractive plant which is easy to grow

an acquired flavour to salads.

An infusion of the leaves makes a cooling drink welcomed in hot weather. Lemonade and cider can be improved by the addition of a few borage flowers.

Borage grows 45–60 cm (1½–2 ft) high and can be raised from seed sown in the open from late April onwards. Usually grown as an annual, the plants will sometimes come through the winter in rosette form and flower in early spring. It seeds freely so that new plants appear annually. The grey-green foliage and the somewhat drooping flowers on upright stems are effective plants for raised beds where the blooms can be viewed from below.

There are taller growing perennial members of the family producing showy blue flowers. These however, are not herb plants.

BURNET *Poterium sanguisorba*

This hardy perennial growing 45–50 cm (18–20 ins) high, is sometimes found growing wild. The greenish flowers have red stigmas. Keep removing the blooms to encourage more leaves to form. The foliage has a cucumber-like flavour with a nutty undertone, making it useful in salads and soups and cooling drinks. Seed should be sown in prepared beds in May and the plants moved to their final positions in any good garden soil in October.

CARAWAY *Carum carvi*

A biennial plant about 75 cm (2½ ft) high. Seed is sown in well-drained soil in May, the flower umbels appear the following spring and the seeds ripening in June and July. The seeds are easily lost if the heads are left too long, so cut them as soon as they ripen. Hang them to dry over paper so that the seeds are caught as they ripen and fall.

Caraway seeds are frequently used in cakes or sprinkled on bread as well as for flavouring soups and cheese dishes. The flavour is very distinctive.

Burnet is a decorative plant

CHERVIL *Anthriscus cerefolium*

An annual growing to 30–45 cm (12–18 ins). Select a fairly rich moist soil and sow from early May onwards. Allow 15–18 cm (6–7 ins) between the plants. Chervil is included in mixed herbs for improving soups and salads.

Above: Chervil; below: Caraway

CHIVES *Allium schoenoprasum*

Usually bought as plants, although seed is sometimes available. These make a useful edging to a border and even a very few of these perennials will ensure that onion flavouring is always available. They are easy to grow even in fairly dry soil.

Growing about 15–18 cm (6–7 ins) high, they produce lots of thin, reedy stems and once established they can easily be propagated by division in spring, placing the separate portions 23 cm (9 ins) apart. It is advisable to lift and divide plants every three or four years to maintain a healthy stock.

The green stems or 'grass' should be regularly cut whether or not they are required in the kitchen. This will ensure the continued production of young tender shoots. Never let chives run to seed or they will deteriorate and lose their subtle flavouring.

DILL *Pendedanum graveolens*

Dill has a pungent, aromatic yet slightly sweet flavour. It has a long history and it is believed that the Romans brought this plant to Britain. A couple of hundred years ago dill seeds were taken to church, to be nibbled during long dry sermons and to prevent the congregation from becoming hungry. A tisane made from the seed is said to alleviate persistent hiccups.

The plants grow up to 90 cm (3 ft) high, and the dark green, erect stems are hollow. The white and green flowers are produced in umbels.

Dill is an annual and is propagated by seed sown in the spring. Germination is sometimes erratic. It is best to sow in succession from early April until early July. Draw the drills up to 30 cm (1 ft) apart. Make sure to water the seedlings in times of drought. Space the plants so they do not touch in full growth, or they may harbour greenfly.

The plants can be grown in pots although there they will not grow as tall but this makes them useful where space is limited. Dill grows quickly and the aroma is best just before flowering. Whole or ground dill seeds are useful for adding to vegetable dishes and the attractive feathery leaves make a garnish suitable for salads and open sandwiches.

Below: Chives in flower

FENNEL *Foeniculum vulgare*

This very ancient plant is found growing wild in many parts of the world including Europe, China, South Africa, America, Russia and New Zealand. It will succeed in greatly varying positions. All parts of the plant can be used. One cultivated variety has bronze or coppery foliage, which many gardeners believe is hardier, longer living and of better flavour.

Growing 90 cm–1.80 m (3–6 ft) high, the stems are blue-green, smooth and glossy; the leaves are bright green and feathery.

The form Florence fennel, also referred to as finocchio, has an enlarged leaf base which is cooked as a vegetable.

Fennel was used by country people long before the introduction of synthetic drugs, and one of Culpepper's famous remarks

Above: Use the leaves and flowers of dill

Fennel has decorative foliage

about this plant is 'that it is used in drinks to make people more lean that are too fat'. Certainly the leaves have a pleasantly acid taste that goes well with various sauces. It is also used in the making of herbal teas and syrups and it is of value in dispersing flatulence. The association of fennel with cooked fish is well known.

Propagation is by seed sown in a sunny situation in April or May. Germination is often slow, but once started the plants grow well. The bright yellow flowers are produced in umbels. As the seeds approach the ripening stage, cut the stems and tie them in bundles. Then lay them on some kind of sheeting so that the ripe dry seed can be properly harvested.

GARLIC *Allium sativum*

This first came to Britain and other European countries via the returning Crusaders of the Middle Ages. They brought it from Ascalon from which the name of our shallot is derived. For long widely used in continental cooking, it is only fairly recently that British gardeners have taken a real interest in garlic, which is now gaining popularity. Though hardy, it does best in sunny, fairly sheltered positions. A light, well-drained soil produces the best crops. Ground manured for a previous crop should be chosen, for garlic should not be grown on freshly manured soil. Wood ash and weathered soot are beneficial if raked into the surface soil just before planting.

Garlic forms a number of bulblets or cloves, as they are known, being grouped together in a whitish outer skin. A well developed bulb often consists of up to two

dozen individual cloves and specimens about 12 mm ($\frac{1}{2}$ in) in diameter are best for planting. Planting is usually done in March, but in warm districts in light well drained soil, an October and November planting gives good results.

On wet soils garlic should be grown in raised beds. Space the cloves 20–23 cm (8–9 ins) apart with 25–30 cm (10–12 ins) between each row and plant 5 cm (2 ins) deep. During July or August the leaves will wither and this is a sign that the crop is ready for lifting and drying.

Garlic ready for use

Always lift with a fork. If the cloves are pulled out by the stem there will be injury to the neck and an easy entry for disease spores. Dry garlic thoroughly before storing in a frostproof, airy shed or larder, then it will keep well for many months.

A tiny quantity of garlic in salads improves the flavour of the other ingredients and it is widely believed that garlic eaten in moderation contributes to good health.

'Jumbo' garlic, a comparatively new strain of mild flavour, can be raised from seed sown in a temperature of 16°C. Use boxes of seed compost and eventually plant the seedlings 30 cm (1 ft) apart in the open ground. Keep the flower heads pinched out.

HORSERADISH *Armoracia rusticana*

This is a native of south-east Europe, and now naturalized in parts of Britain.

To secure good thick roots, it is advisable to grow it on well-prepared, deeply dug and manured ground, where lime is not lacking. To prevent the roots spreading, which is a drawback of this crop, the base of the site where the plants are to be grown should be made very firm.

Not more than a dozen roots will be required for the average household. Good strong thongs about 20 cm (8 ins) long, and of pencil thickness are best. Reduce the buds to one. In early March, holes should be made 25 cm (10 ins) apart and the roots or thongs dropped into them so that about 10 cm (4 ins) of soil covers the top.

To prevent horseradish from becoming a nuisance, lift annually and replant each spring. Lifted roots can be stored in moist sand where they will remain firm.

HYSSOP *Hyssopus officinalis*

A native of southern Europe, hyssop likes light soil and plenty of sunshine. An old-fashioned shrubby perennial plant, it makes a nice low hedge of 60–75 cm (2–2½ ft) high. It can be clipped annually to retain its shape but too much cutting back will reduce the show of gentian-blue flowers. Forms having pink or purplish flowers are sometimes available and seedlings from these often exhibit intermediate colourings.

Propagation is by seed sown under glass in March or in the open ground in May or June. Take cuttings of strong shoots in summer. Hyssop is not much used as a herb since the flavour is rather strong. Very few finely chopped leaves are sufficient to include with mixed herbs or in the salad bowl. Hyssop tea made from the dried flowers and used with honey is of value for chest troubles, while an infusion of the green tops relieves coughs and catarrh.

Below: Horseradish should be lifted annually. Right: Lemon Scented Verbena

Choose young delicate leaves of hyssop

LEMON SCENTED VERBENA
Aloysia triphylla

A native of Chile, this plant has been in cultivation for almost a hundred years. It is sometimes known as *Aloysia citriodora* or *Lippia citriodora*. The leaves smell and taste of lemon and make a fragrant tea. They also flavour fruit drinks, jams and jellies, and are used in finger bowls.

It grows in any good garden soil. Do not use fresh manure or growth will be soft and weak. A sheltered position is necessary as it is susceptible to frost damage. Outdoors, mulch the roots with leaf mould to protect them during the winter.

Lemon scented verbena makes an excellent plant for the living room and greenhouse. Propagation is from cuttings in spring. Both leaves and flowers can be harvested in August although leaves can be plucked off at any time.

LOVAGE *Ligusticum scoticum*

This hardy perennial has handsome polished foliage and the scent of the whole plant is reminiscent of celery or parsnips, with an extra sweetness. A native of Mediterranean areas, it has been grown in Britain for centuries, and was probably introduced by the Romans.

The plants thrive in semi-shade or sun, in rich moist soil, and reach a height of 1.20 m (4 ft). The umbels of yellowish flowers open in July and August. Propagation is by seed

sown in spring or division in spring or autumn. Lovage was once greatly favoured as a tisane for fever and colic. It can be used as a substitute for celery and is normally available fresh or dry.

MARIGOLD *Calendula officinalis*

The old fashioned marigold, usually single flowered, has long been used in salads and mixed herbs. While not so showy as the modern varieties it was once greatly valued for its medicinal qualities and culinary purposes. The whole plant was used to make an ointment to help heal ulcers and other wounds. In salads the flowers add colour and a distinctive flavour when dried and they can be added to soups and broth.

MARJORAM *Origanum* species

There are several species of marjoram invaluable for culinary flavourings.

Origanum onites is the French or pot marjoram, a hardy perennial growing 30 cm (1 ft) high, with rich green aromatic leaves and pinkish-mauve flowers.

Origanum majorana, a native of Portugal, is the Italian, sweet or 'knotted' marjoram. It has smallish grey leaves which have a particularly pleasing scent and flavour. A half-hardy perennial, it is frequently grown as an annual, the seed being sown in March under glass and the plants transferred to their growing positions from late May onwards. It can be grown in pots in the cold or cool greenhouse where it will remain productive for several seasons. It is the grey-green bracts surrounding the tiny flowers that give rise to the common name of 'knotted'.

Marjoram is used in bouquets garnis

Above: Lovage grows in any ordinary soil.
Below: Use the dried flowers of marigolds

Origanum vulgare, wild marjoram, is a native European plant. In Britain it flourishes on the Chalk Downs. The south European plants have more flavour than the British and provided the herb, oregano. Growing 30–75 cm (1–2½ ft) high, the flowers produced vary from pinkish-mauve to purple, while occasionally a white form appears.

Origanum vulgare 'Aureum', is the golden marjoram, a variety with golden, sweetly perfumed foliage, and soft pink flowers. This species too, can be grown in the cool greenhouse and should be propagated by division in spring or autumn. All the others are usually raised from seed sown in boxes in spring in the cool greenhouse or frame. Alternatively sow shallowly in the open ground in May, protecting the young seedlings from drying winds and drought.

Grow the plants in good soil adding plenty of compost to sandy ground, which should be kept free of weeds. The fresh or dried leaves add a delightful flavour to many dishes, and are used in stuffings and salads.

MINT *Mentha* species

Of the many known mint species *Mentha spicata* or *M. viridis* is most popular. Usually known as spearmint, mackerel, pea, potato or green lamb mint, its aromatic taste peps up new potatoes and peas. This species often grows to 90 cm (3 ft) high and is distinguished by its pointed, glossy, dark green leaves. Of invasive habit, it should be divided frequently or propagated from cuttings. Grow it in a sunken bucket punched with drainage holes, to confine its invasive root system.

Mentha suaveoleus (syn. *M. rotundifolia*) often known as the apple or round-leaved mint, is fairly strong growing with large leaves. It is excellent for mint sauce and for flavouring jellies. Less susceptible to 'rust' than other species, it can be grown where the fungus is troublesome. Some dislike it because of its rather hairy or woolly leaves.

Mentha piperita, peppermint, seldom grown in gardens, is enormously important commercially for oil of peppermint distilled from the purple flower heads.

There are several mints which are not suitable for eating but which have for centuries been cherished for their aroma in sachets and for keeping moths out of stored linen. Particularly good is *M. piperita citrata*, the Eau de Cologne mint, which when rubbed gives off the odour from which it gets its name. Other mints have a ginger scent and there is one with variegated foliage which has a penetrating scent not unlike pineapple. It was much used with lavender and rosemary in posies carried by Victorian ladies. Old herbals recommend mint infusions for stomach troubles and head colds.

Mint is easy to propagate by dividing established plants in spring or autumn. Quite small pieces of root will produce sturdy plants in a short time. Young succulent growths can be obtained during winter if roots are placed in boxes or pots of ordinary soil and kept in the warm greenhouse, in full light in the living room, or on the kitchen windowsill.

NASTURTIUM *Tropaeolum majus*

Very well known as a flowering annual, nasturtium is a valuable salad plant. Use the young and clean leaves to provide a piquant flavouring. The seeds can also be included in the salad bowl, although they are rather hot. The flowers, too, can be eaten and provide a bright and appetizing display.

Nasturtiums flower best in poor soil. In rich soil they are apt to produce leafy growth at the expense of flowers. The large seeds can be sown individually 13 mm ($\frac{1}{2}$ in) deep. Watch the plants for aphids since these pests can soon cripple growth. Control aphids with a derris or pyrethrum based insecticide.

There are many varieties and it is best to depend on the dwarfer bushy strains rather than the trailing or climbing forms, unless one wishes to use the plants for ground cover or to hide a fence.

Left: Peppermint is grown not for its fresh leaves but the oil of peppermint it exudes

Below left: Round leaved or apple mint has a good flavour

Below: Nasturtium leaves have a slight peppery taste

PARSLEY *Petroselinum crispum*

This biennial plant has been grown for well over 500 years. It has many health giving properties as well as improving the flavour of food.

Parsley rivals mint for popularity in the kitchen. There are several types although

an improvement with tightly curled deep green leaves resistant to bad weather.

ROSEMARY *Rosmarinus officinalis*

An excellent bee plant, this is one of the best known herbs, around which there are many legends. It is the shrub of remembrance and friendship, as the phrase 'rosemary for remembrance' indicates. Rosemary is eulogized in old books. One states that 'it comforteth the heart and maketh merry and lively'.

Its leaves impart a powerful flavour and one or two are sufficient to enhance a soup or stew. Rosemary has a number of other uses: it is an ingredient of a shampoo, and

Above left: Parsley is the most useful herb

Above: Rosemary is a shrubby plant

Left: Rue 'Jackman's Blue'

the chief kinds now grown are either the numerous curled-leaved varieties or the broad or plain leaved kinds. Freshly gathered parsley is infinitely preferable to dried.

Using cloches and cold frames, it is possible to have sprigs for cutting all year round. Parsley is usually sown for succession, starting in February.

Where the intention is to grow parsley for drying, seeds should be sown early. For summer use, April and early May sowings are the most useful while for plants to stand the winter, July is the time.

There are numerous superstitions in connection with parsley, many arising from the time it takes to germinate, which may be up to seven or eight weeks. If seed is sown in a layer of really moist peat it usually germinates quickly. Little is gained by soaking the seed. Some gardeners believe that parsley keeps away onion fly if a few plants are set in the onion rows.

Early thinning is essential to secure first rate parsley. If flower stalks develop they should be cut down to ground level. As a rule the plants are of little value after the

second year and are best discarded. A fresh sowing should be made annually.

This crop succeeds in any good cultivated soil well supplied with humus. The rows should be 38–45 cm (15–18 ins) apart, and the seedlings thinned to 15 cm (6 ins) apart.

Parsley sauce is in great demand. Finely chopped parsley is added to mixed salads and in soups and stews.

The 'Moss Curled' variety is the most widely used but a newer sort, 'Bravour', is

sugar and the dried leaves are used in pot pourris. The narrow dark green leaves are silvery beneath, the pretty blue flowers appearing in spring. The species grows about 90–180 cm (3–6 ft) high and with regular clipping, keeps shapely for many years. After flowering cut the shrubs back to encourage new shoots. Sun and good drainage suit these plants. There is a rare variegated form. Another, known as 'Miss Jessops' Upright', has an upright habit and is often grown as a hedge 1.20–1.50 m (4–5 ft) high.

RUE *Ruta graveolens*

There are many legends about this well known shrubby plant. One is that it is a symbol of 'repentance and regret'. It was once carried by judges at the opening of Assizes in the belief that it kept away gaol fever. The plant has a penetrating scent, appreciated by some people, disliked by others. It is a perennial growing about 60 cm (2 ft) high. 'Jackman's Blue' is a specially attractive variety with deep steel-blue leaves. The plant is decorative during the cold dark days and only a really severe frost will damage its evergreen foliage. Rue is a great favourite with flower arrangers, and is a useful plant both for the scented and decorative garden.

Above: Leaves and flowers of the common sage.   *Below: Winter savory*

SAGE *Salvia officinalis*

The common sage, a native of Europe, has been grown in Britain since 1597. The greyish leaves are about 38 mm (1½ ins) long, the purple bell-shaped flowers opening in summer. Sage needs a well-drained soil and grows about 60–75 cm (2–2½ ft) high.

Propagation is by seed or division. It is simple to pull off rooted pieces for growing separately. If the soil is drawn toward the plant, the lower parts of the stems will form roots and they can be severed from the parent plant and grown separately.

While the broad-leaved species is the hardiest and best for drying, there are variegated forms which provide ornamental interest. Non-flowering types are best for drying, flavouring and stuffing.

SAVORY *Satureja* species

Although well-known by name this plant is not widely grown. There are two species, winter savory, *Satureja montana* and summer savory, *S. hortensis*. The latter, an annual, is raised from seed in spring. Sow in a sunny position in drills, 30 cm (1 ft) apart. Choose a light, rich soil, and thin the seedlings to 15 cm (6 ins) apart. Winter savory is a perennial. Divide the roots or take cuttings of new shoots in spring. It may

also be raised from seed, the plants flowering in their second year. This is best done on a rather poor soil. Fresh sprays of savory are used for garnishing. When dried, they are used in mixed herbs and for flavouring poultry and veal.

SORREL *Rumex scutatus*

This is a herb for which claims have long been made for its health giving properties. It is said to be of value 'in sharpening the appetite, cooling the liver and strengthening the heart'. Believed to be a source of iron, it used to be thought that cuckoos ate it freely to improve their voice. The leaves are eaten in salads and soups or cooked like spinach.

A hardy perennial growing up to 60 cm (2 ft) it has leaves not unlike those of the

To obtain an adequate crop give plenty of space to sorrel plants

dock. The light green foliage is usually veined red. The reddish-brown flowers are produced in clusters and should be pinched out to make leaves more succulent.

Well-drained soil and partial shade suit the plants, although they will also grow in sunny situations as long as the ground does not dry out badly. If the plants are cut to the ground in late autumn they will produce vigorous new leaves.

'Broad-leaved French' is the best-flavoured strain.

SWEET CICELY *Myrrhis odorata*

A decorative plant with large fern-like leaves, this is well worth a place in the garden. It is a long-lived plant with a penetrating tap root that makes it difficult to propagate vegetatively. The leaves are noted for their sweet aromatic perfume, while they have a pleasing aniseed flavour.

The white flowers are freely produced in terminal umbels during April and May. The seed heads are quite large, and the seeds are dark brown with sharp ribs. Gather the leaves when fairly young and pick the flowers just before they open.

It seeds freely and once plants are in the garden there are usually plenty of self-sown seedlings. It is best propagated by seed sown in April, in a well-drained bed of medium loam which stays moist in dry spells.

Sweet cicely is used in mixed herbs, salad dressings and soups. Chopped finely, it imparts a zestful flavour to food. The roots can also be boiled and eaten with oil and lemon, or included in mixed salads. It is used for flavouring various liqueurs, and herbalists used to recommend it for digestive disorders.

TARRAGON *Artemisia dracunculus*

The common name of this perennial comes from the French word meaning 'dragon', possibly from the flower's slight resemblance to the shape of a dragon's head.

Used with other herbs and salad plants such as lettuce, tarragon imparts an acquired rather 'hot' flavour. Leaves are plucked as required. Avoid stripping individual plants. The sharp flavour is then present but once dried, it fades. Tarragon vinegar is often made by steeping the leaves in vinegar while the foliage is used in preparing French Mustard and Sauce Tartare.

French tarragon growing 60–90 cm (2–3 ft) high is the best for flavour but is not so hardy as the sharper flavoured Russian tarragon.

Not particular about soil, it does best in a sunny situation where the ground is well drained and not too rich. Propagate by division or from cuttings taken in Spring or early summer, as French tarragon rarely sets seed. The inferior Russian variety is the usual kind offered from seed.

THYME *Thymus* species

This family of plants varies in size from the creeping form, *Thymus serpyllum*, to little bushes 30 cm (1 ft) high. All like sun and to be sheltered from cutting winds, while well-drained, humus rich soil encourages leafy growth. Harvest the leaves for drying before the flowers appear.

The garden thyme, *Thymus vulgaris*, a small bushy plant essential in mixed herbs, has had the reputation of 'promoting courage and vitality'. Excellent as a bee flower, it is occasionally possible to get thyme honey. Used fresh or dry, its flavour improves the taste of many culinary dishes and it is invaluable in stuffings, although it needs to be used judiciously. Oil of thyme has a medicinal value.

Lemon thyme, *Thymus citriodorus* has a refreshing, less pungent flavour, and is used in stuffings and with fish. Caraway

Thyme needs a choice position

thyme, *T. herba-barona*, has, as its name suggests, a scent reminiscent of caraway. Apart from its culinary uses, it is an excellent rock garden plant.

Left: Sweet cicely grows wild in grassy places

Below: French tarragon

A-Z GUIDE TO FRUIT GROWING

The majority of gardens are not big enough to have a very large plot set aside for fruit growing, so it is essential to use the space to the best advantage. Fortunately, there are a number of dwarfing stocks on to which apples and pears can be grafted so that they will not grow too large and compete with other features in the garden for light, moisture and nutrients.

More recently dwarfing rootstocks have become available for cherries and plums – trees that would previously have been too large to contemplate growing in many gardens except perhaps as an intensively trained wall tree. The dwarfing cherry rootstock to ask for is 'Colt'. This, combined with the self-fertile variety 'Stella' grafted on to it makes an ideal combination for a small garden where there is not enough room for several trees. 'Pixie' is the dwarfing plum rootstock to look for, although it does need a rich soil ('St Julien A' may be a better choice where space is not at such a premium).

The letters EMLA against certain stocks signify that quality rootstock has been used (EMLA stands for East Malling and Long Ashton research stations, where much fruit selection work has been pioneered).

Another way of making full use of all the space available is to grow single cordons planted at an angle of 45° against walls or fences or as divisions throughout the garden. Espalier trained trees can also be used, while plums and cherries can be trained as fans against walls and fences. Cultivated blackberries and loganberries are also useful for clothing walls and arches.

The so called Family Trees help to solve the problem of limited space. These are trees on which up to five different varieties are grafted on to one stock. Obviously, not a

lot of fruit is produced from any one variety but a single stock can have grafted on to it say, dessert apples or pears that cross-pollinate well to yield a succession of fruits over several months.

Although there are very many possible combinations, any that you buy from a reputable nursery-man will provide a succession of compatible varieties. The following are examples of good combinations:

Dessert apples: 'James Grieve' (September–October), 'Spartan' (October–November), 'Cox's Orange Pippin' (November–January).

Pears: 'William's Bon Cretien' (August–September), 'Conference' (October–November), 'Doyenne du Comice' (November–December).

As far as possible, it is advisable to group together the same kinds of fruit trees, for this makes spraying and pruning easier. Also, plant close to each other varieties which cross-pollinate well, to ensure a good crop of fruit. It is advisable to discover the size to which particular trees are likely to grow for some are unsuitable for small gardens.

One of the secrets of success is to buy good healthy stock – particularly certified virus-free black currants, raspberries and strawberries. These will have been grown at an approved nursery where the stock has

Fruit tree blossom is of decorative value in any garden

been checked by Ministry inspectors.

Garden centres do not often state whether the plants are certified stock, and you may find it worth buying from a specialist nursery if you plan to start a proper fruit garden. You will find advertisements in gardening magazines for nurseries offering certified plants.

Before planting fruit, dig the ground and manure – the trees and bushes will be in position for many years. For the same reason it makes sense to choose the site carefully, ideally in a sunny but sheltered spot.

Basic Guide to Pruning and Training

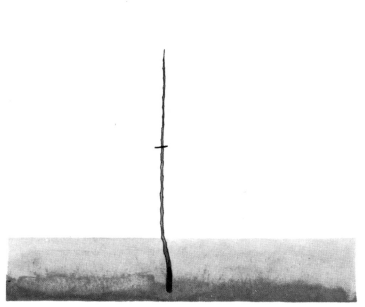

Pruning techniques for apples provide the model for treatment of most fruit trees. The bush is the most easily managed form. The four illustrations show cuts for winter pruning. Above: The maiden tree. Plant to the depth of the soil mark on the stem. After planting, cut back to 60 cm (24 in).

In the next (second) winter, the tree will have put forth several branches. Skilful pruning at this stage will determine the shape of the established tree. Choose up to four branches as leaders, and cut these back by up to two-thirds their length, to an outward pointing bud.

Winter pruning encourages strong growth while directing the tree to a shape which will admit adequate light and air to the developing fruits and facilitate picking the crop. In the third winter, cut back leading shoots again by about two-thirds, laterals (side shoots) to about three buds.

In the fourth and subsequent winters, the extent of pruning depends on the growth made by the tree. Leading shoots of weak trees should be cut back by two-thirds. Vigorous trees (above) should have the leaders shortened by a third their length. Cut laterals back to about three buds.

Red (and white) currants are commonly grown as bushes although, like gooseberries, they can be trained successfully as cordons. In bush form, the aim is to establish about eight branches radiating evenly from the short central stem or 'leg'. Fruit is borne on short spurs made on the previous year's growth of these main branches.

After planting (above left), cut the branches back to about half. New plants can be grown from these cuttings. Winter pruning of an established bush (above): first cut back side shoots to two buds, then cut back the leaders to about half, more if growth has been weak. Summer-prune sub-laterals only back to five leaves.

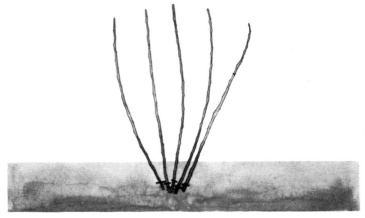

Blackcurrants should be encouraged to produce maximum new growth from the base as they produce fruit on one-year-old wood. Buy certified two-year-old bushes and plant slightly deeper than in the nursery. After planting, cut back all the shoots to 2.5 cm (1 in) to direct the plant's energy into producing new shoots.

Established bushes should be pruned annually by removing entirely about $\frac{1}{4}$ to $\frac{1}{3}$ of the old wood to allow the new wood to ripen. At the same time cut down weak shoots. Improve neglected bushes by removing all the old wood and cutting right down to soil level. The best time to prune is after all the fruit has been picked.

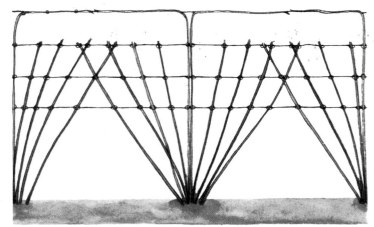

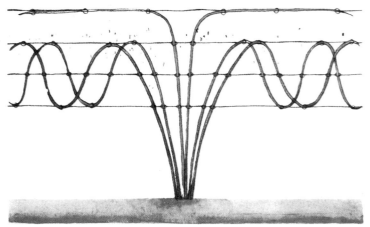

The two training systems shown above are suitable for blackberries, loganberries and hybrids of the two. The aim is to keep old and new wood separate and to train fruiting branches in such a way that the maximum amount of fruit can develop and be picked easily. Wear strong gloves when working with thorny bushes.

Above left: fan training. Current year's growth is tied in along the top wire while the fruiting branches are trained evenly across the wires. Above: weaving. Fruiting branches are woven around the lower wires. After fruiting, cut out the old wood and tie in the new branches in its place. Plant bushes about 3.5 m (12 ft) apart.

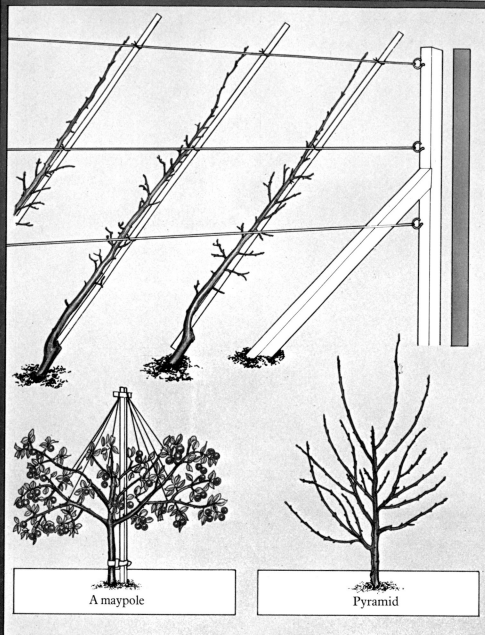

To train cordon apples, tie stakes at an oblique angle to horizontal wires. The stakes need not be driven deeply into the ground. Tie the growing tree to the angled stake.

A maypole (below left) safeguards small bush trees from breaking their branches under the weight of the fruit. Attach wires to the main stake and loop these round fruiting branches. Protect the branches with strips of hessian to stop the wire from digging into the bark.

| A maypole | Pyramid | Bush form |

Gooseberries – double upright cordon (left), triple upright cordon (right). Prune fruiting spurs but never cut main stems unless diseased or damaged.

Blackcurrants – cut back to 16 cm (6 inches) off the ground after planting and remove one third of the old wood after fruiting.

Redcurrants – like gooseberries, prune only fruiting spurs and leave the main framework uncut.

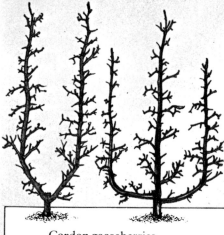

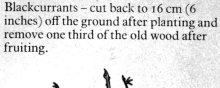

| Cordon gooseberries | Blackcurrant | Redcurrant |

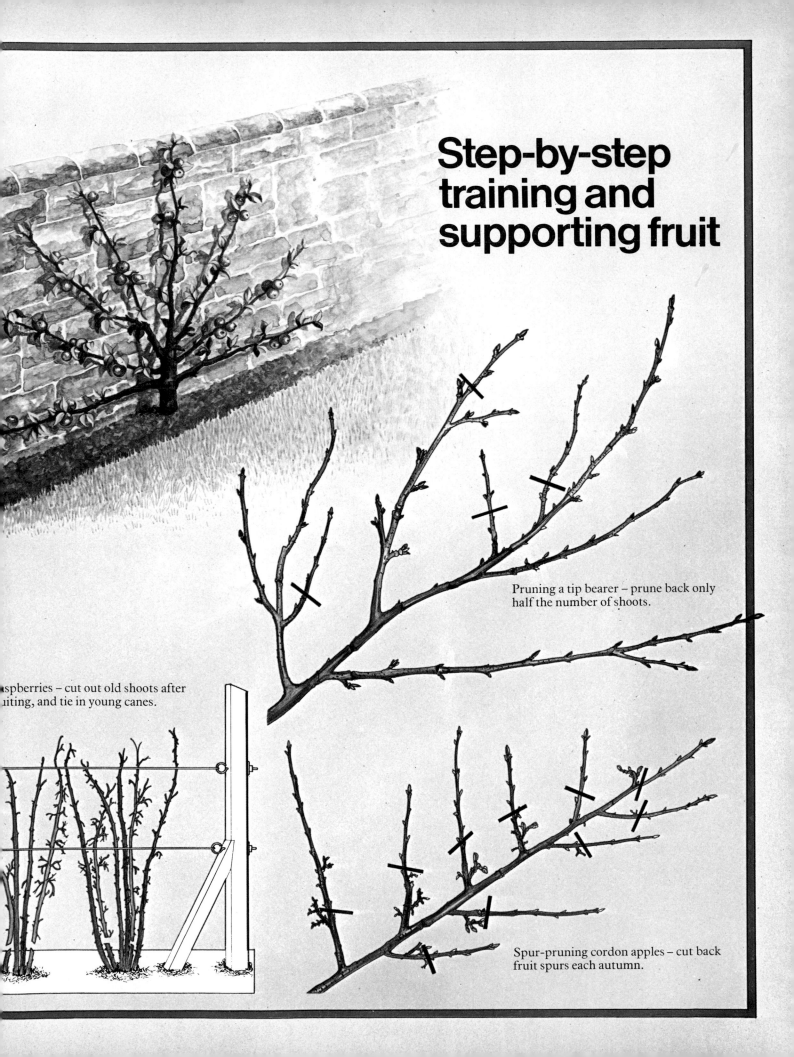

Step-by-step training and supporting fruit

Pruning a tip bearer – prune back only half the number of shoots.

Raspberries – cut out old shoots after fruiting, and tie in young canes.

Spur-pruning cordon apples – cut back fruit spurs each autumn.

Fruit growing

The trend towards increasingly smaller gardens and the need for quick results have brought about many changes in home fruit-growing. Modern high-yield compact trees and plants can be grown in confined spaces and bring home-grown, vitamin-rich fruits within the grasp of a wide public.

Climate, soil and site are as important in fruit-growing as in other crops. Rootstocks, pollination, varieties and pruning are of particular significance for promoting rich crops.

Fruit in the small garden

Growing fruit, flowers and vegetables close to walls and buildings can present problems. To cultivate these successfully and maintain an attractive appearance in a small space demands considerable forethought.

When considering plans to plant fruit, it is useful to bear the following points in mind. Firstly, if you do not grow it, can you obtain such fruits in season? If not, is it necessary or just a luxury? For instance, cooking apples, pears or plums can usually be bought more cheaply than good dessert varieties, which may be more difficult or impossible to obtain. Good dessert fruit of any type is more expensive than cooking sorts, and may lack the flavour of fruit ripened on a bush or tree. In the smallest spaces, grow cordon or trained forms of hard and soft fruits. Dwarf pyramid and dwarf bush types produce a greater weight of fruit per plant than cordons, but need more space.

Siting and aspect

Cordon and similar forms of tree make useful screens and can be sited in a north/south or east/west direction. In southern districts reserve sunny south facing walls for dessert pears.

Use east or west facing walls for dessert plums, gages and pears, or red currants.

All fruits thrive in a sheltered, sunny situation but crops such as raspberries, blackcurrants, gooseberries, blackberries, loganberries and early cooking apples will crop on north-facing walls in the South. The results will obviously be inferior to similar varieties grown in more favoured positions.

In gardens north of the River Trent position dessert apples against south-facing walls, and cordon cooking apples, currants and gooseberries on east or west-facing aspects.

Avoid planting fruit where it may be covered regularly with sea spray, or in heavy shade under trees. Trees in grass are the most likely to suffer from drought and starvation and need a clear 30cm (12in) minimum width of earth around each stem. Keep the grass short to reduce the competition for summer moisture.

LEFT Cordon-trained gooseberry bushes take up little space and are useful in small gardens.
ABOVE Spring mulching of a blackcurrant bush to preserve moisture.
RIGHT Fruit bushes hide the vegetable plot from the view of the house in this small garden.

Rootstocks

Apples, pears, plums and many other kinds of fruit trees consist of two or more plants—a scion, or fruiting wood, which is budded or grafted on to the rootstock.

There are various combinations of these and the home gardener should select grades which have vigour, resistance to pests and disease, and a strong formation of stem or trunk.

Healthy dwarf-growing rootstocks are most useful for the production of small-sized fruiting trees and bushes. Outstanding examples of this are the apple rootstocks M1X and M26 which not only enable small trees to be grown in confined spaces, but induce earlier and heavier cropping (see page 186).

Pollination

In most years healthy fruit trees of named varieties produce an abundance of blossom, but certain sorts of cherry and plum in particular, and some apples and pears, may fail to set fruit. This problem can be overcome by planting two different but compatible varieties together which flower at the same time.

Variety

New and improved varieties have brought increased crop yields, a longer season and a greater resistance to disease than many kinds grown a century ago. Many home gardens are more concerned with quality than quantity, and 'Cox's Orange Pippin' apples, for example, are still preferred to the heavier-cropping newer varieties, which are of inferior quality.

The more exotic fruits such as figs, apricots, peaches, nectarines, and grapes are best left until some gardening experience has been gained. These are specialists' subjects and also take up a fair amount of space.

Training

This is an important part of fruit growing. It is closely bound up with manuring and feeding, and is essential for intensive production.

The training of different forms of tree, such as standards, bush forms, cordons, pyramids and any other, is inseparable from pruning and feeding and pest and disease control.

Even when a framework of branches has been formed, pruning remains necessary to regulate the amount of fruiting wood and to counteract any tendency to biennial cropping (heavy fruiting in alternate years) rather than a reliable annual crop.

The principles of feeding are much the same for fruit as any other plants. Nitrogen promotes growth of leaf and shoot, phosphates encourage good root action and earliness, and potash increases hardiness, improves quality and resistance to disease.

APPLE *Malus sylvestris*

The apple is probably the most popular fruit. It was Edward Bunyard, a pomologist of a past age who wrote, 'no fruit is more to the English taste than the apple. Let the Frenchman have his pear, and the Italian his fig. The Jamaican may retain his farinaceous banana, and the Malay his durian, but for us, the Apple.' This assertion seems to limit the enjoyment of apples to the English but this fruit is valued in many parts of the world.

It is thought by some that not only does the eating of apples help to keep the doctor from our doors but helps to keep ourselves from the dentists. No other fruit compares with the apple for the length of its fruiting season, from August to June. By careful selection and storage, it is possible to have *home*-grown sun ripened fruit for ten months of the year.

Climatic conditions affect both flavour and colour, and different varieties reach their climacteric, or peak of flavour, at different times. We cannot pretend that all good-flavoured apples have the same taste. This is evident by comparing 'Cox's Orange Pippin' and 'Blenheim Orange', both long keeping dessert varieties and both of excellent though quite different, flavour. To quote Bunyard again 'there is in Blenheim a mellow constancy, a reminder of those placid Oxford meadows, which gave it its birth in the shadow of Blenheim Palace. Although I like to wear the light blue favour, what can Cambridge put beside the Blenheim? – only a "Histon Favourite" of poor quality, indiscriminate and undistinguished.' There is still room for old favourites

Cooking apple 'Bramley's Seedling'

but how often do we today come across 'American Mother', 'Gravenstein' and 'Wagener'? All have a superb flavour.

As a result of generous feeding with nitrogenous fertilizers each year the crop weight is usually very heavy, but flavour is almost non-existent. It is not suggested that the manurial system is the only factor involved in the production of flavourless fruit. Rootstocks are to blame in some degree. Soil too, affects the problem.

The good grower does not feed his trees, he feeds the *soil* and gives supplementary dressings or foliage sprays only when the trees indicate their need for them. The aim should be to keep the roots really active.

Colour is always a feature of apples, and we have only to think of 'Charles Ross', 'Rival', 'Lord Lambourne' and 'Scarlet Pimpernel' to know how attractive some apples can be. 'James Grieve' and 'Miller's Seedling' are showy, too. While many

Other showy varieties of apples of fairly recent introduction include 'Red Ellison's Orange' a highly coloured bud sport from 'Ellison's Orange'. It was discovered in a tree near Wisbech, showing crimson coloured fruit. The remaining trees yielded fruit typical of the variety. Sufficient wood was available to 'work' a few scions on to a young 'Bramley's Seedling' tree. It was possible to increase stock and the fruit produced has the same distinctive crimson colouring while the trees have inherited the valuable characteristics of 'Ellison's Orange'.

'Scarlet Pimpernel' is another striking new variety which came to Britain from Holland although it originated in America. 'Scarlet Pimpernel' keeps in excellent condition for a month or so after picking. Growth is vigorous and the branches are upright and spreading. It is highly resistant to scab and is not susceptible to canker. It is self fertile and flowers at the same time as 'Egremont Russet'. If fruit spurs are thinned during winter, instead of the end of May which is normal with other varieties, the apples grow to a good size.

RECOMMENDED VARIETIES:

The following is an alphabetical list of the best dessert and culinary apples and those which do well in gardens. The months mentioned are those when the fruit is at its best although often it is eaten beforehand. When buying apple trees check the pollination requirements with the nursery.

'Beauty of Bath', dessert, early August, medium, flattish pale yellow with a red flush, sweet and brisk flavour, a free bearing

early variety, party self-fertile.

'Blenheim Orange', culinary and dessert, November–February, fairly large, handsome, flattish, round fruit, yellow striped and flushed, red and russet, of vigorous growth and a heavy bearer when established; does well on heavy soils, partly self-fertile.

'Brownlee's Russet', dessert, January–March, splendid variety of medium size, brownish-green, tender flesh of good flavour, self-fertile. A good choice for the small garden.

'Court Pendu Plat', dessert, December–May, bright green changing to yellow marked with russet, and rich red on the side exposed to sun, crisp, juicy, rich flavoured; of moderate growth. This variety is hardy and an abundant bearer, flowers late and usually escapes frost damage.

'Cox's Orange Pippin', the best known dessert apple, October–February, raised at Slough in 1830 from a pip of 'Ribston Pippin'. The greenish skin is streaked and flushed with red, especially where exposed to the sun, flesh yellowish, crisp, juicy and sweet. It is not self-fertile so should be planted with other apples such as 'James Grieve', 'Worcester Pearmain' and 'Sunset' to ensure pollination.

'Cox Pomona', culinary, October–November, yellow streaked bright crimson, flesh white, tender and good flavoured.

'D'Arcy Spice', dessert, March–May, of roundish flattened appearance; yellow covered with brownish-russet, sweet, juicy and aromatic; found at Tolleshunt D'Arcy in Essex many years ago.

'Egremont Russet', dessert, October–December, golden-yellow with broken russet, flesh greenish-yellow, firm and of excellent

Dessert apple 'Egremont Russet'

flavour; heavy cropping, hardy, ornamental when in flower, a good pollinator for 'Cox's Orange Pippin'.

'Ellison's Orange', dessert, September–October, dull green streaked red. The flavour is reminiscent of aniseed. It grows and crops well, the flowers rarely being touched by frost.

'George Cave', dessert, July–August; showy red skin on the sunny side, overlying greenish-yellow; flesh firm, juicy and sweet.

'Golden Delicious', dessert, December–February, a good variety provided virus free stocks are grown; splendid flavour.

'Gravenstein', dessert or culinary, October–December, yellow, streaked crimson and orange, flesh crisp and juicy with rich aromatic flavour. The tree is hardy, vigorous and a good bearer; a grand old apple of German origin, now coming into favour again.

'Grenadier', culinary, August–September, large handsome fruit, greenish-yellow skin; very fertile variety most valuable for garden and orchard, cooks to a froth.

'Howgate Wonder', culinary, December–February; fruit large, flattish with yellowish-green skin, flushed and streaked red, firm flesh, good cooker, a dependable cropper.

'James Grieve', dessert, September–October, good shaped fruit, with pale yellow skin, flushed and striped with red, juicy and of good flavour; vigorous, compact cropper.

'Lane's Prince Albert', culinary, November–April, large, handsome shiny flushed red green fruit; flesh tender, slightly acid; a dwarf grower of spreading habit, very free bearing.

'Laxton's Fortune', dessert, September–November, yellow, flushed and streaked red, flesh yellow, 'Cox' flavour; strong growing.

'Laxton's Superb', dessert, December–March, a cross between 'Cox's Orange Pippin' and 'Wyken Pippin', of similar appearance to 'Cox' but rather larger, flesh white, sweet and crisp; a strong grower and good cropper.

'Lord Derby', culinary, November–December, large, yellow-fleshed; cooks to a lovely deep golden colour, sturdy, upright growth, does best on well drained soils; susceptible to scab.

'Lord Lambourne', dessert, October–

'James Grieve' is a popular and fine-flavoured variety

December, yellow, flushed red firm and juicy, an upright, strong grower and a good cropper.

'Mother'; also known as 'American Mother', dessert, October, medium size, good flavour.

'Rev W. Wilks', culinary, October–November, large, pale yellow, excellent apple for dumplings, hardy, vigorous grower, good bearer, liable to canker on heavy soil.

'Ribston Pippin', dessert, November–January, dull yellow shaded red, with russet markings, flesh yellow, firm, crisp and juicy; an old favourite of superb and distinct flavour; subject to canker on heavy soils; needs regular pruning; grow with other varieties.

'Scarlet Pimpernel', dessert. August, well-coloured fruits of good shape; crisp, juicy and sweet with an acid tang.

'St Edmund's Pippin', September–October, smallish round golden-russety fruit, tender and aromatic; a tip bearer and sometimes liable to scab.

'Sturmer Pippin', dessert, January–June, the green skin is almost covered with dark brown russetings; excellent flavour; raised at Sturmer in Suffolk nearly 100 years ago from a pip of 'Ribston Pippin'; prolific; leave fruit to mellow as long as possible. Best grown in warm districts.

'Sunset', dessert, October–February, golden-yellow with red and russety markings, delicious 'Cox'-like flavour, and succeeds where 'Cox' often fails; strong growing and a good fertile variety; blooms late and almost always escapes frost damage.

'Tydeman's Late Orange', dessert, April–May, yellow, richly flavoured flesh, deep green brightening to golden yellow.

'Wagener', culinary and dessert, December–July, first class for eating from March onwards; yellowish green with red cheek, fresh, firm, crisp and juicy, easy to grow, rarely affected by pests, mildew or scab.

'Winston', sometimes wrongly known as 'Winter King'; dessert, January–April, skin crimson, flesh firm, crisp and sweet, compact grower and resistant to mildew and disease, keeps well.

'Worcester Pearmain', dessert, September–October, one of the best known apples, skin red, with minute fawn coloured dots, flesh tender, juicy and sweet, free fruiting, hardy and much used as a pollinator for 'Cox's Orange Pippin'.

6 Dessert apples for October–November use

Allington Pippin	Gravenstein
American Mother	Ellison's Orange
Egremont Russet	St Edmund's Pippin

6 Dessert apples for December–January use

Blenheim Orange	Golden Delicious
Court Pendu Plat	Ribston Pippin
Cox's Orange Pippin	Wagener

6 Dessert Apples for January–March use

Brownlee's Russet	Sturmer Pippin
D'Arcy Spice	Sunset
Laxton's Superb	Tydeman's Late Orange

APRICOT *Prunus armeniaca*

Generally speaking, it is more difficult to bring apricots into a fruitful condition than peaches or nectarines. They are cultivated successfully and on a large scale, in France, Italy, parts of the United States and Australia and other countries. Apricots will grow on greatly differing soils but they appear to prefer a medium loam over lying limestone.

The rootstocks on which the trees are grafted have a tremendous influence on their vigour. The most popular commercial rootstocks are the vigorous Brompton and the more dwarfing Common Mussel. St Julien A, a plum stock of East Malling origin, is also first class for producing smallish trees.

Apricots can be raised from stones and it is sometimes possible to get good fruiting trees by sowing in May. Bury the stones at least 5 cm (2 ins) deep, and move the resultant seedlings the following autumn to a sheltered position against a warm, sunny wall or fence. To be sure of fruiting it is best to rely on grafted stock. Trees raised from stones sometimes fail to fruit or if they do the fruit is of poor quality.

Apricots flower early in the year, so the blooms are liable to frost damage. Low lying sites should be avoided, or exposed windy situations which may deter bees and other pollinating insects from visiting the flowers.

A warm sheltered garden is best for growing apricots

Bush trees usually do well in sheltered places and wall trained specimens have the advantage of extra shelter and warmth. Avoid north facing walls.

Since apricots start into growth early, the autumn is the best time for transplanting. Heavy soils are unsuitable although the trees will not flourish where the roots dry out in summer. If a deficiency of lime is suspected, dig in lime rubble or hydrated lime when the site is being prepared. As a guide, wall trees should not be planted closer than about 3 m (10 ft) and the stem should be about 15 cm (6 ins) from the wall.

Prevent frost damage to the flowers of bushes or wall trained trees by covering them with old curtains or fish-netting. If the weather is unfavourable for pollinating insects, hand pollinate the flowers. Most varieties are self-fertile.

Apricots require nitrogen and potash for good results and established trees will benefit from top dressings of a fertilizer, preferably of an organic nature, which is rich in these properties. A mulching of good compost or old manure and peat in the spring helps much to curb fruit drop.

Take care not to knock or bruise the trunk or branches or gum may spill from the wounds. If there are signs of a very heavy crop, some thinning out should be done when the fruit is the size of a hazel nut.

The fruit should be picked when it has coloured well, but before it becomes soft, for then wasps fancy it! Keeping apricots in

the warm and light for a day or two after harvesting brings out the full flavour.

Prune with care. The plan for bushes should be to produce open-centred specimens, while for wall trees a good fan-shape is ideal. Because of the tree's susceptibility to die back disease and silver leaf, keep pruning cuts as small as possible, and apart from shortening the leaders, all other cutting should be done in spring or summer. If it becomes necessary at any time to make big cuts, cover the wounds with Arbrex or Stockholm Tar. A simple guide to pruning: cut back one-year shoots to half their length, to just above an upward pointing bud. Nip out with the thumb nail any unnecessary or badly placed shoots.

Die back disease can be destructive; blossoms wilt and later the affected spurs die back.

Brown rot fungus affects both wood and fruit. Its incidence is less likely if no jagged wounds are ever left. Bordeaux mixture sprayed on at the bud swelling stage is a good control. Silver leaf should be dealt with as recommended for plums.

RECOMMENDED VARIETIES: 'Breda', one of the hardiest, producing a heavy crop of orange-flushed, good flavoured red fruit in August; 'Hemskerke', orange-yellow blotched red, good flavour, end of July; 'Moorpark', probably the best known variety, large deep orange with red spots, August–September; 'Royal' or 'Royal Orange', oval shape, good

'Parsley-leaved' blackberries have an excellent flavour

flavour; yellow skin with purple spots, early August; 'Shipley's Blenheim', a strong grower, hardy and prolific; the oval-shaped fruit has an orange skin dotted crimson. It seems to do best as a bush and the fruit is excellent for bottling and jam – mid-August.

BLACKBERRY *Rubus fruticosus*

Apart from their heavy cropping value these most useful plants can be used for covering unsightly fences or for screening an untidy corner of the garden, or for dividing one part of the plot from another.

They need some kind of support on which their long growths can be trained. While they can be planted in a shady position, they prefer an open, sheltered, sunny spot, then crops will be heavy and well flavoured.

Although not particular about soil, drainage should be good and, in preparing the site, it is wise to dig the ground deeply. If humus is lacking, work in plenty of decayed manure. Failing this, any other bulky matter such as peat, leaf mould or spent hops can be used. To this, add sea-weed fertilizer, fish meal or bone meal, to provide nourishment over a long period. Unless the ground is naturally limy, complete preparations by dressing the surface soil with hydrated lime, at the rate of 140 g per m² (4 oz per sq yd).

Where more than one blackberry is grown, it is advisable to space them at least

2.70 m (9 ft) apart, and a post and wire structure is necessary if plants are grown in the open garden. The posts should stand up to 1.80 m (6 ft) above ground level. Three strands of taut wire 60 cm (2 ft) apart are run between the posts. Such a support is suitable for the strongest varieties.

Nurserymen usually supply blackberries as sturdy one-year-old plants and send them out from November to early April. They should be planted immediately on arrival although if the soil is sticky, or frost bound, they can be 'heeled in' until conditions improve. When planting, spread the roots out and retread the soil around the stems after frosts have loosened it.

Once they are planted the canes should be shortened to about 90 cm (3 ft) and tied loosely to their supports. When it is obvious the plants are beginning to grow in spring, it is best to shorten the canes to about 23–25 cm (9–10 ins) from ground level, cutting immediately above a stout bud. This will encourage the production of strong young fruiting canes for the following season. If fruit is required the first year the second shortening of the growths should not be carried out and initially the canes need not be cut back so severely. This will mean less shapely plants and the probability that the following season's growth, or some of it, will develop from the older canes instead of from the base. When stems come from ground level they are easier to train, the fruit is better and annual pruning is easier

as the stems are less tangled.

To prune established blackberries, cut out the old canes and tie in the new ones to bear fruit the following season. Any surplus canes, that is, those which cannot be conveniently tied in or would lead to over-crowding, should be cut out completely. See page 189 for training systems.

RECOMMENDED VARIETIES: The following varieties return a heavy yield:

'Bedford Giant', ripen in July and August with shiny berries of fine flavour; 'Merton Early', a fine mid-season sort; 'Parsley-leaved', a fairly old variety, vigorous on heavy soil; matures in August and September; 'Himalaya Giant', very robust, producing its excellently flavoured berries from early to mid-season; it should be pruned very severely annually, not only to keep it under control but because most of the fruit is carried on young canes; but beware, for it is extremely thorny.

Thornless varieties include 'Merton Thornless', which requires a really rich soil, and produces sweet fruit in August, and 'Oregon Thornless' which has cut, paeony-shaped leaves and fruits in August and September.

Other berries which may conveniently be included here are some of the more unusual edible fruited *Rubus* species and hybrids derived from blackberries and raspberries.

Fruits of the boysenberry

Boysenberry The Boysenberry is a hybrid which produces large dark wine coloured fruit of good flavour with few pips. A strong grower, the plant bears fruit on long spurs which stand out from the prickly canes making it easier to pick them. A hardy variety, it will succeed on drier soils than other berries. Allow 1.8–2.1 m (6–7 ft) between the canes which, when newly planted, should be cut down to about 30 cm (1 ft) from the ground to induce new growth from the base.

A thornless variety of loganberry is easier to prune, train, and pick from

Loganberry *Rubus loganbaccus* It is nearly one hundred years since Judge Logan of California found this plant in his garden. It was named the loganberry and was introduced to Great Britain well over 75 years ago. It has been grown under varying conditions and has proved to be an abundant bearer and absolutely hardy. The large dark red berries ripen over a period of many weeks in summer. The juicy good flavoured fruit is specially valuable for stewing and jam making.

It is essential to grow a good stock. Perhaps the reason that the loganberry is not appreciated as much as it ought to be, is that poor fruiting stocks are grown – cropping indifferently with poor disease resistance.

When well grown, the true loganberry yields heavily. Although some people like the fruit when it is ripe for dessert, it lacks the sweetness of both the blackberry and raspberry. It is, however, suitable for cooking, jam making and bottling, as well as for the manufacture of fruit juice. Loganberries ripen from July onwards.

Planting can be carried out from November until March, the normal spacing being 1.80–2.40 m (6–8 ft) apart. The canes should be cut back after planting, to encourage strong basal growths to develop. These should be tied into place and not left to flop about for it is on these new canes

that fruit is borne the following year.

Where a good vigorous stock is available, it can be propagated by tip layers. Bend the young canes over during July and August and bury their tips in the soil. Leave them in position until the following spring, when they should be moved to nursery beds. After a year they will be good strong specimens, suitable for planting out. Encourage heavier crops by mulching with strawy manure or compost each spring. Once the tips have rooted well and have been severed from the parent plant a new set of canes will develop to furnish further material for propagation.

Obviously only really healthy plants should be propagated. Virus infected stock is usually seen as weak, spindly growth and small anaemic foliage.

Cane spot disease is often spread by the spores falling from the old canes on to the new. This is why some specialists keep the new growths trained more or less upright in the centre of the plants until the old canes have been cut out. Should the disease be suspected at any time, spray the plants with colloidal copper fungicide.

The thornless loganberry was introduced to Britain well over 30 years ago. The fruit is large and good flavoured, excellent for stewing and jam making. Growth is strong and attractive and plants are as easy to grow as the ordinary loganberry. This is the best variety to grow alongside a path.

The attractive wineberry will happily grow against a trellis or fence

The youngberry is a cross between the blackberry and the raspberry

Youngberry This is a vigorous hybrid with large well-flavoured fruit containing few seeds and little core. As the berries ripen they change from deep red to a pleasing black. As the fruit is produced on short stems from the main canes it is easy to gather, and there are few thorns to contend with.

Since the plants are semi-trailing, plant them at least 1.80 m (6 ft) apart, in soil which does not dry out badly in summer. Well-drained, moisture retentive soil encourages heavy cropping.

Propagation is simple: layer the tips of the long stems as previously described.

Wineberry *Rubus phoenicolasius* Wineberry, also known as the Japanese wineberry, is an attractive fruiting plant with bright orange berries that turn a rich crimson when ripe and have a slightly acid flavour. The softly hairy canes assume an attractive reddish hue in winter. Allow at least 1.80 m (6 ft) between the plants.

BLUEBERRY *Vaccinium corymbosum*

The Blueberry is one of several species of *Vaccinium* bearing edible fruit, others being the cranberry and whortleberry.

The finest are the Highbush varieties. Blueberries thrive in acid, peaty soil where little else will flourish; but they cannot stand drought conditions.

The soil should have plenty of humus with moisture always available but it should never be waterlogged. Treated well and pruned regularly, the bushes are kept to a height of about 1.8 m (6 ft). In good conditions, they will fruit well for fifteen years or more. Apart from their fruiting value, blueberries are most ornamental in the autumn when their leaves assume yellow and crimson tints.

Choose an open, sunny situation and prepare the soil thoroughly for the plants are long-lived. Do this well in advance of planting. Small plants move best and those supplied by the growers are usually no more than 15–30 cm (6–12 ins) high.

To allow for future development, they should be spaced up to 2 m (6 ft 6 ins) apart each way. Newly planted bushes should be mulched with compost or decayed manure and peat. In subsequent years a top dressing in early spring is beneficial, but avoid lime in any form.

Little pruning is necessary for the first two years after planting. Subsequently, the older, thicker stems are cut out to encourage basal growths. The white bell-shaped flowers are borne on the previous season's growth. They appear from March onwards and are resistant to frost damage. The fruit ripens from July to September. Established bushes will bear about 2 kg (4½ lb) each year.

Let the fruit mature on the bushes where it will remain in good condition for some days. Ripe berries are a dark bluish colour at the stem end but a reddish tinge indicates immaturity.

General cultivation is simple; keep the ground clean of weeds and net the ripening fruits against birds.

RECOMMENDED VARIETIES: In Holland and Germany research workers have long been engaged in breeding improved varieties to give really worthwhile crops. Apart from wild plants, from which fruits are often gathered, there are a number of named hybrids available in Britain. You can prolong the picking period by planting a selection of these. Some are of American origin, and many have been tested at Long Ashton Research Station. Among the best are: 'Earliblue', strong upright growth and large berries ripening from mid-July; 'Blueray', spreading habit with large pale-blue berries in branched clusters; 'Jersey', an older variety, long sprays of large fruit. Plant with another variety for pollination.

Blueberry 'Blueray' can be eaten raw but is best stewed

BULLACE *Prunus domestica* var *insititia*

These old fashioned fruits are closely related to and grown in the same way as damsons, but sadly are little cultivated today. They were once plentiful in hedgerows but are now rare as land continues to be used for building. In the small garden one bullace tree or bush should be adequate, since all varieties are self-fertile. If more than one is grown, the distance between them should be 4.5–6 m (15–20 ft). They are useful plants, for they prolong the fruit season, and as large bushes form attractive hedges. Bullace are best for stewing or jam-making.

RECOMMENDED VARIETIES: The following can still be obtained from fruit specialists:
'Black Bullace', October, almost black fruit with a purplish 'bloom', juicy but sour.
'Langley Bullace', November, a prolific cropper of good flavour, the large black oval fruit keeping well; introduced by Messrs Veitch in 1902 it is said to be a cross between 'Farleigh Damson' and an early 'Orleans' plum. It makes an upright tree.
'Shepherd's Bullace', October, large round-oval, greenish fruit; growth upright; delicious for fruit pies.
'White Bullace', October, fairly small, attractive fruit with a creamy bloom.

CHERRY *Prunus* species

Although flowering cherries are widely grown in all parts of the country the fruiting varieties are very much less common. There are several reasons. They grow best as standards or half-standards and take nine or ten years to come into full bearing. They are unable to set fruit with their own pollen and only certain varieties will cross-pollinate. Bushes can be obtained but they are of a rather spreading habit. Standard trees too, take up a lot of room and it is not always easy to gather fruit from the higher branches, and birds often take their toll of the crop.

For the smaller garden, the solution to the problem of large trees is to grow cherries as fans, planting them against a wall or fence. Then it is easier to gather the fruit and protect the crop from birds.

Cherries grow best on light loam over chalk, and where potash is not lacking. Over-rich soil can cause the trees to 'gum'.

Established trees and bushes can be encouraged to bear good crops by scattering bone meal over the root area at 70 g per m² (2 oz per sq yd) in February. Dried blood at 35 g per m² (1 oz per sq yd) is also beneficial.

trees, although two-year old specimens are satisfactory if one is prepared to wait longer for the fruit. November is the ideal planting

The 'Morello' or sour cherry is best for small gardens

month but trees can be moved up until the end of March. Do not attempt to push the roots into a very small hole but spread them out fully and plant firmly. Make sure too, that the standards are supported with stout stakes. These should be in position before the trees are planted to avoid damaging the roots.

If you are planting in established grassland or are going to sow grass seed after the trees are in, leave a circle about 1 m (3 ft) in diameter around the trunks to prevent the grass taking all the moisture and nourishment while the trees are becoming established. Do not over-manure trained trees. They should be kept growing slowly. A spring mulch of ordinary compost or sedge peat will ensure that the roots do not dry out in summer. Manure or very rich compost should not be used since it encourages exuberant stem and leaf growth and over-fed trees are more susceptible to disease.

Little pruning is needed the first year for, at transplanting time, the shape of the head will have already been formed. Whenever pruning is necessary, always cut immediately above an outward pointing bud. Crowded, crossing and rubbing branches should be well cut back.

The only sure way of protecting the fruit from birds is to net the trees. Other methods include automatic bird scarers and scarecrows in the trees, although birds often get used to the latter after a few days. Not all the fruit ripens at the same time, so pick carefully so as not to spoil the unripe fruit.

There are many varieties, several having Bigarreau as part of their name. This name was originally applied to varieties which were two coloured but now it applies to any cherry with firm flesh whether it is white or black. Cherries with soft flesh are often known as Geans.

RECOMMENDED VARIETIES: *Sweet Cherries* 'Bigarreau de Schrecken', late June, shiny black, good flavour. 'Bigarreau Napoleon', mid-July, yellow and red, good cropper. 'Early Rivers', June, crimson-black, juicy, delicious flavour. 'Frogmore Early', late June, yellow marked red. 'Governor Wood', early July, yellow and pink, juicy flesh. 'Merton Bigarreau', mid-July, black, rich flavour. 'Merton Heart', late June, dark red, juicy, good flavour.
Acid Cherries The most commonly grown acid or sour cherry is the 'Morello', which unlike sweet cherries is very well suited to garden cultivation. It matures from August onwards, is blackish-crimson, hardy and excellent for north walls. A reliable heavy cropper, fruit rarely splits.

Sour cherries should always be given a winter tar oil spray, since they seem more liable to aphid attacks than sweet cherries.

CRANBERRY *Vaccinium oxycoccus*

This is another undeservedly little grown fruit in Britain though it is grown in quantity in Holland and North America. However, investigations are being made into the possibilities of growing cranberries on a larger scale in this country, and there is no reason why they should not be grown in gardens. The cranberry is a spreading plant with upright branches of 15–20 cm (6–8 ins) high. It flowers in June and July and the fruit is ready for harvesting from September onwards.

Cranberries have a shallow rooting system, so the soil need not be very deep. They thrive in a layer of shallow peat over sand or clay. While peat may not be absolutely essential, the soil should stay fairly moist throughout the year, but never waterlogged.

The cranberry is readily increased from cuttings. Use shoots 7–10 cm (3–4 ins) long and root them in sandy, peaty soil in late April. For striking a small number, boxes may be used, but for larger quantities insert them directly in rows in frames or in the open ground. Some gardeners leave the cuttings untrimmed since they appear able to root quite well if they are simply scattered on the surface and lightly covered with soil, but undoubtedly it is best to plant them in the ground in the usual way.

Sweet cherry 'Bigarreau Napoleon'

CURRANTS

All currants are species of the genus *Ribes*. The black currant grows wild across the whole of Europe and Northern Asia.

BLACK CURRANT *Ribes nigrum*

One of the most important soft fruits, the black currant is rich in vitamin C and its juice is used in health drinks. The name currant is derived from the ancient Greek city of Corinth. Heavy yields can be expected from healthy established bushes which normally bear well for at least twelve years.

In the garden, there is rarely much choice of site but avoid a low lying shady position. Ideally, provide a deep loamy soil with a high organic content. This will ensure moisture is retained during long spells of dry weather. Black currants like moisture during the growing and fruiting season, but stodgy cold, clay soil will not produce the heaviest crops. Such ground can be made more suitable by working in compost and well rotted manure.

If the bushes are exposed to cold north and east winds insects are discouraged from visiting the flowers and distributing pollen from bloom to bloom, necessary to ensure a good set of fruit. Also the bushes should not be planted where they are in a frost pocket, otherwise the open flowers will be damaged. Prepare the soil well before planting.

At one time black currants suffered

'Hatton's Black' black currant is a heavy-cropping variety

badly from big bud mite and the related reversion disease, but now, because of a scheme worked out by the Ministry of Agriculture, leading fruit specialists supply only certified virus-free bushes. Only grow best quality named varieties.

It is most satisfactory to buy two-year old specimens. These normally have three or four shoots and will establish more quickly than older bushes. One year bushes are sometimes offered. They take longer to come into bearing and it is not so easy to detect any virus infection then. Against this of course, if the cuttings were taken from certified stock, there would be little fear of big bud mite. By the time a bush is two years old the presence of any reversion will have shown.

Although black currants can be planted from late October until the end of March, early planting is preferable, ideally in November. It is advisable to cut down newly planted bushes to within 5 cm (2 ins) of their base in the February after planting. Plant firmly and space the bushes 1.5 m (5 ft) apart to allow room for proper development and free air circulation. Many growers find that a thick annual mulch of farmyard manure gives the heaviest crops.

Black currants are pruned annually, the object being to encourage the production of new wood, preferably from the base. There should be no forming of a 'leg' or central

stem; all shoots should arise from the soil. By cutting down bushes to ground level the first year after planting, a good supply of new shoots during the summer is ensured.

Black currants bear fruit on one-year old, light coloured wood. Unpruned bushes produce only a small amount of new wood, usually at the ends of the branches. This leads to unproductive bushes with much unwanted old, basal wood. Older branches should be cut back to strong young shoots. The dark colour of the old wood makes it easy to determine which is the new growth.

Good soil conditions and adequate nourishment is the way to build up plenty of fruiting branches, but regular pruning is required if a weighty crop is to be produced annually. A few varieties have a spreading habit and produce their branches very near the ground. These will have to be cut right out, or where possible, pruned back to an upright growing shoot.

Some gardeners prune their black currants in winter when, of course, one can see all the growths clearly but the best time is September, after picking the fruit. This early pruning stops the bushes wasting their energy on shoots that will be cut out later and, more important, next season's fruiting wood is able to ripen better.

By growing several varieties, it is possible to extend the picking season and thus avoid a glut. The fruits of some varieties hang longer in good condition than those of other varieties and also keep better in wet weather. The best among them are 'Seabrook's Black', 'Baldwin' and 'Westwick Choice'.

Pick the berries on the 'strig', not separately, then 'strig' them indoors, with a table fork. Time of picking is important, for sometimes the berries look ripe before they are. Harvesting should begin when the top berries on the strig have softened. If gathered too early a lot of weight may be lost, for in the last few days of maturing the berries rapidly increase in size.

Not all the berries on individual bushes are ready at the same time and it is usually necessary to 'pick them over' more than once.

Black currants are usually propagated from cuttings in the autumn. You can also increase them from soft wood cuttings in summer, and by layering the lower branches.

Autumn hardwood cuttings should be made from healthy one-year-old shoots. Do not propagate from old bushes – it is asking for trouble. The cuttings should be 20–23 cm (8–9 ins) long and trimmed neatly, top and bottom, to just above a bud.

Select a well-drained patch of sandy soil and take out a straight backed trench 40–50 cm (15–20 ins) deep. Insert the cuttings so that only a couple of buds are showing. When returning the soil to the trench, make sure that the cuttings are really firm. This deep planting encourages the growth of basal shoots and lessens the possibility of a 'leg' forming. If more than one trench is necessary they should be 60 cm (2 ft) apart. Different varieties should be clearly marked. It has been found that freshly taken cuttings root much better than those taken some time before being planted.

RECOMMENDED VARIETIES:

'Baldwin', one of the best maincrops. It forms a compact upright bush, responds well to good feeding but does not like really heavy soils.

'Boskoop Giant', an established early variety which colours evenly and is not prone to splitting; rather tall growing, becoming leggy if not pruned regularly.

'Mendip Cross', an early variety of great vigour. The large fruits appear on long strigs, making picking easy.

'Seabrook's Black' ('French Black'), an old sort which crops well although it is sometimes shy in producing basal growths.

'Wellington XXX', a heavy cropping, mid-season variety. Growth is vigorous but

occasionally sprawling, so prune carefully to counteract this tendency.

'Amos Black' is an erratic cropper but it has the virtue of ripening very late, so extending the season.

RED CURRANT *Ribes sativum*

Although the origin of the red currant is somewhat uncertain it is generally reckoned that three species have contributed to the constitution of present day varieties. These are, *Ribes vulgare*, *R. rubrum* and *R. petraeum*. Less popular than black currants, red currants are used for jams, jelly and pies.

'Laxton's No 1' is a good early variety for the garden

The bushes grow well on ordinary soils but dislike heavy, poorly drained land. Light ground can be improved by adding strawy manure, compost or anything that will increase the humus content. A good supply of potash is needed to colour the berries, produce a good firm wood and to maintain healthy foliage. Leaf scorch – a condition in which the edges of the leaves

turn brown – is usually caused by a shortage of potash. Every four years an application of fish manure at 70 g per m² (2 oz per sq yd) in February or early March will keep the bushes vigorous. Wood ash or sulphate of potash at 70 g per m² (2 oz per sq yd) is an excellent alternative.

November or February and early March are ideal months for planting, provided the soil is workable. Bushes are usually available as two or three year olds. A sunny situation suits the bushes but avoid frost pockets and windy positions.

If you intend to train red currants as single, double or triple cordons to clothe a wall or fence, the younger specimens are the easiest to manage.

When several red currant bushes are planted, space them about 1.80 m (6 ft) apart. This will give them plenty of room to develop and allow for the eight or nine strong branches each should have. Single stemmed cordons should be spaced 45 cm (18 ins) apart at an angle of 45°. Apart from growing them against fences or walls they can be trained on light trellis work and used for dividing the fruit from the vegetable garden without taking up much room.

It is best to keep red currant bushes to one leg (clean stem) of about 15 cm (6 ins) before allowing branches to form. Remove all suckers and buds below this point. This also applies to double and triple cordons and espaliers. Red currants trained as espaliers will grow well on north walls where the fruit will ripen later.

With pruning, the bushes should have four main stems coming from the 'leg'. In the first year, cut these back to within 8–10 cm (3–4 ins) of their base to produce a sturdy, bowl-shaped, framework of branches.

RECOMMENDED VARIETIES: There are fewer varieties of red currants than black currants but among the very best are 'Laxtons No 1', a heavy and reliable cropper of medium sized berries; and 'Red Lake', producing long trusses of good quality, bright-red juicy berries. Two really good varieties of Dutch origin that have recently been introduced are 'Jonkheer van Tets', a very early heavy cropper and 'Random' a late season kind reckoned by some to be the best for yield and quality.

WHITE CURRANT *Ribes sativum*

These are grown just like red currants and repay feeding and watering in a dry season. They do well as cordons or fans when grown against a north wall, but net fruits against the birds. There are several varieties, all rather similar.

Handle white currants with care at picking time and afterwards, for the berries are easily bruised. Propagation is from hardwood cuttings taken in early autumn when rooting is usually quick. Select one year old shoots from strong healthy bushes.

Both red and white currants should be grown on a 'leg', and all buds, excepting 4–5 at the top, are removed from the cuttings. Make the cuttings 23–25 cm (9–10 ins) long and insert them 15–18 cm (6–7 ins) deep. If a quantity of cuttings are rooted, space them 8–10 cm (3–4 ins) apart with 60 cm (2 ft) between the rows. Subsequently, the young specimens must be pruned to shape. To do this always cut to an outward pointing bud to ensure an open, bowl-shaped centre.

RECOMMENDED VARIETIES: 'White Dutch' forms a spreading bush bearing medium sized bunches of berries.

'White Versailles' is an early variety, producing long bunches of large, good flavoured fruit.

DAMSONS *Prunus domestica* var *insititia*

The damson is a native of the country around Damascus, hence its name. At one time damsons were grown on a fairly large scale, but present-day growers do not seem to pay much attention to them. While it is true that some varieties have small fruit which seems chiefly composed of stone and skin, there are several sorts which have really good fleshy fruit. Apart from the fact that damsons make excellent jams and are delicious in tarts and pies they are valuable for bottling and canning, especially since they retain their rich, distinctive flavour for a very long time.

The trees make good shelter belts thriving in exposed places and able to withstand the bitterest of winds. As damsons which are

Currant 'White Versailles'

late-flowering, hold their foliage well into autumn, they provide excellent protection for other late maturing fruits.

This tree also succeeds in soils quite unsuitable for apples and pears, which is one reason why it is seen growing in certain exposed and northern districts where the cultivation of other more tender types of fruit might be less successful.

With very few exceptions, damsons are self-fertile but there is no doubt that heavier crops are carried where two or more varieties cross-pollinate. Damsons crop most freely when there are regular and plentiful supplies of moisture available.

RECOMMENDED VARIETIES: 'Bradley's King', a dessert or culinary variety with medium, oval black fruit having a thick bloom. The firm, acid flesh becomes sweet when fully ripe; of moderate growth, it forms dense twiggy heads and is remarkably fertile; raised by Mr Bradley of Halam, Notts; mid-September.

'Cheshire Damson' ('Shropshire Prune' or 'Prune Damson'), a small tree which is sometimes a shy bearer. The oval fruits which taper to the stem are a deep purple, with a dense bloom; first class for canning and bottling. They are often found in hedgerows in the Midlands; September.

'Farleigh', sometimes known as 'Cluster' or 'Crittendens'; has small oval black fruit with greenish-yellow flesh which are excel-

'Prune Damson' makes a compact tree

lent for cooking; growth is compact and very fertile. It was found wild by Mr Crittenden of Farleigh, Kent; mid-September.

'Merryweather', one of the best cooking damsons, the quite large fruit is round and black, the flesh being firm and of the true damson flavour, a good cropper. This variety was introduced by Messrs Merryweather in 1907; September–October.

FIG *Ficus carica*

Most of us are familiar with those tightly packed boxes or blocks of dried fruit so much in demand at Christmas time. They come from the East, the fig being a native of Syria and surrounding countries.

Figs are not suitable for growing in the open ground in all parts of this country. Certainly, a few may be found growing fairly happily against sheltered south facing walls in the south or west, but they thrive best under glass.

Young plants in small pots are offered by nurserymen and although there is usually a choice of varieties 'Brown Turkey' is perhaps the most reliable, followed by 'Brunswick'. The former has brownish-red fruits with red flesh, and is very fertile, while 'Brunswick' ripens rather later, is larger, green in colour with white flesh. Both are vigorous and usually crop well. 'White Marseille' is an early large pear-shaped variety with pale green skin and sweet red fruit.

The end of March or during April are good times to move figs from their pots to the greenhouse border, or into bigger containers.

The greenhouse border should be well prepared and dug to a depth of 60 cm (2 ft) or so, working in plenty of drainage material such as brickbats, stones, mortar rubble, etc. A good loamy soil is suitable while the addition of really old decayed

Figs need care if they are to ripen

horse or stable manure is beneficial. Bone meal at the rate of 100–140 g per m² (3–4 oz per sq yd) well-worked into the compost will provide additional feeding material over a long period.

Fruit is produced on the new season's growth and if the plants are trained into a more-or-less fan shape they will yield well. The greatest amount of the best fruit is usually carried on the lower branches so that some growers encourage the branches to develop fairly near the ground, or to pull them into that position. With this system some kind of support with stakes or wire is necessary, but even with bush specimens, the branches can be trained to encourage them to grow horizontally.

Once established, the fruit begins to ripen toward the end of May and develops on the new shoots which are produced on the previous season's stems which were pruned back. Further fruit develops intermittently during the summer.

Pruning is important both to keep the trees in shape and to provide new fruit bearing shoots. Often, only very little cutting is necessary, this being done during July and August. Although good drainage is essential figs must have plenty of moisture throughout the growing season.

A moist atmosphere during the summer is advisable and can be ensured by frequent overhead sprayings of clear water, which at the same time, will deter red spider mites — which cause leaf bronzing and spoil the fruit. Occasional applications of liquid manure are helpful. The temperature is best kept at about 15°C (60°F) although naturally it will rise during spells of strong sunshine.

Outdoor figs can be grown against sunny walls. The best method of training is the fan system. This means spreading out the shoots and tying them in position. Never crowd the growths since only with sufficient room, sunlight and warmth, will a crop mature. Avoid rich heavy soils for these lead to rank leafy growth with little fruit. Firm, well-ripened wood is needed for crop bearing.

If the trees are to fruit well it is essential to restrict the root system. The bed should be dug out about 60 cm (2 ft) deep and the bottom of the hole filled with bricks or stone slabs. This will allow for drainage but prevent deep probing tap roots. It is essential to bear in mind that fruitfulness is dependent on a restricted root system.

The fig is unique in the way it fruits. A fruiting branch will usually carry quite large

figs on its lower portion, and tiny embryo fruits no larger than peas at its apex. The latter are the crop for the next season.

To develop full flavour, figs must ripen on the trees, although there are several, if old fashioned, ways of inducing earlier ripening. One of these is to dip a needle in olive oil and push it into the eye of the fig.

Propagation is from cuttings in September, by layering low-placed shoots or detaching suckers in autumn.

In prolonged severe weather, protect figs by spreading straw around the base of the tree and over the branches. Branches damaged by frost should be cut out.

GOOSEBERRY *Ribes grossularia*

For centuries this fruit has been popular in British gardens. The bushes will grow in almost every kind of well-drained soil. Where possible, provide fairly deep soils with a good humus content that are unlikely to dry out in summer. Make sure the soil is not short of potash, for a deficiency leads to poor development and small leaves, which are scorched at the edges. The rooting system is widespread and near the surface, so do not cultivate deeply.

Planting can be carried out from the end of October until the end of March, the earlier the better. The site should be prepared in advance by deep digging and working in farmyard or other bulky manure; bonfire ash is a valuable extra. Never use quick acting fertilizers, for they will force growth and the soft lush foliage is liable to mildew.

Two or three-year-old bushes usually establish quickly. Spread the roots out well but do not plant deeply, for the bushes are best grown on a single stem or 'leg'. Deep planting results in unwanted shoots from below soil level. These make it difficult to clean the soil of weeds and pick fruit. Allow 1.50–1.80 m (5–6 ft) between the bushes or, if you are growing single cordons, space them about 45 cm (18 ins) apart. Espalier gooseberries will need to be 1–1.20 m (3–4 ft) apart and all trained specimens should be given a support at planting time.

Pruning should be carried out annually. Well-shaped, open headed bushes allow the sun to penetrate and ripen the wood as well as making it easy to pick the fruit. For the first few years, shorten the new growth by about a half. This will lead to the formation of strong branches which will be able to bear the weight of fruit the laterals produce. If the laterals are kept cut back to 5–8 cm (2–3

The popular gooseberry 'Leveller' has an excellent flavour

growers catalogued over a hundred varieties, many having been raised specially for exhibition for the large gooseberry shows that were then very popular. Today it would be difficult to find a dozen different sorts. While a good gooseberry has a distinct flavour, crops are sometimes gathered too early, before the flavour has fully developed. Unripe fruit is frequently offered in shops and markets.

VARIETIES: Of the yellow fruiting varieties, 'Leveller' is particularly good. Red varieties should be eaten for dessert at the right moment: 'Whinham's Industry' and 'Lancashire Lad' are delicious. Of the so-called white sorts, 'Whitesmith' is excellent. Green varieties include 'Lancer' and 'Careless'.

GRAPE VINE *Vitis vinifera*

There is plenty of evidence to show that grapes have been grown for centuries. They were greatly valued by the Israelites who esteemed them for their health promoting qualities. The Romans brought them to Britain and no doubt to other countries too. Good wine from them was once produced in several English regions including Gloucestershire, Worcestershire and East Anglia, and it is difficult to understand why production ceased. Happily, though, new and productive vineyards are being developed on a small scale in the south and west.

It may have been at least partly due to the dissolution of the monasteries, where the cultivation of vines was regularly practised, that their cultivation died out. Gradually it seems, the idea became widespread that grapes could be grown successfully only in heated greenhouses. Whatever the cause, the British seemed to have accepted the idea that grapes needed warm greenhouse culture. However, during the last thirty years there has been a remarkable revival in grape growing outdoors as well as under glass and many people have learned the skills of producing a good crop and making acceptable wine. It is largely due to the work of the Viticultural Research Station at Oxted, Surrey that so much more is now known about the successful growing of grapes outdoors.

Dealing first with glasshouse cultivation, ideally, the site should drain naturally and there should be a good depth of light chalky loam. Much can be done to provide congenial rooting conditions. Gardeners have

ins) from their base, they will make plenty of fruiting spurs. Cut right out all weak and badly placed shoots. Always prune to an outward pointing bud so that the centre of the bush remains open. Cordon, espalier and standard gooseberries must be pruned carefully to keep them to their particular shape.

Pruning can be done once the leaves have fallen. The exception to this is where birds, particularly bullfinches, are troublesome. Then it is best to wait until just before the buds begin to burst.

Although rarely practised commercially, summer pruning is beneficial. Do it from the end of June onwards, shortening all lateral growths to about five leaves. This leads to the formation of more fruiting spurs. Thin the clusters of fruit to get really large berries.

Propagation of gooseberries from cuttings is simple, the best time being from October to December. Select strong, well ripened shoots about 30 cm (12 ins) long from the current season's growth. Remove all buds except the top four. This ensures that the developing bushes have a 'leg'. If shoots are pulled from the branches with a 'heel' of old wood, they will root very quickly. Having prepared the cuttings insert them 15 cm (6 ins) deep in a shallow, straight backed trench, lined at the base with sharp sand or clean grit. Firm the soil round them.

Once rooted, the cuttings are planted out and training started to develop good framework. Gooseberries are productive for many years if they are properly treated and mulched with manure or compost each spring.

More than a century ago specialist

'Black Hamburgh' is the best greenhouse grape for the amateur gardener

long planted their vines on an outside border and worked the rods through holes in the greenhouse wall to train them on wires in the usual manner inside the greenhouse.

When this is done drainage must be good for vines will not tolerate stagnant moisture round their roots. The one disadvantage in planting outside is that in very wet weather during the ripening period, the fruit may split.

When planting inside the greenhouse some gardeners make sure they have complete control of moisture by making a brick lined planting hole. This should be about 90 cm (3 ft) deep at the back sloping to 75 cm (2½ ft) at the front, in order to prevent waterlogged roots. Width of the site will depend on the size of the house, but should certainly not be less than 1.35 m (4½ ft). Rubble should be placed at the bottom of the hole before filling in with good rich loam, decayed manure and leaf mould plus a good sprinkling of bone meal.

Vines should be transplanted while dormant and it is advisable to buy pot grown plants. These need to be removed carefully from their pots so as not to damage the rods. Some gardeners believe in thoroughly disentangling the coiled up, often pot-bound, roots before planting. Spread the roots evenly, covering them with about 10 cm (4 ins) of soil and making it firm. Then give a thorough soaking of water which has had the chill taken off it.

If growing more than one vine at least 1.80 m (6 ft) should be allowed between the plants while individual rods should not be spaced closer than 90 cm (3 ft).

Vines are natural climbers having tendrils with which to grasp anything they can find for support. They are normally vigorous growers with many branches and leaves. Various methods of training are adopted when cultivating vines under glass and outdoors. If left untrained a vine will become untidy and unproductive. The training starts the first summer after planting. By then the rod and new growth will be supported by a cane, pushed into the soil about 15 cm (6 ins) deep. The top of the cane should reach just past the first horizontal strand of wire to which it is tied. Next a 2.70–3 m (9–10 ft) bamboo cane must be fixed to the top of the cane and wire supporting the vine, and to a wire along the roof. As growth proceeds the young leading shoot should be tied to this second cane as it grows towards the roof.

Keep rubbing out side shoots that grow from the leaf axils until the last leaf from the wire is reached. From this point allow the growths (laterals) to make two or three leaves before the shoots are pinched out.

Keep removing the tendrils for if left in they will grasp the wires, leaves and laterals and become a nuisance. As a result of stopping the laterals they too will almost certainly produce further shoots. These are known as sub-laterals and they in turn are pinched back to the first leaf. After the rod has been stopped, it is quite a good plan to allow some of the sub-laterals to develop. This not only helps strengthen the rod but keeps the roots active, supplying nourishment to the new growths.

Although pruning sometimes appears to be complicated, it is not at all difficult. The thickish lateral buds that form in the axil of each leaf should be cut off at the end of the first growing season. If growth has not been good and the rod seems unable to make real progress cut it back to within three strong buds from ground level. Such action will stimulate good growth the following year.

In subsequent years when the vine has reached its allotted space, each lateral is cut back to two, sometimes one strong bud from which sub-laterals develop the following season. This means that the fruiting spurs gradually lengthen as a result of cutting the laterals back regularly.

Top dressing the root area can do a lot of good. First very carefully remove the surface soil around the vine, taking care not to damage the shallow fibrous roots. Then, top dress with a mixture of three parts good loam and one part each rotted stable manure and bonfire ash, plus a good dusting of lime and bonemeal.

Where heat is available it is possible to start vines into growth towards the end of November. This is done only where grapes are wanted in April and May. Very often however, the vines are not started until early March. This means that fruit will be ready for gathering from August onwards. Early maturing grapes such as the popular 'Black Hamburgh' and 'Madresfield Court' can usually be cut within five months of being started, but the majority of varieties need six months to ripen their fruits.

Some greenhouse vines will not set heavy crops without being artificially pollinated – 'Muscat of Alexandria' is one of these. If

'Black Hamburgh' or 'Alicante' are grown in the same house as 'Muscat of Alexandria' it will be easy to go from flower to flower with a camel hair brush and distribute pollen to fertilize the flowers.

Once fruit has set the berries develop quickly and some thinning is necessary. No rod should be allowed to carry more than ten to twelve bunches, for overcropping can weaken the tree. Having retained the right number of bunches the next step is to thin out the berries. This is best done with specially pointed vine scissors. The shape of the bunches varies according to the variety being grown, some having much broader shoulders than others. Some varieties have very short fruit stalks which makes it difficult to thin the berries if the operation is delayed. With large bushes particularly, it is helpful to tie out the shoulders, especially if grapes are needed for exhibition. When thinning the bunches, avoid touching the berries with your hands.

As soon as the berries colour, increase ventilation without allowing draughts. One problem in giving more air is that birds may be tempted to attack the fruit. They can be stopped by covering the vents with perforated zinc which, incidentally, will keep out wasps. It is unwise to gather the bunches before the berries are mature for then the sugars have not completely changed and the berries are still acid.

RECOMMENDED VARIETIES:

'Alicante', freely produced, large oval black berries, good flavour.

'Black Hamburgh', probably the best known; large tender berries; sweetly flavoured.

'Madresfield Court', an early muscat, freely producing tender, juicy, rich flavoured berries.

'Mrs Pearson', the round whitish-amber berries turn pink when ripe.

'Muscat of Alexandria', inclined to be a shy setter, large oval berries, pale amber with a sweet, rich muscat flavour.

MEDLAR *Mespilus germanica*

Native to southern Europe, the medlar is widely distributed and can be found both wild and cultivated. At one time this tree was to be found in the gardens and grounds of large estates, the fruit being used in sauces and served with game.

The trees vary in size and appearance, probably influenced by the soil and climate.

Generally, the trunk is rough and on the short side. The spreading branches are irregular in shape, and wild specimens are furnished with thorns. The bark is nearly always an ash-grey colour. In early summer the tree bears large showy white blossoms.

The medlar is usually grafted on to quince stock, very suitable for fairly moist soils. Seed is another means of propagation, but it is about two years before seedlings appear. It is better for the grower to concentrate on grafted or budded trees.

Where large standard medlars with a good straight stem are required, seedling pear stocks are used.

Medlar fruits are more or less round with a slight depression at the top crowned by the sepals of the calyx, giving them a distinctive appearance. They are generally reddish-brown in colour and contain five hard, rather rugged kernels.

When the fruit ripens towards the end of the autumn, it is astringent. It is, therefore, advisable to allow them to remain on the trees, gathering them during November after they have been exposed to light frosts. They are ready for picking when their stalks part readily from the fruits. Gathered then and laid on straw or a rack in a dry frost proof place they become pleasant to eat after a few weeks, and have a somewhat vinous flavour.

The best way to store the fruits is to place them eye-end downwards. After two to four weeks they change from green through yellow to brown; the process is known as 'bletting'. They are then ready for use, and will remain so for several weeks. As well as being eaten raw, medlars may be made into jelly or sauce. To reduce the risk of fruit rotting in store, it is advisable to gather it when the weather is dry and sunny. Some growers have found that dipping the stalks in a solution of ordinary table salt, reduces

'Muscat of Alexandria', fine-flavoured grape, needs careful cultivation

or even prevents rotting.

The fruit borne by really old trees is usually small and flavourless, but the trees compensate for this by the showiness of their white or pink blooms.

Well-shaped specimens with an open, evenly branched head are produced by early training and pruning. Once this has been developed, subsequent treatment consists of removing dead wood and rubbing out badly placed shoots.

Medlars ready for picking

Medlars are not prone to any particular pests or diseases. Occasionally leaf eating weevils are troublesome in the spring, but they can be controlled by dusting or spraying with derris.

RECOMMENDED VARIETIES: 'Nottingham' has an upright habit. The fruit is on the small side, but is freely produced and when ripe has a rich sub-acid flavour.

'Royal' is also an upright grower, producing heavy crops of medium sized, good flavoured fruits.

'The Dutch', which is sometimes known as 'Monster', forms a decorative tree with large leaves. It has a semi-weeping habit and the large brownish fruits remain sound longer than other sorts, often keeping until after December.

MULBERRY *Morus nigra*

The black mulberry is an attractive tree. It is almost always grown as a standard as bushes are seldom satisfactory because of their spreading habit.

Mulberries like a good sandy loam, well-supplied with moisture, but never water-logged. They prefer an open sunny situation and the same conditions as for plums.

Mulberries are very juicy fruits

Although the tree may be small at planting time, and grows slowly at first, it will make a fine large specimen after a few years.

Prepare the soil deeply, working in well-rotted manure and compost, and a 140 g per m² (4 oz per sq yd) dressing of bone meal. Lime is not essential, although mulberries thrive when it is present. Planting time is from the middle of October until the end of March, the earlier the better. Where several trees are planted, allow up to 9 m (30 ft) between them. It is advisable to spread out the roots fully and not to cramp or damage them by putting them in holes which are too small. Cover the roots with about 13 cm (5 ins) of soil and stake the tree before refilling the planting hole with soil.

Initial pruning consists of shortening all leading growths by about a third, and cutting back the laterals to within a couple

of buds from the base. Because mulberries are somewhat slow in coming into bearing it is advisable to start with trees which are about five years old.

Once the main framework is formed, little further pruning is needed. This makes early training important and any later cutting should be done immediately after leaf fall. Mulberries are self-fertile and that is why isolated trees are often seen fruiting heavily. Fully established trees regularly bear heavy crops of sweet, raspberry-looking fruit.

Mulberries are among the latest trees to produce foliage in the spring, but they are certainly most showy in the summer, when most other trees are beginning to lose their attractiveness for the season. The fruit ripens over a period of weeks, and when it turns dark crimson during August and September, it is ready for harvest by laying a cloth beneath the tree and shaking the branches. Surplus berries may be bottled.

Mulberries may be propagated in various ways, the simplest being by layering. In this case, healthy young branches are selected and pegged into the ground in autumn. They should remain there until the following autumn, when they may be severed if they have made a good root system.

Take cuttings of young shoots in October. These should be about 20–45 cm (12–18 ins) long and prepared in the usual way. Insert them firmly 13–15 cm (5–6 ins) deep in sandy soil in a sheltered place. Grafting can be done in March, and consists of selecting suitable shoots from trees of good form, and 'working' them on to strong seedling mulberries.

Seed is another method of propagation, and it should be sown in gritty compost in March. Germination however, is often irregular and it could be some years before saleable trees are available.

The black mulberry *Morus nigra* is distinct from *Morus alba*, the white mulberry, which is grown for its leaves which are used for feeding silkworms.

PEACH *Prunus persica*

Of great antiquity, this fruit is said to have originated from China and to have come to this country by way of Persia, Greece and Italy. In records it is referred to variously as peske, peshe and peche. Its popularity has steadily increased in Britain and other European countries. In 1768 Thomas Hitt described twenty varieties of peaches and nectarines. In 1925 Edward Bunyard mentioned 50 distinct kinds of peach and 23 nectarines commonly grown in England.

Much credit for the development of peaches in England must go to Thomas Rivers of Sawbridgeworth, Herts, which is reputed to be the oldest fruit tree nursery in the country. Thos. Hogg, in his Fruit Manual (1875) mentions about 100 varieties of peach and 35 nectarines. Of these, 24 peaches and 13 nectarines were raised at Sawbridgeworth.

Peaches are sometimes spoiled by careless gathering. Edward Bunyard says, 'They should be neither pinched or pulled off but rather stroked off. A fond and delicate hand is applied and a gentle rotatory movement should suffice if they are ripe. A small basket should be their final mission'.

The culture of peaches and nectarines can be dealt with together as the nectarine is really a sport of the peach with a smooth skin and a rather less robust constitution. At one time it was thought that peaches could only be grown successfully in greenhouses or perhaps, against a sheltered wall in a warm district. Now however, they are cultivated in a similar way to plums and there are established peach orchards, usually of bushes, in various parts of the country.

Many growers depend on peaches grafted on to the Brompton plum stock, on which they make quite large bushes. Fruit is produced on spurs which develop as a result of shortening the stems. The Common Mussel stock is useful because it does not produce such large trees as Brompton although it is sometimes inclined to die back and to produce blind shoots.

Because of the peach's pithy wood, the stocks are usually budded rather than grafted. The experts use triple buds which consist of two fruit buds with a shoot bud between them.

When planting peaches dig holes large enough for the roots to be spread out evenly. The soil mark on the stem indicates the depth at which the tree was planted – do not exceed it. After working in some fine soil among the roots, fill the hole very firmly, finally raking the surface level to a tilth.

The best time to plant is November, although the trees can also be moved in March. Two or three-year old trees transplant best. Fan-shaped specimens are useful for growing against a wall. If several are being planted allow up to 5 m (15 ft) between them, spacing them 15 cm (6 ins) from the wall. Any broken or bruised roots should be pared clean.

When buying a peach bush get a tree with an open centre and well-thinned sides. Fruit is produced on the previous seasons shortish wood growth. If any bush shows signs of producing an extra heavy crop, the fruits should be thinned to 10–15 cm (4–6 ins) apart.

Outdoor peaches A few years ago, it was considered a waste of time to grow peaches

Choose a sunny sheltered spot for growing peaches

outdoors in this country. Since the last War however, it has been proved that this crop can in many districts be brought to maturity without difficulty.

Because peaches are exotic fruits, many amateurs are reluctant to grow them, believing that expert knowledge is vital for success. The excellent results obtained by one or two specialist firms which have cultivated bush peaches on a fairly large scale, have not only created much more interest in this fruit, but many gardeners are actually planting peaches, not only as wall trees, but are growing them in bush form with good success. Peaches will grow successfully in similar positions to 'Victoria' plums, producing first-class crops.

A problem which often presents itself to amateur gardeners is how to prune the bushes or train trees. The framework of a

well-shaped tree will have been developed by the grower, skilled in the knifework necessary, during the first two or three years.

For bushes, a stem of 50–75 cm (20–30 ins) should be left clear of branches, the 'feathers' (side shoots) being cut so as to produce a good open head. If for three years the young branches are cut back annually to half their length, a proper framework will be formed, and from this, branches producing the fruiting shoots will develop.

Peaches are very free croppers, and many gardeners are inclined to let heavy crops mature on very young trees, which are then liable to become stunted and badly shaped. Trees under three years should not be allowed to carry fruit. One is sometimes confronted with trees making extremely strong fruitful growth. This calls for corrective treatment. Pinch out branch tips in June to induce the production of fruiting laterals, and remove new unwanted growth at an early stage.

When bushes of fruiting age bear very heavily, some thinning is necessary. Do this when the fruitlets are quite small, say about the size of marbles; some fruitlets fall naturally, too. Once the stoning process is complete, a good liquid fertilizer is beneficial.

Mulching is invaluable, and a thick layer

of peat, leaf mould, or compost, applied after watering and feeding, will check rapid loss of soil moisture, which can be most harmful to the developing fruit. Avoid deep cultivation as suckering will often follow root injury.

Peaches flower early when it is often cold and windy, and pollination can be poor through the absence of bees and other insects. It is, therefore, a good plan to hand pollinate. This can be done about mid-day when the blooms are open, using a camel hair brush to transfer ripe pollen on to the female stigmas.

RECOMMENDED VARIETIES: *Peach:* 'Barrington', mid-September, large, greenish yellow with crimson stripes, pale yellow flesh, rich and good.

'Bellegarde', mid-September, large very dark crimson fruit, flesh pale yellow and a rich flavour.

'Duke of York', mid-July, large brilliant crimson with tender melting flesh; a reliable variety which bears well.

'Hale's Early', end July, medium-sized crimson with pale yellow tender flesh, excellent for outdoor and indoor culture.

'Peregrine', early August, large fruit with brilliant crimson skin and melting juicy flesh.

'Rochester', mid-August, good sized fruit of high quality; hardy and prolific. The best choice for growing outdoors in bush form.

'Royal George', early September, large, pale yellow skin with red cheek, flesh pale yellow, sweet and rich, first class under glass and excellent outdoors.

Nectarine: 'Early Rivers', late July, large crimson on light yellow ground; the greenish white flesh has a rich flavour; a heavy cropper, it is suitable for outdoor or under glass.

'Elruge', late August, of medium size, the greenish white skin is flushed deep red, the flavour good; this very old sort does well under varying conditions.

'Victoria', delicious late variety.

PEARS *Pyrus communis*

Pears are a little more difficult than apples and if neglected, deteriorate more quickly but they repay good cultivation. Many varieties are self-sterile, so it is necessary to grow two or more different varieties for pollinating purposes – not always easy in a small garden.

Pears are not simply sweet. Edward

Bunyard said 'the pear flavour must stand as a basis upon which may be laid the various overtones of flavour and acidity. Acid gives pears a zest and raises them to a higher plane. The next addition is musk . . . it requires great discretion in its disposal. Some pears seem to have an almond flavour, others a vinous quality while in some, it is possible to detect a perfume not unlike that of the rose or of honey.'

'If', says Bunyard, 'the duty of an apple is to be crisp and crunchable, a pear should have such a texture as leads to silent consumption.'

Soil plays a great part in determining whether or not pears are going to be successful. Very light ground is unsuitable, and it is not worthwhile growing pears on thin soil that retains little moisture. Good medium or heavyish soil is best, so long as it has been deeply cultivated and contains plenty of organic matter.

Generally speaking, pears need more nitrogen than apples and perhaps less potash. Top dressings of compost or decayed manure are beneficial, while in the spring, 90–100 g per m² (2½–3 oz per sq yd) of sulphate of ammonia stimulates sturdy growth. Pears usually bloom fairly early so avoid planting in exposed areas and low lying frost pockets.

Select varieties carefully. Comparatively few pears are self-fertile and two or more suitable varieties must be grown to ensure cross pollination and a good fruit set.

Pears can be planted in mild weather throughout the dormant season, although November is the best month. Having made sure that the soil has been well prepared by

Below: A heavy crop of nectarines

deep digging and manuring, dig out a hole about 20 cm (8 ins) deep and wide enough for the roots to be spread out fully. Trim back any damaged roots with a sharp knife or secateurs.

Stake standards or half standards before the planting hole is filled in to avoid damaging the roots. Plant the young tree to the depth marked on the stem by the soil in which it was raised in the nursery. Sprinkle a layer of soil over the roots and tread it down firmly, for good anchorage is important. The soil around the stem must be trodden down fairly frequently during the winter, since frost is liable to loosen the roots.

If you have ordered trees from a distance and they arrive and cannot be planted immediately, they will be alright in their bundle for a few days. If the trees cannot be planted for several weeks, unpack them and heel them in, in a trench in a sheltered part of the garden.

Pruning is as important for pears as for other fruit trees. Excepting for a few tip bearers (those which fruit at the tips of the shoots) such as 'Jargonelle', 'Josephine de Malines' and 'Packham's Triumph', pears on quince root stocks produce plenty of fruit spurs and are pruned normally. The strongest growing sorts such as 'Beurré Hardy', 'Bristol Cross' and 'Doyenné du Comice', are pruned more lightly for very hard pruning usually results in excessively vigorous growth.

Remove dead, crowded or badly placed branches from all trees. If standards produce extra long, upright branches, they should be shortened to a suitable length.

Prune hard the leaders of young trained trees during the winter for the first few years, to build up a sturdy framework. Some summer pruning may also be necessary according to growth made. This usually consists of pruning the side shoots to four leaves and to one leaf in the winter. Generally pruning for pears is the same as that described for apples on page 188.

Although there is usually a natural fall of fruit (the June drop), some thinning is advisable if there are signs of a very heavy crop developing. This will prevent many small second quality fruits.

Having grown and harvested the fruit it is disappointing to discover that the flesh is dry and mealy (sleepy) instead of rich and juicy. Externally, the pears look perfectly sound, but it is a different matter when you cut them open.

The trouble in many cases is related to the

Above: 'Doyenné du Comice' is the finest flavoured pear
Below: The best-known variety of pear is 'Conference'

time of gathering the fruit. This seems especially so with late keepers such as 'Winter Nelis' and 'Glou Morceau'. If gathered too soon, and especially if stored under very dry conditions, they are liable to become 'sleepy' before they are edible. Similarly, if 'Pitmaston Duchess' and 'William's Bon Chrétien', are harvested a little too early, perhaps to avoid wasp damage, they may quickly become over-ripe and then sleepy, all within a few days. So rapidly can pears ripen that fruits should be examined every few days. It is often difficult to tell when a pear is ripe. Many varieties are more or less covered with russet markings, so appearances do not always help. A good plan is to cut one or two fruits at short intervals when they are beginning to ripen. This will show up any tendency to sleepiness.

RECOMMENDED VARIETIES: Many of the older varieties are no longer grown but the following is a list, given in order of maturing dates, of first class pears which are still available from fruit specialists:

'Clapp's Favourite', early September, medium-sized, thin smooth skin, pale yellow with bright scarlet flush, very fertile.

'William's Bon Chrétien', September, golden-yellow, russet dots, red stripes; fairly large, excellent flavour, juicy and sweet; good for bottling or canning. Known in the USA and Australia as 'Bartlett'.

'Beurré Hardy', October, large, very fertile and good flavour.

'Louise Bonne of Jersey', October, medium, yellowish-green, red flush, red dots, sweet and delicious. Cross-pollinates with 'Conference' and 'Williams' Bon Chrétien'.

'Emile D'Heyst', October–November, medium, pale yellow, marbled russet, sub-acid, pleasantly perfumed.

'Durondeau', October–November, fairly large, long pyramidal, skin rough, golden-yellow, very fertile. Good for small gardens.

'Conference', October–November, large, long, pear-shaped, very juicy, good for bottling, or canning; sweet, regular bearer, the best mid-season to late variety.

'Beurré Superfin', medium-sized fruits, yellow with russet patches, juicy and sweet, deliciously aromatic.

'Pitmaston Duchess', October–November. very large, yellow marbled russet, very juicy and pleasantly flavoured. Plant with 'Conference'.

'Packham's Triumph', November, medium-sized, greenish-yellow, pleasant flavour sweet, very juicy.

'Doyenné du Comice', November, large, pale yellow with fine russet, the best flavoured pear, crop is improved with 'Conference', 'Glou Morceau' and 'Williams'' as pollinators.

'Winter Nelis', November–January, small, rich melting flavour, good cropper.

'Glou Morceau', December–January, smooth pea green skin ripening to pale yellow, good flavour, planted as the most reliable pollinator of 'Doyenné du Comice'.

'Catillac', in season until April, the best culinary pear; large, cooks deep red, no other stewing pear is necessary.

PLUM *Prunus domestica*

Properly grown, plums are among the choicest of fruit for dessert and cooking. They like a reasonably heavy soil with good drainage. It is often thought that all stone fruits need lime but while the soil should not be acid, too much lime or chalk can be harmful. This is apparent in some districts when the foliage turns whitish yellow. The vigour and cropping capacity deteriorates because the trees are unable to obtain enough iron from the soil. Highly alkaline conditions make the iron unavailable to the plant roots. If the soil pH is 8, then lime-induced chlorosis is likely to occur and this, unfortunately, may not be evident until the trees have been planted for three or four years.

It is a good plan to mulch the soil around the trees with sedge peat or leaf mould, but whatever is used, it helps to smother annual weeds; and worms pull some of the organic matter into the soil. When it is decided to enrich the soil, decayed farmyard or cow manure can be used as a mulch, or if these are not available, hoof and horn meal at 90 g per m² (2½ oz per sq yd) can be used. If there are signs of leaf scorch indicating potash deficiency, it can usually be cured by top dressing with wood ash at the rate of 120 g per m² (3½ oz per sq yd), or 35 g per m² (1 oz per sq yd) of sulphate of potash. Avoid situations exposed to high winds and severe frost. Gusty wind can easily break fruit-laden branches.

Whether bush, standard or trained specimens are planted, they move most easily when two or three years old, when they do not have a very large root system, and soon become established after planting. Plant as soon as possible after November, while the ground is comparatively warm. Always stake half and full standards at planting time.

Firmly tied to the supports, the trees will not rock in windy weather and soon produce new fibrous roots. The top of the stake should come just below the crotch, where the branches start. So often the lower branches become chafed by rubbing on ill-placed stakes. Sometimes it is necessary to support heavily laden branches otherwise they break off. Plum wood is brittle and when loaded, branches split easily if not supported.

Many plums produce sucker growths from the base. These should be removed as soon as seen, by tracing them back to their source, and pulling them off the roots from which they arise. If cut off, fresh suckers replace them.

'Czar' is a good cooking plum

Although the temptation is to plant closely, one should remember that bushes and trees make considerable growth over a period of years. Bush plums should not be planted closer than 4–4.6 m (13–15 ft), half standards up to 5 m (16 ft) apart, with full standards about 6 m (20 ft) apart. Fan trained specimens used against walls and fences will need a distance of 5–5.5 m (16–18 ft) between them.

Bush plums yield freely if treated properly. For preference, a bush should have an open centre with low spreading branches. This can be obtained by simple light pruning, the idea being to remove all shoots growing towards the centre and any which cross or die out. It is not essential to tip the shoots for even if the upright leaders are not cut, the weight of the fruit usually brings these branches down to maintain the correct, open shape.

Fruit thinning is necessary, not only to

Still the queen of plums – 'Victoria'

reduce heavy, indifferent crops but to check biennial bearing, a tendency to which many varieties are prone. Before doing so, wait until it is certain that all the fruit will develop, for usually quite a lot falls naturally.

Since it ripens at different times all the fruit cannot be picked at one time. If it is gathered too early the full flavour will not have developed. Do not harvest fruit when it is wet or it will soon become mildewed. All decaying and imperfect specimens should be gathered and destroyed.

RECOMMENDED VARIETIES: Of the many plums in cultivation today the following are the most reliable for general garden culture:

'Cambridge Gage', early September, a

sport from the old Greengage, but a better cropper; partially self-fertile.

'Coe's Golden Drop', end September, oval golden-yellow, dotted red, good flavour, excellent on walls.

'Comte d'Althann's Gage', mid-September, roundish, rich purple, with firm, well flavoured flesh; a good cropper.

'Czar', early August, roundish, almost black, a heavy cropper, greatly used for market, an excellent cooking variety, self-fertile.

'Denniston's Superb', mid-August, round greenish yellow fruit, excellent flavour.

'Early Laxton', early August, smallish yellow fruit, with red flush, sweet and juicy, a reliable cropper, useful for cooking.

'Giant Prune', end September, large, long and oval, dark red, of vigorous growth and a good cropper; a fine culinary variety.

'Green Gage', (also known as 'Reine Claude') early September, of medium size, leaf-green with a white bloom, the flesh is also green and most deliciously flavoured; well-known and much grown; fine as a standard or for growing on walls.

'Jefferson's Gage', early September, large, oval golden-yellow, with reddish spots, a fine reliable variety.

'Kirke's Blue', mid-September, medium-sized round, very dark purple, golden flesh of rich flavour, sometimes a shy bearer.

'Marjorie's Seedling', late September, blue-black fruits with yellow flesh. One of the best late varieties.

'Myrobalan', late July, the 'Cherry Plum',

Delicious fruits of the 'Green Gage'

both the red and yellow varieties are excellent for cooking and bottling; sometimes known as 'Roblets'; a self-fertile variety.

'Old Transparent Gage', early September, yellowish-green, red spots, sweet and juicy; good for pot culture.

'Oullins' Golden Gage', early August, large pale yellow firm sweet flesh, a good grower and useful for dessert and bottling.

'Pershore Yellow', August, medium-sized, oval yellow fruit; good cooker, first class for jam.

'Rivers Early Prolific', end of July, a roundish, deep purple fruit with yellowish brisk flesh; although really a cooking plum it is fit for dessert when ripe; partially self-fertile; plant with a pollinator such as 'Jefferson's' or 'Cambridge Gage'.

'Victoria', late August, the surest cropping and most reliable all-round variety; large oval pinkish-red fruit, the yellow flesh is firm and of excellent flavour.

Although a number of plums will fruit freely on their own, many crop more heavily if a pollinator is growing nearby. The following are examples of how to ensure heavy crops.

Variety	Pollinators
'Cambridge Gage'	'Pershore Yellow'
	'Victoria'
'Coe's Golden Drop'	'Denniston's Superb'
	'Early Laxton'
'Czar'	'Marjorie's Seedling'
	'Pershore Yellow'
'Marjorie's Seedling'	'Cambridge Gage'
	'Czar'
'Oullin's Golden Gage'	'Czar'
	'Marjorie's Seedling'
'Pershore Yellow'	'Czar'
	'Kirke's'
'Rivers Early Prolific'	'Denniston's Superb'
	'Early Laxton'
'Victoria'	'Marjorie's Seedling'
	'Rivers Early Prolific'

'Coe's Golden Drop', 'Jefferson's Gage', 'Kirke's Blue' and 'Victoria' often fruit quite well on their own.

QUINCE *Cydonia oblonga*

This old fashioned fruit is seldom grown as much as it used to be. It delights in damp soil but also does quite well in dryish positions. Quince is often grown as a rootstock for pears.

Apart from its fruit it is beautiful when in flower and enhances the shrubbery. It is also handsome as a specimen tree on the lawn, growing to about 4·5–6·5 m (15–20 ft). When it is grown principally for its fruit, it is advisable to thin the branches. Quinces make extremely good jelly, and when cooked with apples the highly scented fruit imparts a pleasing flavour. One quince to twelve apples is about the right quantity.

RECOMMENDED VARIETIES:

'Bereczeki', a remarkable Serbian quince of great size; once established, it fruits heavily and even two- or three-year-old trees carry reasonable crops; vigorous; the fruit is pear-shaped and particularly tender when cooked.

'Champion' is a splendid greenish-yellow, pear-shaped variety.

'Portugal' produces large yellow downy pear-shaped fruits which turn red when

Devote some garden space to the rewarding quince

cooked; not as prolific as other varieties, it is a strong grower and is said to have been introduced to Britain as long ago as 1611.

'Vranja' is almost identical with 'Bereczeki'.

RASPBERRY *Rubus idaeus*

Although raspberries are not really fussy about their growing conditions they give best results in a fairly rich medium-heavy soil containing plenty of humus. This encourages the development of many fibrous roots and strong canes which carry heavy crops of fruit.

Newly planted canes should be cut down to a bud 20–25 cm (8–10 ins) above soil level in early April. The remaining buds will produce a few fruiting shoots but the effect of hard pruning is to induce one or two stout canes for cropping the following season.

Newly planted rows should be mulched with compost or well-rotted manure against spring droughts.

Very light ground, unless generously manured before planting and mulched annually, produces only poor crops. On such soils there is often a lack of potash which shows itself in the scorched edges of the leaves. This shortage can be remedied by dressings of a good organic fertilizer while bonfire ash placed along the rows and lightly pricked in is helpful. Sulphate of potash is sometimes sprinkled along the sides of the rows but not on the crowns of the canes.

Sites are important and if possible, the rows should run north to south. An open, sunny but not exposed position is best. Avoid frost pockets and other low lying areas, otherwise some of the flowers may be damaged and crop will be light. Clear the ground of weeds before planting. If not it will be very difficult to get rid of tenacious weeds such as bindweed, couch grass and convolvulus.

Plant from October onwards. Autumn planting is best since by the early spring the basal shoots are developing and are easily broken off. Even so, many gardeners do plant successfully up until April.

Space rows from 1.2–1.50 m (4–5 ft) apart and allow from 38–60 cm (15–24 ins) between the canes. It is immaterial whether one permits the clumps to grow into each other or keeps them separate. Plant firmly, and no deeper than the soil mark on the stems. Fruit should not be picked the first year, but strong suckers from below ground will bear fruit the following season.

Some means of support is necessary to prevent the canes from snapping in the wind and make it easy to gather the fruit.

The simplest method is to erect posts at each end of the rows running two strands of wire between them, the lowest being about 45 cm (18 ins) from the ground, the second strand being 1.50 m (5 ft) from the ground. If the canes are not very strong use more wires and space them about 30 cm (12 ins) apart.

Once picking has finished, cut out all fruited canes, tying in the new canes to replace them. Allow four or five new canes to each stool, removing all others, particularly those that are weak or small. Always keep the crop well picked, for over-ripe fruit left on the canes is liable to attract mildew and other fungus disorders.

RECOMMENDED VARIETIES: Although many varieties have been grown, not all have stayed the course, but the following are available and are reliable in every way:

'Baumforth's Seedling', sweet berries.

'Deutschland', dark red, delicious flavour.

'Lloyd George', heavy cropping, rich red well-flavoured berries.

There are a number of excellent varieties

'Glen Clova' raspberries ripen early

raised at the East Malling Research Station; these include 'Malling Promise', 'Malling Jewel' and 'Malling Exploit'.

Among the autumn fruiting sorts, 'Lloyd George' must be included, for it frequently goes on bearing until October or later; others are 'Hailsham' an excellent variety with large dark red fruit.

'November Abundance', medium sized, dark red sweet and juicy fruits.

'September' is a firm red variety.

'Glen Clova' is a fairly new early ripening variety cropping over a long period; of

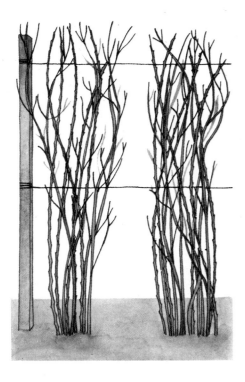
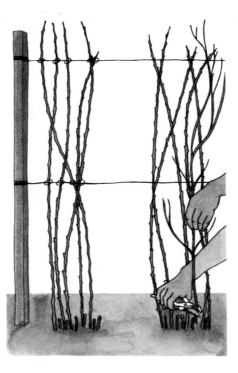

Above: Training and pruning raspberry canes. Below: Ripe fruits.

excellent flavour, it is valued for dessert, jam, bottling and freezing.

Of the yellow raspberries 'Antwerp', although introduced well over a century ago is still very good and in fair demand; it is a firm grower, freely producing large, roundish sweet berries.

There are also a few autumn fruiting yellow sorts:

'Exeter Yellow' produces a good crop of very sweet rich coloured fruit.

'Lord Lambourne' is a splendid sort, rather like 'Lloyd George' excepting colour;

'Fallgold' is a new golden-yellow raspberry bearing a heavy crop of large sweet berries over a long period.

'Zeva' is known as the perpetual fruiting raspberry. Of Swiss origin, it fruits on young canes from July until November; the berries are large and of superb flavour.

STRAWBERRY *Fragaria* x *ananassa*

The delicious strawberry, colourful herald of summer, is probably the most popular of the soft fruits. Whether new plants, or runners taken earlier from one's own healthy plants are used for new plantings, it is never advisable to replant an old strawberry bed. Ideally, change the site every three years, to prevent a build up of pests and diseases. The soil can get 'tired' of strawberries and should be well cultivated before being used for them again.

A fertile, sandy soil is probably most suitable, but success can be obtained in almost any soil, although really heavy land should be drained. It is a good plan, after autumn cultivation, to dig lightly between the rows and place the soil towards the plants, leaving a shallow furrow between the rows, to drain off surplus water.

Select a site which has been recently cultivated and well manured for a previous crop such as early potatoes. Alternatively, deeply dig and manure a patch of ground. If wireworms are present, scatter HCH powder over the soil before planting.

Since deep cultivation will not be possible once the bed is planted, preparation should be thorough and the soil may be further enriched with a 120 g per m² (3½ oz per sq yd) dressing of bone meal. The phosphates this will supply are probably more important than any other ingredient.

Autumn planting should be carried out when the soil is in good condition from September onwards. From an early planting one can allow a fair crop to develop the following summer.

Pot grown runners will be easy to plant with a trowel, but with open ground runners care must be taken to plant firmly. A good method is to plant with a dibber and to press the soil firmly round the roots to remove any harmful air pockets.

The crown of the plant should be kept at soil level: deep planting is as undesirable as shallow planting. Frequently, early frosts lift the plants above soil level and they should be refirmed immediately, or growth may be checked.

Deep cultivation at any time of the year should be avoided for the roots may be damaged. Build up the plant's strength by working a 120 g per m² (3½ oz per sq yd) dressing of bone meal or other phosphatic organic manure into the soil as soon as fruiting is over.

All decayed and drying leaves and runners should be removed, except when the runners are required for propagation. When hoeing, draw the soil lightly towards the plants. This will act as a dust mulch during hot summer days and help to feed the new roots which, each autumn, grow above the previous set.

Many growers propagate their own plants. Where this is done, ensure that runners are taken from strong healthy plants, free from virus diseases, eelworm or aphis. Soon after the stolons (runners) appear, they will produce a cluster of roots at each leaf joint. Peg down the first and strongest plantlet on each runner, cutting back the rest. When well rooted, the plantlets are severed from the parents and moved to their permanent places. If the plantlets are pegged into small pots of rich compost sunk rim-level in the soil, they will crop more readily the first year after planting.

Strawberries can be grown successfully in the greenhouse or the garden frame and will give an earlier crop of really clean fruit than can be obtained from the open ground. Plants for forcing should come from strong runners rooted early directly into pots plunged into the soil. These young plants must be kept well supplied with moisture. They can be severed from the parent plant as soon as it is obvious they are well rooted.

When this has been done move them to a shady spot. Keep them fresh with overhead syringings of water during the evenings in warm weather. After two or three weeks remove them to larger, well drained pots of John Innes No 3 potting mixture. Pot firmly, but avoid burying the crowns. Keep the plants in a shady position for a week or

two. Then transfer them to the cold frame, standing them on weathered ashes or similar material exposing them to full sun. Continue watering as necessary and give feeds of liquid manure until the end of September. Do not cover the plants with the frame lights for they must be grown so that they are quite hardy. In late October, lay the pots on their sides with the crowns facing the light. Alternatively, lay the pots on their sides at the base of a north wall, but in either case once severe weather arrives place straw or bracken over the pots to prevent frost damage. And with plants in frames, put the lights on during very wet weather. Frost will not injure the plants. In fact, after frost they will be better for forcing.

Strawberry barrels need little space

About the middle of January the first batch of plants can be taken into the cool greenhouse, warmth being gradually increased as growth develops. Keep the plants on a shelf in full light and take off any early runners so that the plant's strength goes into flower and fruit production. Ventilate freely to avoid mildew and other diseases. Make sure the roots are nicely moist.

Apart from these standard methods of cultivation strawberries may be grown in barrels and by the Verti-strawb system.

Strawberries in barrels. Growing strawberries in barrels provides an interesting and often profitable means of obtaining fruit, being particularly valuable where space is restricted or where there is no garden at all.

It also gives less active gardeners the pleasure of growing plants with the minimum attention, while weed and pest control is easy. They can easily be covered with netting to prevent birds spoiling the fruit.

First obtain a large barrel. One made of oak, chestnut or similar hard wood will usually last for years. Avoid those which have been creosoted or have contained substances harmful to plant life. Drill the barrel with holes 5–6 cm (2–2½ ins) in diameter, staggering them 23 cm (9 ins) apart.

The barrels can be painted any colour and be used as a feature. To render the barrels weatherproof for a long period, two undercoats of paint are recommended before the final hard gloss colour is applied.

Stand the barrel on bricks, so that water can run away through drainage holes in the bottom. Place a 15 cm (6 in) layer of stones at the base, for drainage. Then fill in with a soil mixture of three parts loam, one part good leaf mould, half part each granulated or similar peat and sharp sand, mixing in about 680 g (1½ lbs) of bone meal, 450 g (1 lb) hoof and horn meal and 450 g (1 lb) of wood ash to each barrel of compost, thoroughly mixing all in a semi-dry state. These organic fertilizers will release their food gradually over a long period.

Ideally, place a column of rubble down the centre of the barrel for extra drainage. A way to do this is to insert a drain pipe, fill it with rubble and pull it out when the barrel is filled with soil.

Planting: Work in the soil firmly and as each hole is reached, insert the plant's roots from the outside, spread them out, and make sure that the growing point is left exposed. Work in fine compost around the roots, taking care not to damage the plants when doing so. Continue to fill the barrel with soil and plants, until each hole is planted. Then the surface of the barrel can be planted.

Little further attention is necessary apart from ensuring that the central drainage duct is kept well supplied with water and occasional doses of liquid manure to help the plants along.

Strawberries particularly suited to growing in barrels include 'Royal Sovereign' and 'Cambridge Favourite', and perpetuals such as 'St Fiacre' and 'Baron Solemacher'. All can be planted from August until November and should yield the following year. Large sized barrels will hold 28 plants and the medium sized, 18, allowing for some on the top of the barrel. White stacking plastic pots are now available which are very useful for this type of growing system.

The Verti-strawb system of culture The Verti-strawb system has been evolved to satisfy the need to obtain maximum crops from limited greenhouse space.

Although the name of the variety used for the first experiments has never been divulged, there seems to be no reason why 'Royal Sovereign', 'Cambridge Favourite' and similar varieties should not be used. Originally strong medium-sized runners, probably from cold storage, were used. In the early part of July, polythene tubing 10 cm (4 ins) in diameter and up to 6.50 m (21 ft) long is filled with suitable compost. This is placed or fixed on raised horizontal supports up to 3.20 m (10½ ft) high.

while for those who have or can make the right conditions.

It has been claimed that the Verti-strawb system returns up to 1.4 kg (3 lbs) of fruit per plant, compared with 340 g (¾ lb) from conventionally grown plants. The fruit will be clean, free from weather, bird and slug damage. Verti-strawb plants can also be grown in a sun lounge or on a sheltered patio.

RECOMMENDED VARIETIES:

'Royal Sovereign' has for long been the most popular of garden strawberries, its large scarlet fruit possessing a rich delicious flavour and scent; a medium cropper, some-

'Domanil' also heavy cropping, mid-season.

'Tamella' produces attractive looking berries of good flavour, excellent for dessert, freezing, bottling and jam.

'Grandee' is a vigorous grower with exceptionally large fruit.

Alpine strawberry Although alpine strawberries are much smaller than the standard varieties they are well worth cultivating. They will grow in partially shaded places, specially if the soil contains plenty of compost, peat or other humus-forming matter. They are splendid for edgings and should be spaced 30 cm (12 ins) apart with 45 cm (18

Ripe berries of the variety 'Tamella', protected by straw

Holes are punched in the tubes with a suitable iron 15 cm (6 ins) apart and the rooted strawberry runners planted through them. Feeding and constant but controlled watering is carried out for up to eight weeks, when the autumn crop is ready for picking.

After a rest period, the plants are started into growth again in early January. Warmth, water and feeding will lead to the production of flower trusses in late February. Fruit will be ready for picking in April, the crop continuing for months so that with the July and January plantings, fruit should be available over a very long period. Some of the earliest fruits may not be of perfect shape but quality and flavour is unaffected. This is a novel if rather expensive way of producing strawberries but well worth-

times spoiled by botrytis, susceptible to virus and best grown under really healthy clean conditions.

'Cambridge Favourite' is a widely grown mid-season variety of moderate flavour; a heavy cropper, resistant to disease and suitable for preserving and freezing.

'Cambridge Vigour' is a second early variety bearing medium sized fruit of good flavour.

'Cambridge Premier', an early large fruiting sort is useful for cloche culture.

'Cambridge Rival', good early variety.

'Red Gauntlet' is another vigorous heavy cropping variety.

'Talisman' is quite widely grown.

'Merton Dawn' is a heavy cropping mid-season variety.

ins) between the rows. The fruit is borne on erect stems clear of the ground and is less often attacked by birds.

If the first flush of flowers is picked off, the plants will crop heavily from August to October, a time when the larger strawberries have finished.

Propagation is from seed sown in trays of John Innes seed compost or a similar mixture in spring, or the plants can be divided after flowering, making sure that each offset is healthy with one or two strong buds.

Varieties not producing runners include 'Baron Solemacher', which is the best known variety, and crops heavily over a long period; the smallish dark red fruits have a buttery texture; there is also a white form.

'Red Alpine Improved' is said by some gardeners to be better than 'Baron Solemacher'.

Remontant or perpetual varieties which bear large fruits from September onwards include:

'Hampshire Maid', excellent for dessert and jam.

'Red Rich', strong growing with dark red berries.

'Sans Rivale', vigorous, heavy cropping, often continuing until late November.

'St Claude', sweet, juicy and disease resistant.

Propagating strawberries from runners

Climbing strawberries At one time quite a lot was heard of the so-called climbing strawberries. This is really a misnomer since there are no actual climbing varieties for none have tendrils. One or two of the remontant sorts produce long stolons on which develop a number of little plants. If these stolons are trained upright they can be used to cover low walls, fences, lattice work or similar supports. The top growth will die down in late autumn.

NUTS

As nuts growing wild in the hedgerows become less common, it is a good idea to find some space for a nut tree in the garden.

WALNUT *Juglans regia*

Apart from their elegant appearance and the crops they bear, walnut trees are of value for the timber they produce. It is not essential to grow them as full standards and some nurserymen offer half standards. A large number of walnuts are eaten in this country.

The Romans are said to have known the walnuts as the Nut of Jove or Jupiter from which comes Jooglans, or Juglans, a nut superior to others and fit for the gods. When its cultivation extended to France it became known as the Gaul Nut, corrupted into Walnut by the British.

Once established, walnuts need a good deal of space and are rather erratic croppers. The majority of nuts in England today are grown in woodland conditions, and there is a large nuttery in Gloucestershire, and two or three smaller plantations in Kent.

They will grow in almost any soil provided it is well-drained with a fair lime content. Avoid low-lying ground and frost pockets. November until the end of March are the best months for planting. The ground should be prepared as for other fruit trees. Never allow the roots to dry out, for failure to protect them is a main cause of trees failing to become established. Trim clean any roots damaged at lifting time.

Plant firmly, keeping the graft union just above ground and provide standards with a stout support. Wire netting round the stem will protect the bark from grazing animals or rabbits.

A mulching of compost after planting will prevent the soil from drying out in the spring and summer. Subsequently, it will be helpful if a dressing of bone or meat meal is scattered round the trees at the rate of 70 g per m² (2 oz per sq yd) each spring.

If the trees are grown in grassland, keep the grass well away from the trunks until the trees are really established, when the turf can be allowed to grow right up to the stem.

Walnuts are usually sold as standards or half standards with at least a partially formed head. Trees with laterals (side shoots) on their stems are best, as these encourage the stem to thicken. This avoids the possibility of a large bushy head on a thin trunk. These laterals, or feathered side shoots, should be kept from growing too large or they will compete with the head.

In the second winter's pruning, the shape of the head is determined. This is done by selecting four or five well-placed shoots and cutting them back so that they are 20–23 cm (8–9 ins) long. Cut to an outward or downward bud, so that the resultant growth does not point towards the centre. Remove entirely any vertical shoots to avoid trouble later. Subsequently, until the head is fully developed, cut out badly placed shoots and shorten any that are excessively long.

The feathers on the stem will of course also be removed when the head has formed. Any large scars can be treated with a proprietary protective paint to keep out disease. Never leave snags and keep the trees well supported until they are twelve to fifteen years old and capable of resisting strong winds and storms.

All pruning should be done before the

Walnuts at the immature stage

end of January, otherwise the trees are liable to 'bleed' when cut.

Walnuts bear male and female flowers on one-year shoots on the same tree. The pollen comes from the catkins and the reason why some trees do not fruit well is that the pollen is shed before the sticky stigmas of the female flowers are ready to receive it. There is, therefore, an advantage in having more than one walnut in the vicinity so that the flowers can more easily be wind pollinated.

RECOMMENDED VARIETIES:

'Franquette' starts into growth late, so usually misses May frosts;

'Mayette', a late starter like 'Franquette'. The large roundish nuts have easy-to-crack shells.

FILBERT & COBNUT Corylus species

The easiest nuts for the gardener. They are closely related botanically, but are distinguished by the long husk of the filbert, (*C. maxima*) which sometimes almost hides the nut and the short husk of the cobnut (*C. avellana*), which leaves the nut exposed.

All are easy to grow and do well on most types of soil but crops are smaller where the land is poor. To allow for development the bushes should be spaced at least 3.65 m (12 ft) apart, although if they are being used as hedges or screens space them closer together.

Harvest cob nuts from September onwards

Nut bushes bear male and female flowers so there is no difficulty about pollination. The conspicuous male flowers, generally known as catkins, are easy to see, but the small red female filaments are easily overlooked. It is from these, of course, that the nuts develop. Choose a frost-free site so the female flowers open when the catkins are ripe with golden pollen.

Propagate the bushes from layers pegged down in the autumn and raise plants from seed. The nuts are stratified between layers of sand in a box buried in the soil in autumn. In spring, they are unearthed and sown in drills to germinate within a few weeks. The resultant bushes are likely to vary greatly both in growth and cropping ability.

RECOMMENDED VARIETIES: Cob: 'Cosford', thin-shelled, of excellent flavour, Filbert: 'Kentish Cob', pollinated by 'Cosford'.

WHORTLEBERRY Vaccinium myrtillus

This plant is also known variously as the bilberry or blueberry, although the true blueberry is *Vaccinum corymbosum*. It bears racemes of little bell-shaped flowers in early summer. The variety *leucocarpum* has white berries.

Growing about 45 cm (18 ins) high, it is a heath-like shrub with small, ovate foliage

and sprays of pendant pink flowers which are followed by showy bluish-black, round, edible fruit. These are delicious in whortleberry pie topped with cream.

Plants thrive in moisty peaty, lime-free soil and are best transplanted in March or April. Old, badly placed stems should be cut out in late winter or early spring.

Propagation is from half-ripe cuttings 8–10 cm (3–4 ins) long. Insert them under glass where there is bottom heat, in late July or August. Other means of increasing stocks are by offsets, divisions, layering in autumn, or by seed sown in early autumn.

The worcesterberry crops heavily

WORCESTERBERRY Ribes divaricatum

Although this American native has long been regarded as a hybrid between a gooseberry and a blackcurrant, it is in fact a small black gooseberry. Certainly the fruit resembles in appearance both these subjects, being smaller than a gooseberry and usually larger than a blackcurrant. The flavour is similar to both. The abundant berries are borne in clusters, and are a deep reddish-purple, often turning purple-black.

The vigorous stems are closely furnished with thorns, undoubtedly one reason why the Worcesterberry has never been popular. If properly trained, however, this is a valuable addition to the fruit garden.

Cultivation and pruning is identical for that recommended for gooseberries. The Worcesterberry is resistant to mildew. Set plants in rich well drained soil containing plenty of humus. For sulphur-shy varieties, like 'Leveller', 'Early Sulphur- and 'Golden Drop', use a colloidal-sulphur spray.

SPECIAL-PURPOSE GARDENS

The special gardens discussed here are designed to suit peculiarities of site or personal circumstances or preferences. The differences of style and methods of application are merely modern adaptations of old concepts; water gardens, for instance, have been in existence for thousands of years. The only comparative newcomer is the busy man's garden below, designed for minimum time spent on upkeep.

The busy man's garden
The aim here is a garden which serves its purpose and can be kept neat and tidy for 52 weeks of the year with a minimum of attention. The busy owner can solve this by paying someone else to look after the garden or by streamlining the work. Here we consider the latter alternative.

With time at a premium, reduce or eliminate time-consuming repetitive tasks. Annual bedding schemes, climbers and plants require constant tying and attention and should be kept to a minimum. Where the aim is primarily to keep the garden tidy and presentable, incorporate labour-saving surfaces and avoid fussy planting.

Lawns should be formed of finer grasses like fescues and bents, or a blend of these and special hard-wearing rye grass. Avoid farm grass mixtures which require heavy mowing. Changes in level are best dealt with by the use of retaining walls, or shrub and grass banks, or terraces, all of which are much less demanding than rock gardens, unless these are heavily planted with permanent subjects.

Plants and planting
A few well chosen and carefully sited plants can look most attractive as well as being easy to manage. Select slow growing perennial plants, preferably evergreen, such as dwarf conifers, heathers, and hollies. The herringbone cotoneaster and pyracantha are both useful for covering walls. Colourful bush roses require little care.

Keep planting in lawns to a minimum to cut out obstacles to mowing.

Lawn edges should be as straight as the site will allow. Hard kerbs round beds and borders will reduce grass edging problems.

Trained forms of fruit, like cordon apple and pear trees or cordon gooseberries and redcurrants, require more attention than bush forms. Fan-trained trees are best avoided as they require considerable attention. Vegetable growing is also time-consuming. As a guide, a vegetable plot requires about ten times as much attention as a comparable area of lawn. On the other hand, perennial herbs such as sage, thyme, mint, and chives require little attention or space.

Avoid container-grown subjects, which need regular watering. Crocus, snowdrop, muscari and daffodil are excellent bulbs for this type of garden. They can safely be left year after year, apart from the occasional lifting, dividing and replanting.

For surfaces, use flagstones, concrete or other easily-brushed materials, which are longer lasting and less trouble than gravel, loose chippings or even grass. Confine your equipment to basics, stored under cover and well maintained.

Formal and town gardens
Modern gardens, which are mostly small, of regular outline and dominated by buildings, are well suited to formal treatment.

As with the wall and herb garden, these gardens are typically bounded by straight sides and laid out in geometric patterns such as squares, rectangles and circles. The plants are generally naturally compact or severely pruned and trained to conform to the character of the architectural environment. Although regimented straight lines are not everyone's choice, the horizontal and vertical lines of buildings considerably influence the design of the town garden.

Town gardens are much restricted by size and are often overwhelmed by walls and buildings. The main difficulties are drab surroundings, pollution and shade.

Only the hardiest evergreens such as laurel and skimmia can survive the combination of these conditions. Although many towns are not as grimy or

dirty as even ten years ago, many evergreens look jaded when compared with the fresh green leaves of deciduous plants as they unfold in spring.

In these surroundings, where colour is so important, spring bedding plants or bulbs like tulips and daffodils, or summer pelargoniums and begonias stimulate the eye. As these plants are raised in nurseries in good conditions of light and air, their accumulated food reserves are useful for flowering in the less congenial conditions. Hardy deciduous shrubs like forsythia, winter flowering jasmine, and flowering currants or lilacs are invaluable for town gardens.

Paved surfaces are harder wearing than grass. Changes in level are better solved by steps, terraces and retaining walls in confined areas. Drainage must be checked for flooding in your own garden and neighbouring gardens.

Formal gardens are not confined to towns and can be used in country areas. Features include clipped hedges, hard surfaces, paved or flagged floor area, terraces and beds, borders or pools of regular shape. Bush roses are often planted in square or rectangular beds in lawns or surrounded by paving, a formal setting which seems to suit them.

Plants for town gardens resemble those listed for container gardening and roof gardens, together with the following trees: Amelanchier; Betula; Crataegus; Ilex; Laburnum; Malus; Prunus; Pyrus; Robinia; Sorbus. Recommended shrubs include: Aucuba; Berberis; Buddleia; Chaenomeles; Cotoneaster; Escallonia; Forsythia; Hydrangea; Hypericum; Magnolia; Mahonia; Philadelphus; Pyracantha; Rhododendron; Ribes; Rosa; Spartium; Spiraea; Syringa; Tamarix; Weigela.

LEFT The busy man's garden can be kept neat and tidy with a minimum of attention. Particular features are hard surfaces and labour-saving plants such as azaleas, greyleaf plants and lavender.
RIGHT An alternative treatment for a small town garden has a formal patio and pathway and is largely planted with foliage plants.

Herb gardens

Herb gardens can be little more than a window box providing household needs or, on the other hand, may have an area devoted exclusively to them. A collection of herbs laid out as a formal garden with separate beds or panels for individual groups can make an interesting and highly fragrant feature but their lack of colour may require compensation.

ABOVE A planned informal garden
RIGHT A herb garden.
BELOW A wall garden.

Informal gardens

Informal gardens do not have to be untidy to merit their title, and are in fact very difficult to design to look natural and continue to look good. In natural or wild gardens plants are allowed to grow almost at will without close mowing, clipping and severe pruning. It follows that the original choice of plants must be expert if they are not to swamp each other.

Wall gardens

Walls are particularly important in confined spaces and provide a great opportunity to display plants to good effect. They must be well maintained and preferably light, south-facing and not too draughty.

Low retaining walls with holes or pockets left in them can house plants such as aubrieta, alyssum and arabis. Walls of 3m (10ft) high can have wires or trellis fixed for training climbing roses, clematis, pyracantha or jasmine. High walls can be topped with troughs or boxes of plants which trail and hang down, such as eccremocarpus or ivy, to meet the climbing plants as they ascend. They will need regular watering.

Water gardens

The formal use of water

In formal settings, water is usually used in pools of regular shape, and each pool is usually surrounded with a paved or flagged area.

Waterlilies and fountains can be seen to best effect in sunlight, so avoid dull or heavily shaded spots.

Fountains can be free-standing or of the wall type. Pumps, pipes and services are best installed before the pools are made or any paving or surround is completed.

Pumps, pools and pipes are vulnerable to the action of severe, prolonged frost in winter. Bury water pipes at least 45cm (16in) deep in the ground.

The colour of the pool is important; blues and greens tend to be more subdued than white, which is also difficult to keep clean.

Water in natural surroundings

If there is a natural pool in your garden, check the continuity of the water supply, especially during the summer months, before you think about incorporating it in a planting scheme. Water always finds its way to the lowest point and the presence or absence of changes in level will, to a large extent, determine the character of the site.

In nature, there are four groups of plants which are found in or near water. First there are the submerged plants such as pond weed, which oxygenate the water and enable fish to thrive. The next category includes plants with floating leaves such as water lilies. The third group consists of plants which grow in shallow water, but hold their leaves and flowers above water. Sedges, yellow flag, bur-reed and water forget-me-not fall into this group. The last class consists of the marginal plants which like moist soil, but are not happy actually growing in water. Examples of this group include primulas, forget-me-not, mimulus, marsh marigolds and other waterside plants.

Plants for the water garden: Bog plants: Andromeda; Astilbe; Caltha; Carex; Hosta; Hemerocallis; Iris; Kniphofia; Mimulus; Myosotis; Myrica; Primula; Ranunculus; Spiraea; Trollius. Water plants: Aponogeton; Juncus; Nymphaea; Osmunda; Sagittaria.

ABOVE A formal water garden.
BELOW A natural garden pond.

Container gardening

Two functions are served by container gardening. Containers are invaluable in built up areas where there is no conventional garden space, while in all areas (including large gardens), tubs and troughs provide a movable feature, greatly easing the gardener's task of giving year-round interest to his garden.

Containers should be strong, durable, and deep and wide enough to hold sufficient compost to support and nourish plants. Other points include good drainage, attractive appearance, lightness in handling, and ease of cleaning.

Teak and oak are the most durable timbers for containers but require treating with wood preservative. Stone, earthenware and plastic receptacles are non-rotting; frost can break clayware holders.

Use loam-based mixtures such as John Innes potting compost, provided these have sand or aggregate included, for plants remaining more than a year in containers.

Trough gardening

Stone or earthenware containers of sufficient depth, can be planted with various small plants to create a novel miniature landscape, or used for standard bedding plants. For alpine plants, put a 6mm ($\frac{1}{4}$in) layer of clean granite chippings on the surface and around the plants, to prevent undue capping of the compost from rain or watering. Use peat for bedding plants. Where particularly choice small plants are being grown, raise the trough on to a firm secure platform before filling and planting for easy viewing.

Balcony planting

This is usually confined to covering vertical surfaces and window sills. Window boxes come into their own in this situation, and both small tubs and hanging baskets should be used where space and watering allow. Attractive window boxes are not always easy to obtain, but can be made by a handyman. Two useful sizes are 60cm (2ft) and 90cm (3ft) long by 15cm (6in) wide and deep (these are internal measurements). Make containers with 12mm ($\frac{1}{2}$in) thick wood suitably treated with preservative, and drilled with 3mm ($\frac{1}{8}$in) holes for drainage. When planting up the boxes firm the compost well and leave a 12mm ($\frac{1}{2}$in) space at the top for watering. Bracket window boxes to a wall if placed above ground level, or place in a bracketed metal cradle.

Hanging baskets

These are a useful means of softening hard walls and providing colour at a height. To obtain the best effects line the bottom with living green moss so that a 10cm (4in) layer of compost can be added. Next work in three or four plants, such as lobelia, so that the shoots jut out beyond the wire frame, with the roots planted in the compost. Place more moss inside the frame, and spread another layer of compost and repeat the planting process if the basket is big enough. Plant the top of the basket as for tubs and other containers, and cover the compost with a final layer of moss. The moss improves the appearance, hides the wire frame, and reduces the loss of moisture.

Plants for containers, balcony and troughs include Ageratum; Alyssum; Arabis; Aubrieta; Begonia; Polyanthus; Salvia; Tagetes; Tulip; Verbena; Wallflower.

Rooftop gardens

Wind is one of the major problems with these sites, and they need a low wall surround. Place containers of plants at the base of the perimeter wall. Additional protection can be provided by securing a trellis to increase the height of the screen. If there are high walls, grow climbers in containers, securing the plants to trellis or wire supports.

Spring and summer bedding plants including bulbs, wallflowers, and forget-me-nots, and summer-flowering pelargoniums, begonias and marigolds, will brighten the surroundings.

Nearby chimneys can be shut out by plants and trellis screening. Weight should be considered where a considerable amount of planting is being carried out, also provision for watering and the disposal of surplus water.

Safety rails should be placed round the edge and if there is seating it should be fixed so that children cannot drag the benches to look over the safety rails.

Plants for roof gardens include those given for container gardens with the following additions: Anthemis; Armeria; Artemisia; Campanula; Cotoneaster; Dianthus; Erigeron; Galega; Hedera; Iberis; Nepeta; Polygonum; Potentilla; Prunus; Rosa; Rosmarinus; Sambucus; Santolina; Statice; Thymus; Veronica.

BELOW Container planting is ideal for brightening up dingy basement entrances, and trailing plants such as ivy help to hide the angularity of the bricks and concrete.

Rock gardens

In the rock garden, copy conditions which prevail in the wild state (see Foliage gardens p. 228) for best effects. Select local stone, and layer pieces of rock as nearly as possible in the way they occur naturally. A few large stones are preferable to many small pieces. Rocks associate well with water or a heath type setting and are a useful means of changing level, but can also be used flat.

Limestone is one of the most favoured materials. Sandstone is also popular, although less durable, and will serve the purpose. A sunny site is preferable, although many plants will grow well in most situations. When constructing a rock garden, avoid sudden changes of materials; do not, for example, mix bricks with stone, or granite with limestone. Secure the stones and ram potting compost or similar soil between rocks as a rooting medium.

When selecting plants, include one or two dwarf conifers to ensure a more balanced type of vegetation rather than concentrating entirely on flowering varieties. Avoid planting acid-loving plants such as lithospermum among limestone rocks. Heathers of the *Erica carnea* type, which flower during autumn, winter and spring, grow and flower well in neutral soil in limestone districts.

ABOVE LEFT A glass roof for a south-facing balcony enables houseplants and a vine to grow satisfactorily outdoors.
LEFT Window boxes and hanging baskets full of colourful bedding plants brighten up city streets.
ABOVE A small rock garden (foreground) can be successfully inset on a wide concrete path.

225

BELOW LEFT A garden for children needs careful planning from both the safety and interest points of view. Hard paths are necessary for cycle riding, but play areas, particularly where there are climbing frames, should be soft – lawns are ideal. A small flower bed can be instructive and amusing – suitable plants range from small pansies to giant sunflowers.

BELOW CENTRE The garden for the disabled should be carefully planned with the particular handicap in mind. Raised flower beds enable many gardening tasks to be carried out from a wheelchair, and hard wide pathways allow easy access.

BELOW RIGHT The scented garden is best kept small for maximum effect. If planted close to the house, the fragrance can be allowed to penetrate through open doors and windows in summer.

Children's corner

This part of the garden is not always easy to blend in with flowers but it is nonetheless an important feature. It is important that you should be able to reach children easily if necessary, and keep them constantly in sight from the house. It must be a safe place with surfaces suitable for play.

Access to and from the play space, especially for the very young, requires careful attention. Provide protection from busy roads and parking areas. Spring-loaded gates with an automatic catch and a good secure boundary fence or hedge are of considerable assistance.

Watch for danger points such as steps, water and machinery. Close off steps and stairs with gates. Water features should be inaccessible, and machinery, tools and all chemicals kept out of reach. Unsafe trees and structures need prompt attention. Always watch for uneven surfaces, nails sticking out from walls or timber, and deal with them without delay. Paved areas, although hard, cause fewer cuts than gravel paths.

Children's play includes imitation and learning. If a small plot of soil is set aside where seeds can be sown or plants grown, a lifelong interest in plants and living things may be kindled. Simple plants are bulbs and bellis, chives, potatoes, shallots and radish. A bird table, bath and nesting boxes can provide hours of pleasure.

Gardening for the disabled

Plants can be of immense value in rehabilitating physically or mentally disabled people. Gardens which find favour with the blind consist largely of small and medium-sized scented plants and those with variously textured leaves. A useful setting for these plants is on a level where they can be handled from a standing or sitting position.

People who are unable to stoop or bend prefer troughs or trays of plants at waist height.

Particular points to watch in gardens for the disabled are that paths are of sufficient width, level and firm. Use ramps in preference to steps, and supply hand rails.

Tool handles may need modifying to enable them to be gripped for use.

Watering sometimes presents problems. Taps that work with a push action instead of twist or thread may be easier. Small light-weight watering cans which can be used single handed are often needed. It is important to find ways and means of enabling disabled people to get to the plants, by extending tools or bringing plants up to within their reach. Another aspect is shelter and warmth. Disabled people are often unable to keep themselves warm so a sunny sheltered spot, out of the wind, is best.

Holding and handling plant pots can present problems: an upturned tray like a tomato box with holes of different sizes can make a useful holder. In these instances time is of less consequence than the ability to carry out various jobs.

Scented gardens

The fragrance of flowers adds much to the enjoyment of most gardens but for some, scent is considered sufficiently important to be classified in categories such as jonquil, violet or roses. Perfume is also found in leaves and other parts of the plants.

With sufficient space it is possible to have twelve months of fragrance in all but the coldest climates, by careful selection of plants. Lavender and rosemary make useful scented hedges for year-round interest. Various herbs like balm, sage, mint and thyme will scent the air, particularly if their leaves are bruised. Bulbs such as hyacinths, daffodils, jonquils and various lilies are strongly perfumed. Roses, stocks, lily-of-the-valley and sweet peas can be included in any planting of this nature.

There are many fragrant shrubs and climbers which add height and colour. A few of the old favourites include honeysuckle, daphne, jasmine, hamamelis, and various viburnums. Among the border plants, no planting would be complete without carnations, pinks, phlox, monarda and violets.

Scent in plants can be unpredictable: it may be particularly noticeable at certain times and less so at others. Very often the fragrance seems stronger in the cooler part of the day, early in the morning or evening for example. To judge from experience the best scents appear to be obtained from plants growing in well-drained soils and warm sunny situations. There is much to be said for having the scented garden close to the house, to let scent and perfume waft in through the open windows.

Scented plants: Flowering shrubs and climbers: Buddleia; Daphne; Hamamelis; Jasminum; Lavandula; Lonicera; Osmanthus; Rosa; Rosmarinus; Syringa; Viburnum; Wisteria. Flowering bedding and border plants: Alyssum; Centaurea; Cheiranthus; Convallaria; Dianthus; Heliotropium; Hyacinthus; Iris; Lathyrus; Matthiola; Narcissus; Nicotiana; Nymphaea; Oenothera; Primula; Tulipa; Verbena; Viola. Scented foliage: Aloysia; Lavandula; Melissa; Mentha; Monarda; Rosmarinus; Santolina; Thymus.

Seaside gardens

The climate and other conditions close to the sea make life difficult for many plants. The chief limiting factors are high winds or lack of shelter, sandy porous soils, salt in the soil, sea spray, and strong sun.

One of the first priorities is effective wind protection. This can be provided by banked earth, walls, screens, fencing and hedging. Light sandy soils are improved by the addition of organic materials such as manure and peat. Good cultivation of plants which tolerate these conditions is the best way of overcoming these limitations.

One problem which is common to gardens in exposed positions is that the erection or growing of screens may shut out some impressive views. The solution may be to leave an opening and settle for low ground-hugging plants at the strategic point.

Some pines and maples withstand coastal conditions as do a number of plants from the southern hemisphere, such as New Zealand Daisy Bush and various close relatives of the olearia family. Various veronicas or hebes, fuchsia, escallonia, and tamarisk are all useful seaside subjects. Hydrangeas, lupins and valerian are well known for their good performance and so are various grey-leaved plants like sea buckthorn, lavender, sea holly and echinops. Brooms, gorse and genista are other colourful plants which seem to flourish near the shore.

Plants for seaside gardens: Small trees: Arbutus; Chamaecyparis; Crataegus; Cupressus; Ilex; Juniperus; Laurus; Pinus; Sorbus. Shrubs: Cassinia; Cotoneaster; Cytisus; Erica; Escallonia; Fuchsia; Griselinia; Hebe; Helianthemum; Hippophae; Hydrangea; Ilex; Lavandula; Olearia; Rosa; Rosmarinus; Santolina; Spartium; Spiraea; Tamarix.

Foliage gardens

Foliage gardens may be laid out formally or in the informal style using a more random arrangement of plants.

In foliage gardens the leaves of plants are exploited to provide an infinite variety of colour, texture, shape and size. With careful choice, year round interest can be maintained. The colour range too is surprisingly wide, ranging through white, grey, blue, gold, copper, scarlet, purple, variegated, brown, pink, near black, and various autumn tints. Leaf textures vary from smooth to hairy and differ greatly in size. The large-leaved *Fatsia* (aralia) when well grown can create the impression of tropical plants.

Foliage is also often used to create a formal setting. Large and small-scale topiary – the art of cutting and trimming trees, plants and shrubs into various shapes – has been used to make gardens of distinction. Archways, hedge-walls, chess figures, peacocks and mazes can be seen in some of the older gardens. The use of clipped box and other evergreens in combination with well-chosen pieces of statuary can give dignity and character. Foliage plants used formally need less space than where the aim is to imitate nature. Colour and texture can be obtained from ground cover plants, such as thymes, ivies, and variously tinted heathers. Hosta, acanthus and fatsia will have a bolder effect. Bamboos, grasses and ferns provide a shapely contrast. Hedges composed of plants of contrasting leaf colour, like green and purple beech, can be very effective but care is needed to avoid a fussy appearance. Red, gold and cream or blue variegated plants, whether of the small-leaved type like dwarf conifers, or broad-leaved plants such as maples, and hollies or climbers are still more variations.

Foliage plants: Evergreen: Aucuba; Buxus; Calluna; Chamaecyparis; Elaeagnus; Erica; Euonymus; Hedera; Ilex; Juniperus; Lavandula; Osmanthus; Pieris; Rosmarinus; Santolina; Sedum; Sempervivum; Skimmia; Stachys; Viburnum; Yucca. Deciduous: Acer; Cornus; Corylus; Diervilla; Hibiscus; Hosta; Pyrus; Rhus; Ribes; Sambucus.

Winter garden

The attainment of colour and interest during the dark and dismal months of the years presents a challenge, but it is not as difficult as it may first appear.

Evergreens provide considerable variety in shape, colour and texture. Hollies, ivies and periwinkle provide greens, golds and whitish shades on leaves. Dwarf and other conifers add blues, greys, olive greens and rusty shades, and mahonia produces holly-like reddish leaves.

Between bouts of frost, the winter-flowering cherry puts on a brave show of delicate pink, as does *Viburnum fragrans*. The bright-yellow winter-flowering jasmine will usually manage a show of colour intermittently throughout the winter against a wall. Among the shrubs, pink or white *Daphne mezereum*, yellow wintersweet, and witch hazel combine to produce colour and scent. Red and pink forms of flowering quince on leafless branches look attractive against a wall. Heathers can provide flower and foliage colour and interest and suit most situations. Winter aconite, the dwarf yellow *Hacquetia* flowering among snowdrops, squills and scillas or the white cups of the Christmas rose all help to cheer up the dull days of winter. Bright red berries of holly, cotoneaster and rose hips provide splashes of colour, and contrast well with white stems and trunks of silver birch.

In mild districts in the South and South West the winter-flowering honeysuckles are well worth planting. The two better known species are *Lonicera fragrantissima* and *L. standishii*.

Winter-flowering plants thrive in sunny sheltered positions, protected from north and east winds.

Plants for the winter season: Trees: Betula; Prunus. Shrubs: Arbutus; Arctostaphylos; Chaenomeles; Chimonanthus; Cornus; Corylus; Corylopsis; Daphne; Elaeagnus; Erica; Garrya; Hamamelis; Jasminum; Kerria; Lonicera; Stachyurus; Viburnum. Flowering bulbous plants: Crocus; Cyclamen; Eranthis; Galanthus; Hacquetia; Helleborus; Iris; Petasites; Schizostylis; Sternbergia. Berry bearing: Aucuba; Arbutus; Berberis; Cotoneaster; Crataegus; Euonymus; Hippophae; Ilex; Mahonia; Pernettya; Pyracantha; Pyrus; Rosa; Skimmia.

BELOW A garden in winter need not lack colour and interest. Planted here from left to right are cornus, viburnum, heathers, daphne, ivy, winter jasmine, holly, cotoneaster, winter aconite, Christmas rose and flowering quince.

GARDEN FRIENDS AND FOES

In dealing with garden pests, disorders and diseases the first aim of the gardener is to get rid of them. To do this efficiently it is necessary to identify the culprits.

Very often the severity of attack is due to faulty cultivation or failure to control the pests when they first appeared. Sometimes they gain a hold because of wrong soil care. Also, weak growing plants are more susceptible to troubles than robust ones growing on soil kept well fed with organic manure. The use of quick acting fertilizers induces soft growth which easily becomes the target of many enemies.

It is comforting to realize that there are many friendly creatures about too so do not work on the principle of killing everything.

Among the most useful garden insects are bees whose activities encourage pollination. Wasps eat greenfly, although they can spoil fruits in late summer. Toads, frogs, hedgehogs and the devil's coach horse (a beetle), are our allies, destroying quite a lot of harmful creatures. The earthworm should be encouraged too, although not in the lawn.

Larvae of the ground beetle are beneficial as well. They look like caterpillars, are a dull brown colour and have three pairs of legs. They move very quickly but should not be confused with the harmful wireworm which is lighter in colour and very much less active. The centipede is another friend. It has a rather flat light brown body and moves very quickly. It should not be confused with the harmful millipedes which are either a slate grey or darkish brown colour and

Ladybirds attacking aphids (greenfly)

very sluggish. Generally, soil creatures that move quickly are friendly while those that are slow are harmful.

Of the flying insects, the familiar ladybird is one of the gardener's best friends. Both the familiar spotted adult beetles and the tiny rather alligator-like larvae destroy countless numbers of greenfly. Some species of hover fly look rather like elegant wasps, but hang motionless in the air between their quick darting movements when they catch all kinds of pests. Their larvae consume many pests.

Many species of ichneumon fly do a lot of good in the garden. One kind parasites cabbage white caterpillars. The common lacewing has a thin pale green body and is very active destroying all kinds of small insects. It lays its eggs in clusters on leaf stalks and the larvae hatch quickly to mop up aphids.

In a well managed garden there is little to fear from pests and diseases. Good plant hygiene leads to healthy growth and if occasional pest attacks are dealt with early, there will be no repercussions.

Most pests that settle on plants can be killed by stomach poisons, mostly in the form of liquid sprays or dusts. Take special care when using any of these products. Follow closely the manufacturer's instructions for use, and store all poisons under lock and key out of the reach of children and where pets cannot find them.With slugs and snails, poison baits can be placed near the plants to lure the pests to their death. Aphids and other suckers can be destroyed by spraying the plants with derris or pyrethrum or its synthetic derivatives – all of which are relatively safe for humans.

Good soil drainage reduces the risk of slugs, snails, millipedes and leatherjackets. There are many predators which do a tremendous amount of good, but unfortunately, they are often unknowingly destroyed.

Some pests favour certain plants, but there are a number which attack all kinds. Similarly some diseases and disorders are common to many plants. The following are some of the troubles you are most likely to encounter.

Common Pests and Diseases

Regular spraying with derris or malathion – dimethoate if you want a synthetic insecticide – is usually sufficient to destroy them. Broad and runner beans are vulnerable, but they will infest almost any plant in the vegetable patch as well as the flower garden. Spring and summer are the danger periods out of doors.

Ants. These are attracted to plants infested with greenfly, which they 'milk' for their sweet honeydew. They may carry aphids which spread virus diseases from plant to plant. Various ant killers based on derris and gamma-HCH, as well as borax, are effective.

Botrytis. A common fungus, most likely to appear in wet seasons and in cold damp conditions. It may settle on plants which are weak and soft-growing, and it flourishes on dead and dying plants. Burn affected plants and treat healthy specimens nearby with benomyl.

Caterpillars. Except those that cover themselves with a web, these can be eradicated by the use of derris insecticide. Since caterpillars are so easy to see, the simplest method is to hand-pick them, and also to destroy the eggs which are laid in clusters, usually under the foliage.

Cockchafers. Together with related species such as the rosechafer, cockchafers usually appear in May and June and lay clusters of eggs below the surface of the soil. From these hatch fleshy, dirty-white grubs with brownish-yellow heads. They feed on the roots and lower parts of the stems, and a wide range of plants can be affected. Try using bromophos or diazinon soil insecticide. Alternatively, use gamma-HCH dust pricked into the surface.

Symptoms of club root on brassica

Club root. Affects candytuft, stocks and alyssum. Calomel dust controls this soil fungus which spreads easily from these flowering plants to vegetables of the cabbage family, as well as turnips and radishes.

Cuckoo spit. The frothy mass of cuckoo spit seen on stems and leaves of garden plants conceals the pale yellow nymph of the frog hopper, a jumping insect not more than 7 mm ($\frac{1}{4}$ in) long. Both adults and nymphs suck sap and distort leaves and shoots. To get rid of them spray the spittle with malathion.

Cutworms (surface caterpillars). The larvae of several species of moths, they feed at night, attacking the plant stem at or just below ground level, causing it to collapse. Plants with fairly thick stems are usually the victims. Where pests are suspected examine the soil and the plants, for cutworms are easy to see. Use bromophos.

Botrytis (grey mould) on strawberries

Damping off. A fungus which attacks crowded seedlings left too long in the seed bed, causing stems to wither at soil level. Avoid over-watering and never grip the tiny stems too firmly. Control by watering the soil with Cheshunt compound.

Earwigs. These sometimes damage foliage and flowers. They are most active at night hiding under rubbish. They can be trapped in inverted pots filled with hay or straw, or eradicated by spraying damaged plants with gamma-HCH.

Eelworms. These damage potatoes, onions, some bulbs and a few annuals. They are microscopic pests which lay their eggs in the tissues of plants. Ultimately the plant dies, first exhibiting twisted stunted growth. Leave affected ground unplanted for three seasons.

Flea beetles. These very active creatures damage vegetables such as cabbage, turnips and radish, and some other crops, especially in dry weather. The remedy is to keep the soil surface moving and to give frequent dustings of derris or gamma-HCH powder. These pests hide in rubbish; eggs are laid on the soil and foliage.

Protect plants from cutworms with bromophos

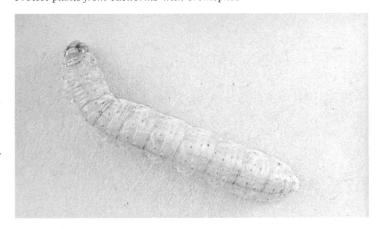

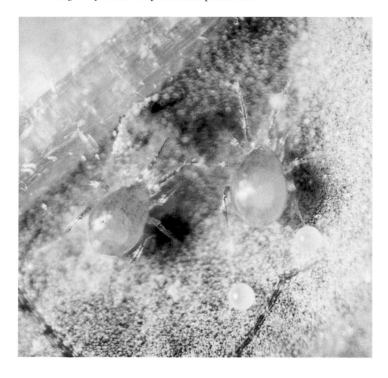

Above: A millipede. Below: Red spider mites can be controlled by introducing the predator Phytoseiulus persimilis.

Leaf hoppers. Minute insects which bite and disfigure foliage: spray with derris or malathion.

Leatherjackets. These are the larvae of the well-known crane fly or daddy longlegs. They attack and kill the roots of plants, especially on newly broken ground that was previously grassland. They occur on damp, badly-drained soil. Birds will often clear the larvae. Naphthalene at 100 g per m² (3 oz per sq yd), or chlordane worked into the ground will usually get rid of this pest.

Mildew. Slight attacks seem to do little harm, but sometimes the white powder-like growth is very bad, causing a whole batch of plants to become disfigured and useless. As soon as the disease is seen, dust the plants with yellow sulphur powder or spray with one of the proprietary fungicides such as benomyl or dinocap.

Millipedes. These are common both in the garden and under glass. They usually feed at night, attacking seed-leaves and early growth. They are easily distinguished from beneficial centipedes by their slower movement and greater number of legs. One species, slate-grey in colour, curls up like a watch spring when disturbed. The simplest method of destroying millipedes is to trap them with scooped-out pieces of vegetables, which should be examined daily and the pests destroyed.

Red Spider Mites. These tiny reddish pests attach themselves to the undersides of the leaves producing whitish specklings on the upper surface. Left unchecked, the pests settle on the growing points and may make a fine weblike growth over them. Although excellent sprays are available, killing both the insects and their eggs, dimethoate has the merit of being systemic. Malathion is also effective but repeated treatment may be needed. Some growers of greenhouse plants prefer to use an aerosol based on malathion as it reaches all parts of the plants as well as the crevices of the greenhouse.

Scab. A disorder sometimes affecting apples and pears. A spraying of mancozeb normally controls the disease.

Springtails. These are wingless active jumping insects in various colours. They feed on decaying plant tissues, as well as attacking living plants, especially delicate seedlings. If they are suspected, dust around the plants with pyrethrum powder or derris.

Stem rot. This works through the roots and affected plants must be burned. Cheshunt compound checks the disease.

Symphalids. These small white pests attack the roots. Soil sterilization has little effect. Plants should be drenched with gamma-HCH two or three days after planting out.

Thrips. These tiny insects attack few plants. Silvery markings on the foliage indicates their presence. They are virus carriers, spreading infection by piercing the foliage. Under glass they can be controlled by fumigation. Outdoors, spraying the plants with permethrin is usually effective; derris is also helpful.

Virus diseases. The usual symptoms are stunted, distorted growth and mottled foliage. All plants suspected of virus should be removed and burned immediately, and if greenfly or other aphis are seen on nearby plants, spray them with a derris wash, for aphis often spread diseases as they feed on neighbouring plants.

Whitefly. These are small aphid-like creatures which may rapidly build up into swarms under glass. Biological control by introducing suitable predators such as *Encarsia formosa*, a type of wasp, is the best control. Alternatively, spray every three days for a fortnight with malathion.

Wireworms. These larvae of the click beetle are most destructive. They attack and spoil a wide range of plants, usually eating the roots, but sometimes they damage the stems too. They are prevalent in grassland and uncultivated ground, which is why they seem so plentiful on freshly broken-up soil. Regular cultivation is the best means of controlling wireworms. They can be trapped by pieces of root vegetable placed in the ground, which can be examined frequently so the pests can be destroyed. There are a number of preparations, most of which contain gamma-HCH, diazinon or bromophos, which can be dusted into the ground when it is being dug.

Woodlice. These are often present in rubbish. They flourish in damp, dull conditions and are frequently found on decaying wood. The remedy is to concentrate on cleanliness. Woodlice can be trapped by placing pieces of root vegetables in the surface soil and examining them frequently so the pests can be destroyed. Alternatively, dust infested areas with derris or gamma-HCH.

Disorders and Diseases of Vegetables

Broad beans are sometimes attacked by what is known as 'chocolate spot disease'. The leaves, stems and often the pods become heavily marked with brown streaks or spots. Attacks are usually worse during wet seasons and are more likely on heavy, badly drained ground.

As soon as the disease is seen or suspected, the plants should be sprayed with a copper fungicide. As far as possible, broad beans should be grown on a fresh site the following year, preferably one which has been dressed with wood ash or some other form of potash.

Dwarf French and runner beans are sometimes affected by a blight which is technically known as anthracnose. This is seen as dark coloured spots and reddish streaks which appear on the foliage, stems and pods. Often the spots increase in size and eventually merge into brownish patches. This trouble, too, is more likely to be serious in damp seasons and where the soil is wet and cold. Spraying with Bordeaux mixture or one of the proprietary fungicides usually controls an attack.

Halo blight causes bean plants to become sickly and wilt. If affected plants are examined, small spots surrounded by a light coloured halo will be seen on leaves and stems. Destroy plants affected.

Cabbages and other members of the brassica family may be attacked by various diseases. Among the most troublesome is club root, often known as 'finger and toe'. See page 231.

Carrots in store are sometimes affected by a rot. It is most likely to appear on roots damaged at lifting time. To lessen its spread, the clamps or boxes used for storing should not be too large and they should be carefully ventilated.

Celery leaf spot can be quite a serious disease in some seasons. It first appears as minute brown spots which gradually increase in size until the foliage is brown and withered. Any plants which become discoloured should be sprayed with Bordeaux mixture or benomyl as a precaution against the disease.

Cucumbers. Under glass, cucumbers are sometimes attacked by rot or canker at soil level. This gradually eats into the stems causing them to collapse and die. The remedy is to keep soil from settling around the stems.

Slight attacks can often be checked by dusting the stems with flowers of sulphur. Sulphur can also be dusted where mildew is suspected. Ventilate freely on all suitable occasions.

Leeks may suffer from rust seen as yellowish spots which turn a

Above: Wireworms. Below: Rust can attack many vegetables, including broad beans

reddish shade. Where the trouble has occurred previously, do not plant leeks in the same soil for a period of three or four years. Affected leaves should be removed and the entire plants sprayed with a fungicide such as mancozeb.

Lettuce are sometimes seen with reddish markings on the stem at soil level. Subsequently, botrytis sets in and the plant wilts and dies. It is more likely to appear on frame grown, winter lettuce. If the plants are put in too deeply they are liable to rot at the centre and this gives rise to botrytis. Sulphur powder or benomyl should provide control.

Another trouble is tip burn. There are various forms. All are related to the water balance within the plant or the size of the root system and degree of soil salinity. The most common form occurs from March onwards during periods of high temperatures and low humidity, when transpiration exceeds the uptake of water, and the tissues wilt. The edges of the leaves covering the heart turn brown and look scorched; rotting by botrytis usually follows.

Onions are affected by a few diseases. A white or greyish mildew can sometimes be seen on the leaves, which begin to discolour and collapse. This mildew is much more liable to occur on badly drained than well-drained land in good condition.

If only a few plants are affected, it is often possible to stop the infection spreading by applying a colloidal copper wash. If this is done three or four times at ten to fourteen day intervals, the disease should be controlled.

Parsnips are liable to canker, which causes the roots to crack at the top and to become affected by a brown rot which sometimes becomes wet and rotten. Canker is less likely on well-drained ground containing a high humus content. The variety 'Avonresister' should be grown where the disorder has previously occurred.

Peas frequently exhibit variegated and otherwise marked foliage. This discoloration is usually due to virus infection. Burn affected plants.

In spite of its name, marsh spot usually appears on light soils which dry out easily. Affected seedlings are distorted and never grow well. Here again, it has been proved that where the soil contains plenty of compost, the disease is less likely to occur.

Potatoes. There are numerous disorders which can affect potatoes.

Common scab is more likely on light soil deficient in humus and where there is a high lime content. Powdery scab, on the other hand, is worse in wet ground. Then there is skin spot, which although not serious, can damage the eyes of the tubers, which, if they are to be used for seed purposes, are spoiled.

Potato blight is a destructive disease and usually occurs in late July. The crop is greatly reduced. This disease is most liable to occur when the temperature is above 10°C (50°F) and when the air is humid. Control by spraying with mancozeb.

Remove and burn leek leaves affected with spot

Potato 'blackleg' is a rot which can occur on all varieties, and in all soils, being most severe in heavy wet ground. The stems become black and rotten at and below soil level, and can easily be pulled out. First symptoms may be a yellowing, rolling and wilting of the foliage in June and July. Be sure to plant sound tubers.

Spinach may become affected by downy mildew especially in a wet season on heavy soils. The undersides of the leaves become coated with a grey or bluish-grey mould and the whole leaf turns yellow and dies. Attacks are more likely in ground over-rich in nitrogen. Pick off and burn all affected leaves or in bad cases, destroy the entire plant. Dust the remainder with yellow sulphur powder or spray with mancozeb.

Turnips and Swedes will not tolerate an acid soil which is conducive to the spread of club root. Since the organism responsible can remain in the soil for years turnips should not be grown in ground previously occupied by other members of the cabbage family. Always grow turnips and swedes on land containing plenty of lime. Dusting the seed bed with calomel prior to sowing reduces risk of attacks. Soft rot sometimes occurs in the centre of turnips, caused by a fungus gaining an entry through wounds or pest attacks.

Dry rot, often known as canker, can occur while turnips and swedes are growing, or while they are in store. It starts in late summer as brown patches. These often enlarge, causing the roots to split or become shrunken. Affected roots should be burnt and a long rotation system practised.

Tomatoes being natives of warmer climes, are subject to several complaints, the most common being cladosporium, a fungus causing a light grey mould on the undersides of the leaves. This spreads and eventually the leaves turn brown and fall. In the greenhouse, good ventilation helps to avoid the disease which does not occur in a temperature over 18°C (64°F). Spray the plants with colloidal copper or mancozeb. Damping off of tomato seedlings is usually due to sowing too thickly and to careless watering.

Tomato canker, caused by *Botrytis cinerea*, occurs where there is a cool moist, stagnant atmosphere. It appears on the fruit as brown rotting spots and on the stems, as swellings. The remedy is good ventilation and low atmospheric humidity.

There are several physiological disorders, including blossom end rot, which is the result of insufficient moisture when the young fruits are developing. Dark brown areas appear where the flower was attached at the base of the fruit. Sometimes, diseased roots prevent the plants from obtaining all the moisture needed.

Blotchy ripening is associated with an unbalanced food supply and one or two dressings of sulphate of potash at 70 g per m² (2 oz per sq yd) will correct the trouble. Greenback is a condition when the top portion of the fruit becomes hard and does not colour. Lack of potash and exposure to strong sunlight encourages this disorder. Grow resistant varieties and take care that the soil does not dry out. Tomatoes must develop under even conditions to be at their best.

Fruit splitting is due to sudden changes in growing conditions. Very high temperatures will often cause the skin to harden, as will happen if the roots dry out. Then, when moisture is applied, the skin cannot expand quickly enough and this leads to splitting.

Very occasionally virus disorders occur, when the foliage becomes mottled to a definite pattern. Virus diseases cannot be cured and affected plants should be destroyed.

Disorders and Diseases of Flowers

Bulbs and corms are susceptible to *storage rots* – they may become soft and pulpy inside or show signs of black spots or fungal growth on the outside. Affected bulbs are best destroyed, and any apparently healthy bulbs in the same batch immersed in benomyl after lifting and again before planting.

Narcissi, including daffodils, that are soft and producing few leaves and flowers may have *narcissus fly* (actually it is the maggot, about 12 mm ($\frac{1}{2}$ in) long that causes the trouble). Lift and destroy affected plants.

If the growth appears distorted and unhealthy, and the bulb is soft when lifted, cut it cross-ways. If there are dark 'rings', *eelworms* are the likely cause. Destroy the bulbs and do not plant other bulbs for at least four years.

Tulip fire is a serious disease of tulips. The leaves look 'scorched' and the flowers may be 'spotted'. Young shoots may reveal a grey mould. The bulbs (together with the leaves) are best burned, but you can try destroying the foliage and soaking the bulbs in mancozeb.

Chrysanthemums frequently succumb to some pest or disease. One of the most disfiguring pests is the *leaf miner*. This pest bores tunnels within the leaf, leaving white trails and blisters. With age these may turn brown. It is wise to remove the worst-affected leaves and burn them, then spray the plant with malathion.

Powdery mildew is an equally unsightly disease. The leaves become covered in a white mealy growth, which can spread rapidly.

Spray with benomyl as soon as the disease is noticed, and repeat a week later. Be prepared to treat again if it shows signs of returning.

Wilt is a puzzling disease that may affect chrysanthemums. As the name implies, the symptoms are similar to those caused by lack of water – drooping leaves. If the stem is cut open, however, it may be stained brown. There is no practical treatment and the plants should be destroyed. Avoid growing chrysanthemums again in the same soil.

Rust reveals itself as raised brown spots on the leaves. Pick off and burn affected leaves then spray with mancozeb at fortnightly intervals.

Earwigs are often a nuisance on chrysanthemums – they chew holes in the leaves and pieces out of the petals. Spray with gamma-HCH.

Dahlias also have more than their fair share of troubles. The most annoying pest is perhaps the *earwig*. The damage is the same as that described for chrysanthemums, and the treatment the same. You can also catch many of them for no cost and little effort by using traps. These are traditionally upturned plant-pots filled with straw and placed upsidedown on the top of the stake. You will have to knock the earwigs out and destroy them, but it does work.

Aphids are also attracted by the succulent growth of dahlias, and they are a particular problem because they spread virus diseases that can ruin the quality of your plants. Spray as recommended on page 230.

Capsid bugs are also serious – the symptoms are similar to those caused by earwigs – holes in leaves – but the holes are brown-edged and the leaves themselves are more puckered. The insect looks rather like a large green or brown greenfly, but much more agile. Spray with gamma-HCH or fenitrothion.

The most serious diseases are the *viruses* that can cause crinkled, distorted and mottled leaves and stunted growth. There is no cure and any suspect plants should be burned. It is not worth risking the rest of your dahlias.

Herbaceous plants are obviously subject to a wide range of pests and diseases, but fortunately many of them are uncommon. Most of the

Prevent potato blight by earthing up the plants well

common problems such as aphids and mildew are easily recognised and have been described on pages 230 to 237. The pests and diseases described here supplement the general information already given.

Slugs and snails are broad in their taste, and will attack most plants if the shoots are tender enough – which is usually just as they are coming through in the spring. Damage later in the season is usually less worrying, though plants such as hostas can be ruined if the ornamental leaves are full of holes.

If you do not want to use bait, it is possible to use traps – which range from grapefruit skins (scooped-out side down) to proprietary 'slug pubs' (a container for beer – into which the creatures fall and drown). But these methods are either tedious to use or expensive, so baits have an attraction (they can be placed under a stone or somewhere out of reach of children and pets). It makes little difference whether you use one based on metaldehyde or methiocarb, but mini pellets are more economical in use.

Leaf miners (see chrysanthemums) and *capsid bugs* (see dahlias) affect a wide range of herbaceous plants, and another widespread pest is the *cuckoo spit* (see page 231).

Rust in its various forms can be a troublesome disease. Hollyhocks are particularly susceptible. Symptoms and treatment are as discussed under chrysanthemums, but frequent treatment may be necessary for hollyhocks.

Roses are wonderful plants, but many of the older varieties are particularly prone to diseases such as black spot and mildew.

Black spot is the dread of many rose growers. The name of the disease describes its symptoms – black spots, irregular in shape, affect the leaves and gradually enlarge until the leaf is disfigured and probably drops off. It is usually worse in rural areas than in the more polluted atmosphere of towns and cities. The disease is difficult to control once established, and it may be necessary to resort to routine spraying, and careful removal of affected leaves from the ground to prevent the disease overwintering in the soil. Mancozeb, copper compound, and the systemic thiophanate-methyl will all give control.

Mildew is the other major rose disease. The white powdery-looking growth can cover shoots, buds and leaves. Benomyl or dinocap should give control, but regular spraying may be necessary in a year when the disease is troublesome.

Roses are susceptible to many of the common pests such as aphids, froghoppers (cuckoo spit), and capsids. But you might also encounter the more interesting kinds such as leaf-cutter bees (they remove notches round the edge of leaves, and leaf-rolling sawflies (leaflets are rolled around a small grub inside).

Pests and Diseases of Fruit

As far as possible, prevention is better than cure when it comes to fruit troubles, since too often the remedy will be the ruthless one of grubbing an infected plant altogether. Always buy certified stocks (where applicable) from a reliable supplier, and never propagate from plants which have shown unhealthy symptoms. When pruning, take great care to leave a clean cut so disease cannot enter. If a large branch is removed from a tree, paint the wound immediately with a proprietary seal.

Apples are most likely to suffer the attentions of aphids (q.v.) and codling moths. The caterpillar of the latter bores into the core of the fruit where it feeds, leaving a small hole in the surface. Spray with malathion in mid-June and again three weeks later. Powdery mildew sometimes distorts young stems and leaves, which are covered with a fine white powder. Regular spraying with benomyl fungicide will hold this at bay. Sawflies are an unpleasant pest. They leave a small brown scar on the skin, and the grubs feed inside on the flesh. Spray with gamma-HCH immediately after petal fall. Fruit tree red spider mites are another problem, but a mid-June spraying of malathion should be effective.

Swollen buds of black currant infested with big bud mite

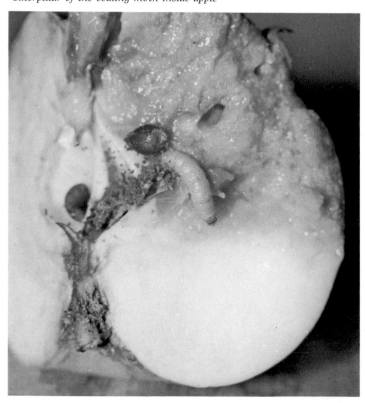

Caterpillar of the codling moth inside apple

Black currants. Big bud mite causes the buds of young blackcurrant shoots to become abnormally swollen and globular. The mites are microscopic and live within the bud. Infested buds fail to open, so that growth is checked and the bush so weakened and ceases to produce profitable crops. The mites leave the swollen buds at blossom time, spend a short period on the flowers and leaves, and then enter the young buds on the new shoots, in which they quickly multiply. This pest can be controlled, first by removing and burning all infested buds, and then you can try spraying with benomyl, which is said to help. Do this when the blossom is at the 'grape stage', that is, the racemes look like bunches of grapes and the flowers have not opened. Spray annually to protect bushes against this pest. Reversion is a serious virus disease of blackcurrants and is carried by the big bud mite. Infected leaves have fewer sub-veins and serrations than normal leaves. The flowers on 'reverted' branches are often distorted and seldom produce fruit. Bushes showing this trouble should be burned, and of course no cuttings should be taken from them. Various types of aphid attack both red and blackcurrants. One of the commonest is that which, attacking the undersides of the leaves, causes red blisters to appear on the upper surface. Spray the bushes with tar-oil winter wash while dormant to destroy the eggs. Directly the pest appears spray with derris or malathion; if necessary, repeat at 10-day intervals. The green capsid bug feeds on the foliage of currants and gooseberries as well as on apples and pears. Winter spraying with a winter wash will kill the eggs.

Cherries. Apart from aphids and, of course, the frequent attacks of hungry birds, the most common problem here is the disease known

The distinctive symptoms of peach leaf curl

graphically as silver leaf. Affected branches should be cut out and burned, and the wound painted with a proprietary seal. If the whole tree is affected, remove and burn it.

Gooseberries. Gooseberry sawfly is a most destructive pest. The adult sawfly lays its eggs on the undersides of the leaves, and the greenish caterpillars, with black heads and spots, quickly defoliate the bush. Two broods of caterpillars are often produced in a season. Spray or dust with derris when the pests are first seen. American gooseberry mildew is a serious disease. The leaves, shoots and fruits are infected and become covered with a whitish, felt-like fungus. Later, it turns a brownish colour and spoils the fruits and causes the shoots to become stunted and distorted. Feeding too generously with nitrogenous manures encourages this disease, as does inadequate pruning to open up the bushes and let in light and air. Infected shoots and fruits should be burned. Spraying with a fungicide such as benomyl just before flowering will give protection from early infection. The bushes are sometimes attacked by a disease called gooseberry dieback which causes whole branches to wither suddenly and die, and unless they are quickly removed the whole bush may soon become infested. Dig up and burn badly diseased plants. Magpie moth caterpillars, which are white and black, with a yellow stripe down each side, eat the leaves of currants and gooseberries. If the pests are numerous they can cause considerable damage. Fortunately, they are easily destroyed by spraying or dusting with derris.

Pears suffer from aphids and scab. If fire blight occurs, with cankers at the base of dead shoots, the Ministry of Agriculture must be

notified, and will advise on treatment. Brown rot may attack fruits if careless pruning has left snagged wounds.

Plums. Aphids, again, are the main problem, causing distortion of the leaves and shoots. Branches affected with silver leaf must be removed and burned and the wound sealed with a good protective paint. False silver leaf is common, and is caused by poor growing conditions.

Peaches. Aphids and red spider mites may cause trouble and the trees should be sprayed before blossom time with malathion. Peach leaf curl will cause affected leaves to swell up and then fall early in the season. Spray with Bordeaux mixture or benomyl early in the year (February) and again in the autumn before the leaves drop.

Raspberries. The maggots sometimes found in the fruits of raspberries and blackberries are the larvae of the raspberry beetle. A spray of derris when the first flowers open and again 10 days later will be helpful. Cane spot causes purplish spots on the young canes and leaves. Cut out and burn affected canes. Spray with benomyl as soon as growth starts, and again before blooming.

Mosaic is a very serious virus disease among raspberries; the leaves become mottled with yellow and the plants are stunted and unfruitful. There is no cure. Infected plants should be grubbed out and burned. Replace with certified virus-free canes. Aphids transmit virus diseases and must be kept under control.

Strawberries. Aphids infest strawberries, birds and slugs eat them, and botrytis (grey mould) attacks weak plants in damp weather. Spray with benomyl and malathion in flowering period. Plants affected by virus disease—seen as stunted leaves and distorted stems—should be grubbed.

Gooseberry sawflies are easily recognized

INFORMATION TABLES

Outdoor Crop Information Chart

Vegetable	Time to sow		Time to plant or transplant
	Under glass	In the open	
Artichokes – Globe	—	—	offsets in March–May
Artichokes – Jerusalem	—	—	tubers in Feb–March
Asparagus	—	April	March–April
Beans – broad	—	November or Spring	—
Beans – climbing French	—	April–June	—
Beans – dwarf French	mid-March under cloches	April–July	—
Beans – runner	April under cloches	May onwards	after frosts
Beetroot	—	April–June	—
Broccoli – green sprouting (Calabrese)	March	April	May–June
Broccoli – purple sprouting; white sprouting	—	April	June–July
Brussels sprouts	February–March	March–April	May–June
Cabbage – spring greens	—	July–August	—
Cabbage – spring	—	July–August	September–October
Cabbage – early summer	February	—	April
Cabbage – summer	—	March	May
Cabbage – autumn (Savoys) and winter	—	April–May	June–July
Carrots	March under cloches	March–July	—
Cauliflower – early summer	September	—	March
Cauliflower – summer	January	March	March–May
Cauliflower – autumn	—	March–May	May–July

Final distance in rows	Distance between rows	Season of use
75 cm (2½ ft)	1.2 m (4 ft)	June–October
30 cm (12 in)	90 cm (3 ft)	November–March
60 cm (2 ft)	90 cm (3 ft)	May–June
15–20 cm (6–8 in)	45–60 cm (18–24 in)	June–July
20–30 cm (8–12 in)	1.2–1.3 m (4–5 ft)	July onwards
15 cm (6 in)	45 cm (18 in)	May–September
20–30 cm (8–12 in)	30 cm (12 in) between each pair of rows: about 1.5 m (5 ft) between each double row	July–October
15–30 cm (6–12 in)	30–40 cm (12–16 in)	June–October (fresh); rest of year from store
75 cm (2½ ft)	75 cm (2½ ft)	July–September
75 cm (2½ ft)	75 cm (2½ ft)	January–April
60–90 cm (2–3 ft)	60–90 cm (2–3 ft)	October–March
23–30 cm (9–12 in)	30–45 cm (12–18 in)	March–April
30–45 cm (12–18 in)	45 cm (18 in)	April–May
45 cm (18 in)	45 cm (18 in)	May–June
45 cm (18 in)	45 cm (18 in)	June–August
45 cm (18 in)	60 cm (2 ft)	October–February
5–15 cm (2–6 in)	20–30 cm (8–12 in)	end May–October (fresh); October onwards from store
45–60 cm (18–24 in)	45–60 cm (18–24 in)	May–June
45–60 cm (18–24 in)	45–60 cm (18–24 in)	June–July
60–75 cm (2–2½ ft)	60–75 cm (2–2½ ft)	August–December

| Vegetable | Time to sow | | Time to plant or transplant |
	Under glass	In the open	
Cauliflower – winter (heading broccoli)	—	April–May	June–July
Celeriac	March	—	May–June
Celery – self-blanching	March	—	May–June
Celery – trench	March	—	May–June
Chicory	—	May	—
Corn salad (Lamb's lettuce)	—	July–October	—
Cucumbers – ridge	April–May	May	May–June
Endive	—	May–August	—
Kale – curly (Borecole)	—	April–May	July–August
Kale – rape	—	July	—
Kohl rabi	—	March–July	—
Leek	January–February	February–March	June–July
Lettuce	March	March–September	April
Marrows and courgettes	April	May	May–June
Onions – bulb – autumn sown	—	August	—
Onions – bulb – spring sown	January	March	April
Onions – sets	—	—	April
Onions – salad	—	August or Spring	—
Parsley	March under cloches	March–July	—
Parsnip	—	February–March	—
Peas – round-seeded	February under cloches	March–June	—
Peas – wrinkle seeded	—	March–June	—
Potatoes – early	—	—	mid-March
Potatoes – second early	—	—	late March
Potatoes – maincrop	—	—	April

Final distance in rows	Distance between rows	Season of use
45–75 cm (1½–2½ ft)	60–75 cm (2–2½ ft)	January–May
30 cm (12 in)	45 cm (18 in)	October onwards
23 cm (9 in)	23 cm (9 in)	August–September
25 cm (10 in)	single rows in 38 cm (15 in) wide trenches. 90 cm (3 ft) between trenches	October onwards
30 cm (12 in)	45 cm (18 in)	Roots lifted October onwards
15 cm (6 in)	30 cm (12 in)	September onwards
60 cm (2 ft)	75 cm (2½ ft)	July–September
30–40 cm (12–16 in)	38 cm (15 in)	August onwards after blanching
45–60 cm (1½–2 ft)	60–75 cm (2–2½ ft)	February–April
45–60 cm (1½–2 ft)	60 cm (2 ft)	May–June
15 cm (6 in)	38 cm (15 in)	mid-June onwards
20–30 cm (8–12 in)	30–45 cm (12–18 in)	November–March
25–30 cm (10–12 in)	30 cm (12 in)	June–October
120 cm (4 ft)	120 cm (4 ft)	July–September
15 cm (6 in)	30 cm (12 in)	July onwards
15 cm (6 in)	30 cm (12 in)	September onwards
15 cm (6 in)	30 cm (12 in)	September onwards
0.5–1 cm (¼–½ in)	20–30 cm (8–12 in)	March–April onwards
15–30 cm (6–12 in)	30 cm (12 in)	All year round
15 cm (6 in)	30–45 cm (12–18 in)	November–March
5–7 cm (2–3 in)	60–150 cm (2–5 ft)	May–August
5–7 cm (2–3 in)	60–150 cm (2–5 ft)	July–September
30 cm (12 in)	60 cm (2 ft)	July
30 cm (12 in)	60 cm (2 ft)	August
45 cm (18 in)	75 cm (2½ ft)	October

| Vegetable | Time to sow | | Time to plant or transplant |
	Under glass	In the open	
Radish – salad	—	March–May and September	—
Radish – winter	—	July–August	—
Rhubarb	—	—	Spring or autumn
Salsify	—	April–May	—
Scorzonera	—	April–May	—
Seakale	—	—	root cuttings in March
Seakale beet (Chards)	—	April	—
Shallots	—	—	February
Spinach – New Zealand	March	mid-May	late May
Spinach – summer	—	March–end June	—
Spinach – winter	—	August–September	—
Spinach beet (Perpetual spinach)	—	April and August	—
Swede	—	May–June	—
Sweet corn	April	April–May	May
Tomato	March	—	early June
Turnips – summer	—	March onwards	—
Turnips – winter	—	July–August	—

Quantities of seeds

It is useful to know the number of seeds to 30 g (1 oz), although many seeds are quite small and a full ounce is not always required.

Beet	234
Cabbage	7,000
Carrot	18,700
Cauliflower	7,000
Celery	50,000
Leek	9,370
Lettuce	16,000
Onion	7,300
Parsley	17,500
Parsnip	7,000
Pea	106
Radish	5,000
Swede	8,000
Tomato	7,500
Turnip	9,300

These are only approximate quantities since variations in variety affect weight.

Planting Guide for Soft Fruit

These are minimum spacings between bushes. Allow more room if your soil is very fertile.

	In Rows	Between Rows
Blackberries (Most varieties)	3 m (10 ft)	1.80 m (6 ft)
,, Himalayan Giant	4 m (12 ft)	1.80 m (6 ft)
Black Currant	1.50 m (5 ft)	1.80 m (6 ft)
Blueberry	1.50 m (5 ft)	1.80 m (6 ft)
Gooseberry, bush	1.50 m (5 ft)	1.50 m (5 ft)
Gooseberry, cordon	38 cm (15 in)	1.80 m (6 ft)
Raspberry	38 cm (15 in)	1.80 m (6 ft)
Loganberry and other hybrids	3 m (9 ft)	1.80 m (6 ft)
Red Currant bush	1.50 m (5 ft)	1.50 m (5 ft)
Red Currant cordon	38 cm (15 in)	1.80 m (6 ft)
White Currant bush	1.25 m (4 ft)	1.50 m (5 ft)

Final distance in rows	Distance between rows	Season of use
Broadcast or: 2–3 cm (1 in)	15 cm (6 in)	May onwards
15 cm (6 in)	23 cm (9 in)	Autumn–winter
90–120 cm (3–4 ft)	90–120 cm (3–4 ft)	Spring–summer
25–30 cm (10–12 in)	30 cm (12 in)	October–March
15 cm (6 in)	38 cm (15 in)	October–March
30 cm (12 in)	45 cm (15 in)	Roots lifted from late November onwards
20 cm (8 in)	40 cm (16 in)	July onwards
15 cm (6 in)	30 cm (12 in)	July
60 cm (2 ft)	90 cm (3 ft)	Mid-summer onwards
15 cm (6 in)	30 cm (12 in)	May onwards
15 cm (6 in)	30 cm (12 in)	October onwards (protect from November)
20 cm (8 in)	38 cm (15 in)	Summer and winter/early spring
30 cm (12 in)	45 cm (18 in)	Autumn–Winter
45–60 cm (18–24 in)	45–60 cm (18–24 in)	August–September
45–60 cm (18–24 in)	90 cm (3 ft)	August–September
10–15 cm (4–6 in)	30 cm (12 in)	Mid-June onwards
20–30 cm (8–12 in)	38–45 cm (15–18 in)	Winter

Planting Guide for Fruit Trees

Distances are given in metres and feet. These are minimum spacings. Allow more room if your soil is very fertile.

Subject	Bush	Fan
Apple	4.50 m (15 ft)	3.60 m (12 ft)
Apricot	—	3.60 m (12 ft)
Cherry (Morello)	4.50 m (15 ft)	3 m (10 ft)
Cherry (Sweet)	9 m (30 ft)	6 m (20 ft)
Damson	3.60 m (12 ft)	3.60 m (12 ft)
Gage	3.60 m (12 ft)	3.60 m (12 ft)
Nectarine	—	3.60 m (12 ft)
Nut	3.60 m (12 ft)	3.60 m (12 ft)
Peach	5.40 m (18 ft)	3.60 m (12 ft)
Pear	3.60 m (12 ft)	3.60 m (12 ft)
Plum	3.60 m (12 ft)	3.60 m (12 ft)
Quince	3.60 m (12 ft)	—

Single cordon apples and pears can be planted 75 cm ($2\frac{1}{2}$ ft) apart at an angle of 45° Pyramid apples and pears need a spacing of 1.80 m (6 ft), while Espalier apples and pears should have 4.50 m (15 ft) between them to allow for development of the 'arms'.

Chemical terms

Common name	
Carbonic acid gas	Carbon dioxide (CO_2)
Gypsum	Calcium sulphate ($CaSO_4 2H_2O$)
Hydrate of lime, slaked lime	Calcium hydroxide ($Ca(OH)_2$)
Nitrate of soda	Sodium nitrate ($NaNO_2$)
Nitrogen	Nitrogen (N)
Salt (common)	Sodium chloride (NaCl)
Sulphate of ammonia	Ammonium sulphate ($(NH_4)_2SO_4$)
Sulphate of iron	Ferrous sulphate ($FeSO_4$)
Sulphate of potash	Potassium sulphate (K_2SO_4)
Superphosphate of lime	Tetrahydric monocalcic diphosphate (H_4Ca2PO_4)
Water	Water (H_2O)

GLOSSARY

Acid soil One containing little lime

Activator Chemical product (normally a powder or granules) to speed decay of material on compost heap

Adventitious Plant organ (bud or root, for instance) that appears other than in normal place

Aerial root One that arises anywhere above ground (for instance, an adventitious root from a stem)

Aggregate Usually, sand and gravel mixture for concrete mixes. Also used to indicate material used to retain moisture on greenhouse benches or as a growing medium in ring culture and hydroponics

Air layering Propagation technique, layering the plant in air instead of soil. The cut stem is usually tightly packed round the wound with damp moss until roots show

Algae Microscopic plants (normally green) that thrive in still water and on damp surfaces

Alkaline soil One rich in lime

Alpine In everyday terms, small plants for a rock garden; strictly, those that grow in mountainous regions

Annuals Plants that are sown, grown, set seed and die within a year

Anther Pollen-bearing male plant organ, normally part of stamen

Aquatic Strictly, a plant that lives entirely in water, but also applied to floaters and marginals whose roots alone are permanently or mainly submerged

Beard Tuft of hair on lower petals (particularly irises)

Bedding plants Those set out in flower beds to give colour and lifted within a year

Biennial plants These require two years from sowing to seeding and death

Blanching Consists of excluding light from plant stems or leaves to make them pale and improve the flavour, as with leeks

Blind Failure of growing point of a plant to develop properly; often applied where flowers do not bloom

Bog plant One that thrives in perpetually damp conditions

Bole Technically, trunk of a tree; loosely used as referring to the base

Bolting Premature flowering and running to seed by vegetables

Botrytis (grey mould) Fungus disease prevalent in damp conditions and badly ventilated greenhouses

Bonsai Trees and shrubs artificially miniaturized by confining the roots and training young shoots to the required shape by tying in with wire

Bordeaux mixture Copper sulphate and lime, used mainly as a fungicide

Bottom heat Warmed soil or compost to give cuttings and seedlings an easier start. Usually provided by soil-warming cables; formerly by placing over a manure heap

Bract Flower 'substitute': modified leaf, often brightly coloured (as in poinsettia)

Brassica Wide range of vegetables of Cruciferae family, including Brussels sprouts, cabbages and cauliflowers

Break Branch or fork produced by pinching out growing tip to induce earlier and better flowering. See also **Disbudding**, and **Pinching-out**

Budding Propagation method (notably with fruit and roses) whereby a bud is inserted into a T-cut made in bark of host plant and securely bound

Bulbs Flowering plants with swollen underground stems

Callus Corky tissue forming over a wound in the bark, or thickened tissue that forms over a wound on a cutting

Calyx Sepals, outer ring of flower parts

Cambium Tissue or layer immediately beneath the bark, the region of active growth

Capillary Syphoning action, raising water to the plant from an absorbent surface such as sand or a flannel-type cloth. Lamp wicks can also be used to transfer water from a container to plants situated at a higher level

Cheshunt compound Copper sulphate and ammonium carbonate spray, used to combat fungus diseases, notably damping off

Chlorosis This occurs when plant leaves turn yellow due to excess lime at the roots

Compost Garden compost is a type of manure; potting compost is a complete growing medium

Conifers Cone-bearing trees, usually evergreen; for example, pine

Container-grown Plant grown in a pot or other container (as opposed to one lifted from the field for transplanting). Container-grown plants can be planted at almost any season as the roots are less disturbed

Cordons A tree form restricted to a single main stem

Crocks Broken pieces of plant pot placed inside a pot for drainage

Crown A term used to denote the branch network of trees, also a root clump

Cultivar A variety raised in cultivation

Damping down A method of increasing humidity by wetting floor and staging of a greenhouse

Damping off Disease normally caused by overcrowding and too-moist conditions in a greenhouse. Fungi attack stem base, causing collapse of the plant

Dead-heading The removal of old flower heads

Deciduous trees Trees that lose their leaves in winter

Dibber Generally, a piece of wood used to make holes to insert small plants in soil

Disbudding Removal of surplus buds or shoots to encourage one flower of exhibition size

Dormant An inactive plant, usually 'resting' for winter

Dot plant One, usually taller than neighbours, used to provide contrast in height, shape or colour in a bedding scheme

Drawn Elongated thin and weak plants grown in dark or too-crowded conditions

Drill Groove made in seed bed for sowing in a line

Dutch light Frame with one top light (pane of glass) usually used for hardening-off plants

Earthing up Act of moulding soil or earth round plant stems

Espalier Fruit training system whereby branches are spread out horizontally, usually trained along wires

Evergreens Plants that retain their leaves all year round

Fı Hybrid The first generation plants arising from crossing two distinct varieties

Falls Outer petals of irises, particularly those hanging vertically

Fan-trained Fruit trees pruned and

shaped so that branches radiate like a fan

Fastigiate Erect, upright form of growth, branches close together

Fertilize Sexual union of two plants, male pollen transferred either naturally or by hand

Fertilizers Concentrated, but not necessarily 'artificial', plant foods

Foliar feed A fertilizer to encourage growth, that can be absorbed by the leaves

Form Variant, or different strain from the normal plant

Frame Low-built structure with removable glass to protect seedlings and other plants against cold; the intermediate stage for greenhouse-raised plants before planting out. Frames can be 'cold' or 'heated' (with bottom heat or heating cables around sides)

Friable soils Crumbly and fine grained soils without lumps

Fungicides Any substances used to control fungus diseases

Gall Abnormal swelling, frequently ball-shaped, caused by insects, bacteria or fungi

Genes Molecular material determining genetic make-up and heredity

Genus A group of plants with similar characteristics, considered as a closely related family. A genus usually contains many species, but can contain only one

Germination The point at which a seed starts to sprout and grow

Graft Union of two plants by merging cambium tissue with the aim of affecting shape or yield. There are several methods, widely used in producing roses and fruit trees

Green manuring Growing and digging in quick-growing leaf crop, such as lupins or mustard to improve soil

Ground-cover Very low-growing plants able to form a compact mat, useful in preventing emergence of weeds

Half-hardy Applied to plants unable to survive winter without shelter

Half-standard Trees with a clear stem of 75–120cm (2½–4ft)

Hardening-off Act of conditioning indoor plants to the outside climate

Heel cutting Shoot for propagation, with a sliver of main stem still attached

Heeling-in Temporary planting to prevent drying out while awaiting transfer to permanent quarters

Herbaceous Plant with non-woody stem that dies away at end of growing season

Hybrid New 'species' resulting from cross-breeding between parents

Inorganic material One containing no carbon, such as superphosphate

Intercrop A crop grown between two other crops; radish between lettuce, for example

Internode The section of stem between leaf joints, or nodes

Larva The name given to an immature form of insect; for example: caterpillar

Lateral A secondary shoot arising from a stem or branch

Lime One of various forms of calcium compounds

Loam A friable soil mixture with neither too much clay nor excess sand

Manure Usually a mixture of vegetable and animal waste

Marginal plant One that grows round the edges of ponds or water

Mulch A thin layer of material such as peat, placed on the soil surface around plants to conserve moisture

Neutral soil One with a pH of 7, neither acid nor alkaline

Node A swelling on the plant stem at the junction with a leaf stalk

Organic A substance containing carbon

Peat Partly decomposed mosses and sedges built up over a prolonged period

Perennial A plant that flowers or lives for more than two years

pH A scale used to indicate acidity or alkalinity, especially of soils. Above 7 is alkaline; 7 is neutral; 6.5 and below, acid

Pinching out Action of removing the growing point of plants

Plunge The process of sinking plant pots up to the rim in soil or peat, or burying bulbs in pots in peat or sand

Pollinator Generally, an apple tree of different cultivar from those around it, pollen from which will enable them to produce a better crop

Potting The act of placing plants in pots containing soil-based or loamless composts

Pricking off Spacing seedlings in pots or boxes after germination

Propagation The term used to denote the process of increasing plants

Pruning The removal of shoots or roots to regulate plant development

Resting period In plants, a phase – usually in winter – when active growth ceases

Rootstock The lower parts of a grafted plant

Runner A small plant produced at the end of a shoot, as in strawberry, for example

Scion The upper parts of grafted plants and different from the rootstock

Seedling The young plant that develops after the seed has germinated

Shrub A plant consisting of many woody stems arising from ground level

Specimen plant An individual plant, such as a shrub rose, grown for its beauty

Spit A spade depth of soil, 25–30cm (10–12in)

Staking Act of supporting plants, with bamboo canes or pieces of wood for example

Standard tree One with a minimum length of clear stem of 1.5m (5ft) from soil to lowest branch

Tender plant One requiring warmer conditions than an outdoor climate provides

Terminal shoot The leading growths of a plant

Tilth The physical condition of the top 5cm (2in) of soil

Top dressing Act of applying fertilizer or soil mixture to the soil surface around plants

Transplanting Lifting plants and re-planting them elsewhere

Tubers Swollen pieces of stem used by plants for food storage, potato or dahlia, for example

Variegated Two or more colours in leaves or petals: generally refers to white or cream markings on foliage

Variety Variant from original species or hybrid. Some occur naturally: those induced by cultivation are now called 'cultivars'

Whorled With three or more flowers or leaves in a ring at one stem joint

INDEX

The publishers would like to thank the following individuals and organizations for their kind permission to reproduce the photographs in this book:

Bernard Alfieri 20 left, 29, 31, 57 above left, 106 above, 121, 123 below left, 143 above right, 154 above right, 158 above left, 181 above, 192 right, 212–213; Bryce Attwell 4–5, 6–7, 16–17, 48–49, 74–75, 110–111, 118–119; A–Z Botanical Collection Ltd. 19 above right, 71, 79 above and below, 95, 101, 102 centre, 122, 150 below left and above right, 155 below, 180 below left and below right, 182 below right, 185 above and below, 198 below, 219 below, 222 centre and below, 223 below; Barnaby's Picture Library 15 below, 25 below right, 204, 215; Pat Brindley 34 below, 53 below, 57 below, 103, 114 above, 119 inset, 120, 139 below, 141 above, 157 right, 168, 169, 177 right, 181 below, 184 above left, 219 above right, 222 above left, 223 above, 225 below right; Dr. C. P. Burham 23 above left, centre and right, below left and right; Steve Campbell 39, 107; R. J. Corbin 51, 76 right and left, 135, 137, 139 above right, 142 left, 146 below, 148 below right, 156 left, 183 right, 231 left; Eric Crichton 138 below, 142 right; W. F. Davidson 19 above left; Derek Fell (Horticultural Picture Library) 13; Brian Furner 53 above, 106 above and below left, 132 above right, 138 above, 139 above left, 143 centre left, 152 above, 154 below left, 158 above right, 163 below right, 176 above right, 178 centre below, 183 below, 192 left, 214 above, 216, 235; Iris Hardwick Library 164, 206; George Hyde 19 below, 106 below right, 136, 159 above, 176 left, 178 below right, 179 centre, 184 above right, 197 above, 208 right, 233 above, 236 above and below, 237 below; Leslie Johns & Associates 8, 9, 10–11, 15 above, 36 below, 94, 168 left, 178; Bill McLaughlin 93 above, 224, 225 above; Murphy Chemical Ltd. 231 above right; National Vegetable Research Station 230, 231 below right, 234; NHPA (M. Savonius) 114 below, 204, (M. W. F. Treadie) 232 above; Ray Procter 117, 170; P. W. A. Services 125; John Rigby 55, Harry Smith Horticultural Photographic Collection 12, 20 right, 30, 35 above and below, 36 above, 37 above and below, 56, 57 above, 77, 88 below, 90 above and below, 93 below, 102 above, 106 centre, 123 above and below right, 126, 127, 128–129, 130–131, 132 above left and below, 133 above and below, 134 above and below, 140, 143 below, 144, 145 above and below, 146 above, 147, 148 left, 149, 150 above left and below right, 151 above and below, 152 below, 153, 154 above left, 155 above left and above right, 158 centre below, 159 below left, 160 above left, above right and below, 161, 162, 163 above left, 165, 171 below, 176 below, 177 above left and below, 178 above right, 179 above, below and left, 181 centre, 182 above and below left, 183 above left, 184 below, 185 left, 187 above, 194 left and right, 195, 196, 197 below, 198 above left and above right, 199, 200–201, 201 above, 202, 203 left and right, 205, 207, 208, 210, 211 above and below, 212 left, 213 right, 214 below, 217, 218, 220, 221 above and below, 225 below left, 228, 233 below, 237; Spectrum Colour Library 14, 34 above, 88 above; Peter Stiles 24; John Topham Picture Library 193; ZEFA Picture Library (J. Pfaff) 141 below.

Front Jacket: Michael Warren
Back Jacket: Bryce Attwell

discovering **nature**

Nature Garden

Sally Hewitt

Franklin Watts
London • Sydney

An Aladdin Book
© Aladdin Books Ltd 2000
Produced by
Aladdin Books Ltd
28 Percy Street
London W1P 0LD

First published in Great Britain
in 2000 by
Franklin Watts
96 Leonard Street
London EC2A 4XD

ISBN 0-7496-3714-5

Editor: Kathy Gemmell

Consultant: Helen Taylor

Designer: Simon Morse

Photography: Roger Vlitos

Illustrators: Tony Kenyon, Stuart Squires – SGA
& Mike Atkinson

Printed in Belgium
All rights reserved

A CIP catalogue record for this book
is available from the British Library.

Original concept by David West Children's Books

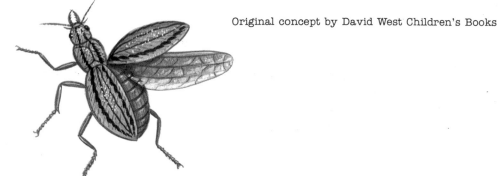

Contents

Introduction

Look closely in a garden and you will find many interesting things. You can have fun learning about creatures and where to find them. Make a worm garden and watch worms at work in the soil. Plot an ant map and attract birds with a bird cake. See what plants need in order to grow and find out who visits the garden when you're not there.

1 Look out for numbers like this. They will guide you through the step-by-step instructions for the projects and activities, making sure that you do things in the right order.

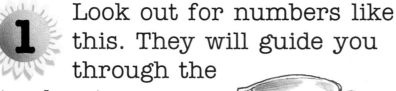

Further facts

Whenever you see this 'nature spotters' sign, you will find interesting information, such as how to recognise animal footprints, to help you understand more about your nature garden.

Hints and tips

- When you look for things in the garden, be careful not to tread on any plants.

- Try to look at creatures without disturbing them. If you do move them, always return them to the place where you found them.

- Before touching soil, always cover any cuts you may have with a plaster.

- Do not rub your face or eyes when working with plants or soil. Always wash your hands afterwards.

DON'T TOUCH ROTTEN THINGS

Wherever you see this sign, ask an adult to help you. Never use sharp tools or go exploring on your own.

Get an adult to help you

This warning sign shows where you have to take special care when doing the project. For example, when looking at rubbish rotting in bags of soil, keep the bags sealed. Don't touch or smell the rotten things. They may give you germs that make you ill.

Soil

Soil is a very important part of your nature garden. It is full of the minerals and water that plants need for growth. Moles, worms and all kinds of tiny creatures make it their home.

Soil settling

1 Find out what makes up the soil in your nature garden. Dig up some soil from the edge of a flower bed and put it in a bucket.

2 Shake some soil in a sieve over the bucket. Sort what is left behind onto some paper. You may find stones, bits of plants or even creatures that live in the soil.

3 Now put some soil into a screw-top jar. Fill the jar nearly to the top with water and screw on the lid.

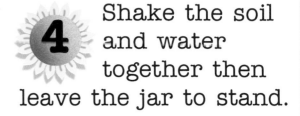

4 Shake the soil and water together then leave the jar to stand.

5 Carefully look at the jar without disturbing it. The soil will have settled down into layers in the water.

Soil layers

Soil is a mixture of dead plants and animals and tiny pieces of broken down rock. Different kinds of rock will make sandy, chalky or sticky clay soil.

Bits of plants

Muddy water

Clay or chalk

Sand

Gravel and stones

Rotting rubbish

Dead plants and animals that rot down into the soil help to make it rich and good for new plants to grow in. Not everything rots down quickly. Some rubbish stays around for a very long time.

Bags of rubbish

1 See what kind of rubbish rots away and what doesn't. Don't throw away banana skins, apple cores, tissues, cans or crisp packets – bury them!

NEVER TAKE RUBBISH FROM THE BIN

2 Put some soil into clear plastic bags. Push one piece of rubbish into the soil in each bag and seal it.

3 Check the bags every few days, but don't open them. You will see that apple cores rot quickly, but banana skins take a long time. Rubbish made of plastic doesn't rot at all.

Natural rotters

There are many different plants and animals that get to work straight away on natural rubbish like leaves, logs or dead creatures. They are called decomposers.

Fungi are not really plants. They grow and feed on dead wood.

Lichens grow on stone and wood and gradually break them down.

Worms pull leaves and bits of dead plant down into the soil and eat them.

Maggots that hatch from housefly eggs eat the bodies of dead creatures.

Woodlice live in dark, damp places and feed on leaves and wood.

Seeds

Gardeners look after the plants and flowers they want to grow in their garden and spend a lot of time pulling up weeds that they didn't plant. You can discover what seeds are hiding in the soil, waiting to grow.

Soil gardens

1 Dig up some soil from two different places in the garden, perhaps from under a tree and by a fence. Put the soil from each place into its own plastic tray and label where it came from.

2 Water both trays every other day. After a while, you will see shoots beginning to push up through the soil, even though you didn't plant any seeds.

3 Some shoots may become grass or weeds. A seed from a tree may one day grow into a young tree. A rose tree may even grow from a rosehip dropped by a bird.

Spreading seeds

Plants have different ways of spreading their seeds to give them a good chance to grow into new, strong plants.

Birds eat juicy berries, such as cherries. The seeds are stones inside the berry, which fall to the ground in the birds' droppings.

Horse chestnut seeds are heavy and fall straight to to the ground. Look for them under a horse chestnut tree.

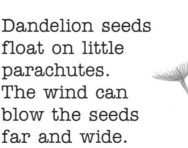

Dandelion seeds float on little parachutes. The wind can blow the seeds far and wide.

Green grass

Grass in the countryside is food for animals and it is like a soft, green carpet in the garden. Grass has another job to do too.

Grass roots hold soil in place in the wind and the rain. Different kinds of grass grow in different soils.

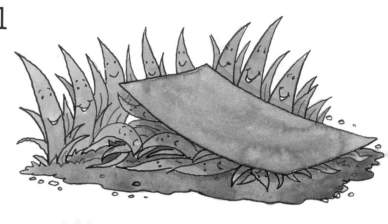

In the dark

1 This project will show you that sunlight is what makes grass green. Find a corner of your lawn.

2 Cover a patch of grass near the edge of the lawn with a thick piece of card. Put a stone on it to stop it blowing away.

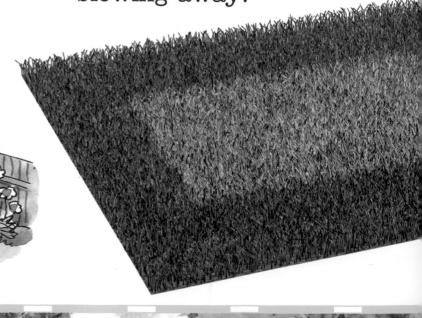

3 Lift up the card after two weeks and see what has happened to the grass. When it is kept in the dark, grass will turn pale green or yellow and begin to die.

Using sunlight

Like grass, other plants also need sunlight to grow and survive. Plants make their own food using sunlight. This is called photosynthesis.

Photosynthesis

Plants need sunlight to make food using the green colour in their leaves, called chlorophyll.

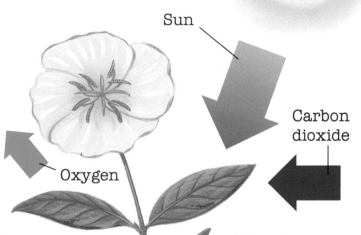

Sun

Carbon dioxide

Oxygen

As part of photosynthesis, plants give out a gas called oxygen.

The green leaves catch the Sun's energy. They use the energy to make food from water and a gas in the air called carbon dioxide.

Without sunlight, plants could not make food and would die.

Plants

We all have veins to carry blood around our bodies. Plants have veins too. They carry the water and minerals a plant needs to grow to every part of it. Watch how water moves up the stem and into the leaves of a celery stalk.

Drinking water

1 For this project you will need a jar of water, some blue food colouring and a celery stalk with leaves.

2 Mix the water and blue food colouring together in the jar and put in the celery stalk. Leave the jar near a window for a few hours.

3 The blue water will slowly rise up the veins in the stalk then into the leaves, turning them blue.

Get an adult to help you

4 Now slice the stalk across the middle. You will be able to see the veins that have been stained blue.

Roots

Roots grow downwards into the soil to hold the plant in place. They have tiny hairs to suck up the water and minerals that a plant needs from the soil. Water goes into the roots, then up the stem into the leaves, then out into the air.

Carrots and potatoes are swollen roots which store food for the plants.

Water in the soil

Flowers

A plant starts life as a tiny egg. Flowers are the parts of a plant where eggs that become seeds are made. The seeds then grow into new plants. If you look closely at a flower, you will see all the parts it needs for making seeds.

Parts of a flower

1 Stamens grow from the middle of the flower. Yellow powder called pollen is made on the tip of the stamens. Pollen gives some people hayfever.

Ovary

Stem

Petal

Pollen

Stamen

2 Petals use colours, patterns and smells to attract insects and birds that feed on pollen and on a sweet juice made by the plant called nectar.

Stamen

3 A stigma also grows from the middle of the flower. Pollen grains that land on the stigma grow a tube down to join an egg in the ovary. The egg can then become a seed.

4 The ovary is the case where eggs that become seeds are made.

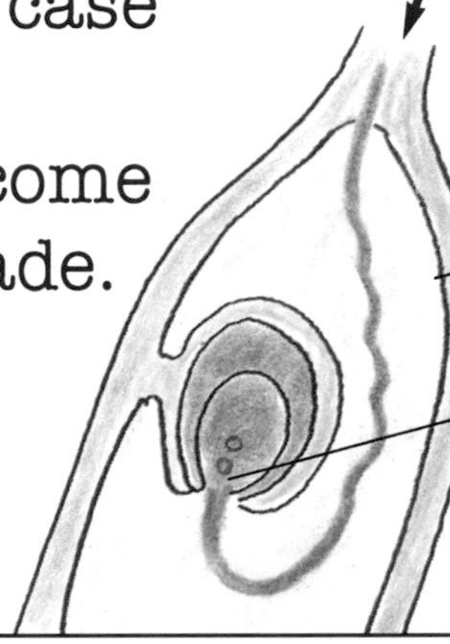

From stigma

Ovary

Pollen fertilises an egg to make a seed.

Flower power

Look out for flowers of all colours, shapes, sizes and smells growing in different places in the garden.

Apple blossom

Apple blossom on an apple tree becomes fruit in the summer.

Daffodil bulbs can be planted in pots and window boxes.

Daffodil

Honeysuckle grows up walls and fences. It smells very sweet.

Honeysuckle

Stigma

Birds

Birds are visitors to the garden, looking for food and water. In the spring, they may find a sheltered place there to build a nest. You can make sure there is always something for birds to eat and drink.

Winter bird cake

1 In winter, there is less food for birds to find. Use breadcrumbs from a stale loaf, uncooked peanuts, bacon rind and lard to make a winter bird cake.

2 Line a cake tin or muffin tray with greaseproof paper. Now mix the breadcrumbs, peanuts and chopped bacon rind together in a bowl.

3 Lard will hold the cake together, as well as give the birds fat to eat to keep them warm. Melt the lard in a saucepan over a low heat until it is all liquid.

Get an adult to help you

5 Leave the mixture to cool. Then turn it out of the tray and put your winter cake outside, out of reach of cats. Put out water too.

4 Stir the melted lard into the dry mixture and pour it into the cake tin or muffin tray.

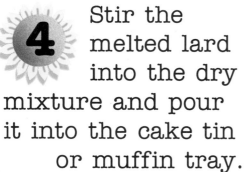

Bird food

Birds will find things to eat all over the garden.

Some birds feed on berries and fruit. Some catch insects in the air.

Caterpillars, snails and worms make a juicy meal.

Small birds peck for seeds and insects on the ground.

In winter, when the ground is hard and there are no berries, birds will eat your winter cake.

Footprints

Birds are not the only visitors to the garden who come looking for food and water. Other shy creatures come at night or when there is no one around. Their footprints will let you know who called.

Hungry visitors

1 Fill a baking tray with damp sand and smooth it over. Put food scraps like brown bread, fruit, vegetables and nuts on a plate. Pour milk or water into a saucer.

2 Put the food and liquid onto the baking tray and leave it in a quiet part of the garden. Check the tray for footprints in the morning and again in the evening.

3 Make a note of who has left tracks in the sand. Did they come at night or during the day? Look carefully, then smooth over the sand.

Identifying tracks

You can use these pictures to identify the footprints that have been made in your tray. These pictures are the same size as real animal footprints.

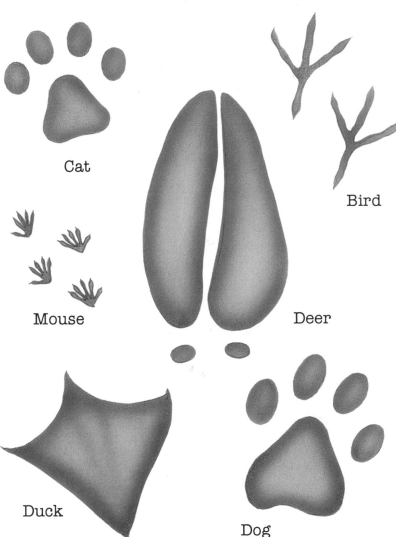

Cat

Bird

Mouse

Deer

Duck

Dog

If you can't see a print to match the ones in your tray, try to find the one that looks most like it. Can you tell if it is a bird or an animal? Is it big or small? Ask an adult to help you work out what any mystery prints are. You could look them up in a field guide.

Insects

Look for insects in the soil, under stones, on plants, resting on walls, hiding in cracks or swimming in water. Make a chart of the insects that live in or visit the garden.

Insect visitors

1 You will need a sheet of card, a ruler, coloured pens and a magnifying glass.

2 Copy the chart in the picture onto your card. You can add extra columns. Draw a moon if you spot an insect like a moth at night.

Where insects live

	Dragonfly	Moth
leaf		x
grass	) x	
flower		
wall		
log	x	

DON'T GO TOO CLOSE TO WASPS AND BEES

	Ladybird	Wasp	Butterfly
			X
		X	

3 Look for insects in the garden. Mark a cross on the chart to show what they are feeding on. Which part of the garden has the most visitors? Do the insects come during the day or at night?

A bug's bits

Insects all have six legs. They have a skeleton on the outside of their body and sensitive feelers called antennae. Many have wings.

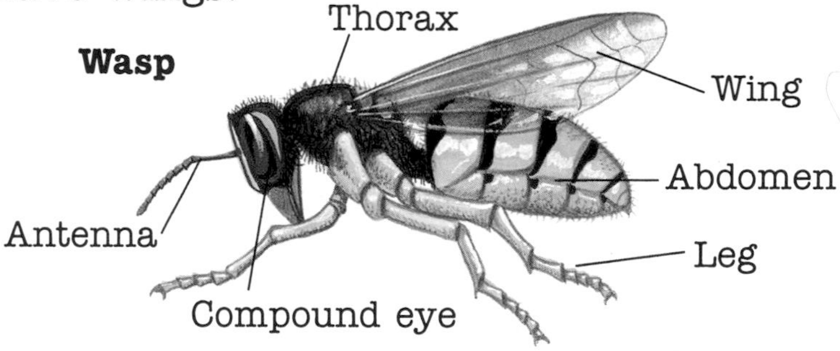

Wasp

Thorax

Wing

Antenna

Abdomen

Compound eye

Leg

Insects can look very different from each other. Beetles have hard, shiny cases to protect their delicate wings. The easiest way to tell if a creature is an insect is to count its legs.

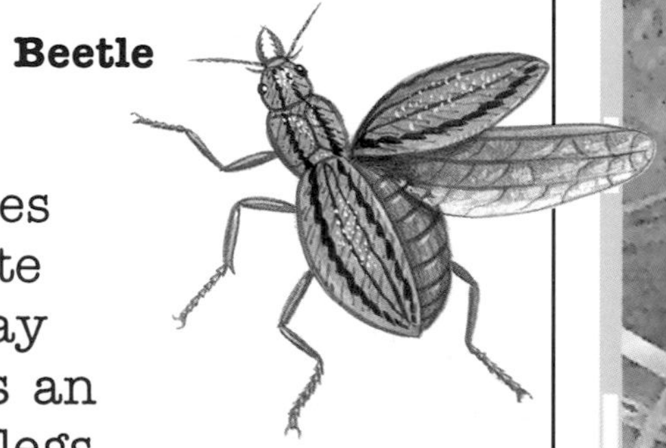

Beetle

Minibeasts

There are many small creatures, such as spiders and slugs, which are not insects. Spiders spin silky webs to catch their food. Slugs and snails slither along on silvery trails. Millipedes scuttle in dark, damp places. Set a trap to catch some minibeasts in your nature garden.

Setting a trap

1 Dig a hole in the soil just deep enough to hold a small container. Put in pieces of fruit and a spoonful of cat food or dog food.

2 Cover the trap with a small rock, propping up one end with a stone to leave a small gap.

3 Leave the trap overnight. Lift the rock to see what you have caught. Before you let your minibeasts go, try to find out what they are.

Minibeast spotting

Use a magnifying glass to see if you can spot some of these creatures in your nature garden.

A snail hides inside its shell when danger is about.

Snail

Spiders are not insects because they have eight legs.

Spider

Millipedes with hundreds of legs eat leaves and dead plants.

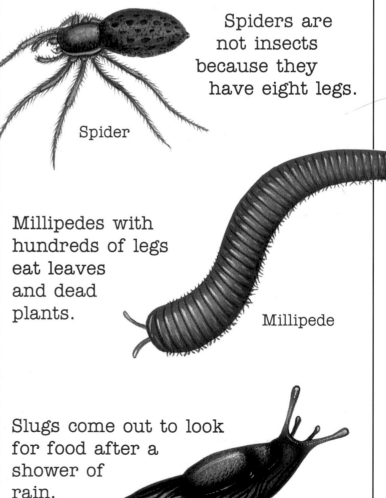

Millipede

Slugs come out to look for food after a shower of rain.

Slug

Ants

Ants have six legs, so you know they are insects. Ants often move around in long trails, following the same path. This project will help you find out if there is a busy ants' nest in your nature garden.

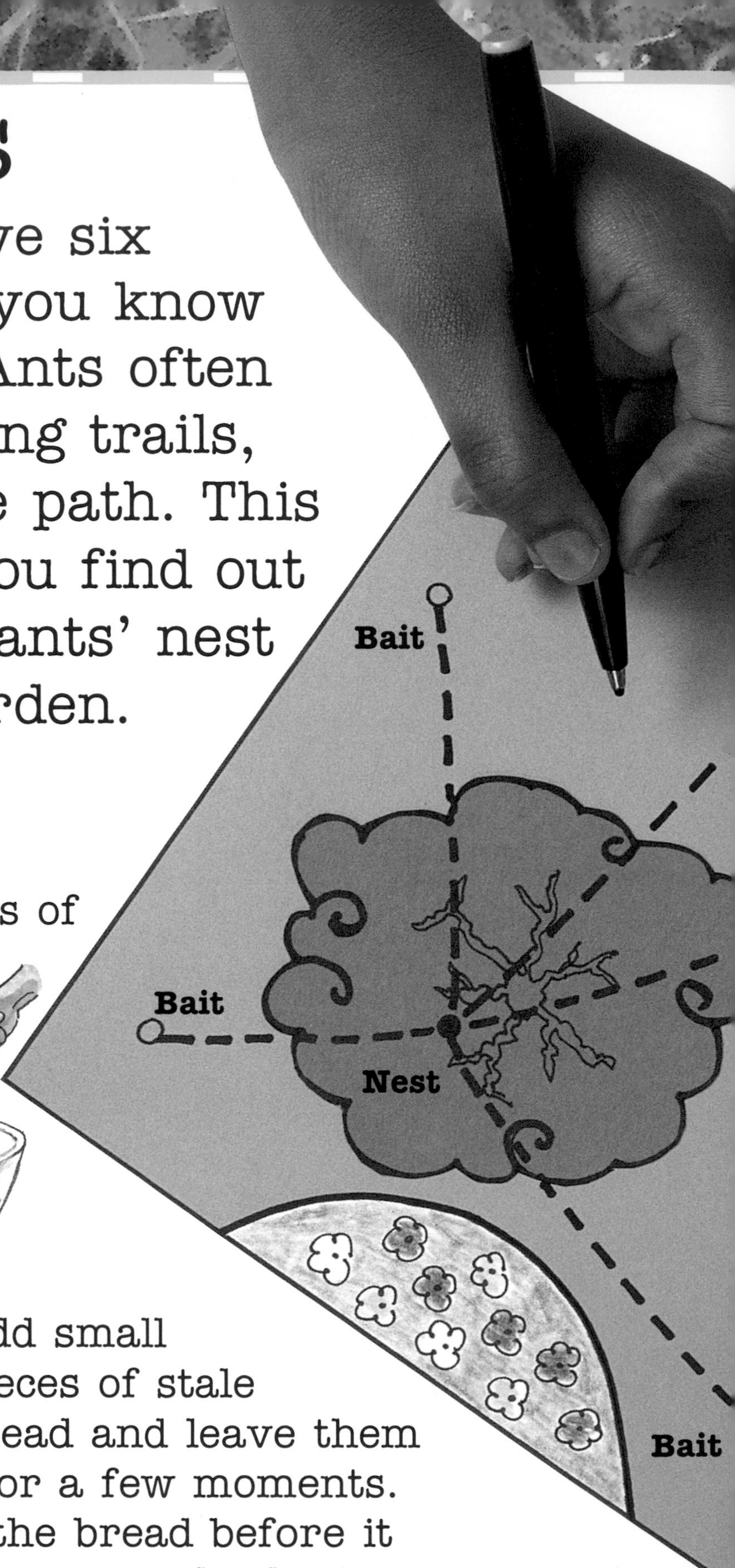

Ant trails

1 Mix two teaspoons of sugar in a bowl half filled with warm water. Stir until the sugar dissolves.

2 Add small pieces of stale bread and leave them to soak for a few moments. Remove the bread before it goes too soggy and take it into the garden.

Bait

Bait

Nest

Bait

3 Put pieces of bread all over the garden as bait. Ants will find the food and carry it off, moving in a line. If you follow the line, you will find the ants' nest.

4 Draw a map of where you put the bread bait. Put in lines to show the paths the ants took to carry their food. The nest should be where all the lines meet.

Bait

Bait

Ants' nests

Ants live and work together in a nest underground. They build lots of tunnels. A queen ant lays eggs. Worker ants look for food and bring it back home along the tunnels.

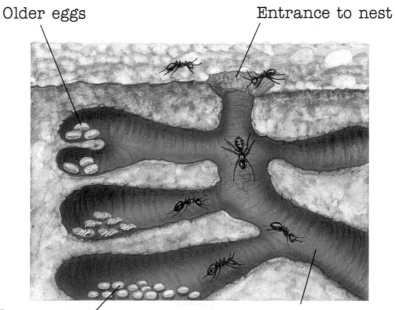

Older eggs

Entrance to nest

Young eggs

Main tunnel

Worms

As worms burrow along under the ground, they eat soil, leaving behind mounds of fine soil called worm casts. You can watch worms pull leaves and dead plants down into the soil to munch.

Worm watching

1 You will need a shoe box, a bin liner, sticky tape, clingfilm, leaves and dead plants, soil and worms.

2 Line the box with the bin liner and fix it in place with tape. This will make the box waterproof.

3 Fill the box with damp soil and put in some worms you have dug up from the soil in the garden.

4 Let the worms burrow down into the soil, then sprinkle on the plants and leaves.

5 Cover the box with clingfilm punched with holes to let in air. How long does it take for the leaves and plants to disappear?

Words on worms

Worms are not garden pests. Gardeners are very happy to have worms in the soil because they help to break it up.
Breaking up the soil keeps it full of air, which is good for growing plants.
Soil without any worms in it is solid, very heavy to dig and not as good for growing things.

Glossary

Ants

Ants are insects that live in a nest underground. They carry food away in long trails.

Turn to pages 26-27 to find out how you can lay a food trail to see if there is an ants' nest in the garden.

Birds

Birds feed on berries and fruit or insects and creatures they find on the ground. In winter, it is hard for them to find enough to eat.

You can learn how to make a winter bird cake on pages 18-19.

Decomposers

Decomposers are creatures or plants that help animals and dead plants to break down, or decompose.

You can find out how long different objects take to decompose in the project on pages 8-9.

Flowers

Flowers are where the seeds for new plants are made. They come in all shapes and sizes, but all have the same parts.

Find out what the parts of a flower are on pages 16-17.

Grass

Grass holds the soil in place and provides food for animals. Grass needs sunlight to stay green.

See how to prove that grass needs sunlight to stay green on pages 12-13.

Insects

All insects have six legs. Any creature with more or fewer than six legs is not an insect. Different insects like to feed in different places.

Chart the best places to spot insects in the garden, and look at the parts that make up an insect on pages 22-23.

Photosynthesis

Photosynthesis is the name for the way that plants use sunlight, carbon dioxide, water and the green colour in their leaves, called chlorophyll, to make their own food.

Look at how photosynthesis works on pages 12-13.

Roots

Roots hold plants firmly in the ground. Water and minerals go up through the roots and into the plant from the soil.

You can watch how plants take up water in the project on pages 14-15, using a celery stick and some coloured water.

Seeds

Plants grow from seeds. Inside a seed is a new plant and the food that it needs to begin to grow.

You can discover if there are seeds waiting to grow under the soil in the project on pages 10-11.

Soil

Soil is made up of several layers of rock and dead plants and animals that have been broken down over many years. Different types of rock break down to make different kinds of soil.

You can look at how to shake up soil so that you can see all the layers in the project on pages 6-7.

Worms

Worms live in the soil. They break up the soil and make it easier for plants to grow.

Most gardeners like to have worms in their garden.

You can learn how to build your own worm garden in the project on pages 28-29.

Index

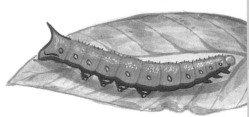